SACR...

SA...

D0201886

STOP!

This is the back of the book.
You wouldn't want to spoil a great ending!

This book is printed "manga-style," in the authentic Japanese right-to-left format. Since none of the artwork has been flipped or altered, readers get to experience the story just as the creator intended. You've been asking for it, so TOKYOPOP® delivered: authentic, hot-off-the-press, and far more fun!

DIRECTIONS

If this is your first time reading manga-style, here's a quick guide to help you understand how it works.

It's easy... just start in the top right panel and follow the numbers. Have fun, and look for more 100% authentic manga from TOKYOPOP®!

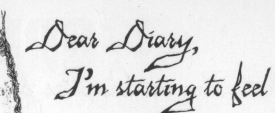

BIZENGHAST

T TEEN AGE 13+

Preview the manga at:
www.TOKYOPOP.com/bizenghast

When a young girl moves to the forgotten town of Bizenghast, she uncovers a terrifying collection of lost souls that leads her to the brink of insanity. One thing becomes painfully clear: The residents of Bizenghast are just dying to come home. ART SUBJECT TO CHANGE © Mary Alice LeGrow and TOKYOPOP Inc.

that I'm not like other people...

Bizenghast™

The gothic fantasy masterpiece
continues in June...

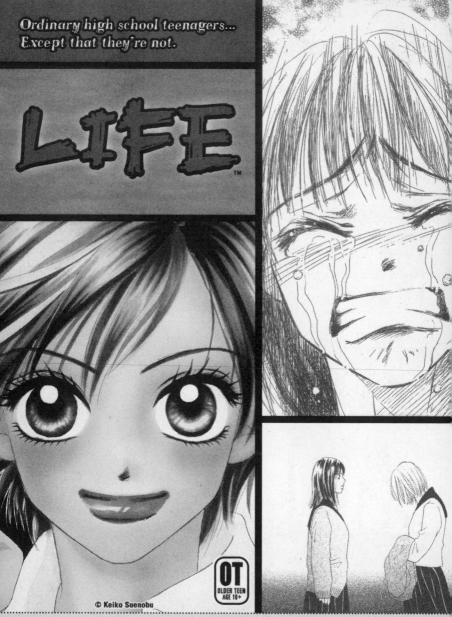

READ THE ENTIRE FIRST CHAPTER ONLINE FOR FREE:

Ayumu struggles with her studies, and the all-important high school entrance exams are approaching. Fortunately, she has help from her best bud Shii-chan, who is at the top of the class. But when the test results come back, the friends are surprised: Ayumu surpasses Shii-chan's scores and gets into the school of her choice—without Shii-chan! Losing her friend is so painful for Ayumu that she starts cutting herself to ease her sorrow. Finally, Ayumu seeks comfort in a new friend, Manami. But will Manami prove to be the friend that Ayumu truly needs? Or will Ayumu continue down a dark path?

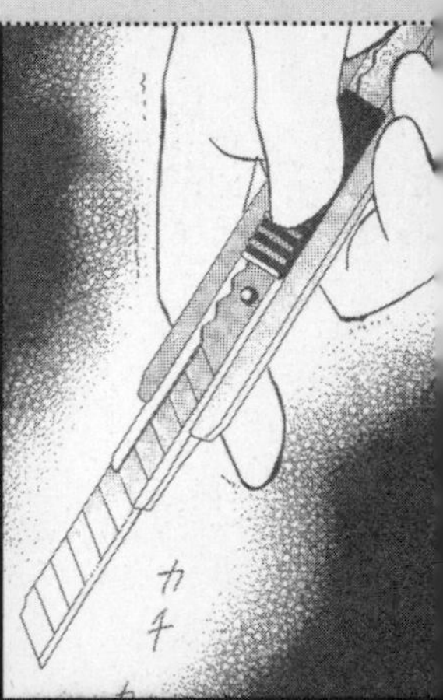
カチ

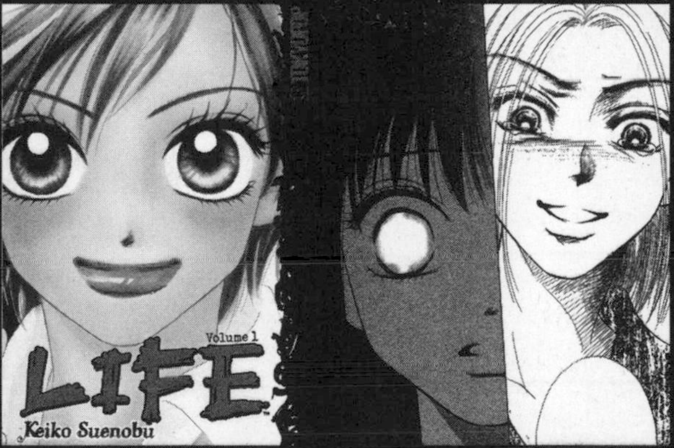
Volume 1
LIFE
Keiko Suenobu

It's about real teenagers...

It's about real high school...

It's about real life.

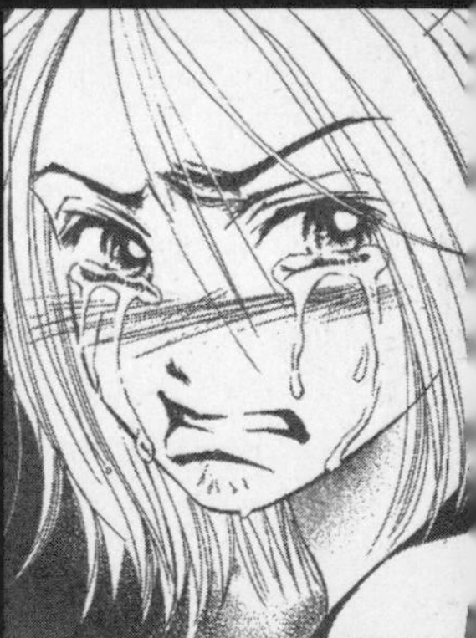

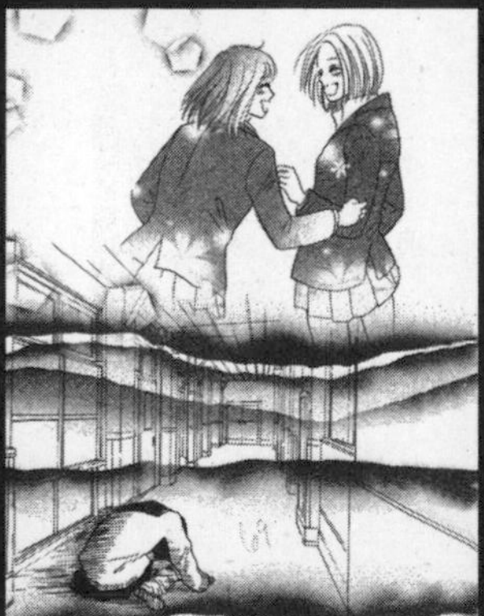

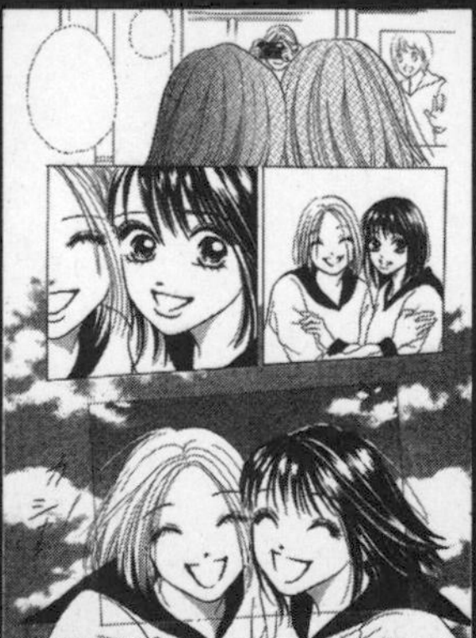

WWW.TOKYOPOP.COM/LIFE

TOKYOPOP SHOP

WWW.TOKYOPOP.COM/SHOP

HOT NEWS!
Check out the TOKYOPOP SHOP! The world's best collection of manga in English is now available online in one place!

Check out all the sizzling hot merchandise and your favorite manga at the shop!

BIZENGHAST POSTER

PRINCESS AI POSTCARDS

WWW.TOKYOPOP.COM/SHOP

0 00000 00000 0

I Luv Halloween Glow-in-the-Dark STICKERS!

I LUV HALLOWEEN BUTTONS & STICKERS

- LOOK FOR SPECIAL OFFERS
- PRE-ORDER UPCOMING RELEASES
- COMPLETE YOUR COLLECTIONS

I LUV HALLOWEEN © Keith Giffen and Benjamin Roman. Princess Ai © & ™ TOKYOPOP Inc. Bizenghast © M. Alice LeGrow and TOKYOPOP Inc.

SPOTLIGHT TOKYOPOP MANGA SUPPLEMENT

FRUITS BASKET
BY NATSUKI TAKAYA

Fruits Basket ™

Tohru Honda was an orphan with no place to go...until the mysterious Sohma family offers her a place to call home. Tohru's ordinary high school life is turned upside down when she's introduced to the Sohmas' world of magical curses and family intrigue. Discover for yourself the Secret of the Zodiac, and find out why *Fruits Basket* has won the hearts of readers the world over!

THE BESTSELLING MANGA IN THE U.S.!

T
TEEN
AGE 13+

© Natsuki Takaya

FOR MORE INFORMATION VISIT WWW.TOKYOPOP.COM

It was so exciting drawing this character!! →

When I was writing, I was thinking about Ms. Tsubaki's youth. I was imagining her having an affair with two men and suffering this very passionate yet complicated love.

What kind of story is that? 💧💧

Even someone like Ms. Tsubakai had a very sad and tough past. She wasn't just an abnormal mother.

By the way, if I was Hagane, I definitely would choose Tsubaki, without a doubt! Forgive me, Ruriha⟿

Anyhow, I will continue to try my best to produce something good. 💧💧

FINALLY, I FILLED UP FIVE PAGES!

I'M GOING TO BED NOW.

Glass Wings

Story & Art by

Misuzu Asaoka

HAMBURG // LONDON // LOS ANGELES // TOKYO

Table of Contents

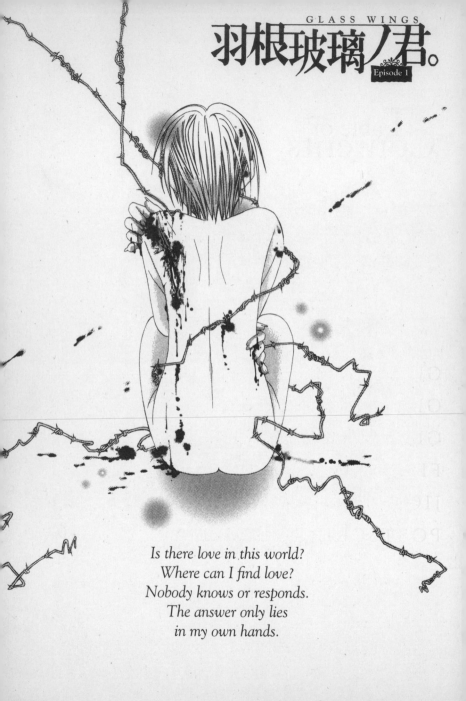

GLASS WINGS

羽根玻璃ノ君。

Episode 1

Is there love in this world?
Where can I find love?
Nobody knows or responds.
The answer only lies
in my own hands.

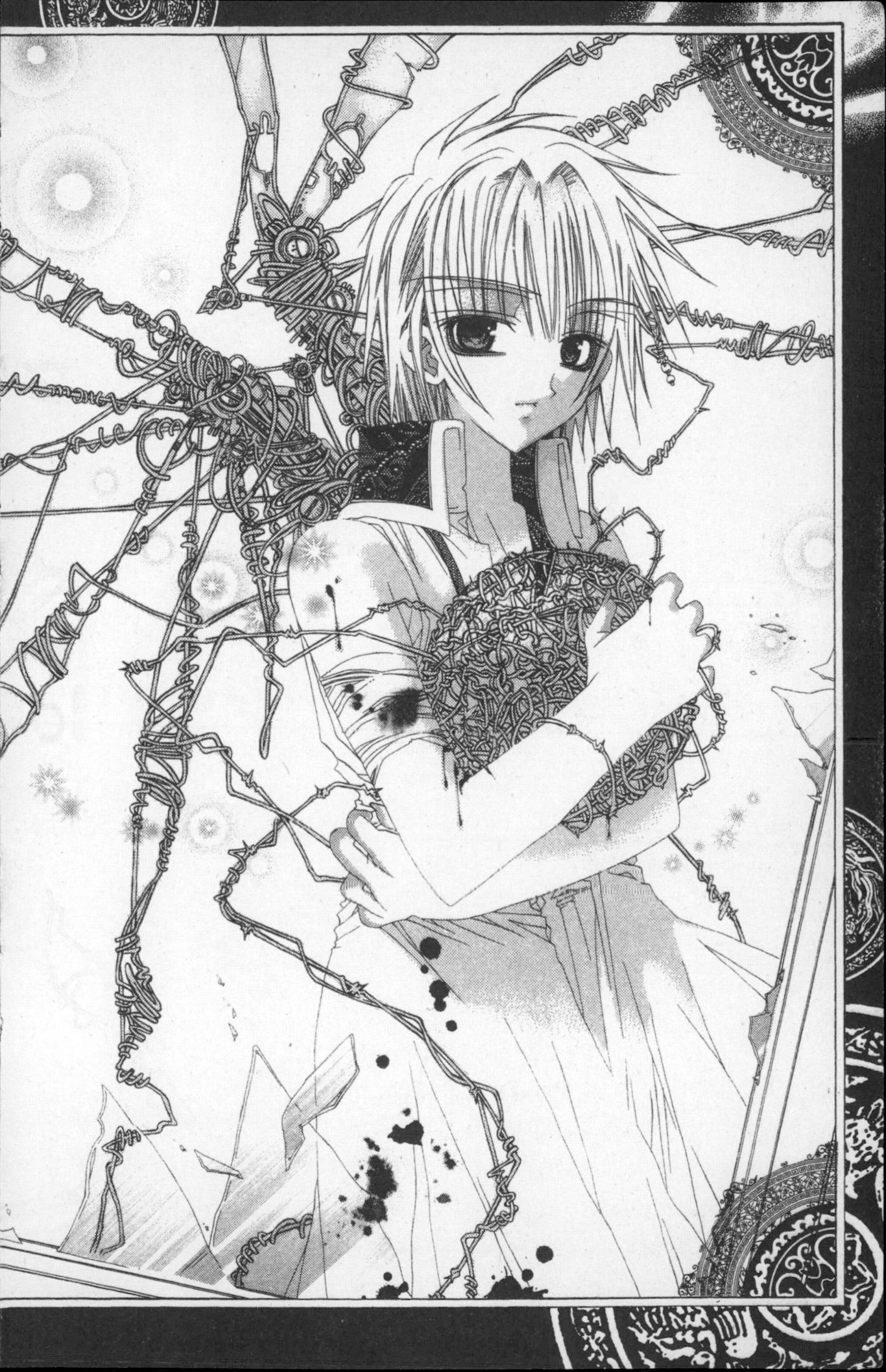

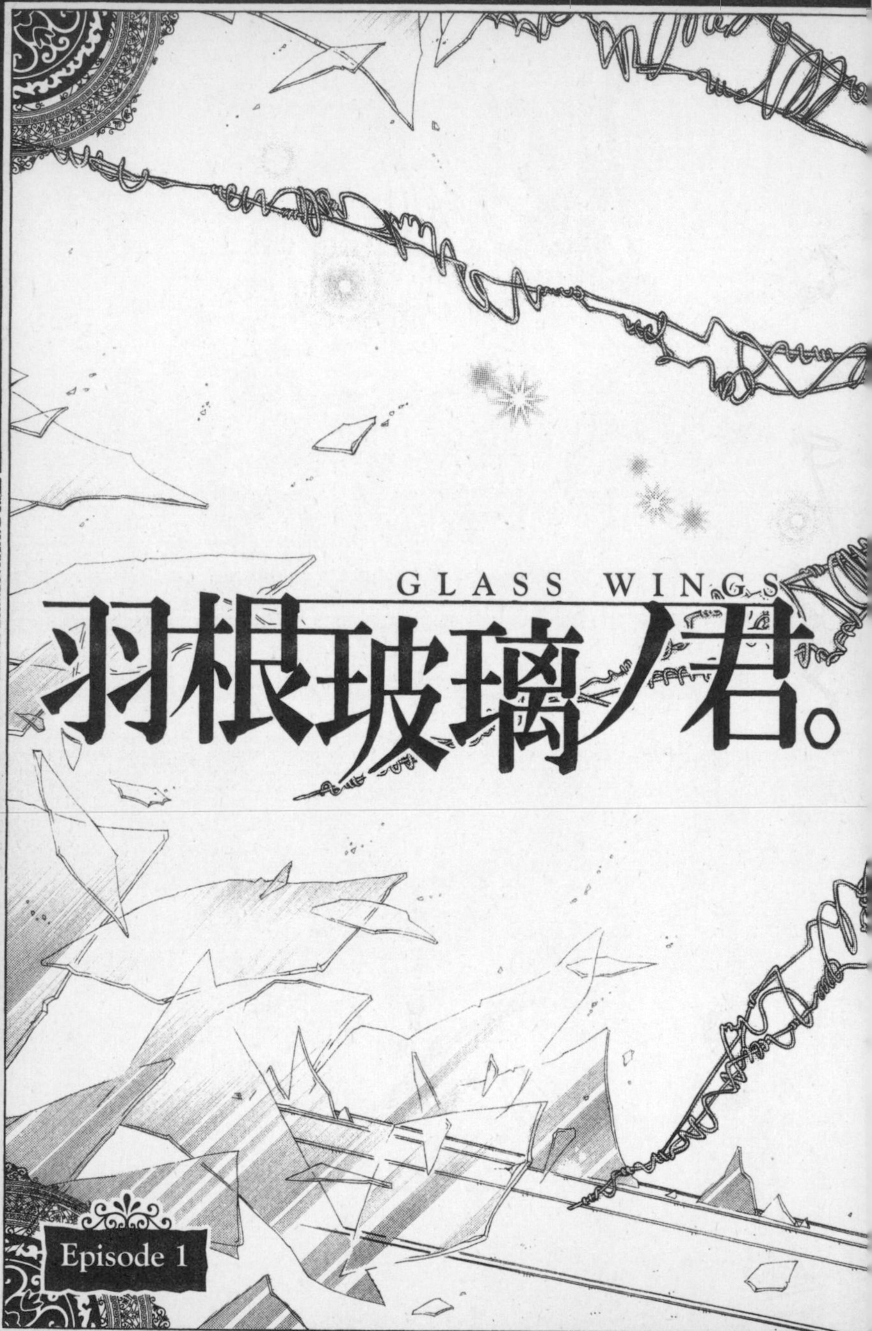
GLASS WINGS
羽根玻璃ノ君。
Episode 1

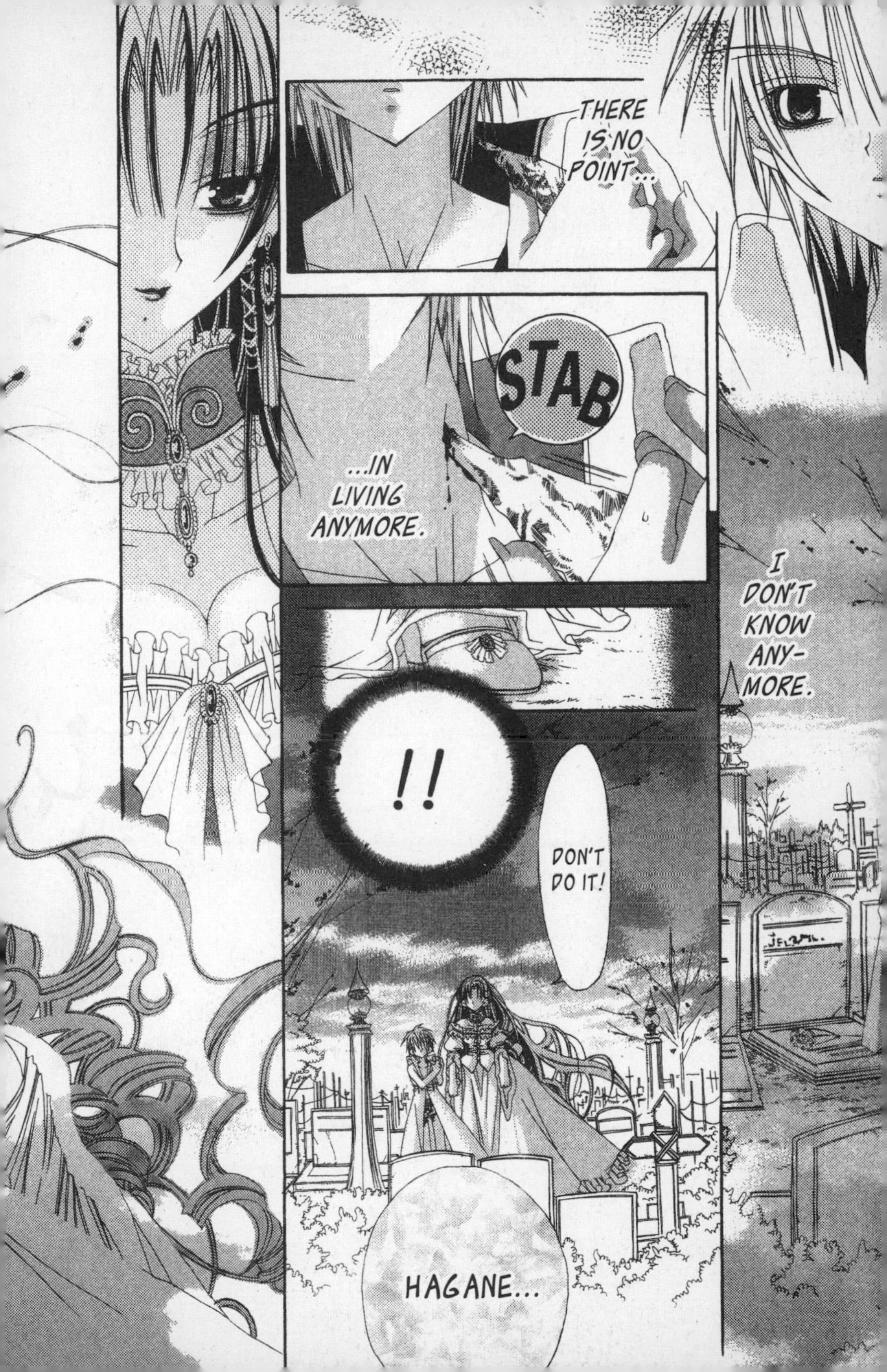
THERE IS NO POINT...
STAB
...IN LIVING ANYMORE.
I DON'T KNOW ANY-MORE.
!!
DON'T DO IT!
HAGANE...

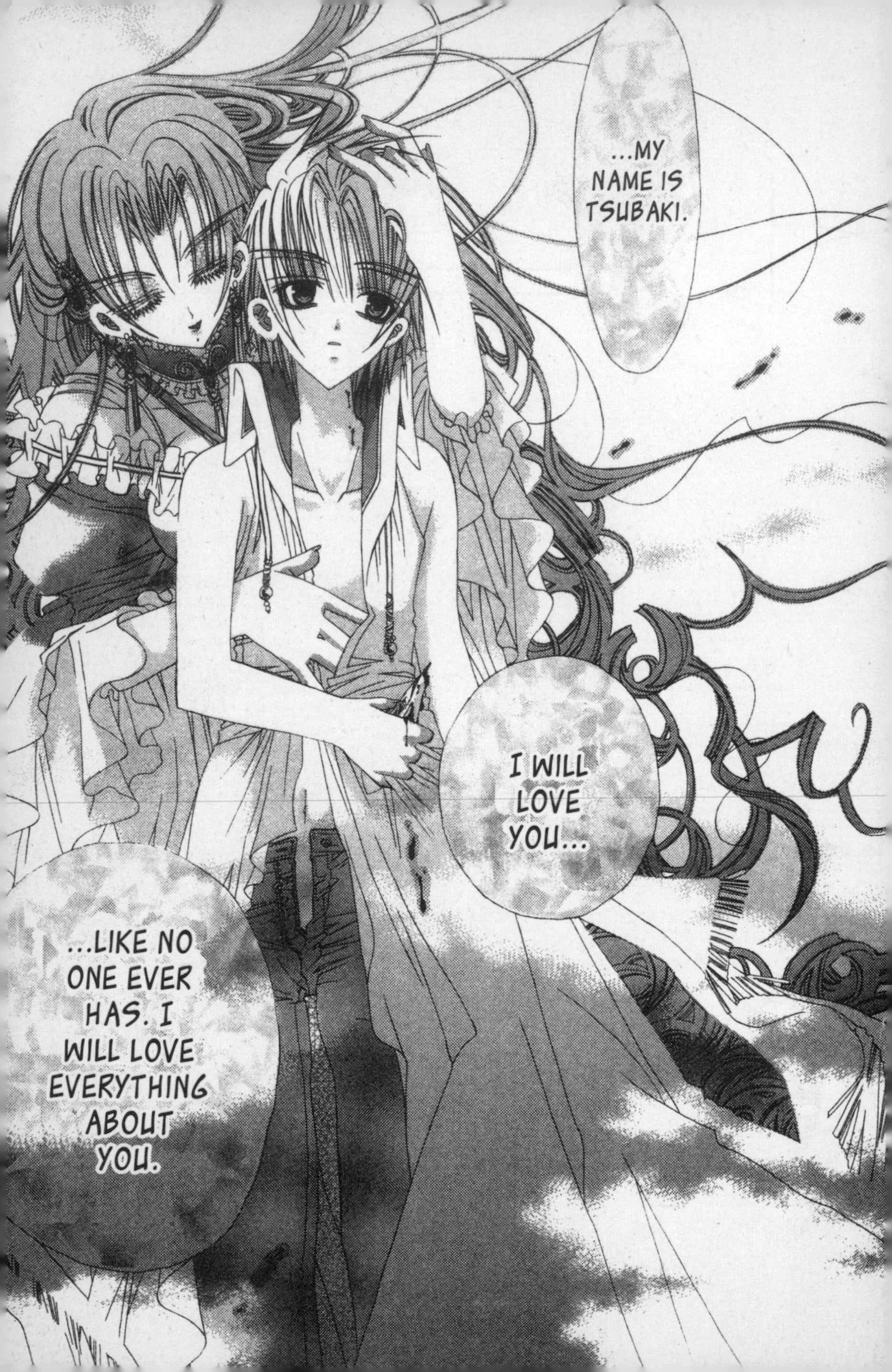
...MY NAME IS TSUBAKI.
I WILL LOVE YOU...
...LIKE NO ONE EVER HAS. I WILL LOVE EVERYTHING ABOUT YOU.

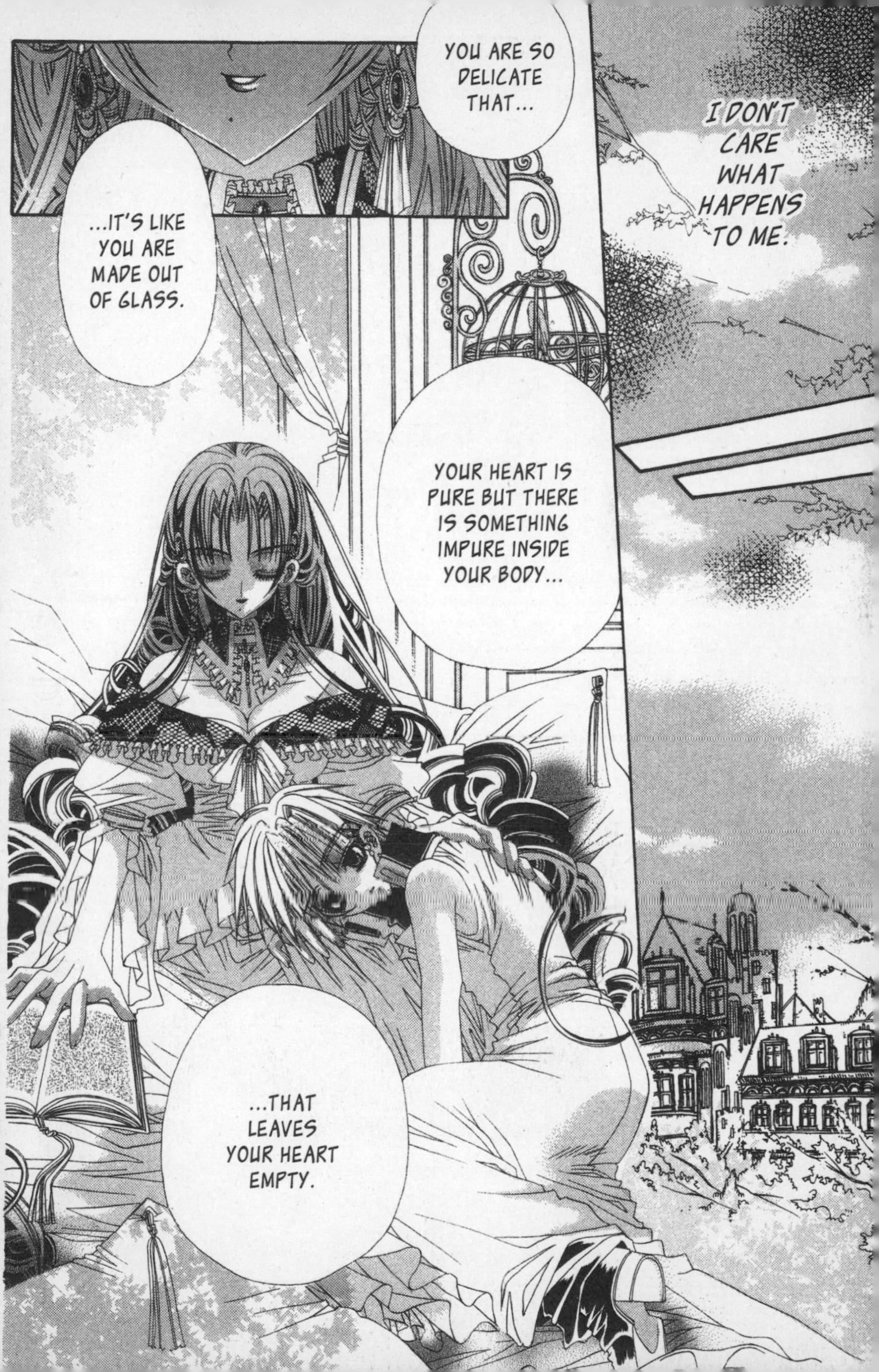
I DON'T CARE WHAT HAPPENS TO ME.
YOU ARE SO DELICATE THAT...
...IT'S LIKE YOU ARE MADE OUT OF GLASS.
YOUR HEART IS PURE BUT THERE IS SOMETHING IMPURE INSIDE YOUR BODY...
...THAT LEAVES YOUR HEART EMPTY.

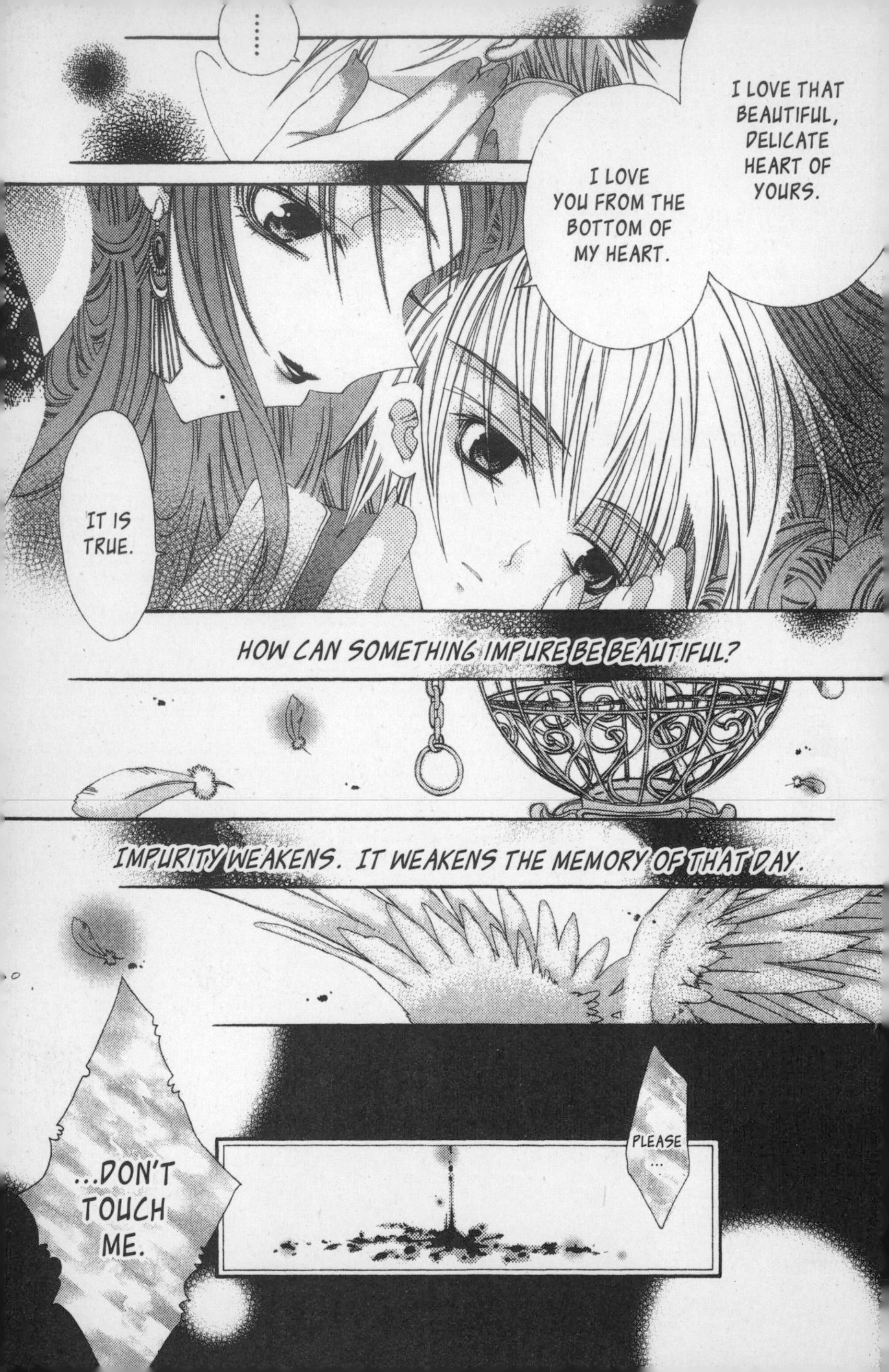

......
I LOVE THAT BEAUTIFUL, DELICATE HEART OF YOURS.
I LOVE YOU FROM THE BOTTOM OF MY HEART.
IT IS TRUE.
HOW CAN SOMETHING IMPURE BE BEAUTIFUL?
IMPURITY WEAKENS. IT WEAKENS THE MEMORY OF THAT DAY.
PLEASE ...
...DON'T TOUCH ME.

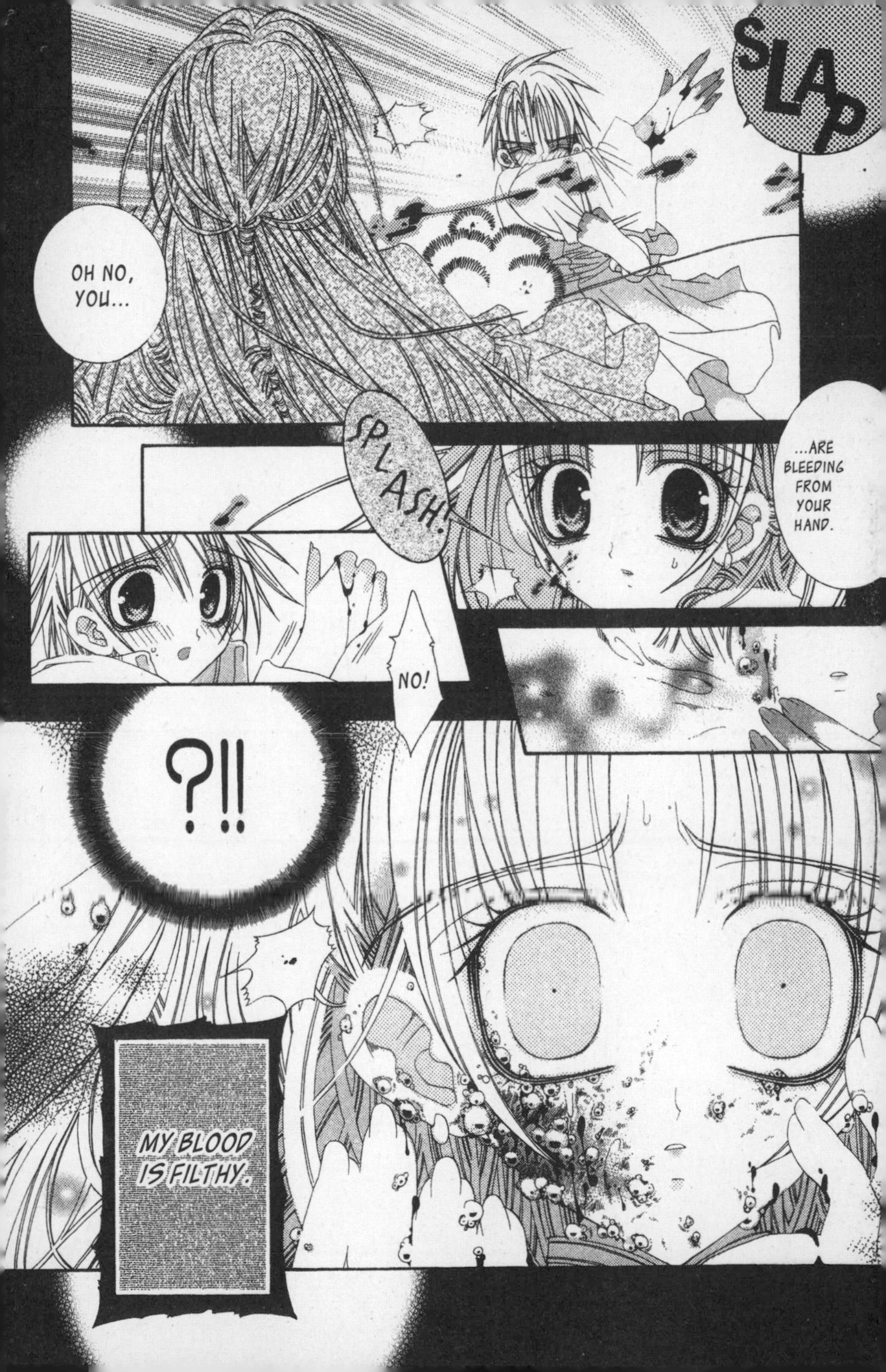
SLAP
OH NO, YOU...
...ARE BLEEDING FROM YOUR HAND.
SPLASH!
NO!
?!!
MY BLOOD IS FILTHY.

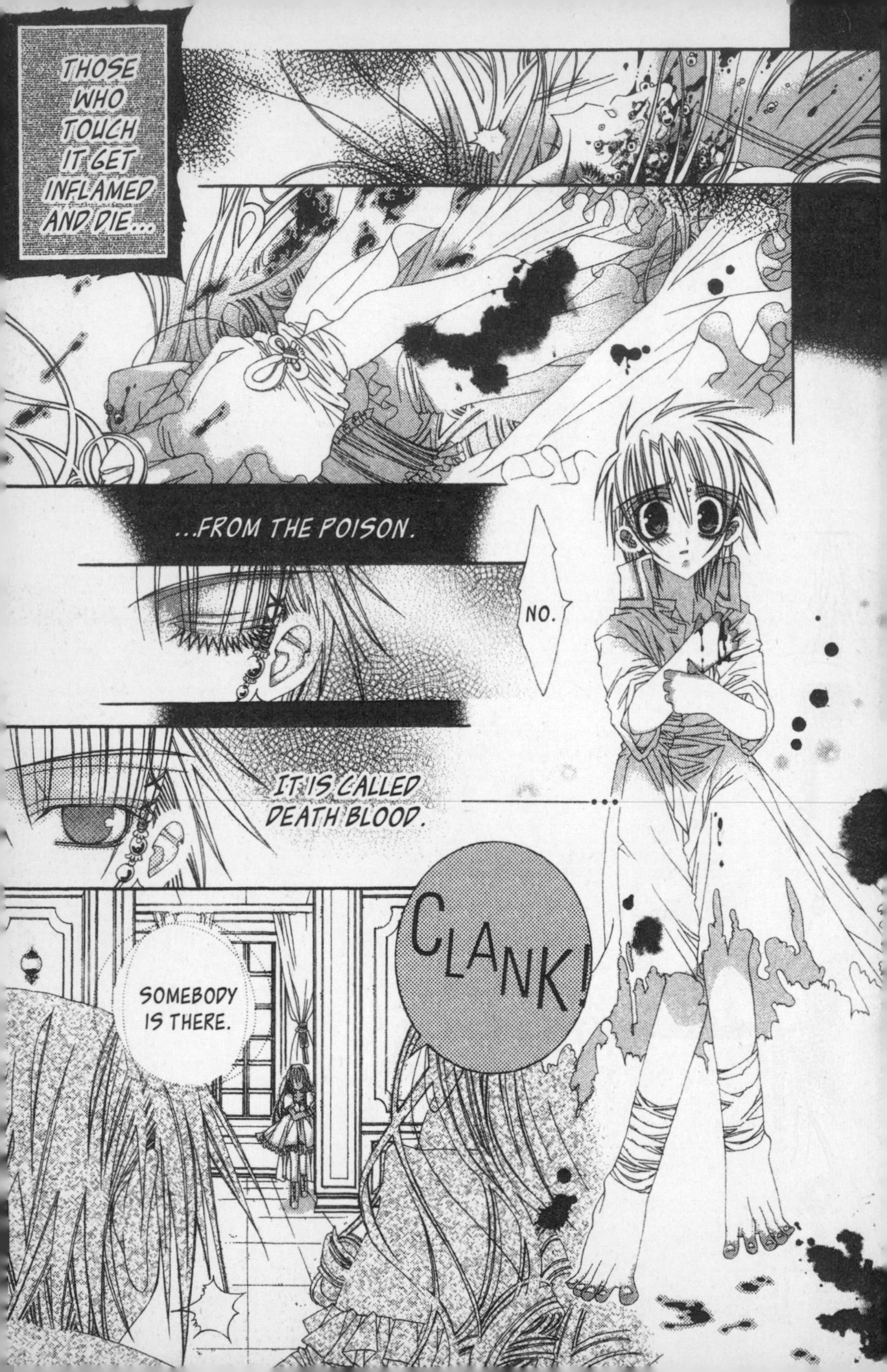
THOSE WHO TOUCH IT GET INFLAMED AND DIE...
...FROM THE POISON.
NO.
IT IS CALLED DEATH BLOOD.
CLANK!
SOMEBODY IS THERE.

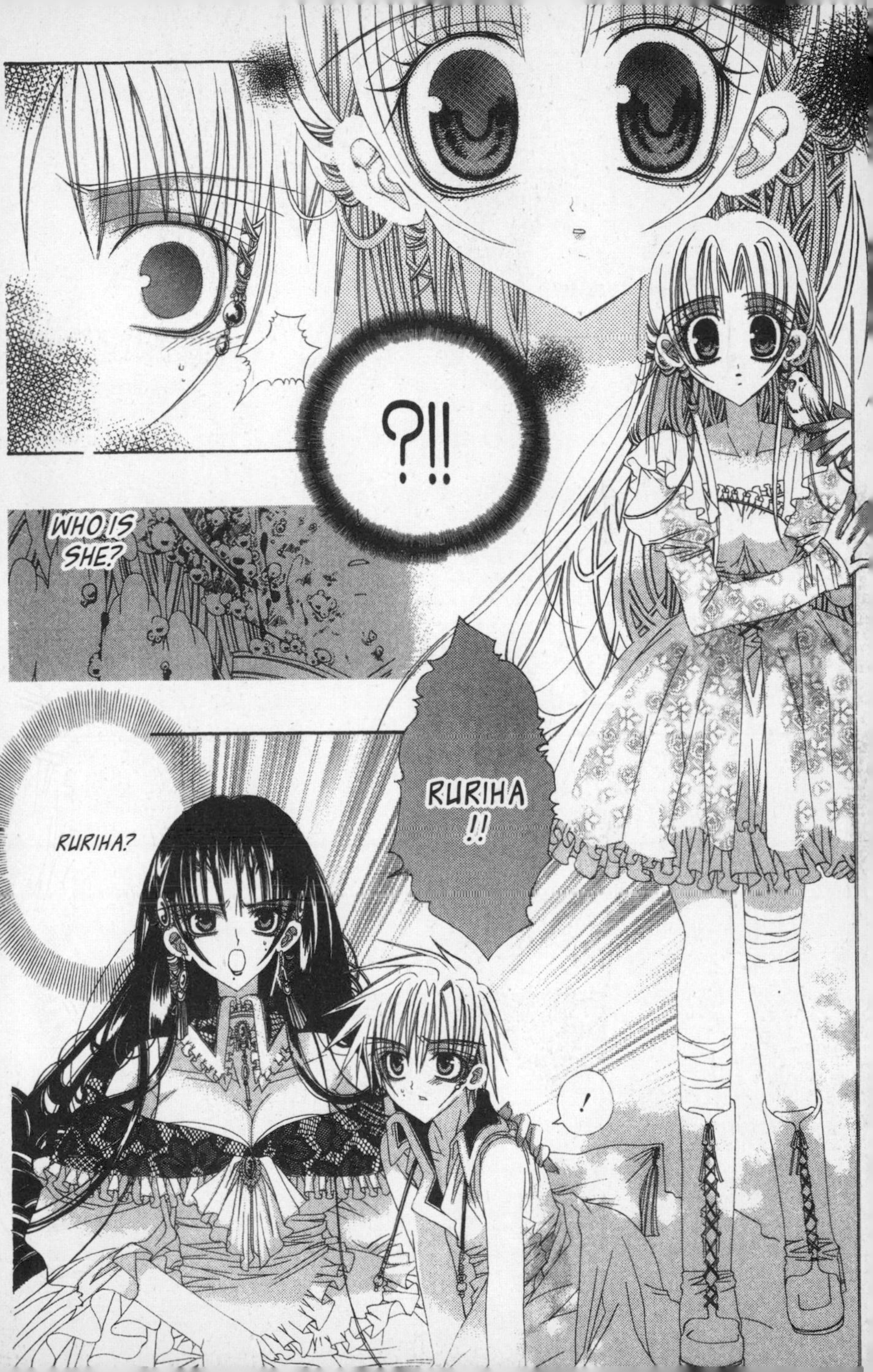
?!!
WHO IS SHE?
RURIHA !!
RURIHA?
!

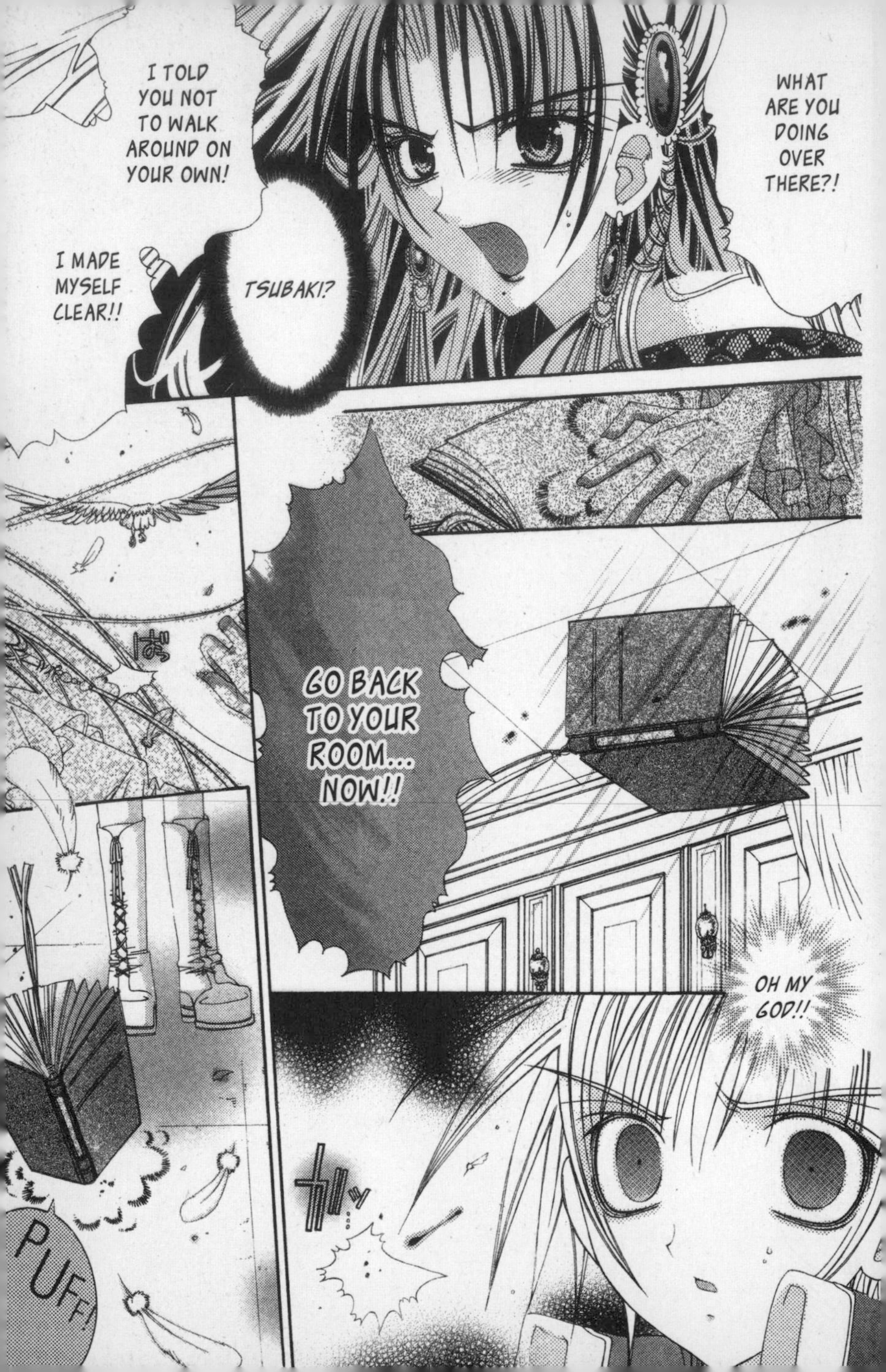
WHAT ARE YOU DOING OVER THERE?!
TSUBAKI?
I TOLD YOU NOT TO WALK AROUND ON YOUR OWN!
I MADE MYSELF CLEAR!!
GO BACK TO YOUR ROOM... NOW!!
OH MY GOD!!
PUFF!

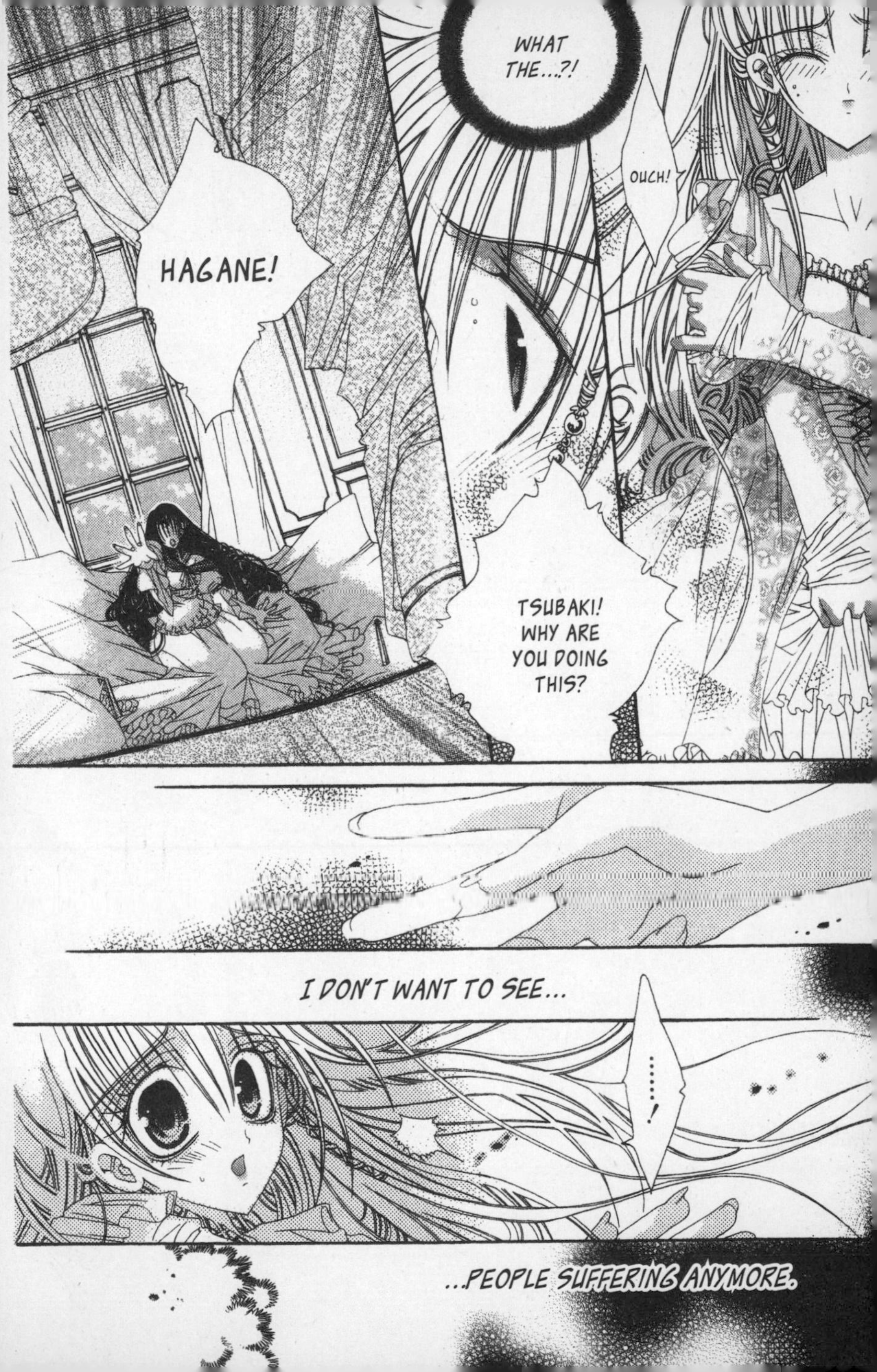
OUCH!
WHAT THE...?!
TSUBAKI! WHY ARE YOU DOING THIS?
HAGANE!
I DON'T WANT TO SEE...
......!
...PEOPLE SUFFERING ANYMORE.

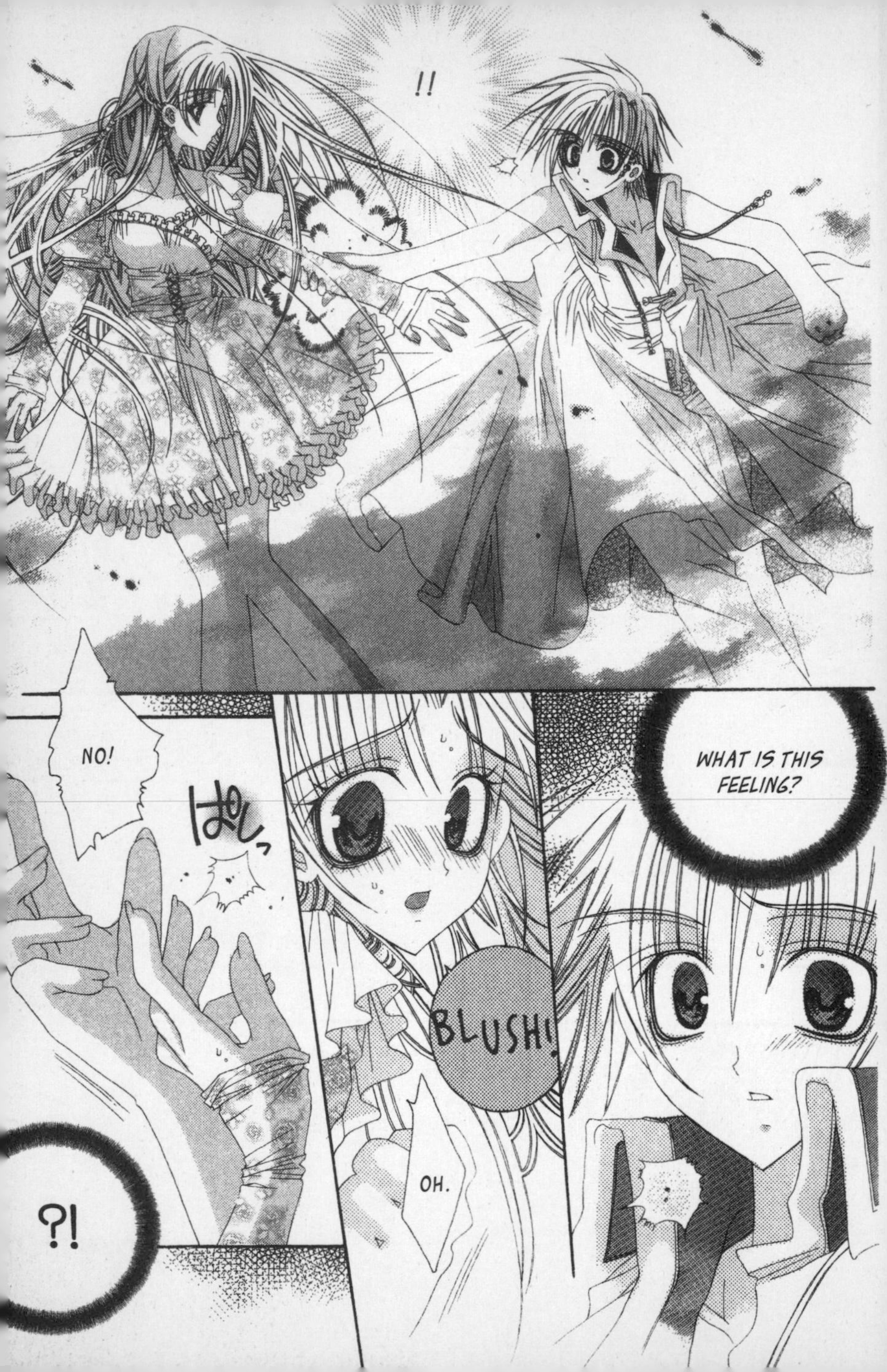
!!
WHAT IS THIS FEELING?
BLUSH!
OH.
NO!
ぱしっ
?!

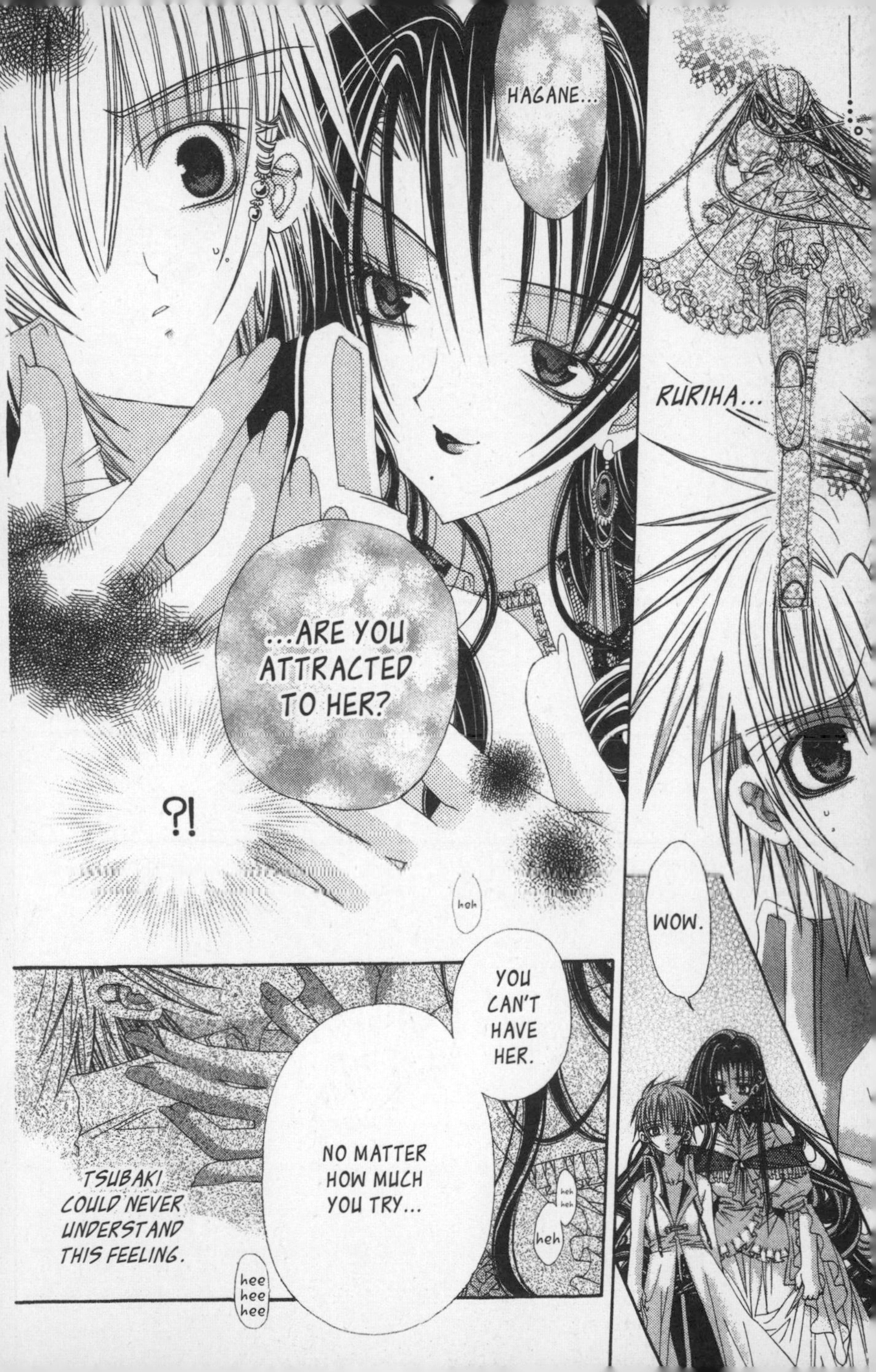

RURIHA...
HAGANE...
...ARE YOU ATTRACTED TO HER?
?!
heh
WOW.
YOU CAN'T HAVE HER.
NO MATTER HOW MUCH YOU TRY...
heh heh
heh
hee hee hee
TSUBAKI COULD NEVER UNDERSTAND THIS FEELING.

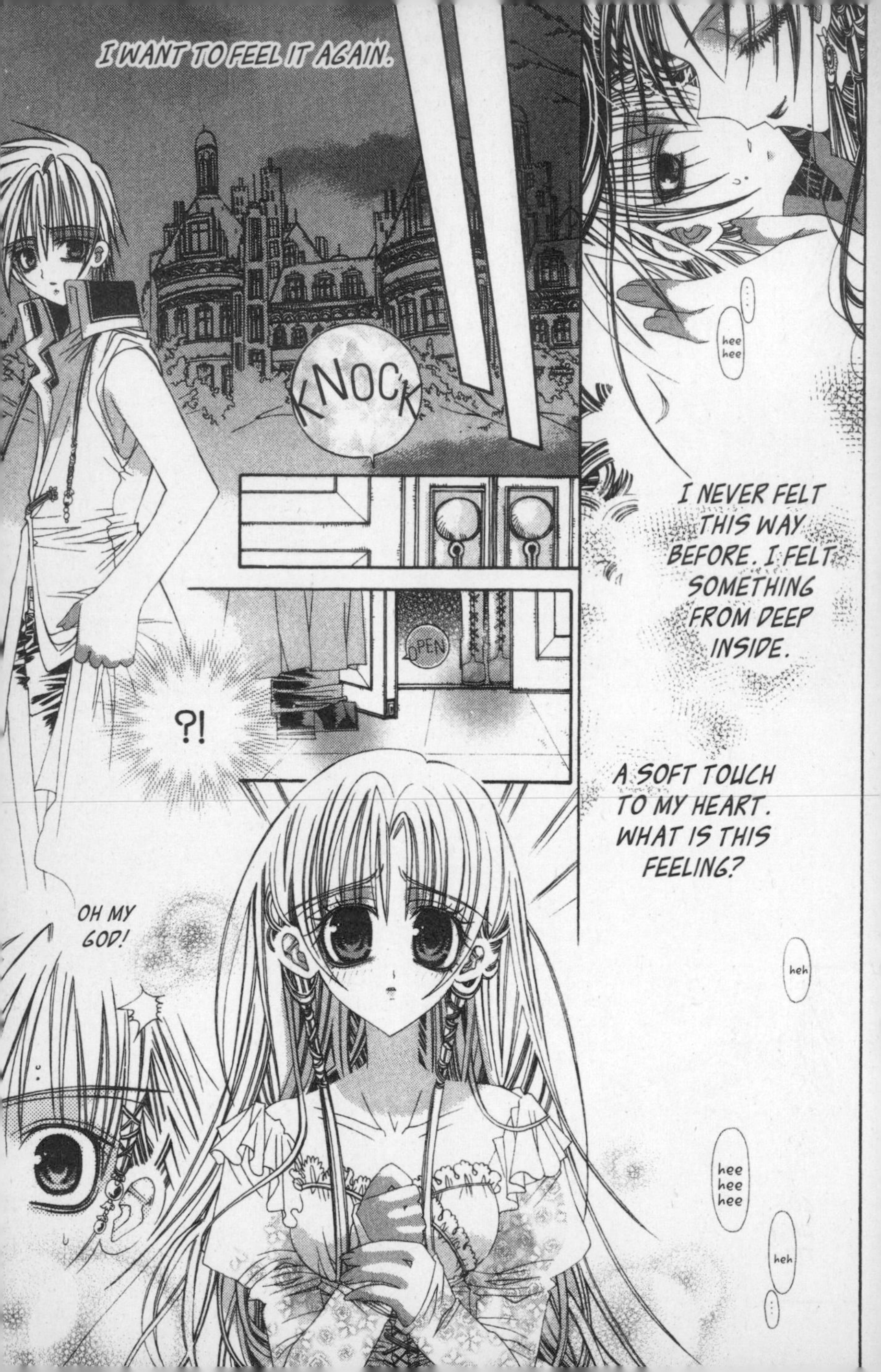
...
hee hee
I NEVER FELT THIS WAY BEFORE. I FELT SOMETHING FROM DEEP INSIDE.
A SOFT TOUCH TO MY HEART. WHAT IS THIS FEELING?
heh
hee hee hee
heh
...
I WANT TO FEEL IT AGAIN.
KNOCK
OPEN
?!
OH MY GOD!

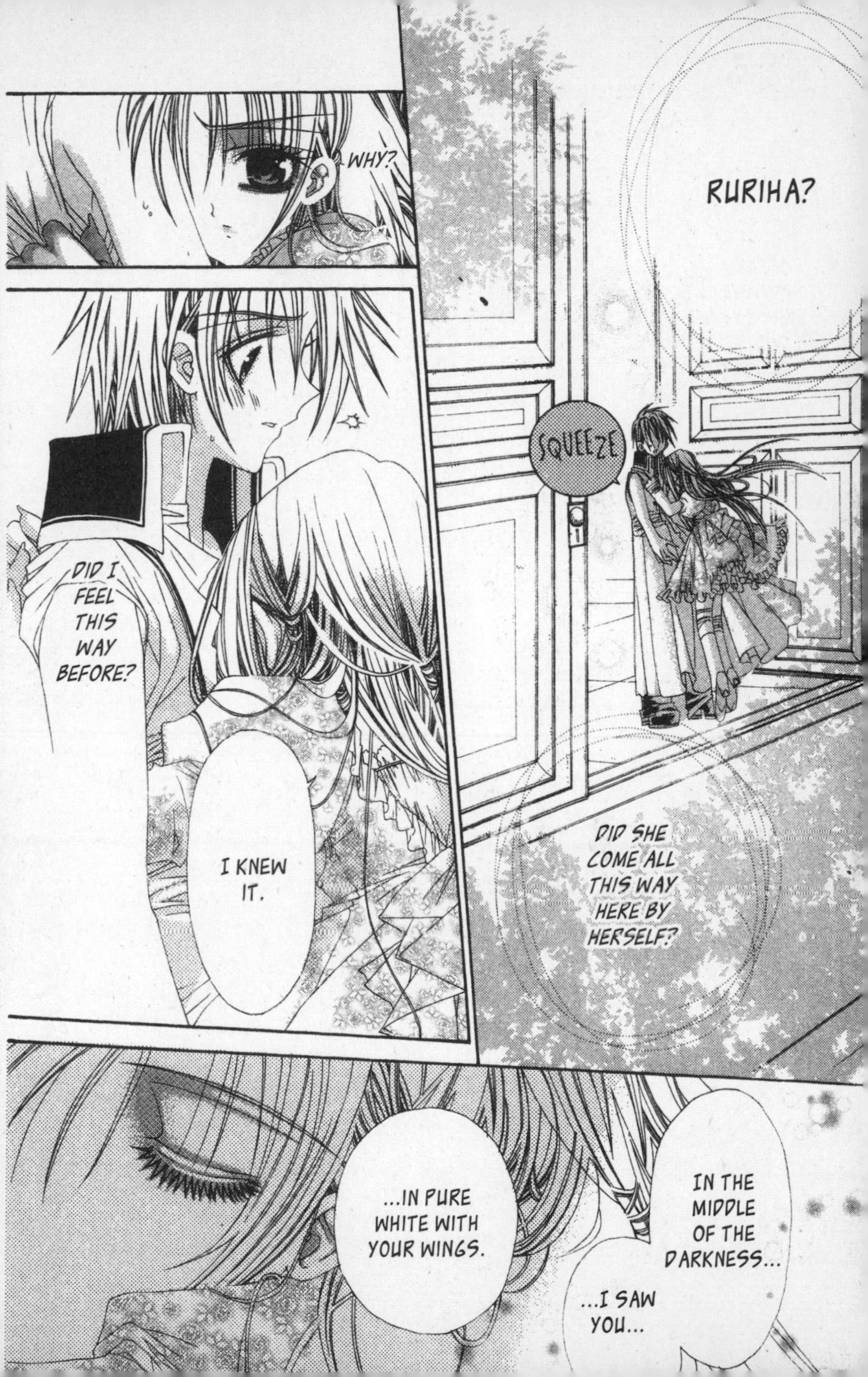
RURIHA?
SQUEEZE
DID SHE COME ALL THIS WAY HERE BY HERSELF?
WHY?
DID I FEEL THIS WAY BEFORE?
I KNEW IT.
IN THE MIDDLE OF THE DARKNESS...
...I SAW YOU...
...IN PURE WHITE WITH YOUR WINGS.

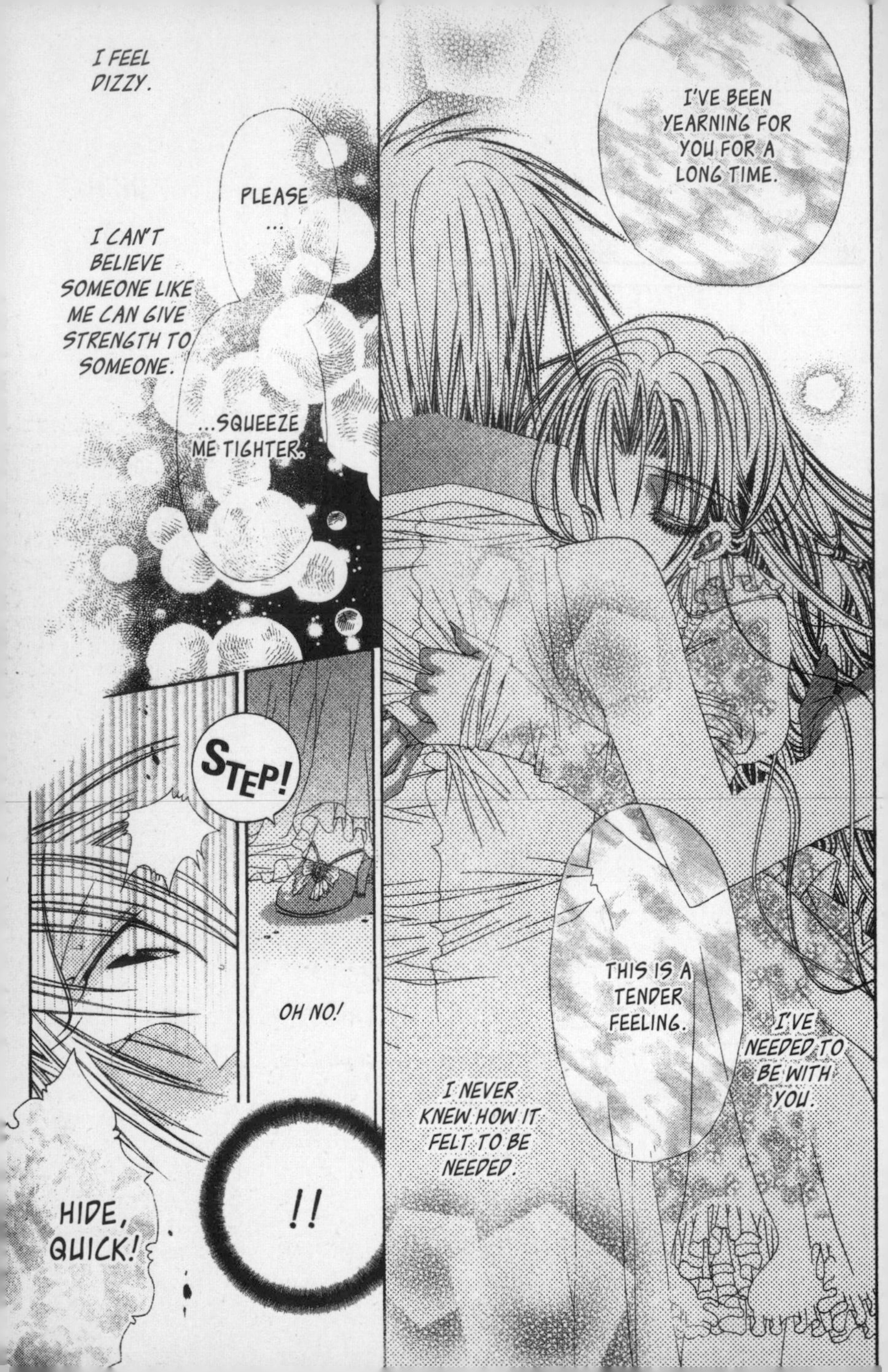

I'VE BEEN YEARNING FOR YOU FOR A LONG TIME.
I'VE NEEDED TO BE WITH YOU.
THIS IS A TENDER FEELING.
I NEVER KNEW HOW IT FELT TO BE NEEDED.
I FEEL DIZZY.
PLEASE ...
I CAN'T BELIEVE SOMEONE LIKE ME CAN GIVE STRENGTH TO SOMEONE.
...SQUEEZE ME TIGHTER.
STEP!
OH NO!
HIDE, QUICK!
!!

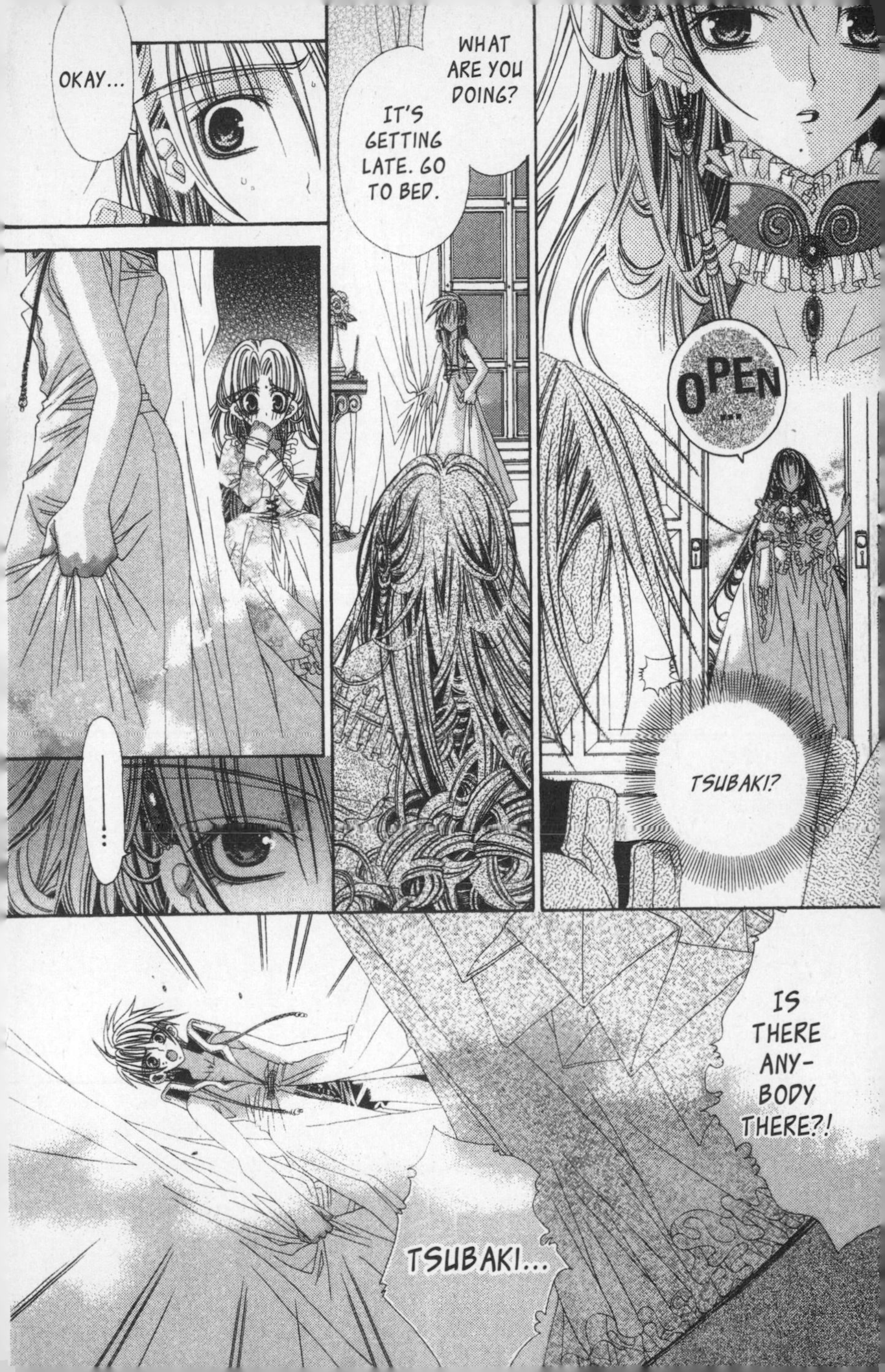

OPEN...
TSUBAKI?
WHAT ARE YOU DOING?
IT'S GETTING LATE. GO TO BED.
OKAY...
...!
IS THERE ANY-BODY THERE?!
TSUBAKI...

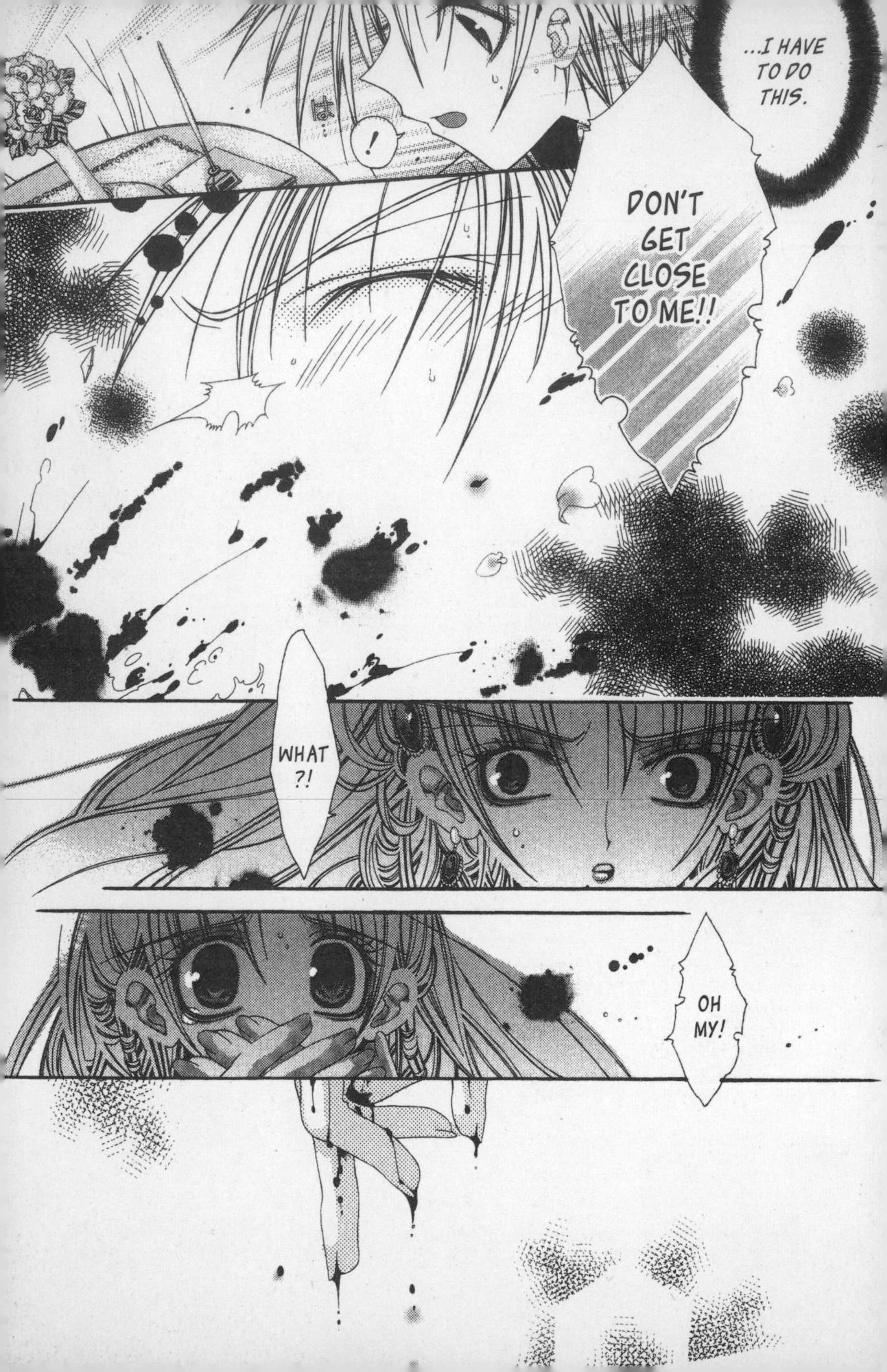
...I HAVE TO DO THIS.
DON'T GET CLOSE TO ME!!
!
WHAT ?!
OH MY!

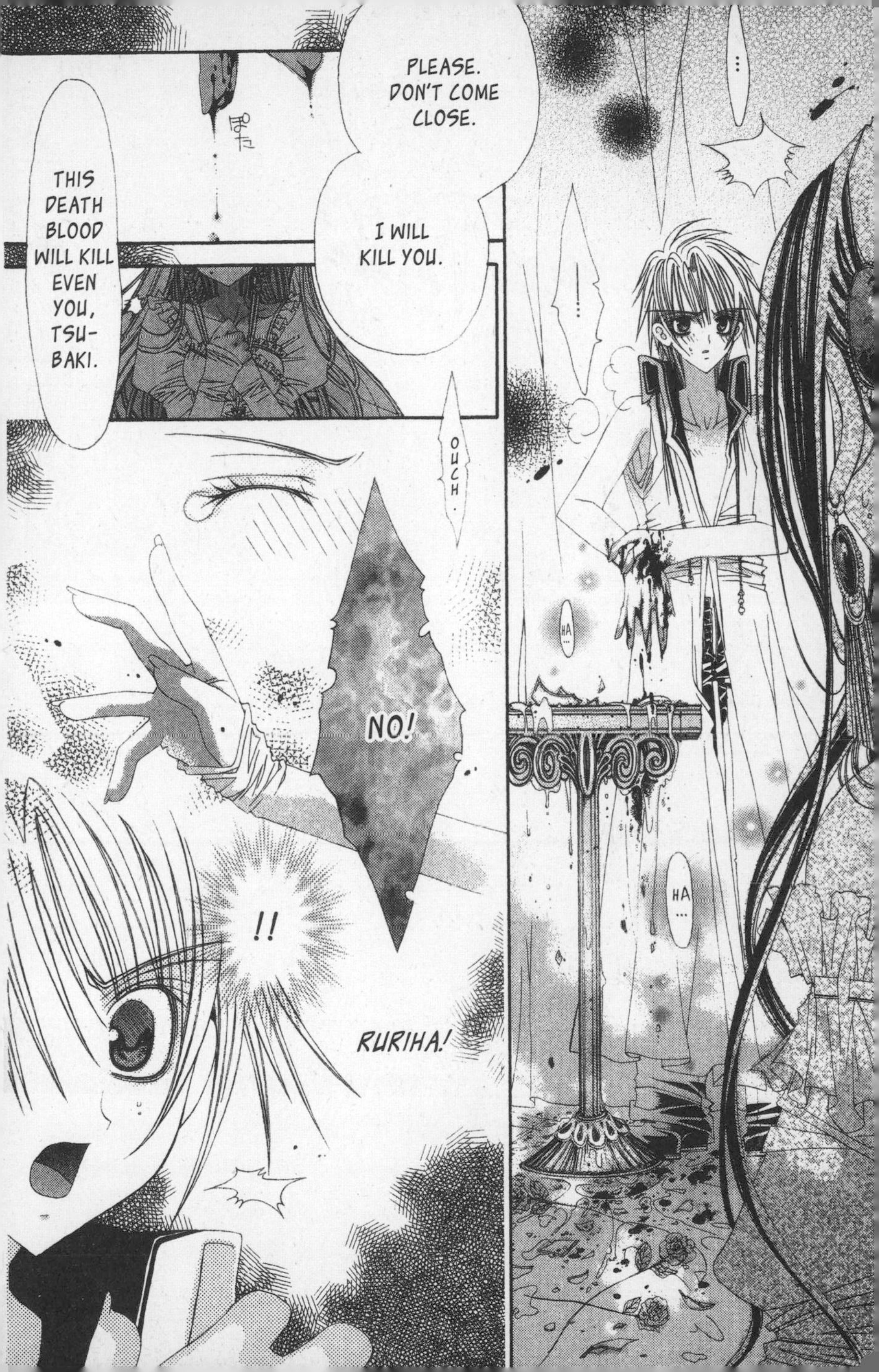
...
!
HA...
HA...
PLEASE. DON'T COME CLOSE.
I WILL KILL YOU.
ぽた
THIS DEATH BLOOD WILL KILL EVEN YOU, TSUBAKI.
OUCH.
NO!
!!
RURIHA!

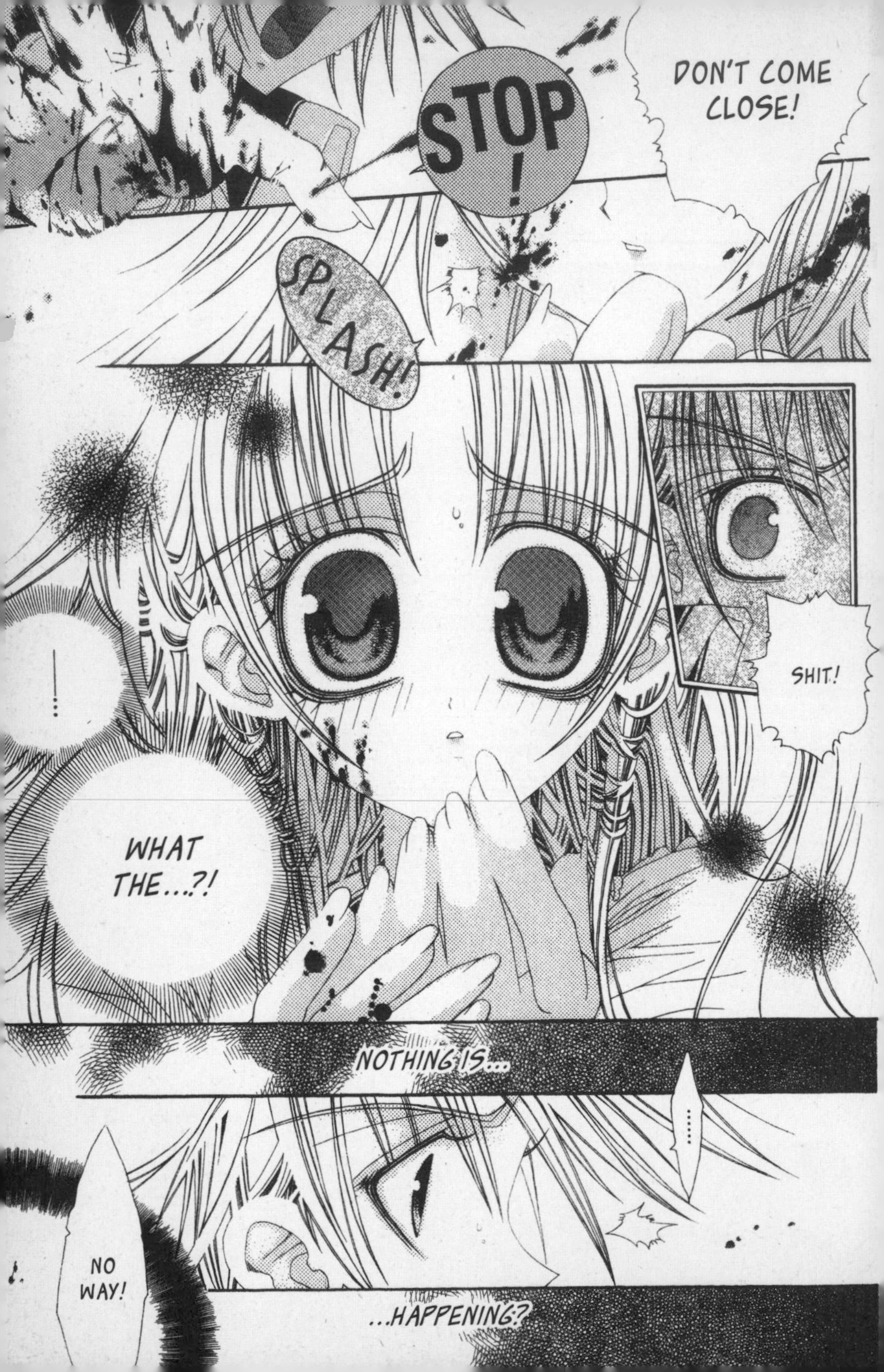
DON'T COME CLOSE!
STOP!
SPLASH!
SHIT!
…!
WHAT THE...?!
NOTHING IS...
……
NO WAY!
...HAPPENING?

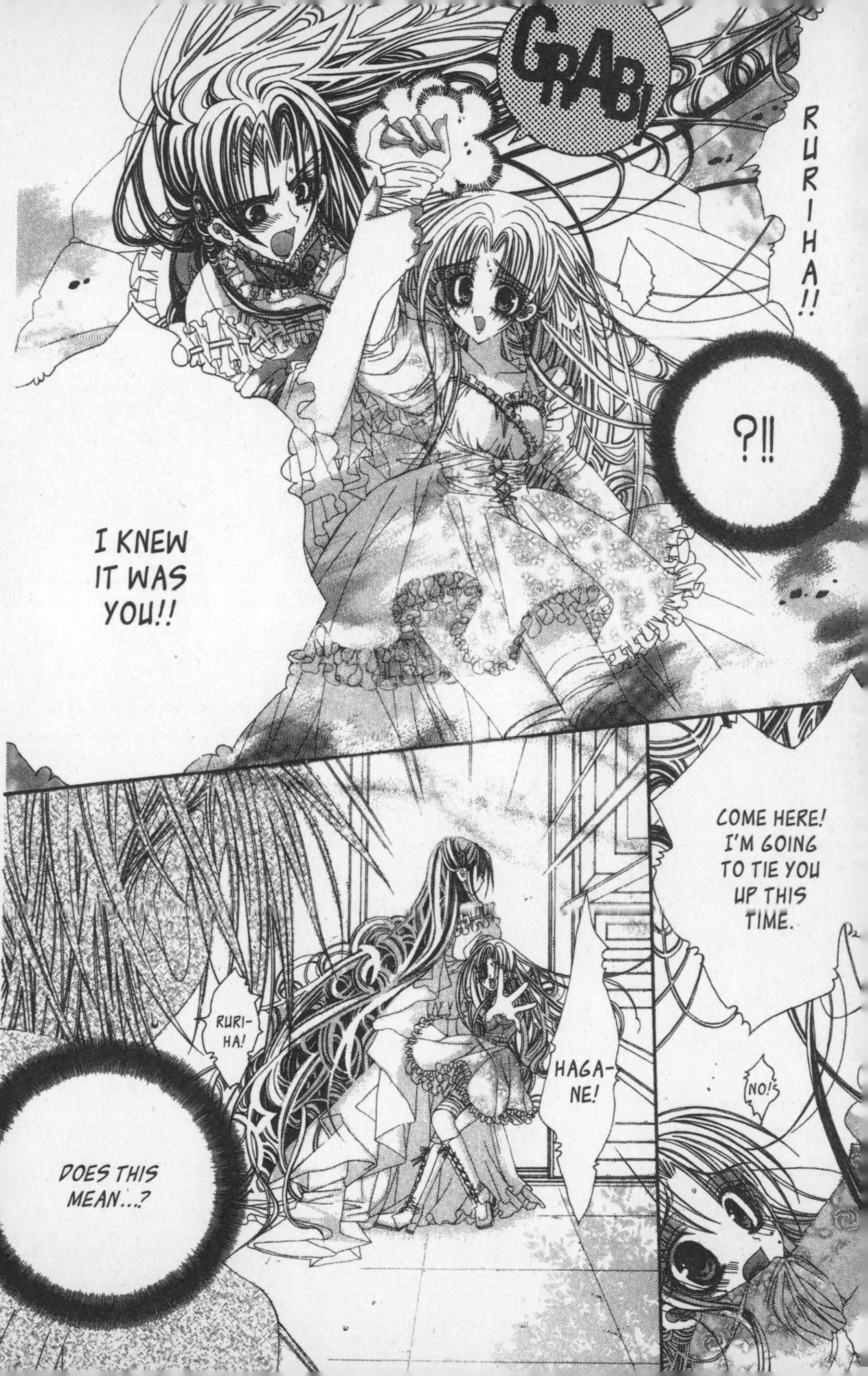
GRAB!
RURIHA!!
?!!
I KNEW IT WAS YOU!!
COME HERE! I'M GOING TO TIE YOU UP THIS TIME.
NO!
HAGA-NE!
RURI-HA!
DOES THIS MEAN...?

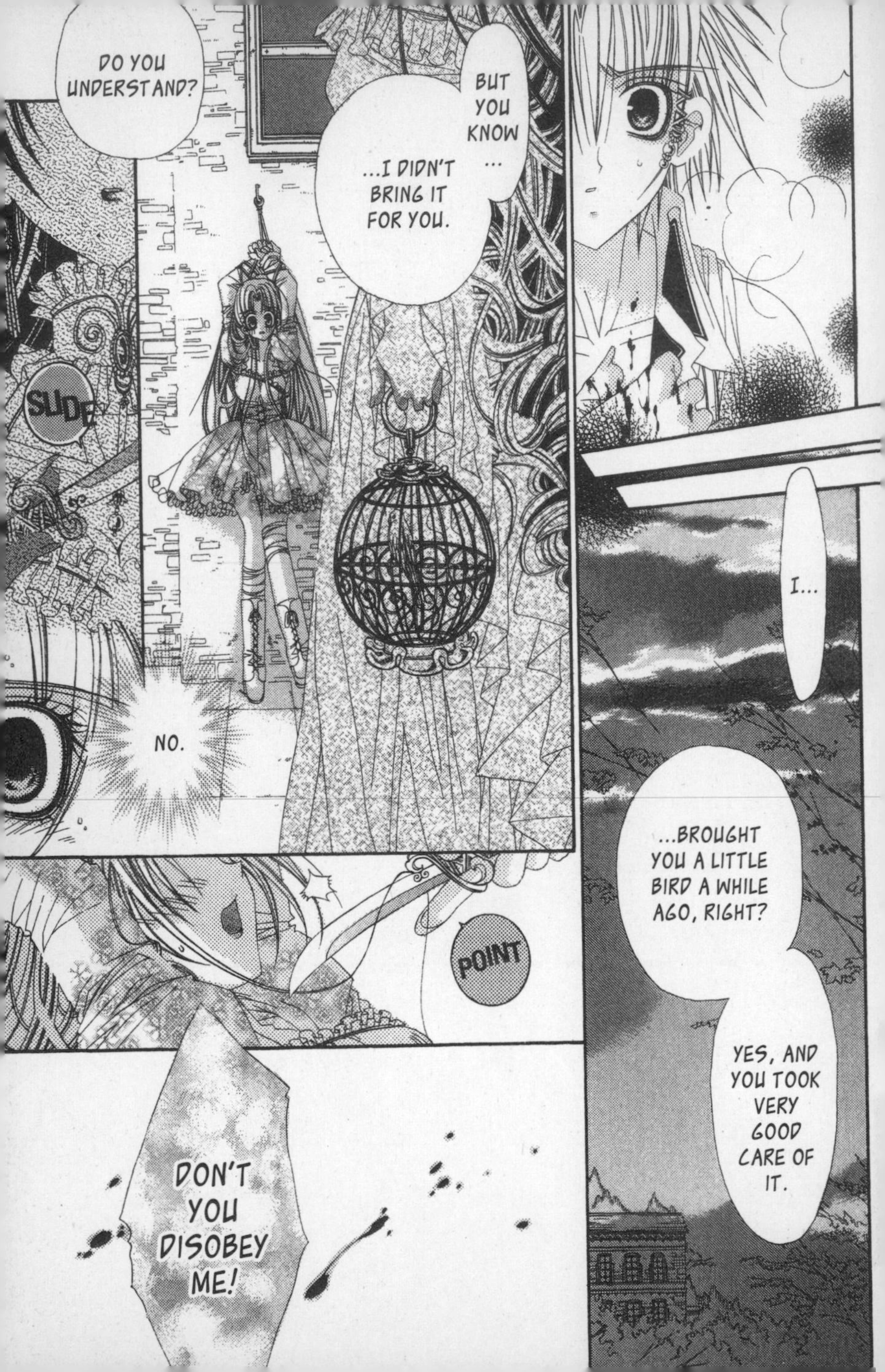
I...
...BROUGHT YOU A LITTLE BIRD A WHILE AGO, RIGHT?
YES, AND YOU TOOK VERY GOOD CARE OF IT.
BUT YOU KNOW...
...I DIDN'T BRING IT FOR YOU.
DO YOU UNDERSTAND?
SLIDE
NO.
POINT
DON'T YOU DISOBEY ME!

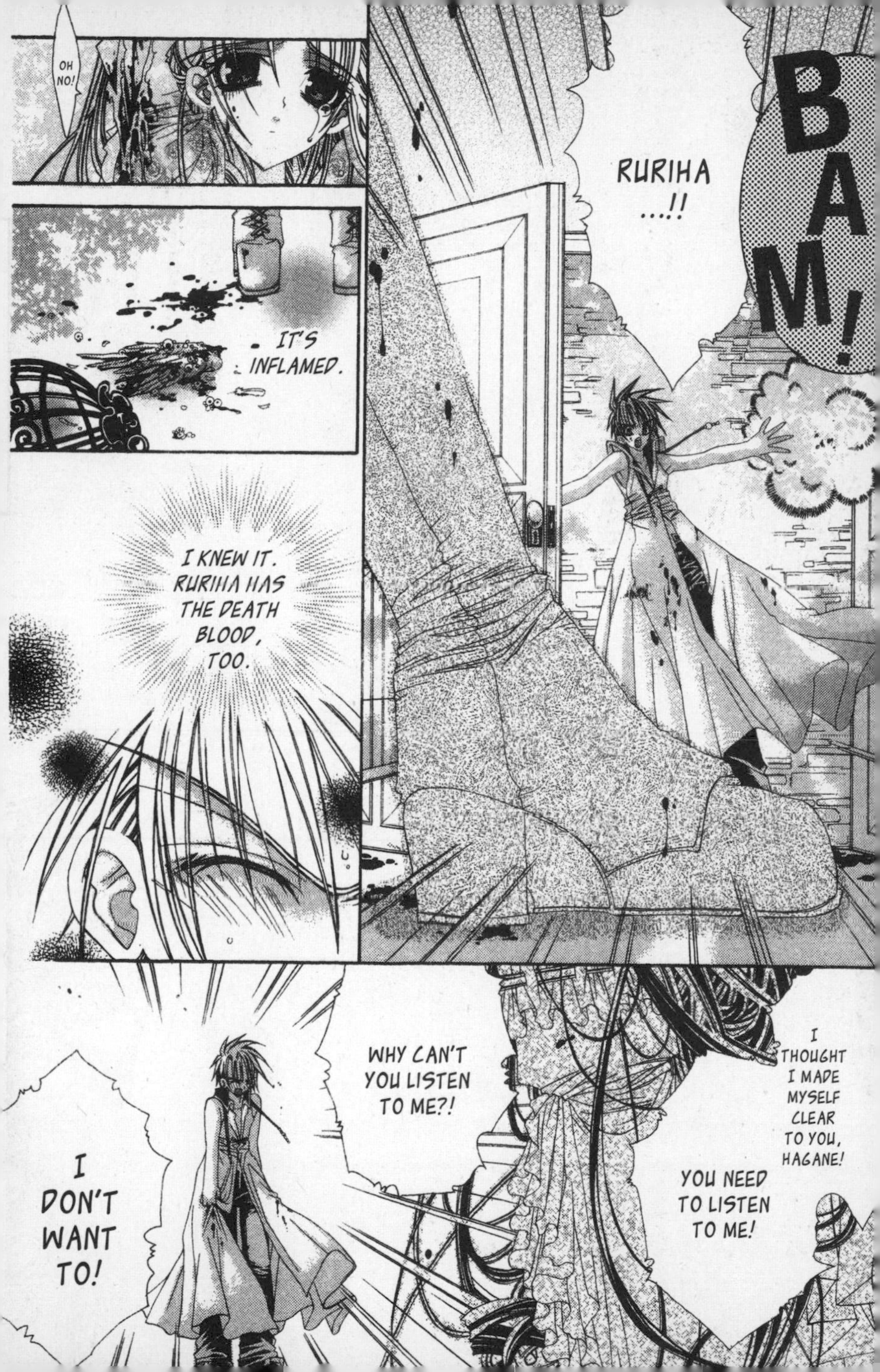
BAM!
RURIHA ...!!
OH NO!
IT'S INFLAMED.
I KNEW IT. RURIHA HAS THE DEATH BLOOD, TOO.
I THOUGHT I MADE MYSELF CLEAR TO YOU, HAGANE!
YOU NEED TO LISTEN TO ME!
WHY CAN'T YOU LISTEN TO ME?!
I DON'T WANT TO!

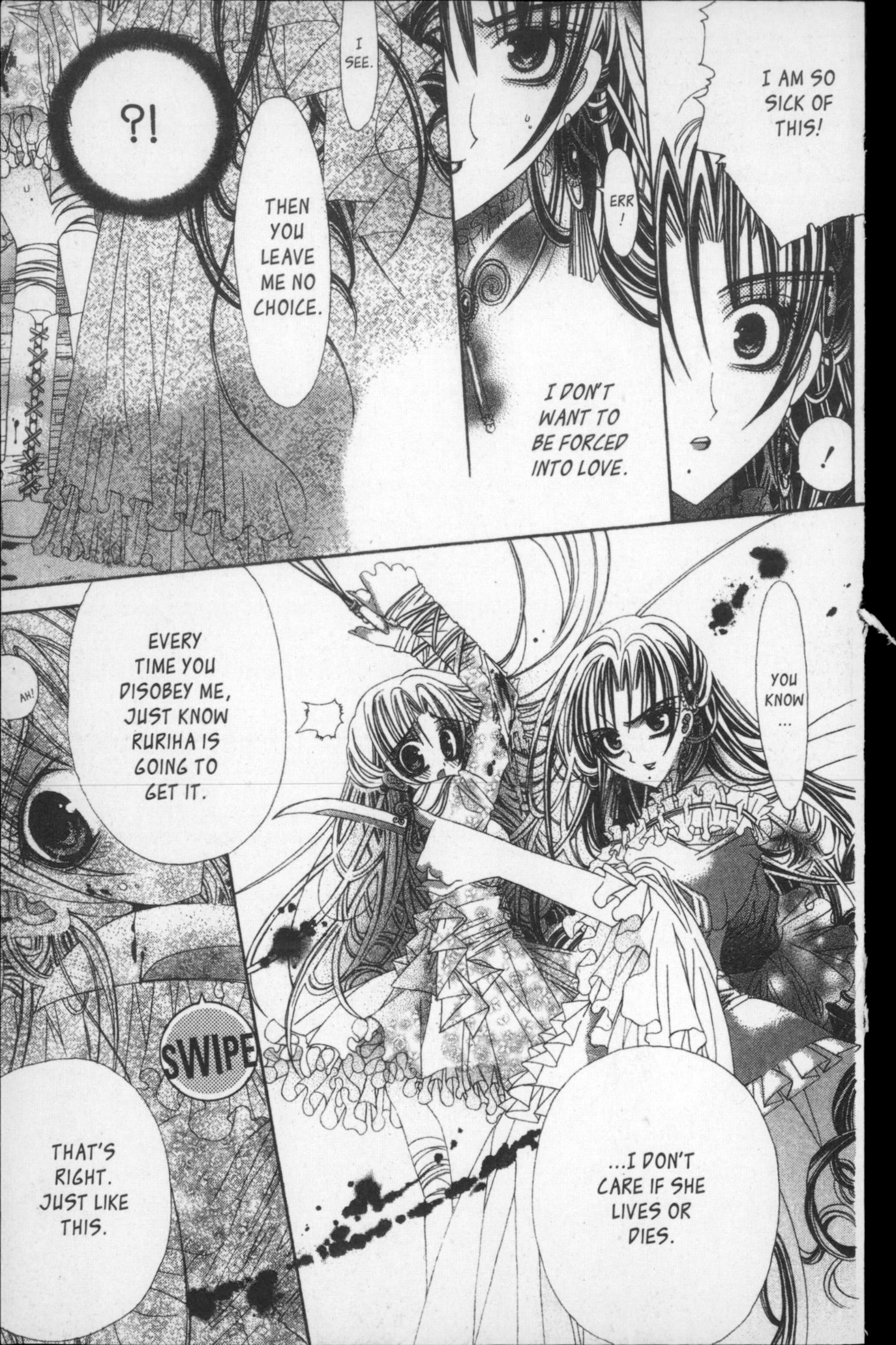
I AM SO SICK OF THIS!
!
ERR!
I DON'T WANT TO BE FORCED INTO LOVE.
I SEE.
THEN YOU LEAVE ME NO CHOICE.
?!
YOU KNOW...
...I DON'T CARE IF SHE LIVES OR DIES.
AH!
EVERY TIME YOU DISOBEY ME, JUST KNOW RURIHA IS GOING TO GET IT.
SWIPE
THAT'S RIGHT. JUST LIKE THIS.

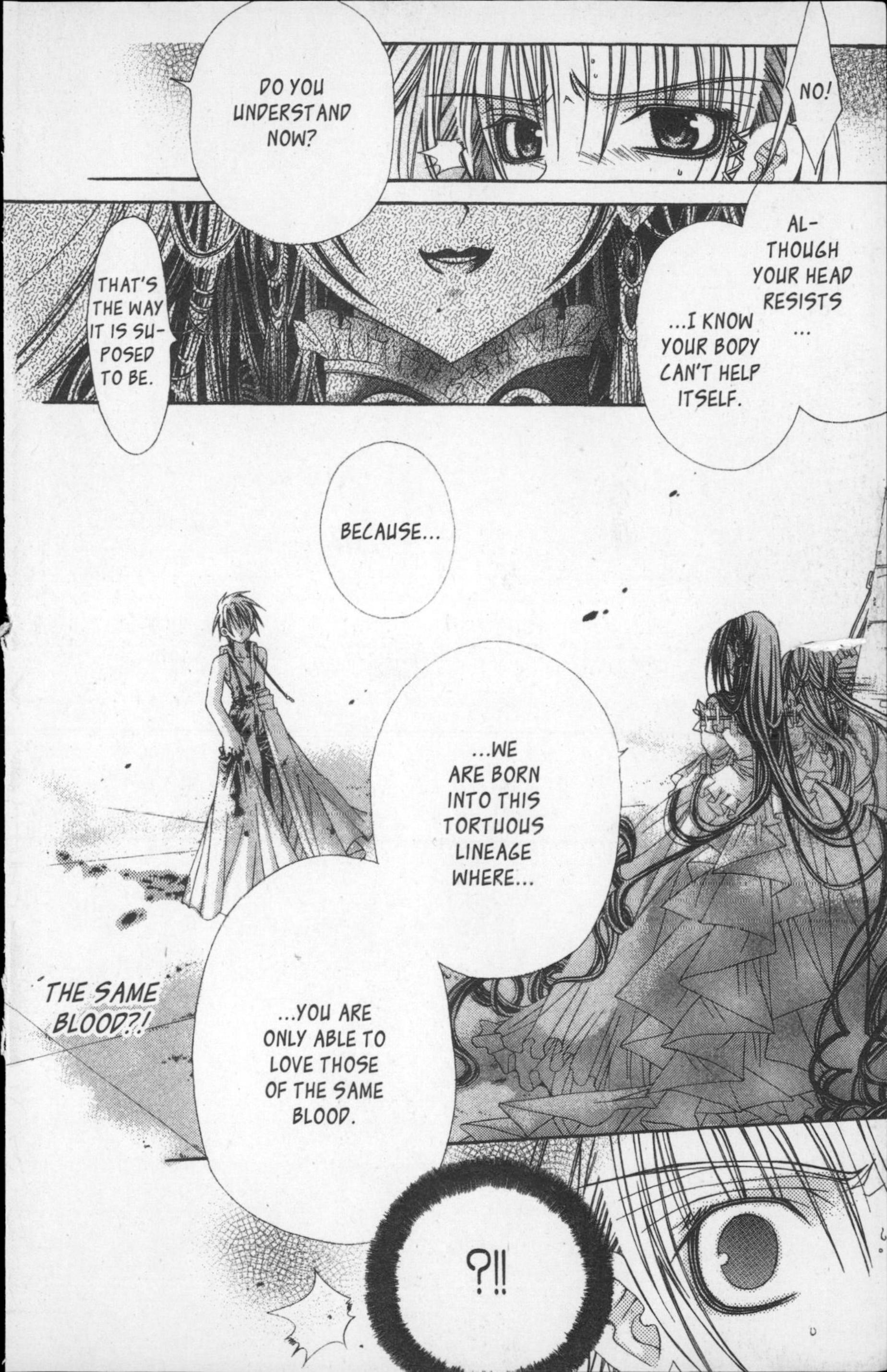
NO!
DO YOU UNDERSTAND NOW?
AL-THOUGH YOUR HEAD RESISTS...
...I KNOW YOUR BODY CAN'T HELP ITSELF.
THAT'S THE WAY IT IS SU-POSED TO BE.
BECAUSE...
...WE ARE BORN INTO THIS TORTUOUS LINEAGE WHERE...
...YOU ARE ONLY ABLE TO LOVE THOSE OF THE SAME BLOOD.
THE SAME BLOOD?!
?!!

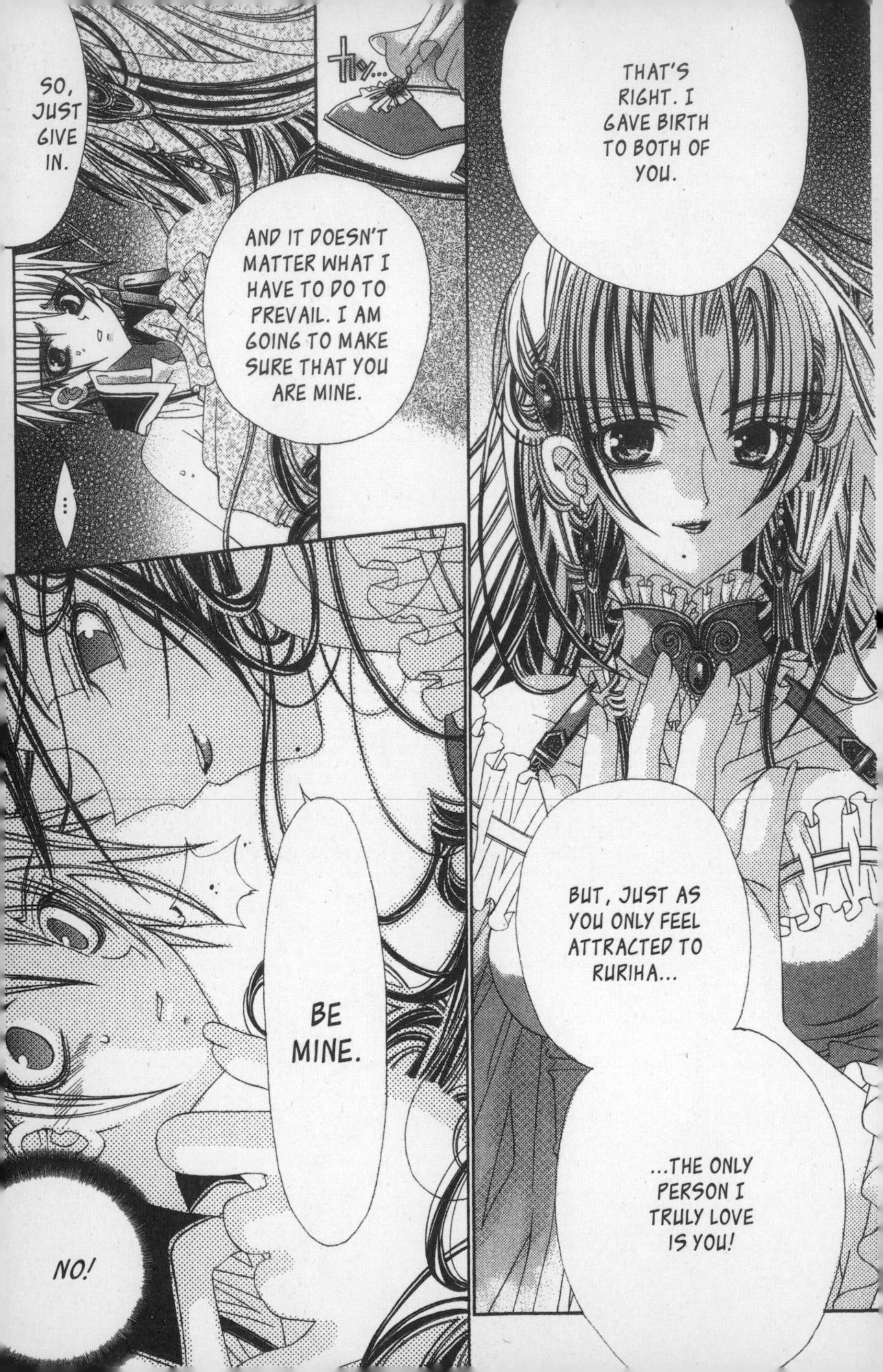
THAT'S RIGHT. I GAVE BIRTH TO BOTH OF YOU.
BUT, JUST AS YOU ONLY FEEL ATTRACTED TO RURIHA...
...THE ONLY PERSON I TRULY LOVE IS YOU!
カツ…
SO, JUST GIVE IN.
AND IT DOESN'T MATTER WHAT I HAVE TO DO TO PREVAIL. I AM GOING TO MAKE SURE THAT YOU ARE MINE.
...
BE MINE.
NO!

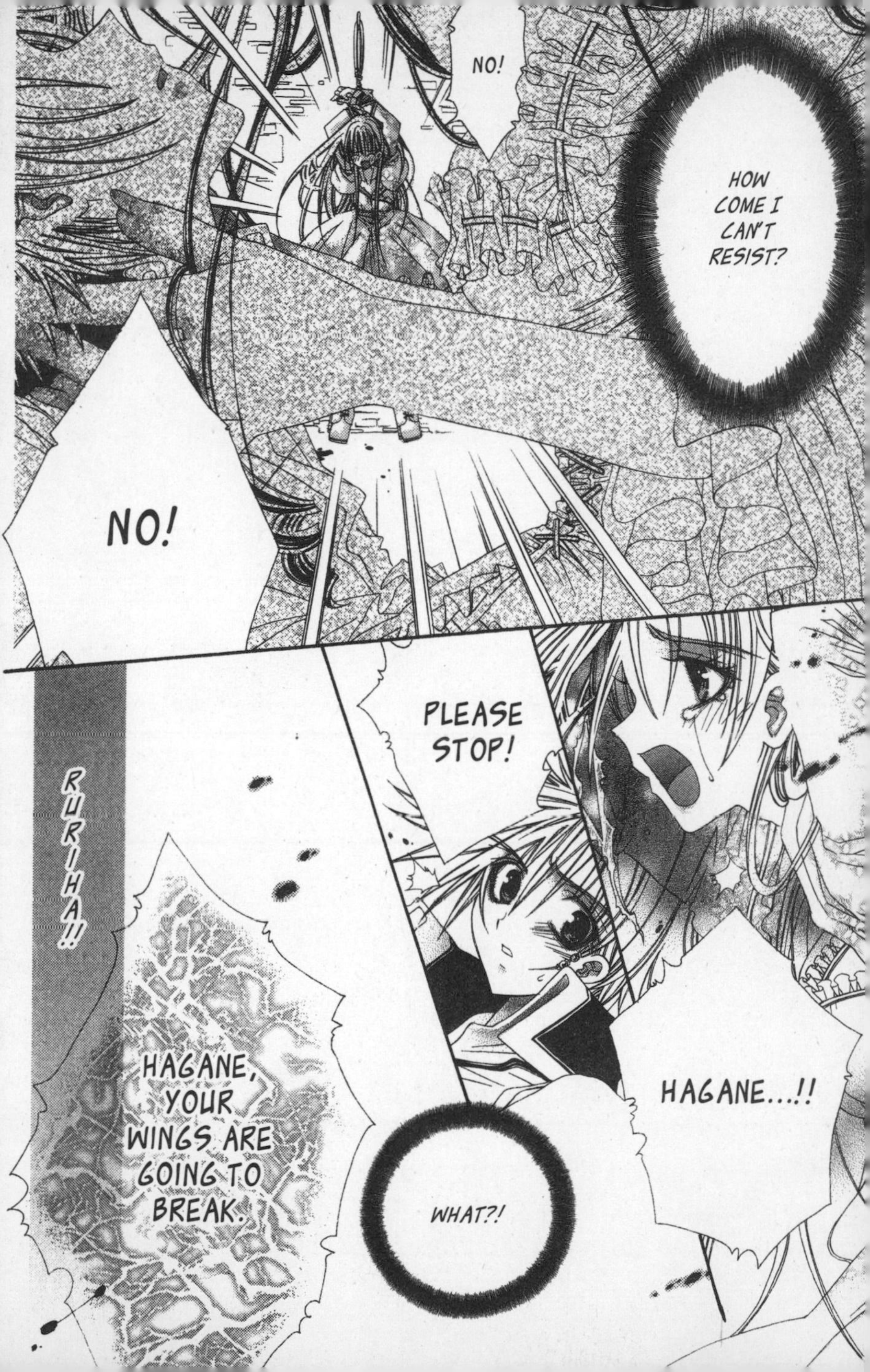
NO!
HOW COME I CAN'T RESIST?
NO!
PLEASE STOP!
HAGANE...!!
WHAT?!
RURIHA!!
HAGANE, YOUR WINGS ARE GOING TO BREAK.

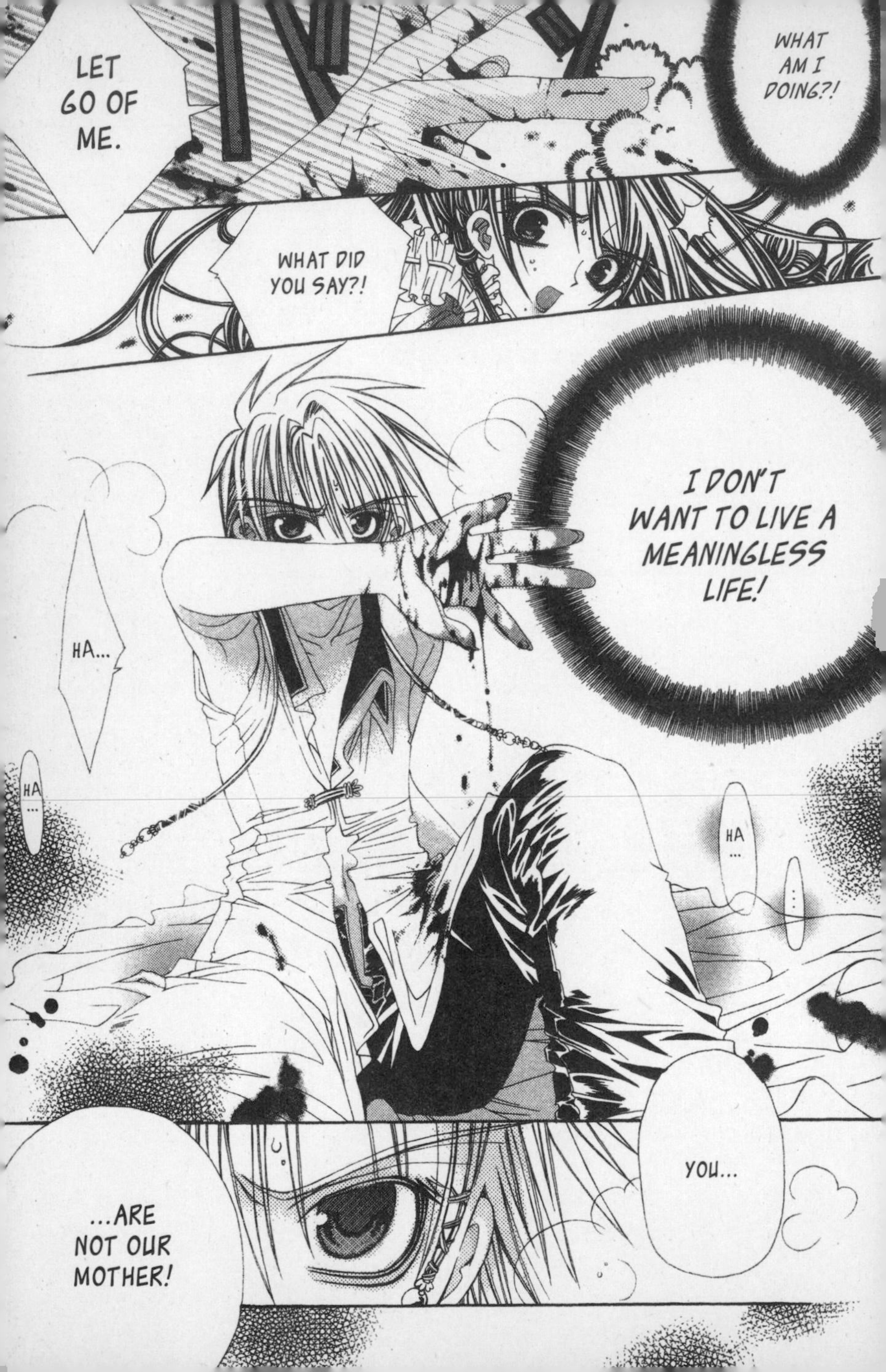
WHAT AM I DOING?!
LET GO OF ME.
WHAT DID YOU SAY?!
I DON'T WANT TO LIVE A MEANINGLESS LIFE!
HA...
HA...
...
HA...
YOU...
...ARE NOT OUR MOTHER!

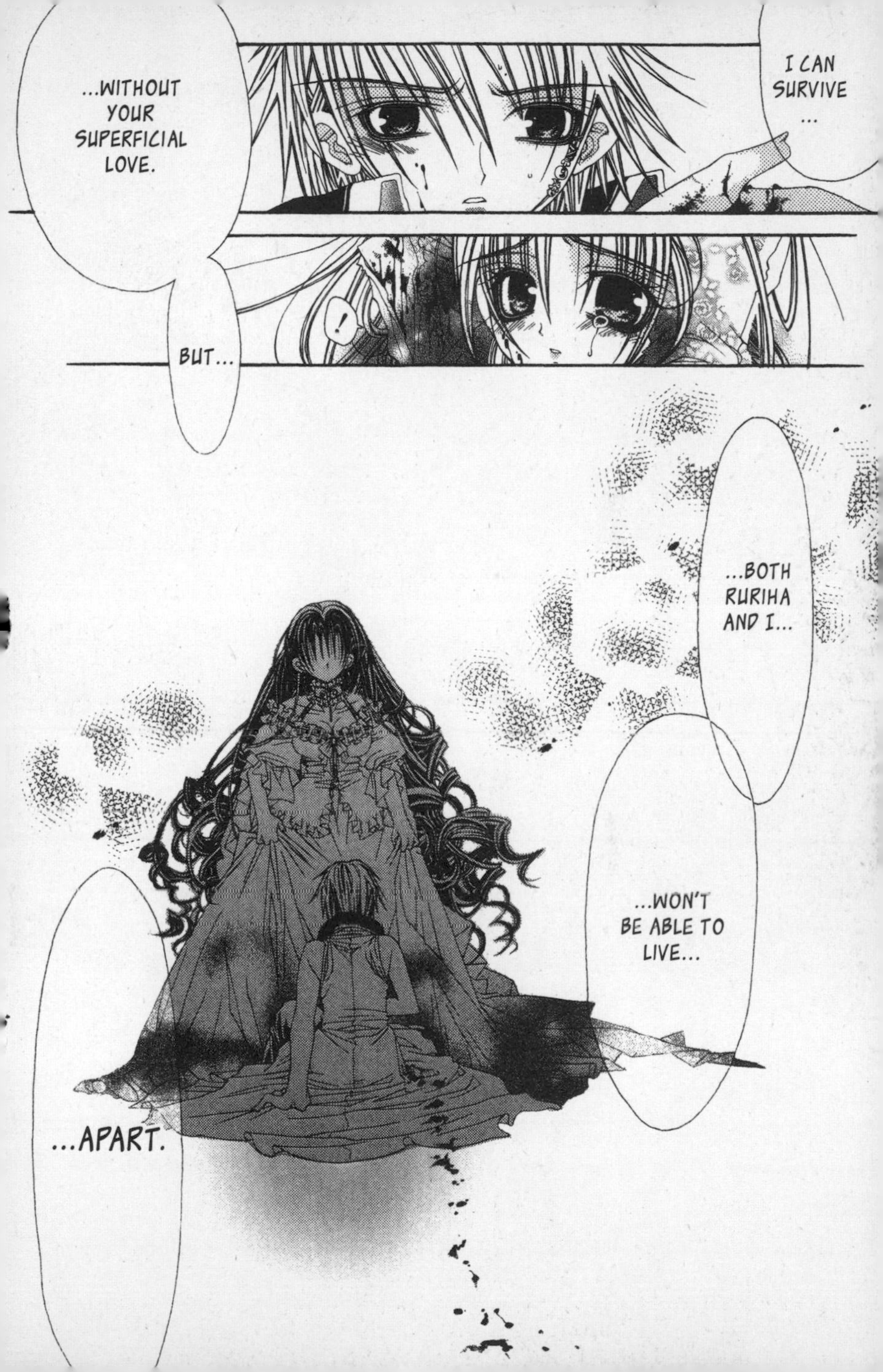
I CAN SURVIVE ...
...WITHOUT YOUR SUPERFICIAL LOVE.
!
BUT...
...BOTH RURIHA AND I...
...WON'T BE ABLE TO LIVE...
...APART.

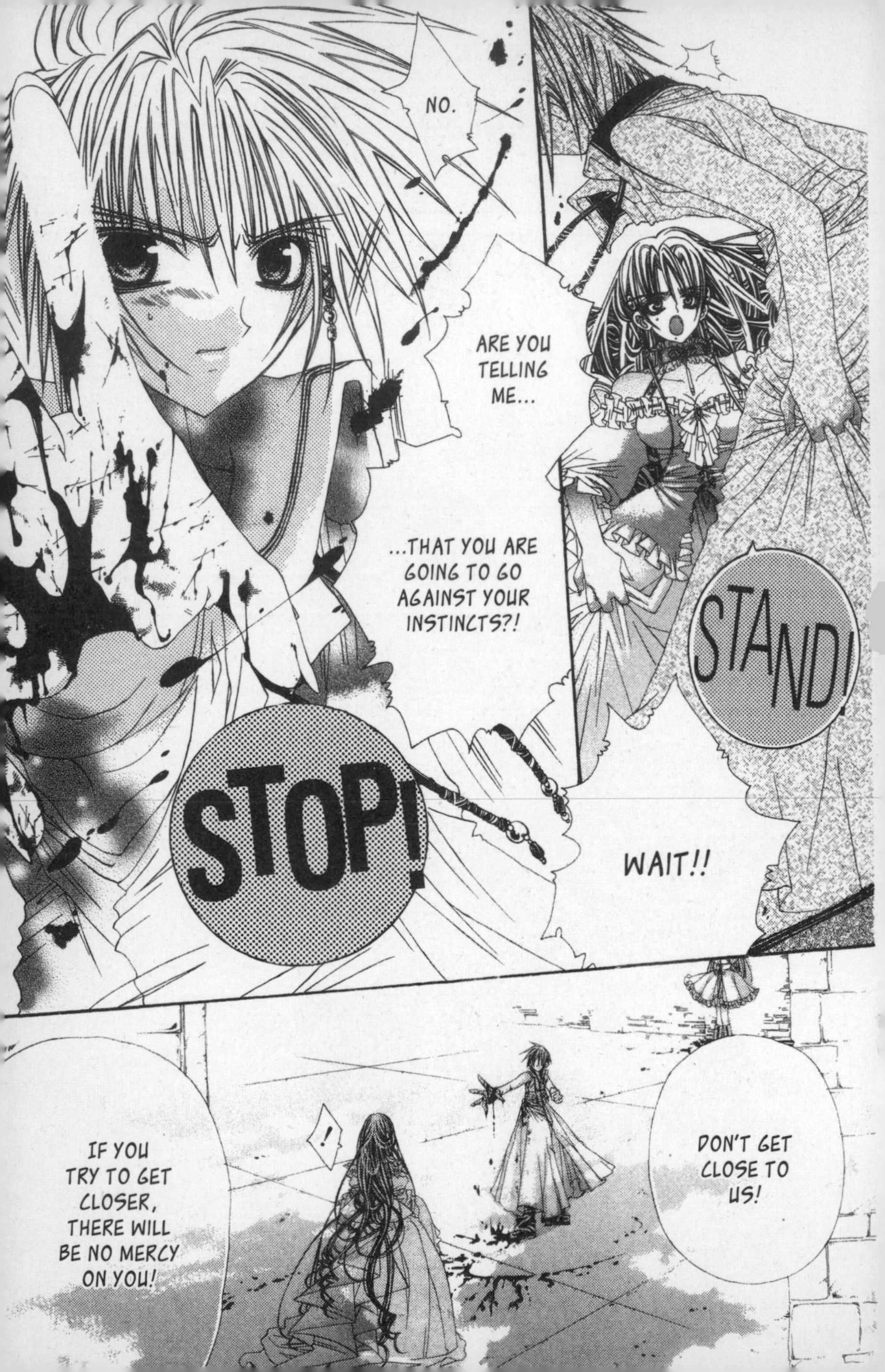
WAIT!!
STAND!
ARE YOU TELLING ME...
...THAT YOU ARE GOING TO GO AGAINST YOUR INSTINCTS?!
NO.
STOP!
DON'T GET CLOSE TO US!
!
IF YOU TRY TO GET CLOSER, THERE WILL BE NO MERCY ON YOU!

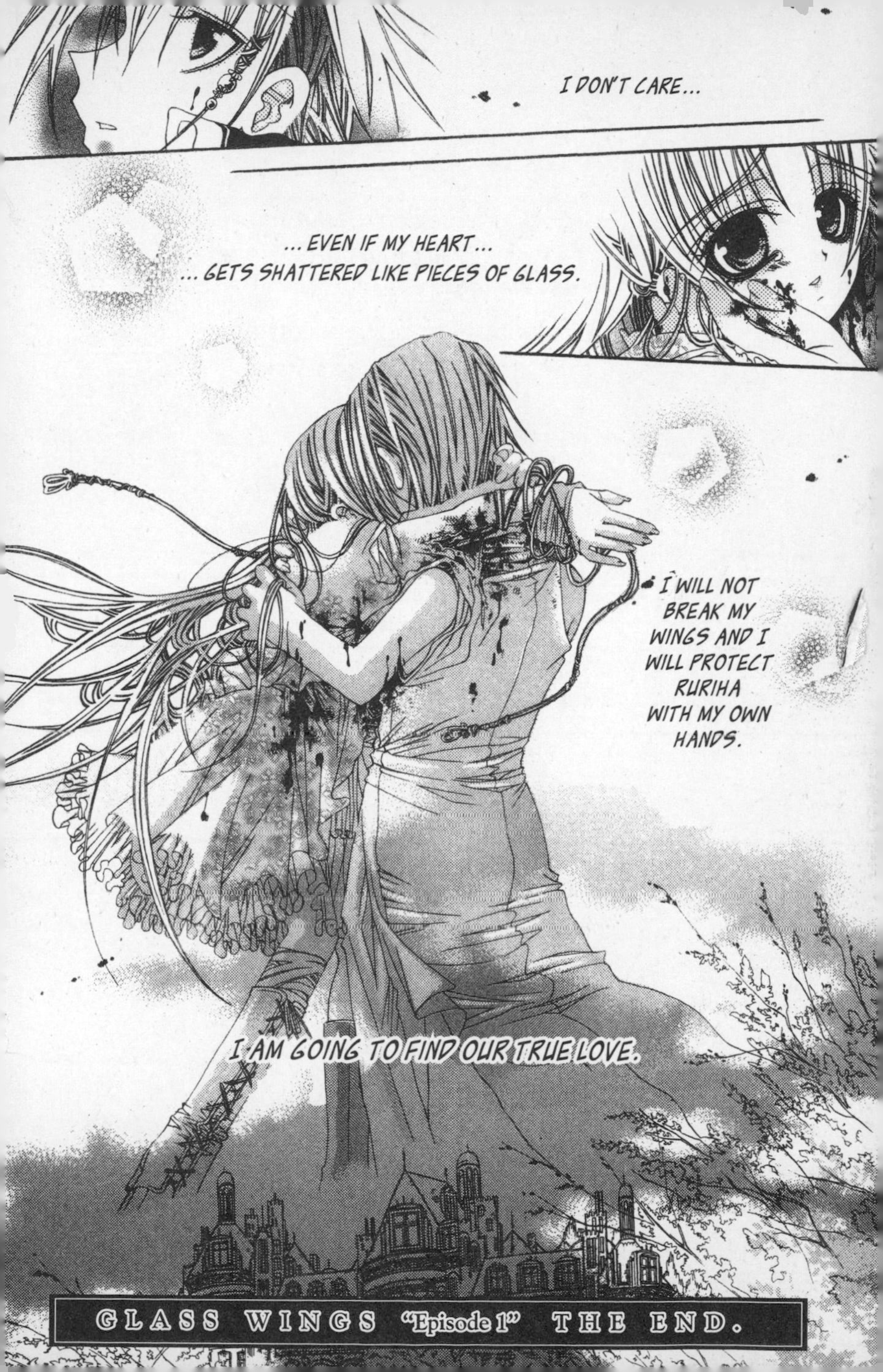

I DON'T CARE...
... EVEN IF MY HEART...
... GETS SHATTERED LIKE PIECES OF GLASS.
I WILL NOT BREAK MY WINGS AND I WILL PROTECT RURIHA WITH MY OWN HANDS.
I AM GOING TO FIND OUR TRUE LOVE.
GLASS WINGS "Episode 1" THE END.

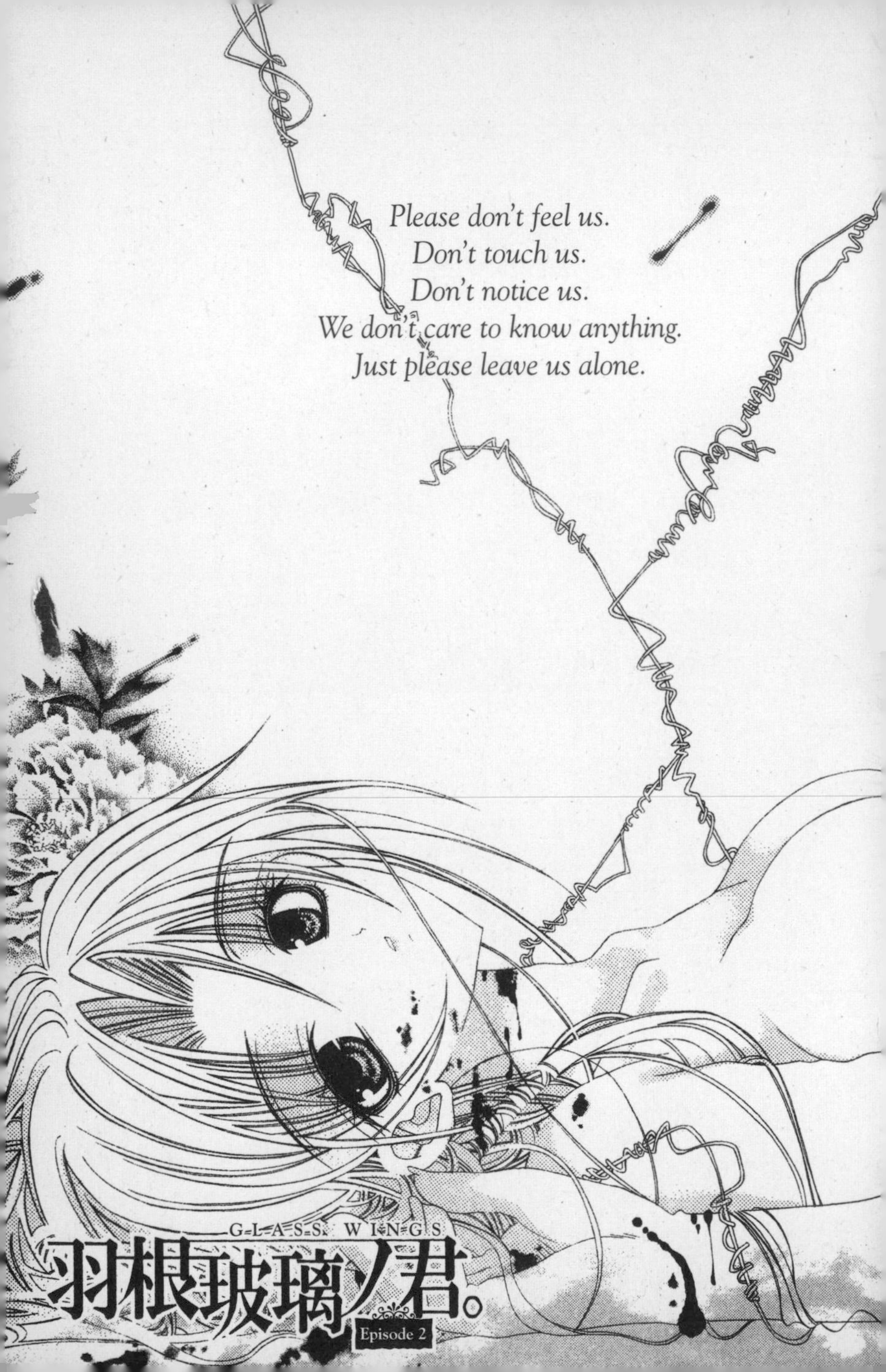
Please don't feel us.
Don't touch us.
Don't notice us.
We don't care to know anything.
Just please leave us alone.
G-L-A-S-S WINGS
羽根玻璃ノ君。
Episode 2

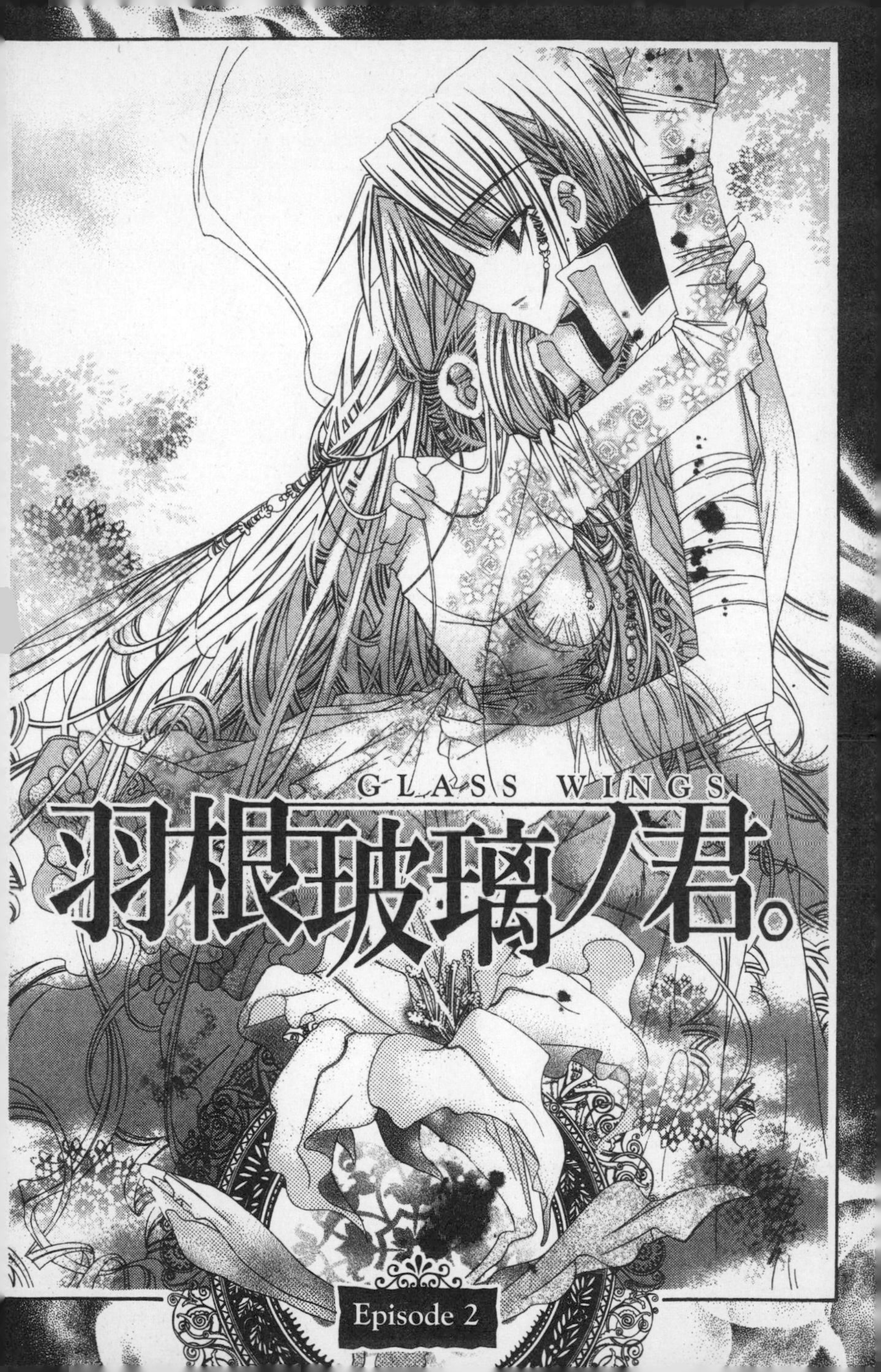
GLASS WINGS
羽根玻璃ノ君。
Episode 2

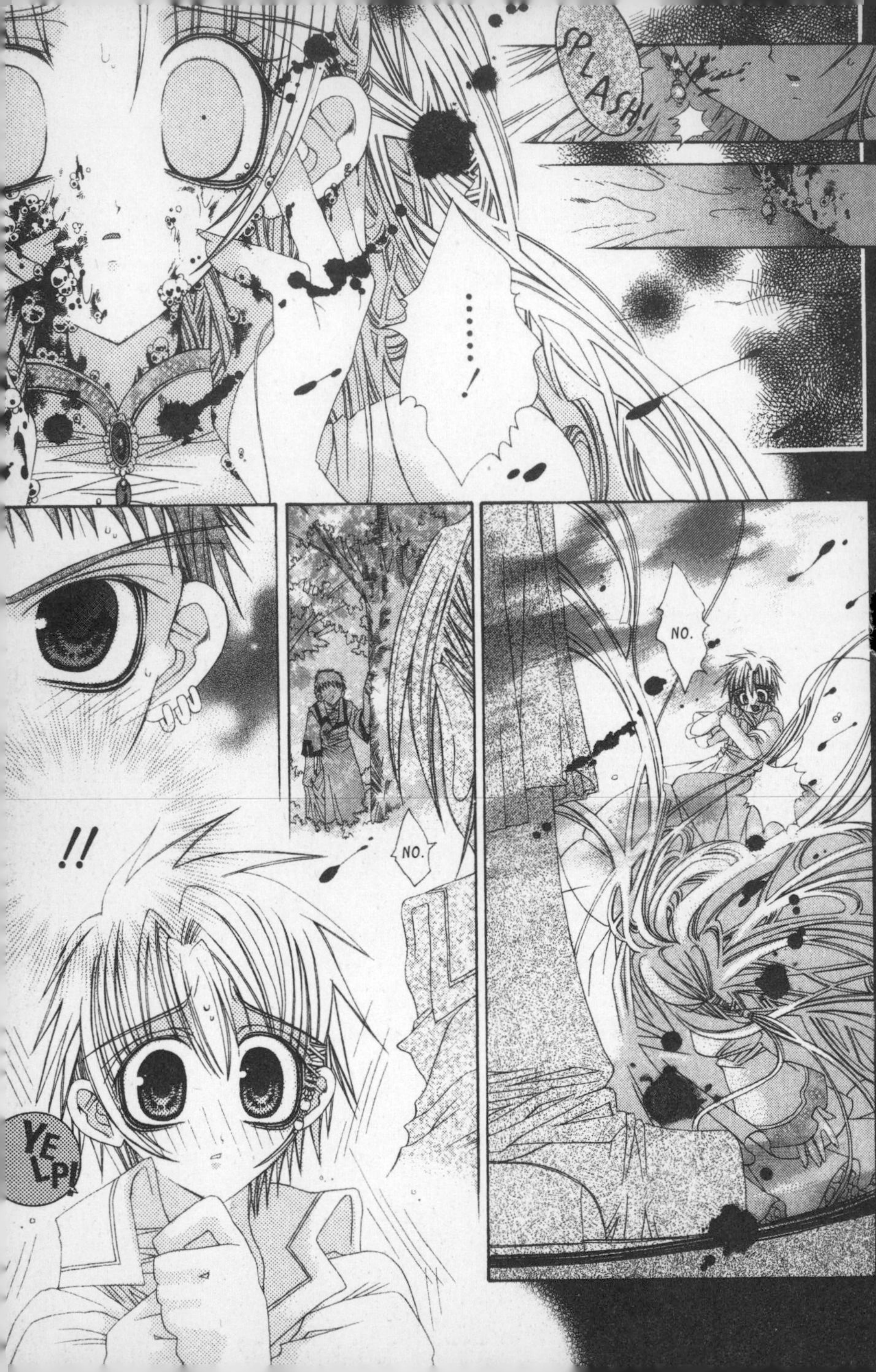
SPLASH!
......!
NO.
NO.
!!
YELP!

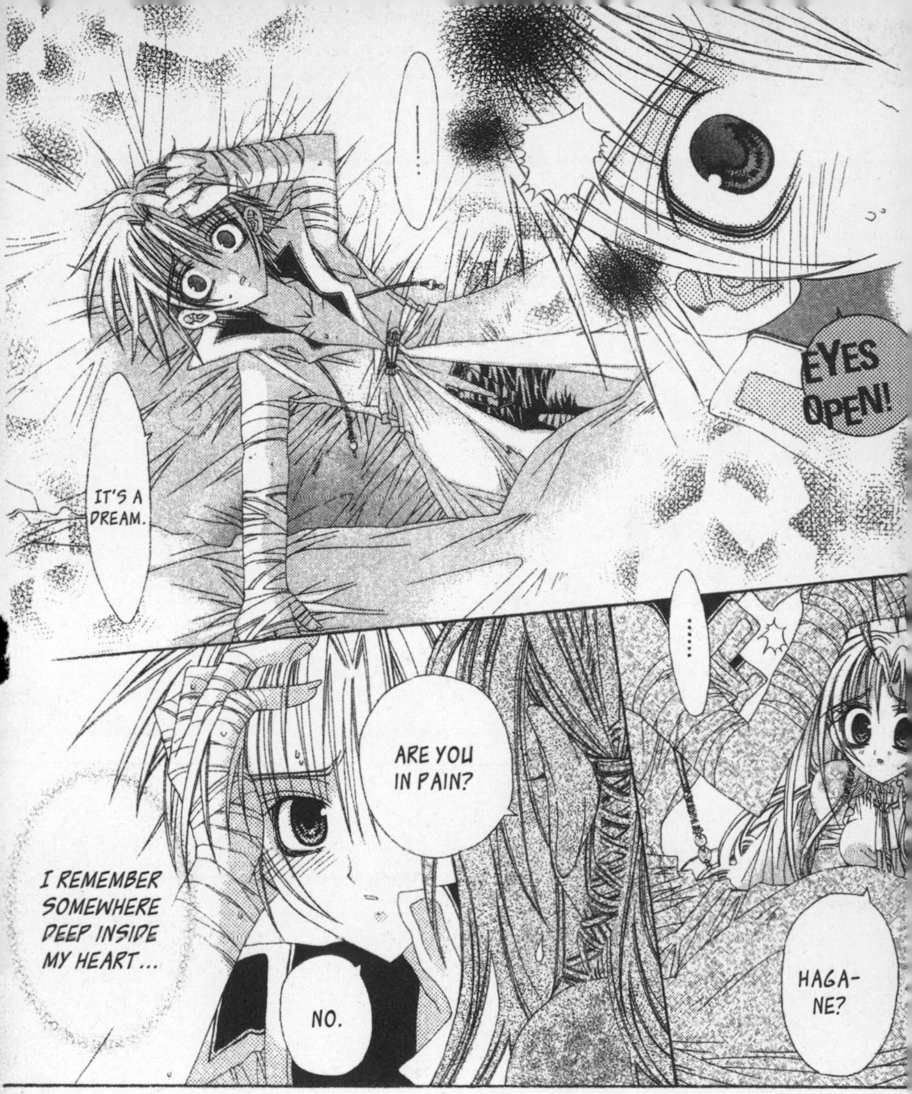
......
EYES OPEN!
IT'S A DREAM.
......
HAGA- NE?
ARE YOU IN PAIN?
NO.
I REMEMBER SOMEWHERE DEEP INSIDE MY HEART...

Glass Wings

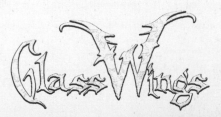

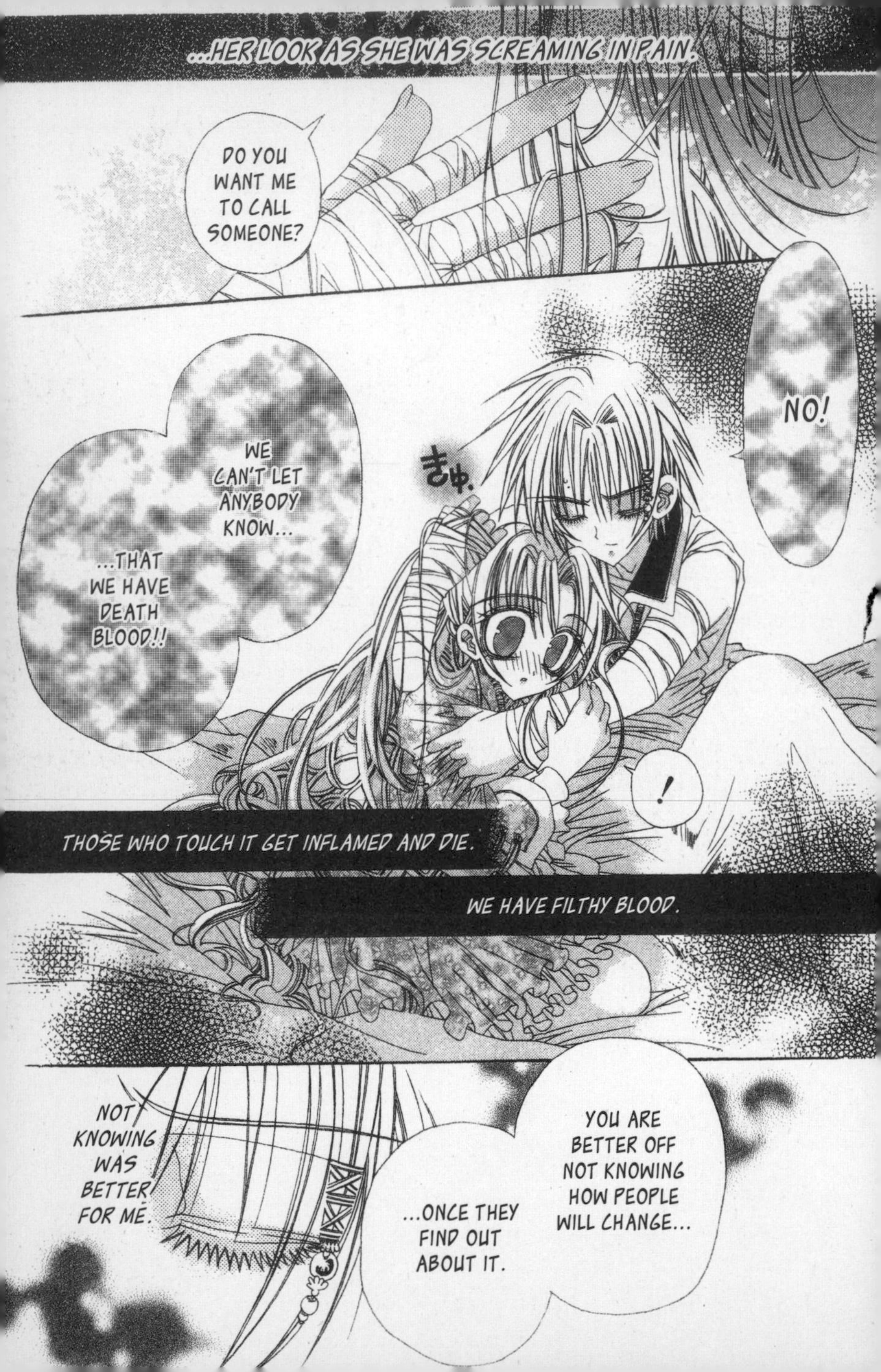
...HER LOOK AS SHE WAS SCREAMING IN PAIN.
DO YOU WANT ME TO CALL SOMEONE?
NO!
WE CAN'T LET ANYBODY KNOW...
...THAT WE HAVE DEATH BLOOD!!
きゅ
!
THOSE WHO TOUCH IT GET INFLAMED AND DIE.
WE HAVE FILTHY BLOOD.
YOU ARE BETTER OFF NOT KNOWING HOW PEOPLE WILL CHANGE...
...ONCE THEY FIND OUT ABOUT IT.
NOT KNOWING WAS BETTER FOR ME.

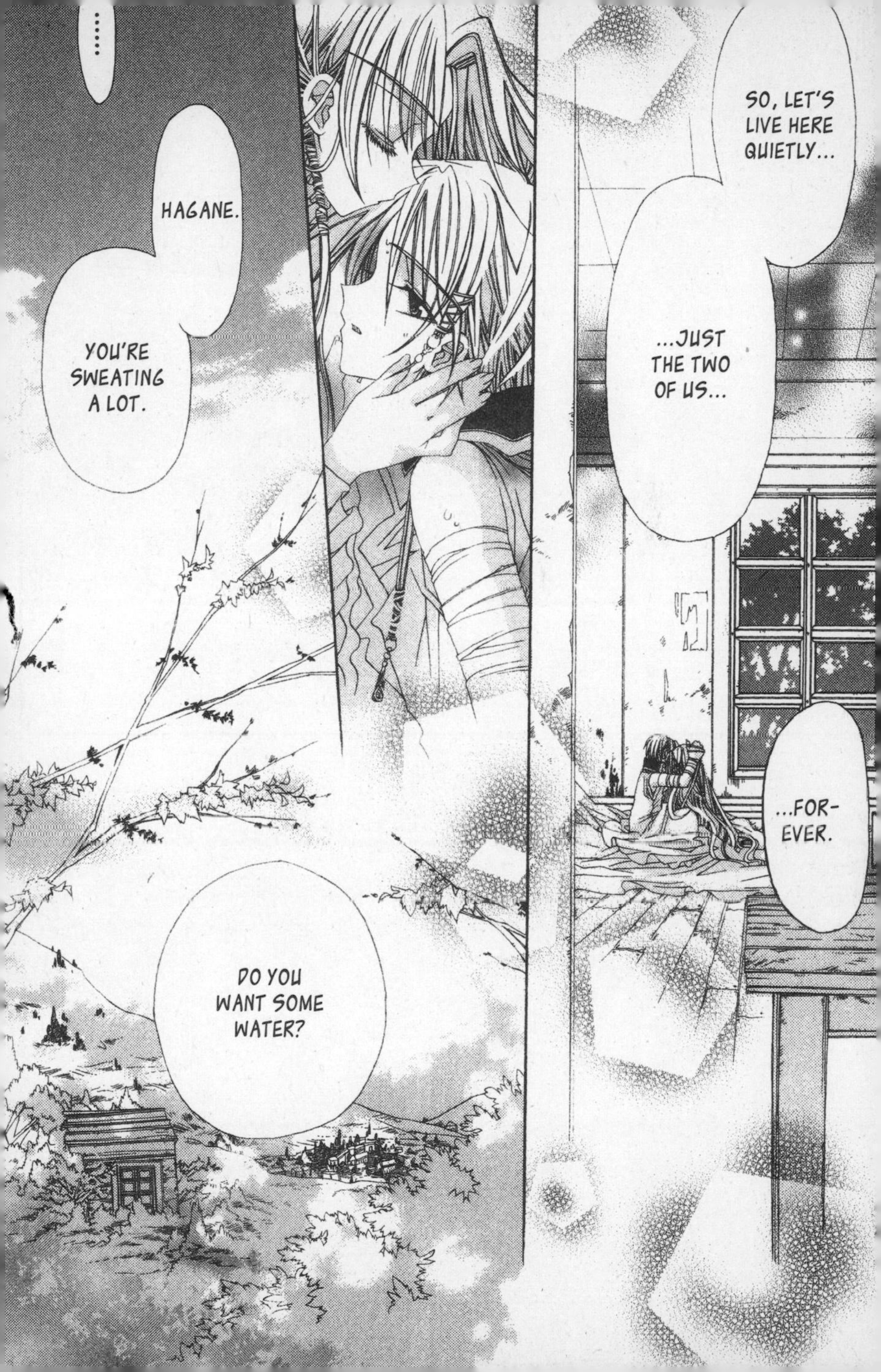
SO, LET'S LIVE HERE QUIETLY...
...JUST THE TWO OF US...
...FOR-EVER.
......
HAGANE.
YOU'RE SWEATING A LOT.
DO YOU WANT SOME WATER?

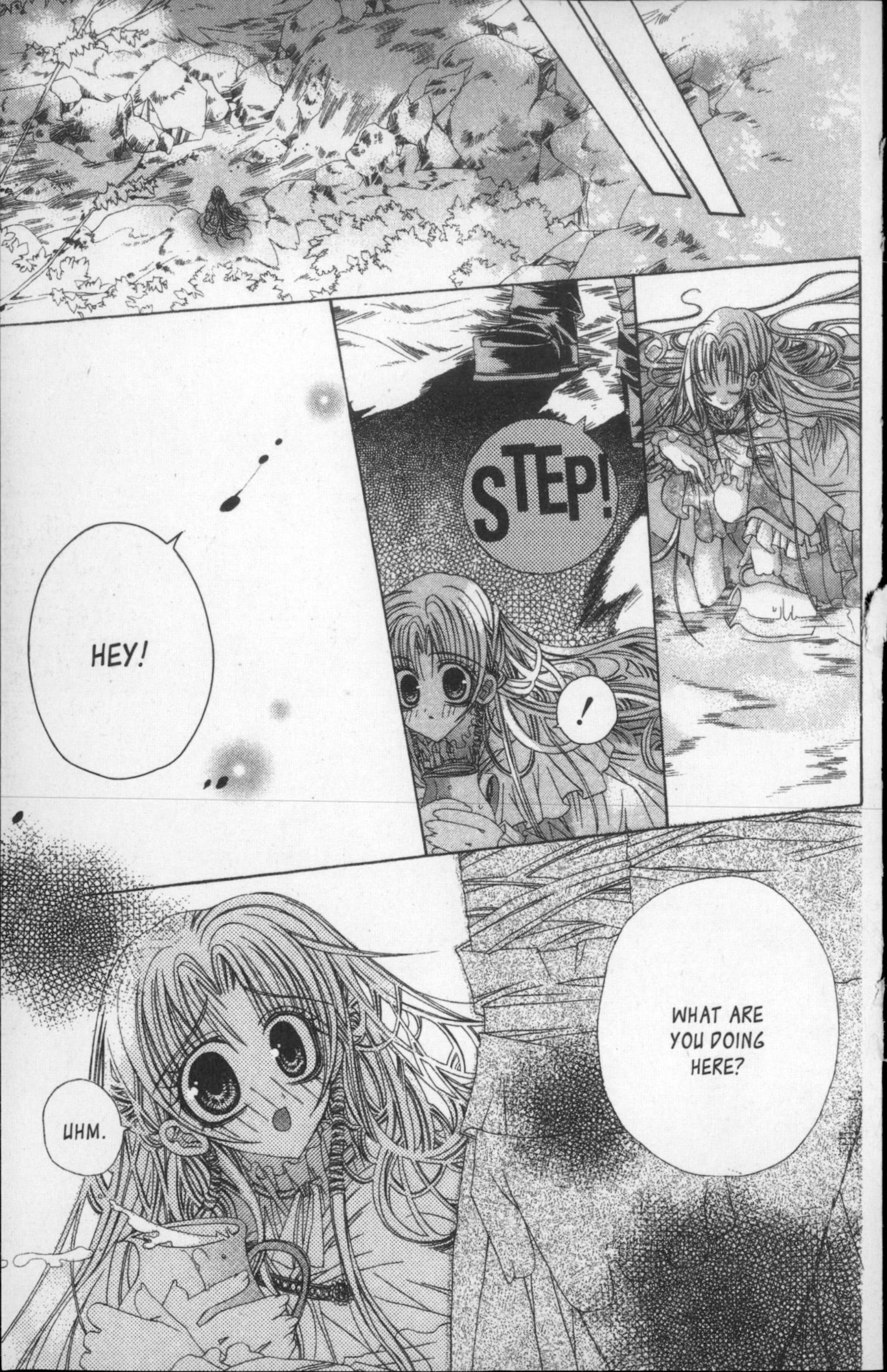
STEP!
!
HEY!
WHAT ARE YOU DOING HERE?
UHM.

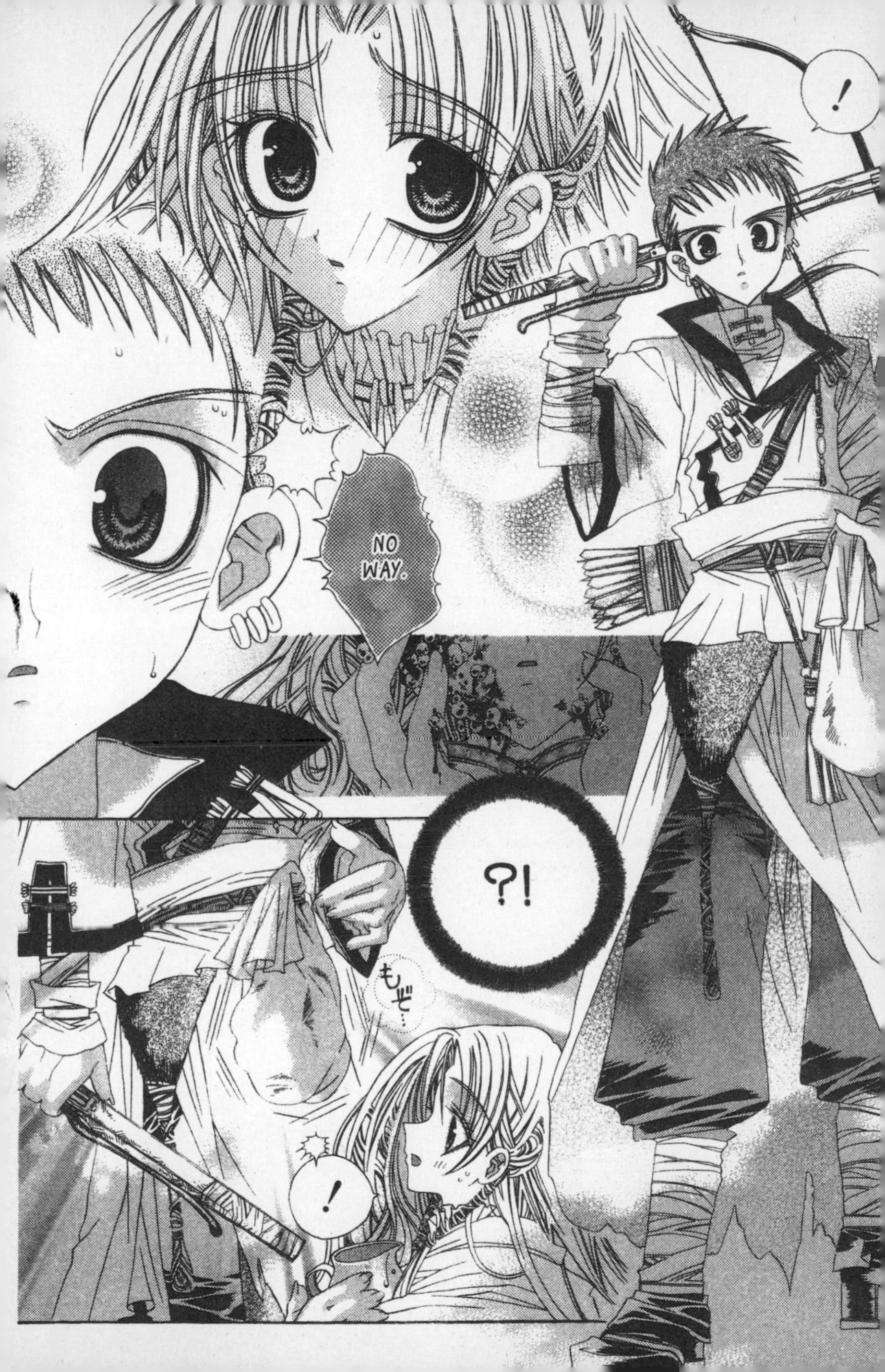
!
NO WAY.
?!
もぞ…
!

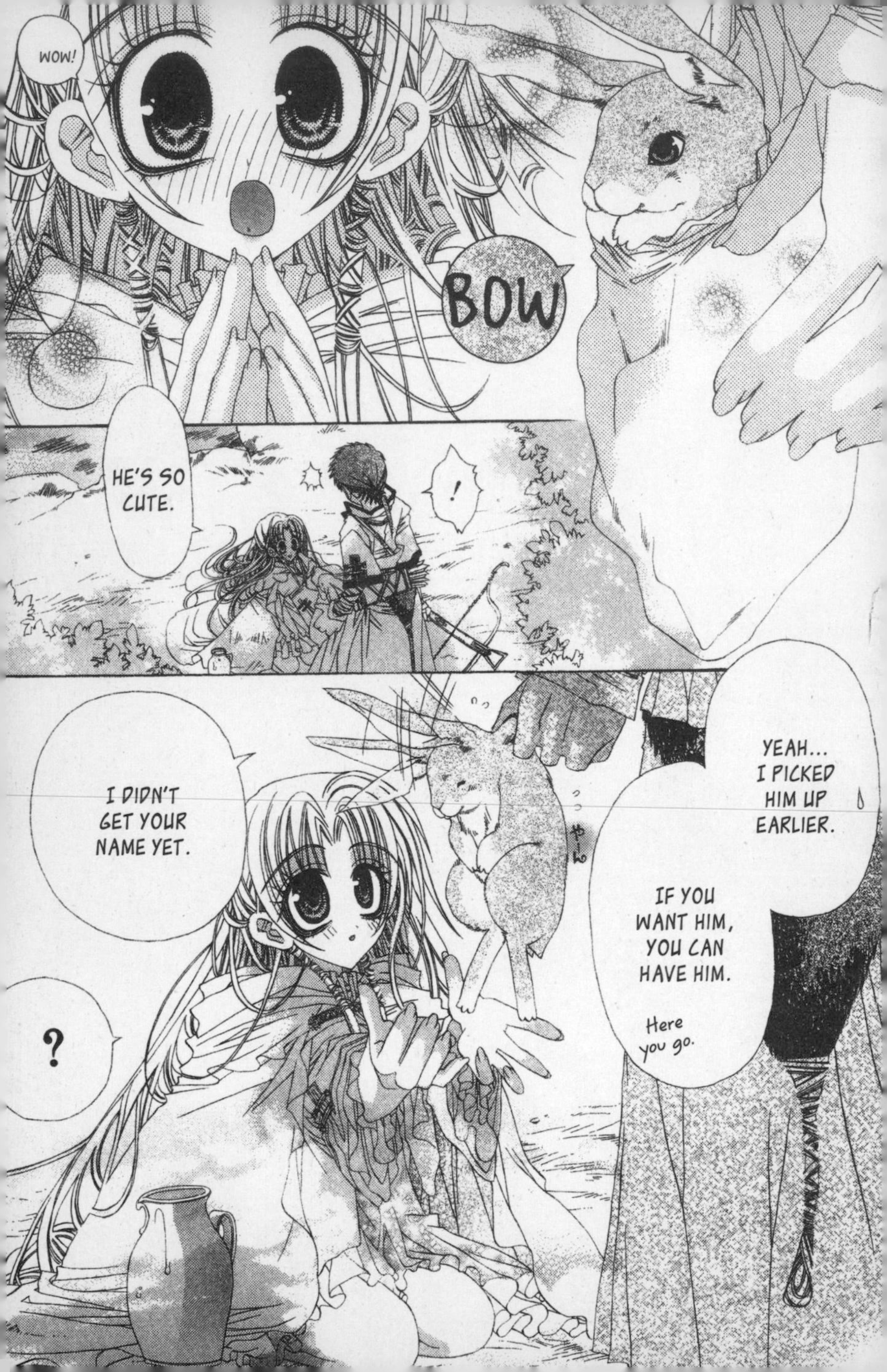
BOW
WOW!
!
HE'S SO CUTE.
YEAH... I PICKED HIM UP EARLIER.
IF YOU WANT HIM, YOU CAN HAVE HIM.
Here you go.
I DIDN'T GET YOUR NAME YET.
?

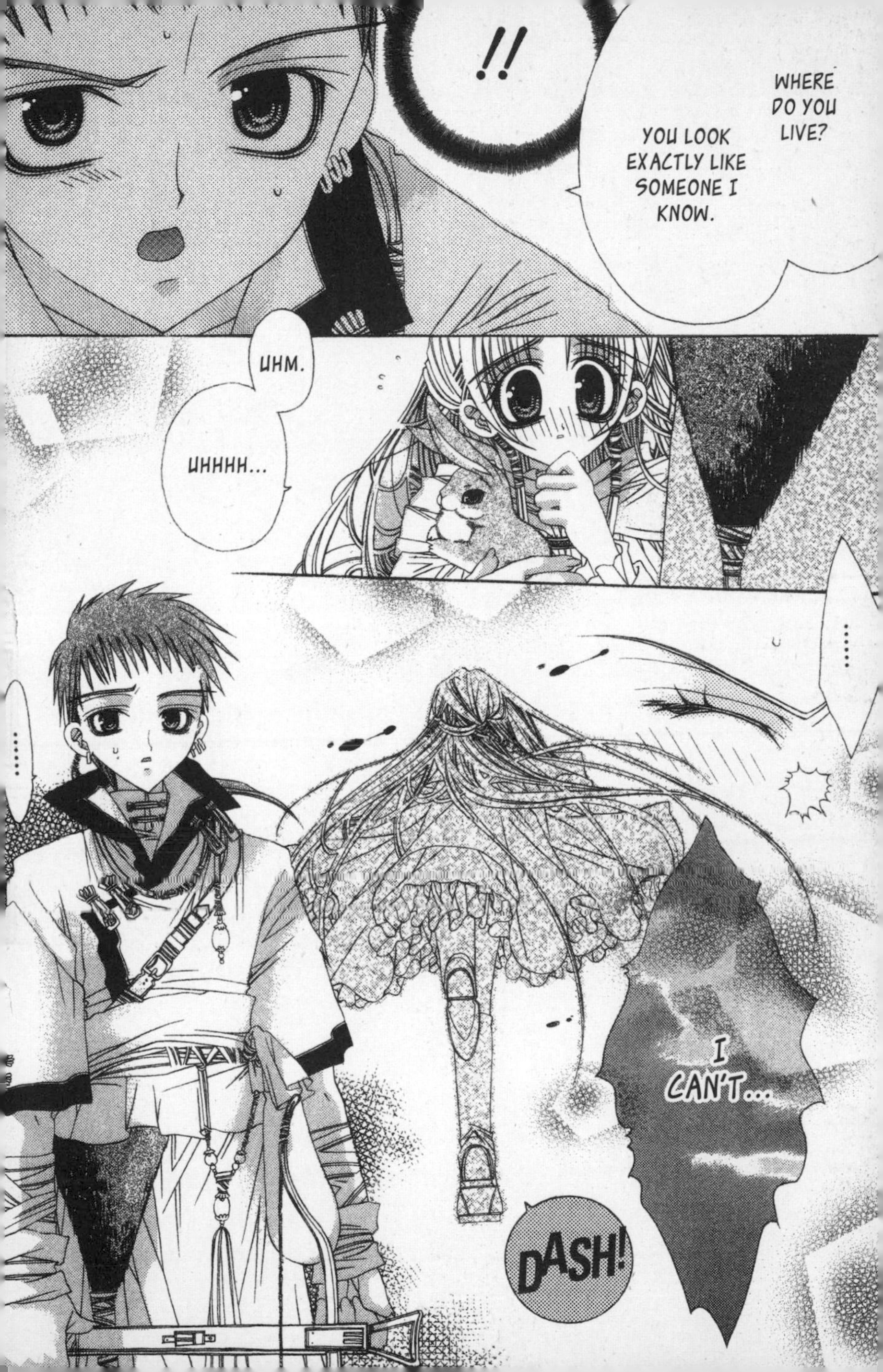
YOU LOOK EXACTLY LIKE SOMEONE I KNOW. WHERE DO YOU LIVE?
!!
UHM.
UHHHH...
......
......
I CAN'T...
DASH!

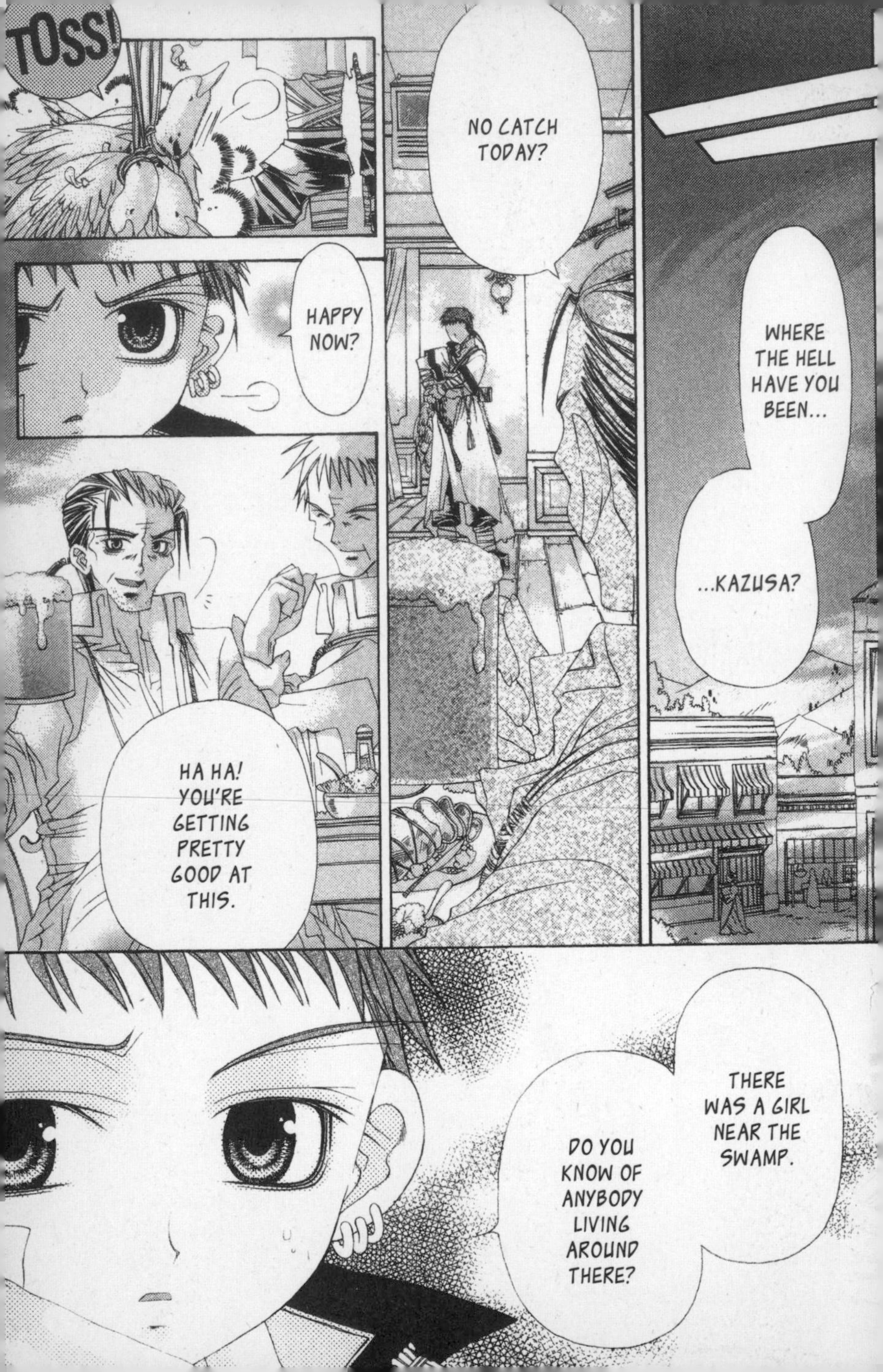
WHERE THE HELL HAVE YOU BEEN...
...KAZUSA?
NO CATCH TODAY?
TOSS!
HAPPY NOW?
HA HA! YOU'RE GETTING PRETTY GOOD AT THIS.
THERE WAS A GIRL NEAR THE SWAMP.
DO YOU KNOW OF ANYBODY LIVING AROUND THERE?

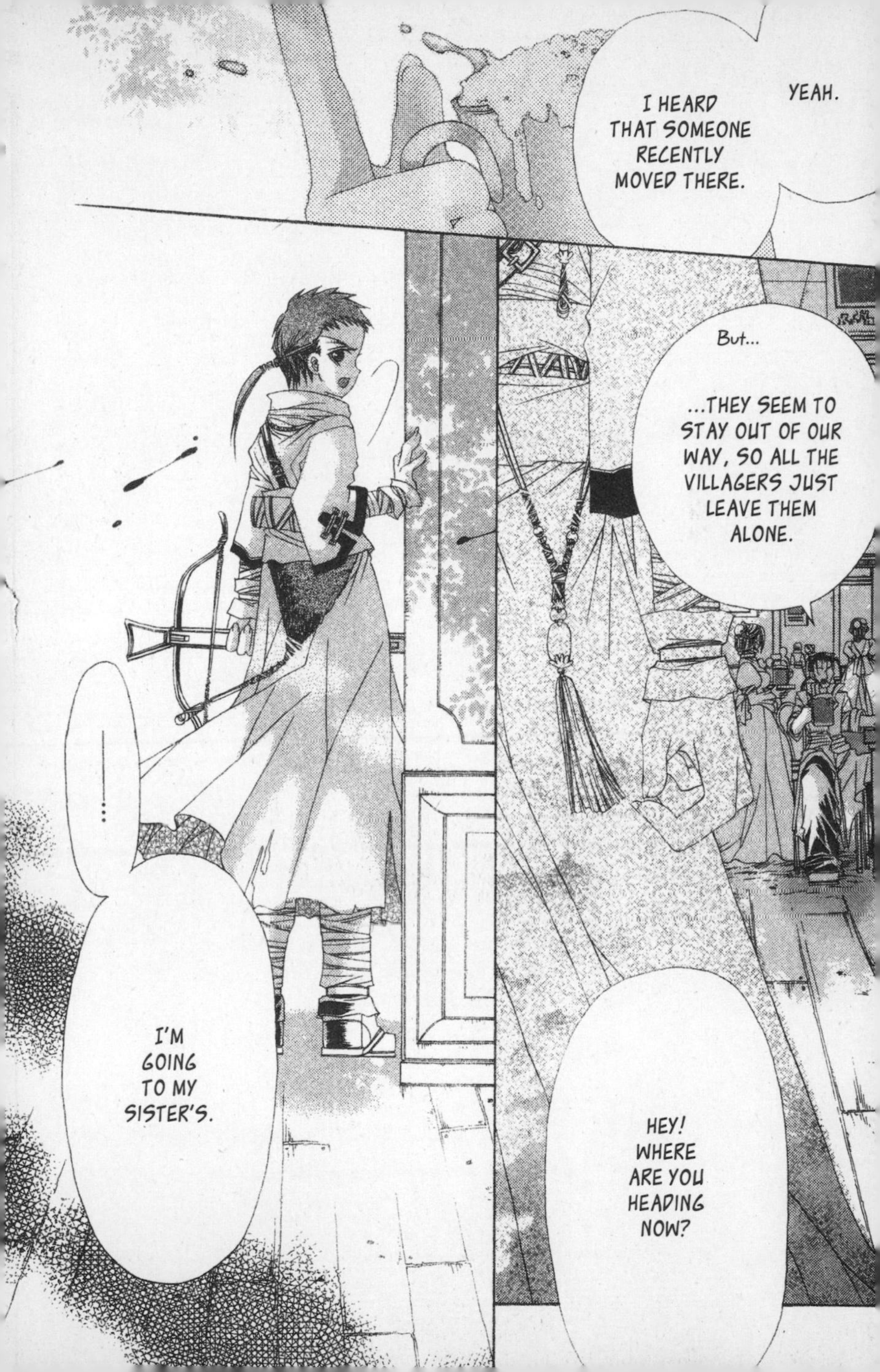
YEAH.
I HEARD THAT SOMEONE RECENTLY MOVED THERE.
But...
...THEY SEEM TO STAY OUT OF OUR WAY, SO ALL THE VILLAGERS JUST LEAVE THEM ALONE.
HEY! WHERE ARE YOU HEADING NOW?
......
I'M GOING TO MY SISTER'S.

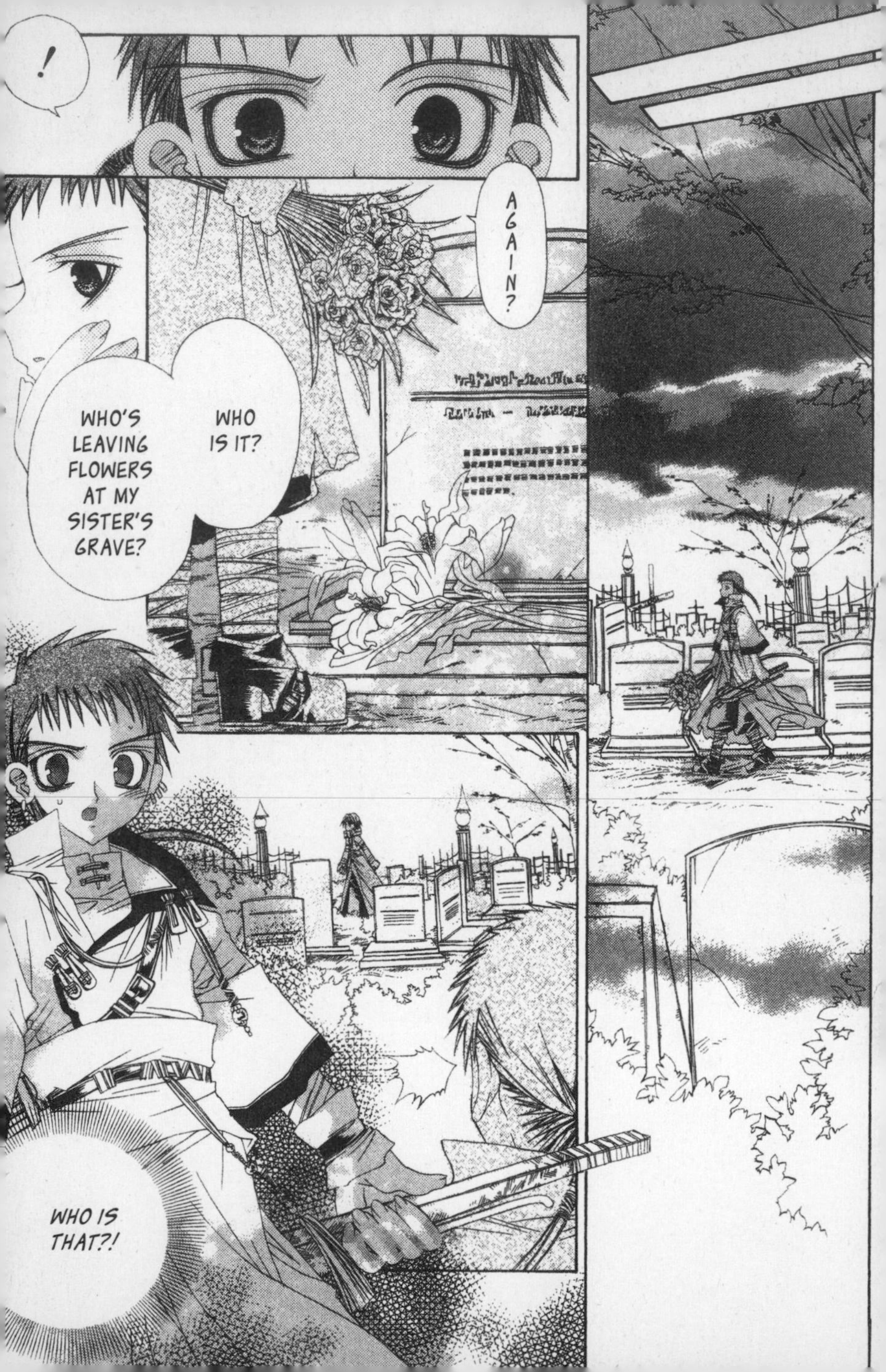
!
AGAIN?
WHO IS IT?
WHO'S LEAVING FLOWERS AT MY SISTER'S GRAVE?
WHO IS THAT?!

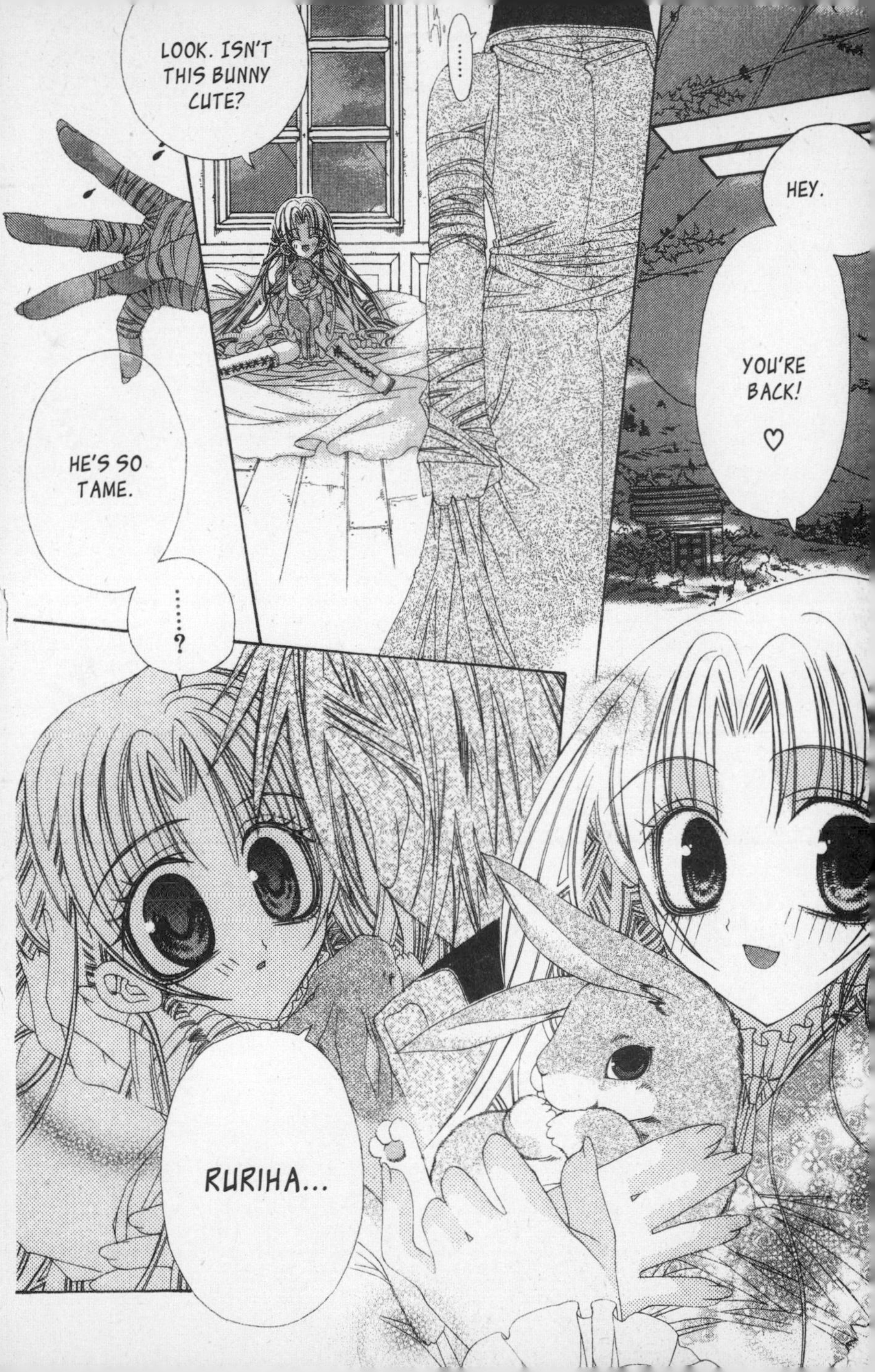
HEY.
YOU'RE BACK! ♡
......
LOOK. ISN'T THIS BUNNY CUTE?
HE'S SO TAME.
......?
RURIHA...

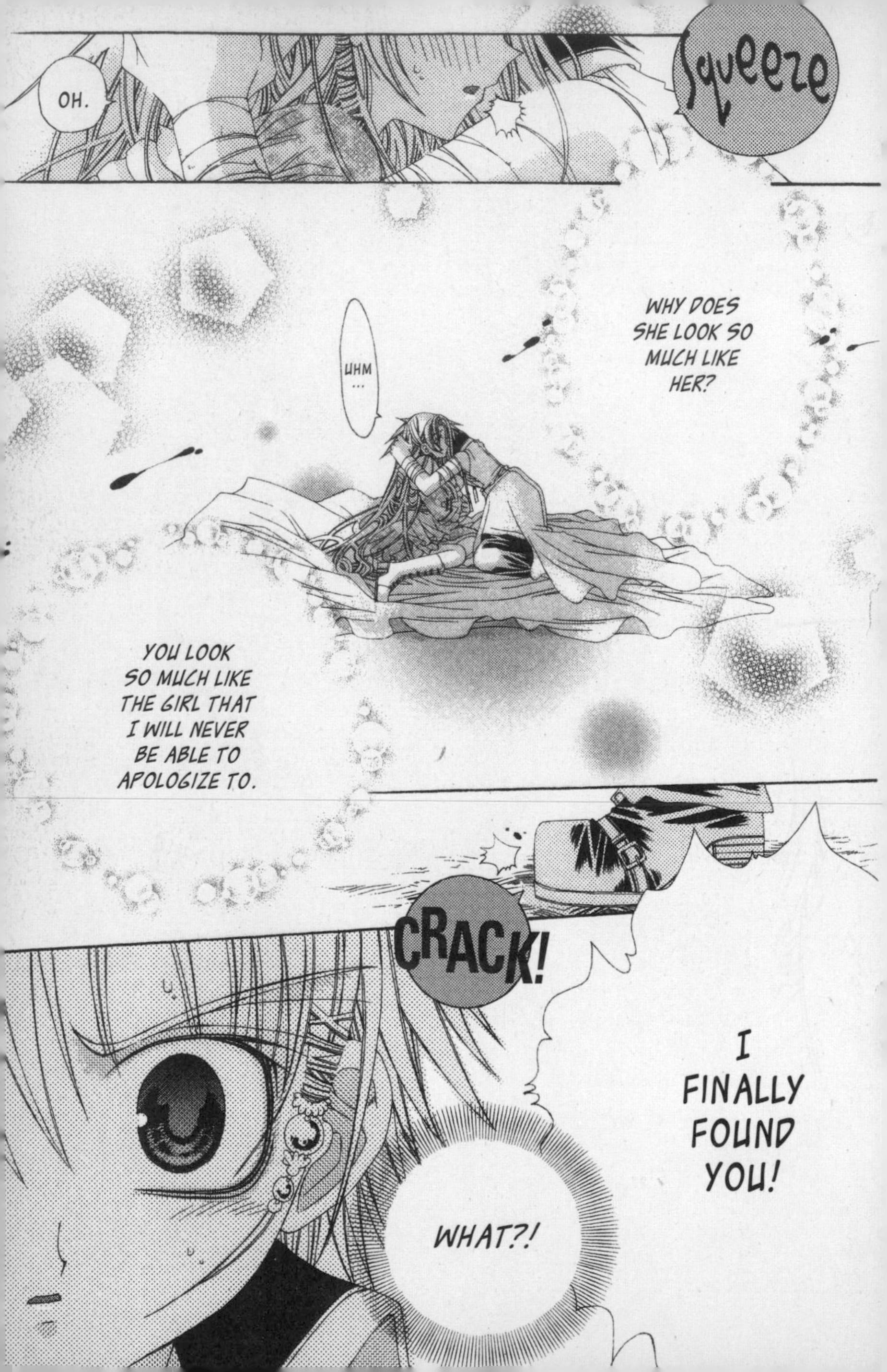
Squeeze
OH.
WHY DOES SHE LOOK SO MUCH LIKE HER?
UHM ...
YOU LOOK SO MUCH LIKE THE GIRL THAT I WILL NEVER BE ABLE TO APOLOGIZE TO.
CRACK!
I FINALLY FOUND YOU!
WHAT?!

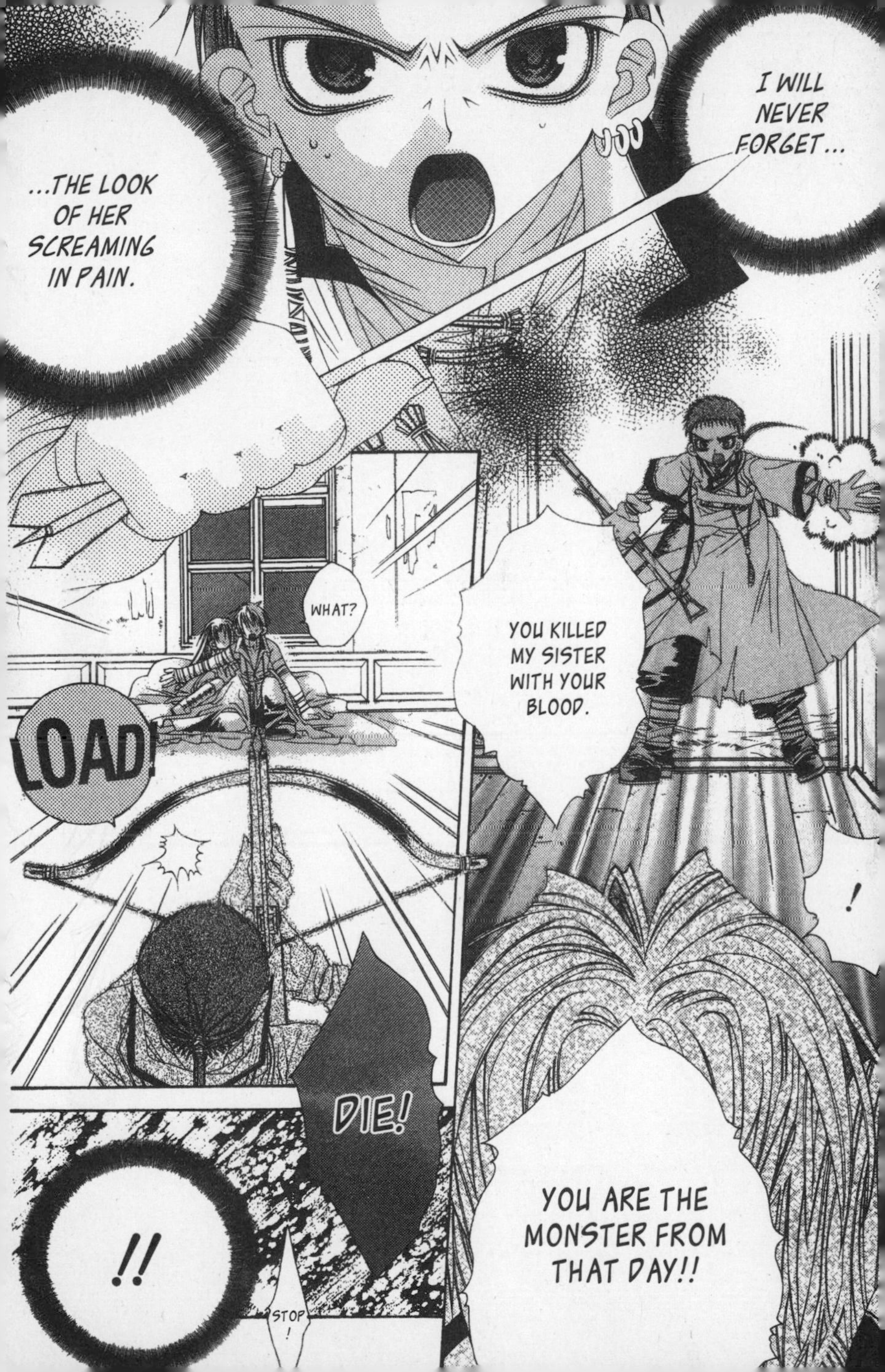
I WILL NEVER FORGET...
...THE LOOK OF HER SCREAMING IN PAIN.
YOU KILLED MY SISTER WITH YOUR BLOOD.
WHAT?
LOAD!
!
YOU ARE THE MONSTER FROM THAT DAY!!
DIE!
!!
STOP!

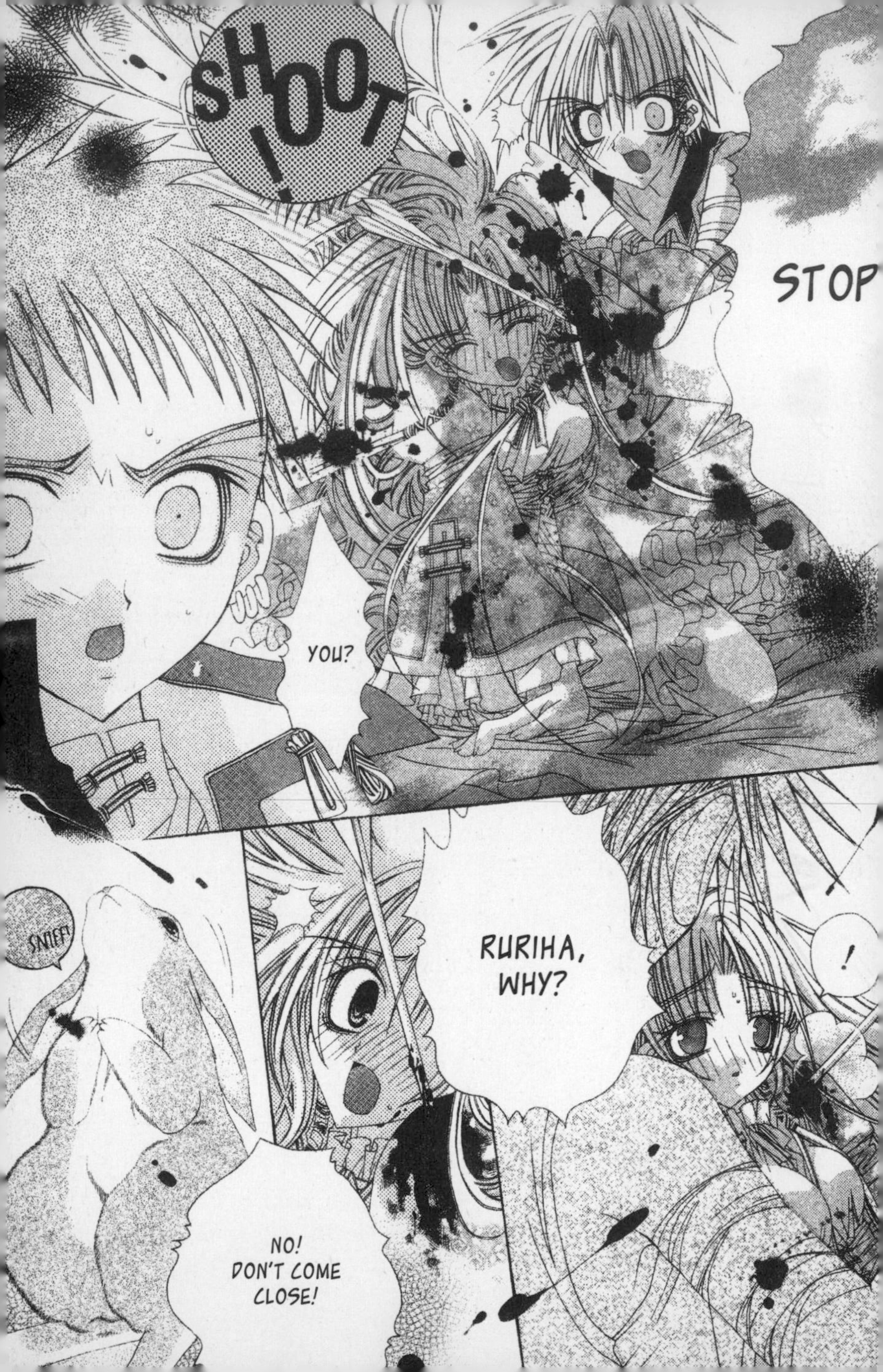
STOP
SHOOT!
YOU?
!
RURIHA, WHY?
NO! DON'T COME CLOSE!
SNIFF!

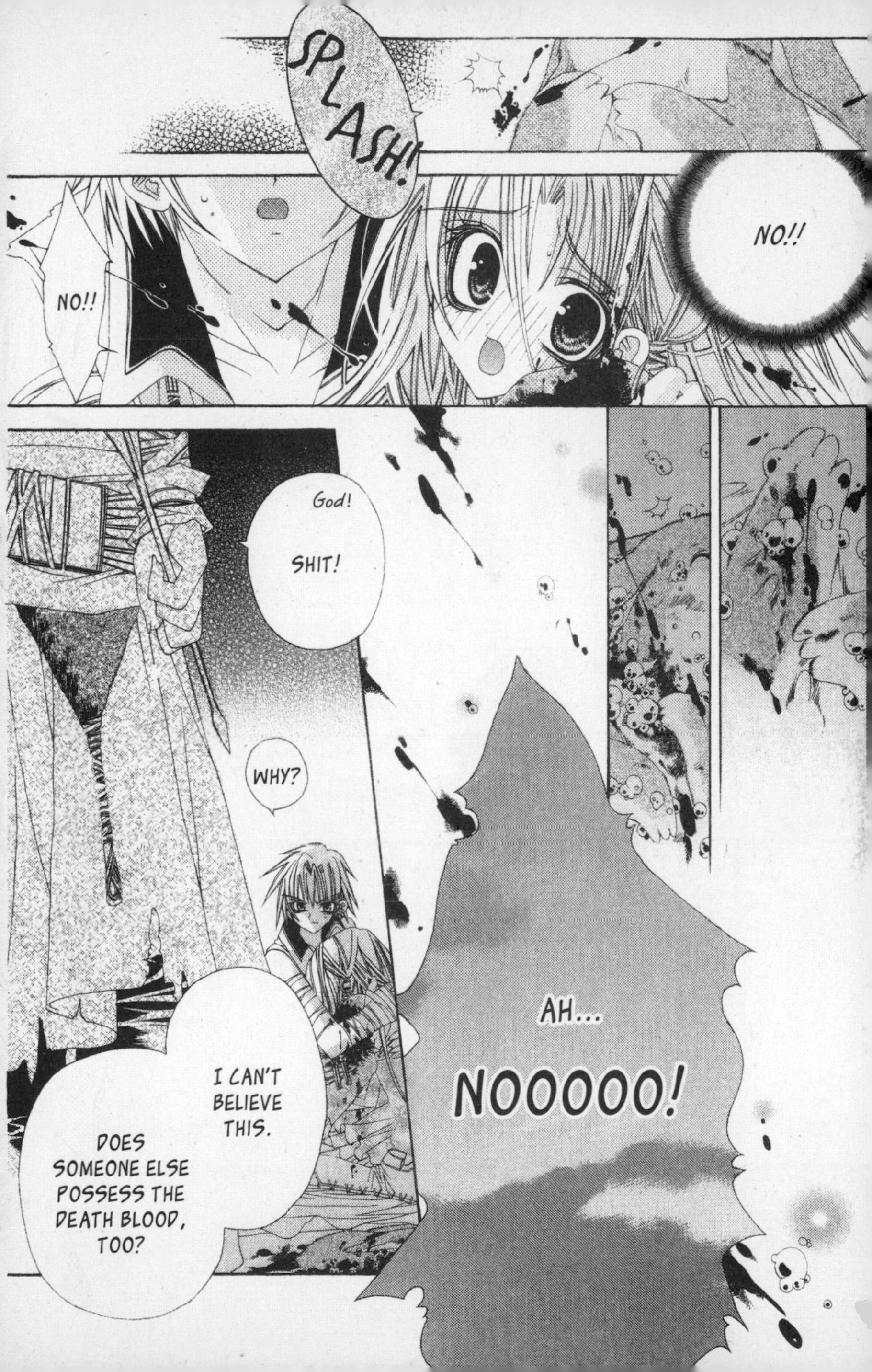
SPLASH!
NO!!
NO!!
AH...
NOOOOO!
God!
SHIT!
WHY?
I CAN'T BELIEVE THIS.
DOES SOMEONE ELSE POSSESS THE DEATH BLOOD, TOO?

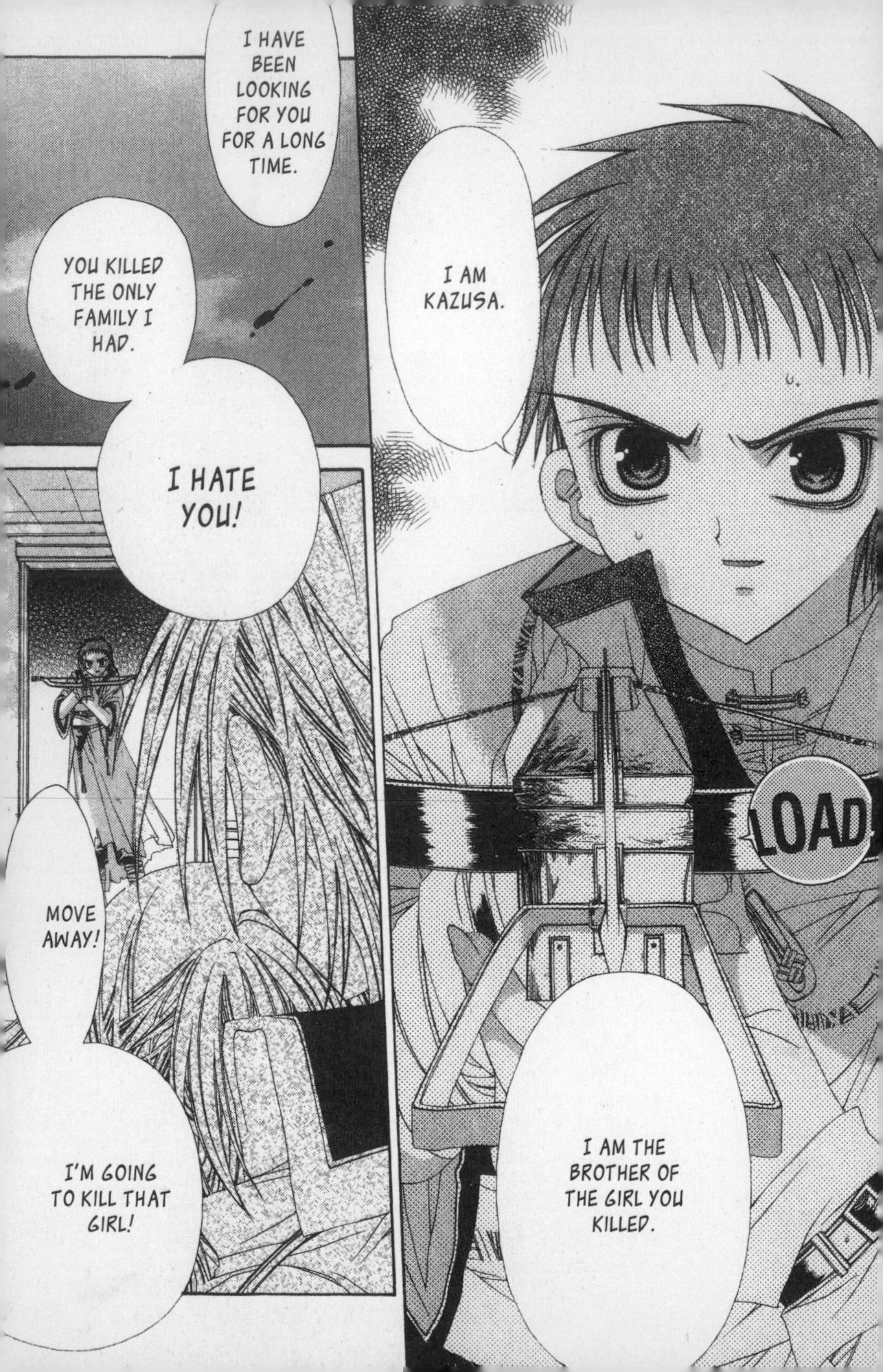
I AM KAZUSA.
LOAD
I AM THE BROTHER OF THE GIRL YOU KILLED.
I HAVE BEEN LOOKING FOR YOU FOR A LONG TIME.
YOU KILLED THE ONLY FAMILY I HAD.
I HATE YOU!
MOVE AWAY!
I'M GOING TO KILL THAT GIRL!

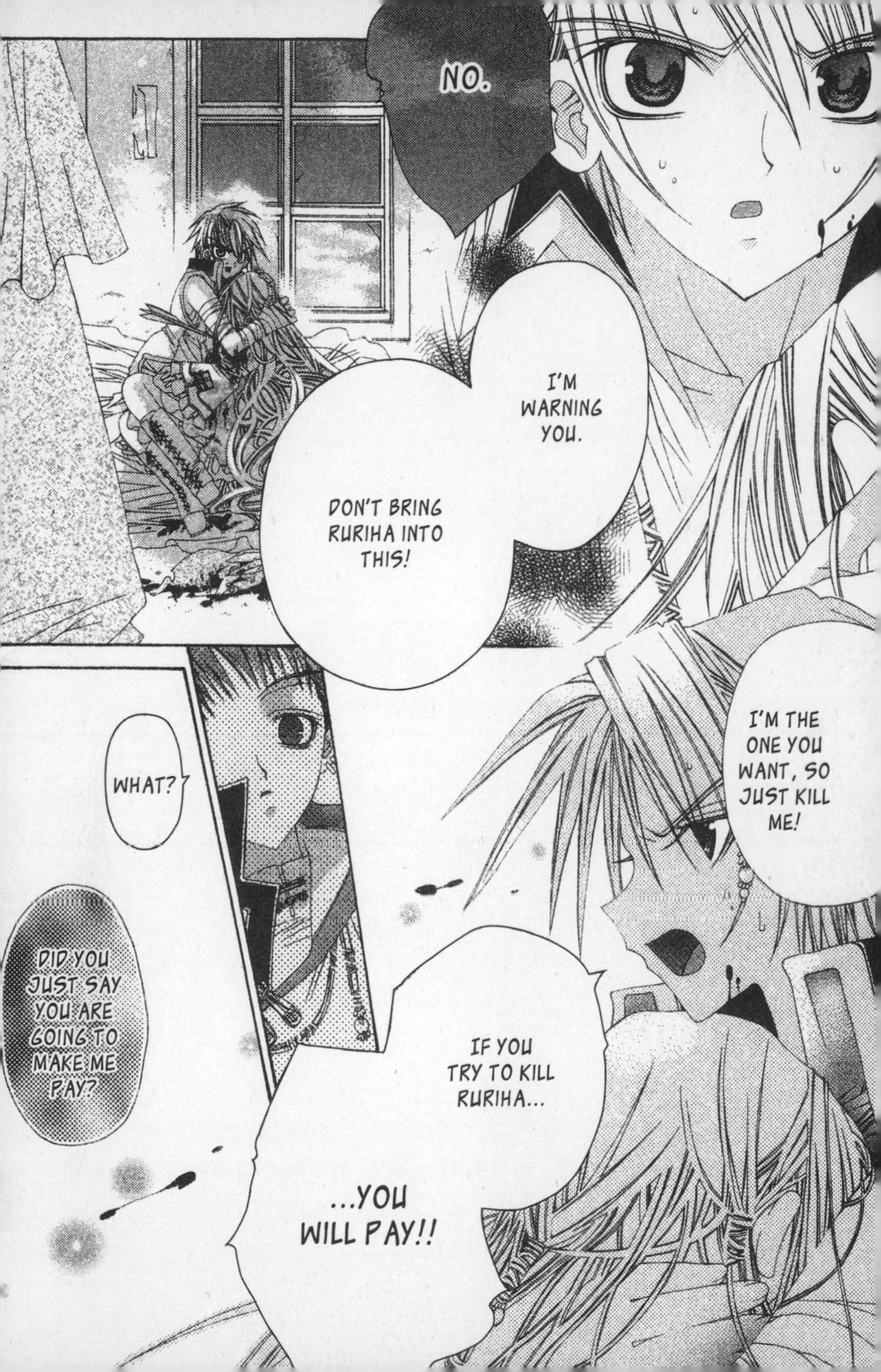
NO.
I'M WARNING YOU.
DON'T BRING RURIHA INTO THIS!
I'M THE ONE YOU WANT, SO JUST KILL ME!
IF YOU TRY TO KILL RURIHA...
...YOU WILL PAY!!
WHAT?
DID YOU JUST SAY YOU ARE GOING TO MAKE ME PAY?

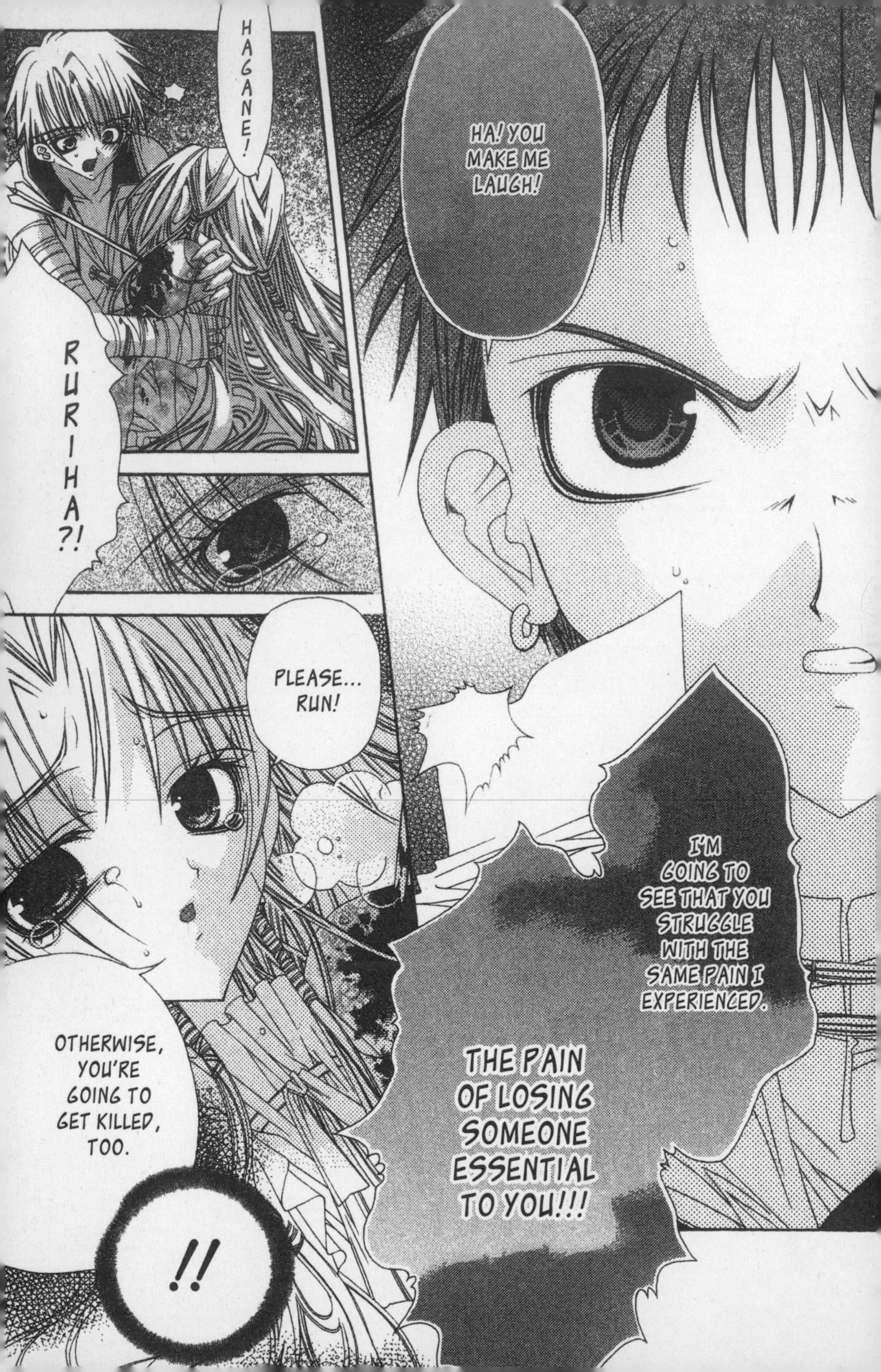
HA! YOU MAKE ME LAUGH!
I'M GOING TO SEE THAT YOU STRUGGLE WITH THE SAME PAIN I EXPERIENCED.
THE PAIN OF LOSING SOMEONE ESSENTIAL TO YOU!!!
HAGANE!
RURIHA?!
PLEASE... RUN!
OTHERWISE, YOU'RE GOING TO GET KILLED, TOO.
!!

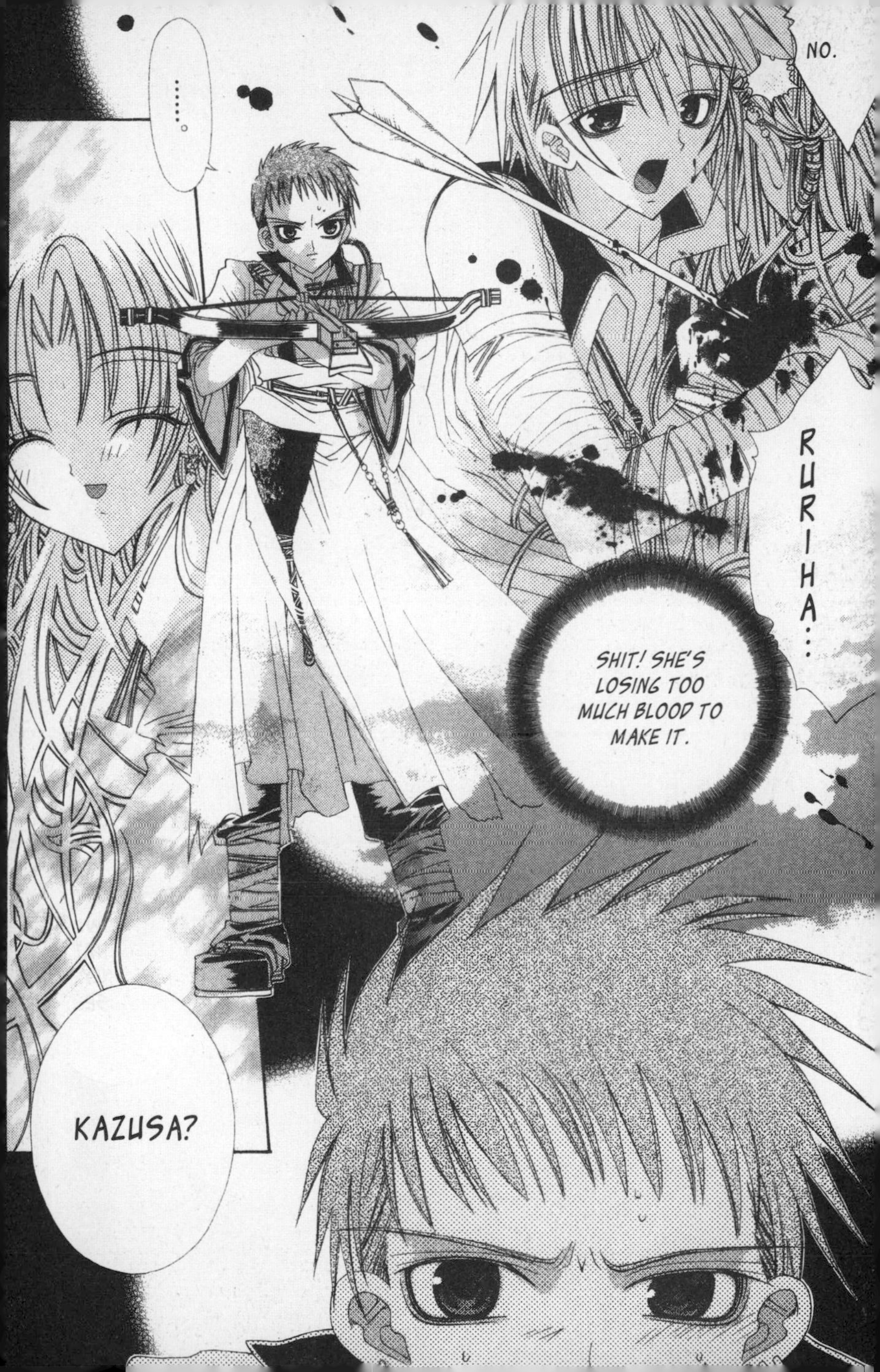
NO.
RURIHA...
......
SHIT! SHE'S LOSING TOO MUCH BLOOD TO MAKE IT.
KAZUSA?

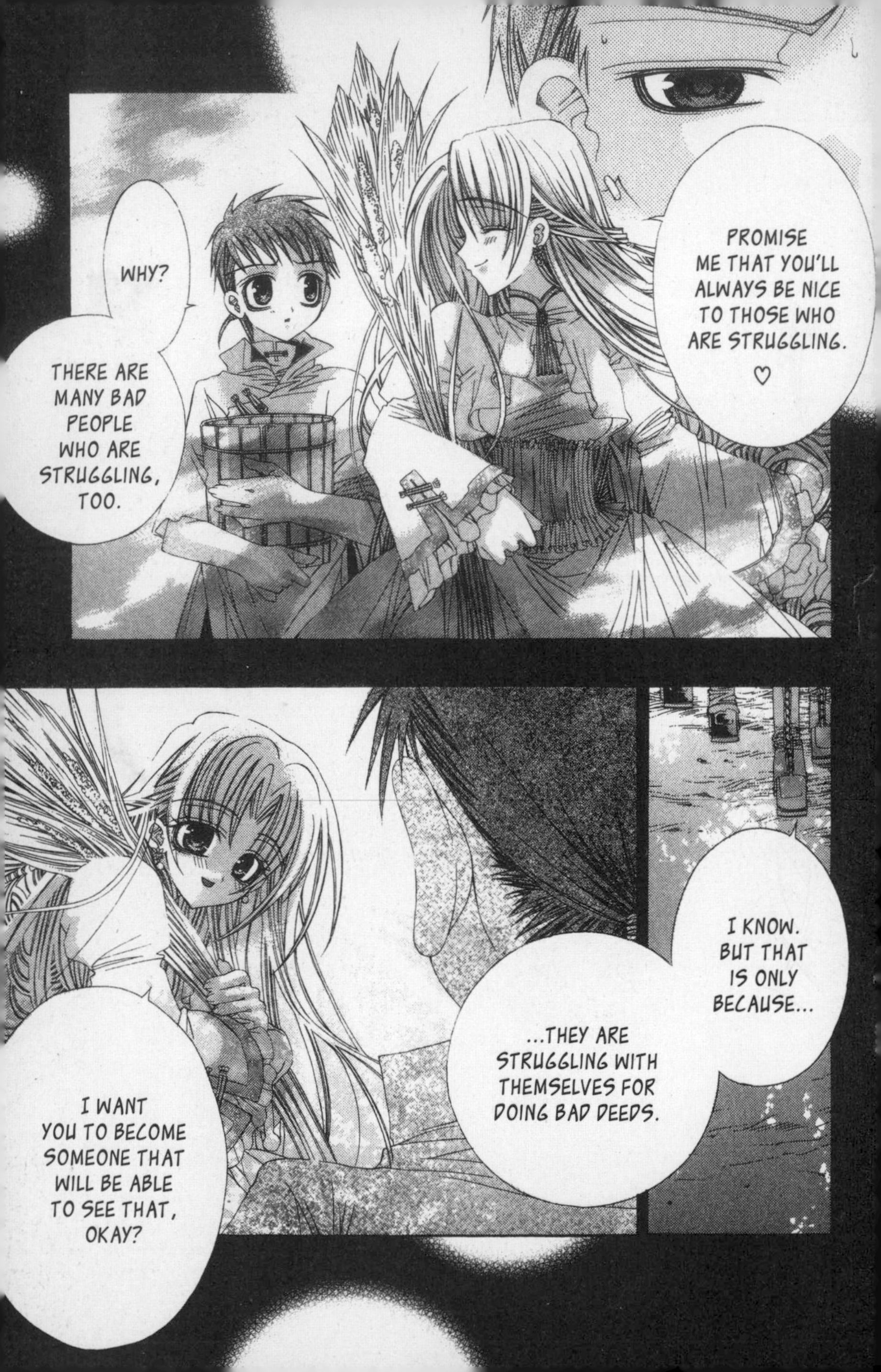
PROMISE ME THAT YOU'LL ALWAYS BE NICE TO THOSE WHO ARE STRUGGLING. ♡
WHY?
THERE ARE MANY BAD PEOPLE WHO ARE STRUGGLING, TOO.
I KNOW. BUT THAT IS ONLY BECAUSE...
...THEY ARE STRUGGLING WITH THEMSELVES FOR DOING BAD DEEDS.
I WANT YOU TO BECOME SOMEONE THAT WILL BE ABLE TO SEE THAT, OKAY?

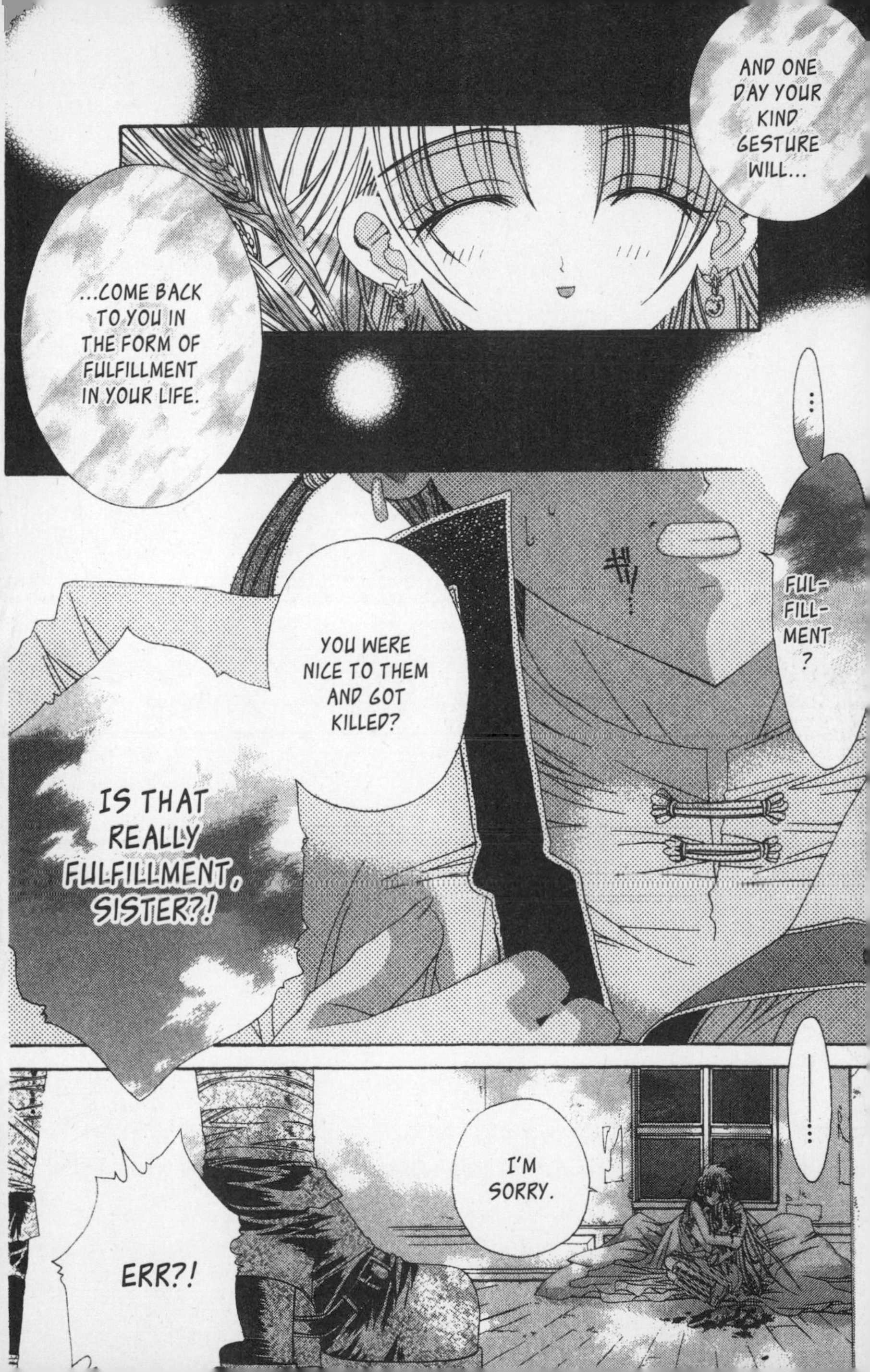
AND ONE DAY YOUR KIND GESTURE WILL...
...COME BACK TO YOU IN THE FORM OF FULFILLMENT IN YOUR LIFE.
...
FUL-FILL-MENT?
YOU WERE NICE TO THEM AND GOT KILLED?
IS THAT REALLY FULFILLMENT, SISTER?!
......
I'M SORRY.
ERR?!

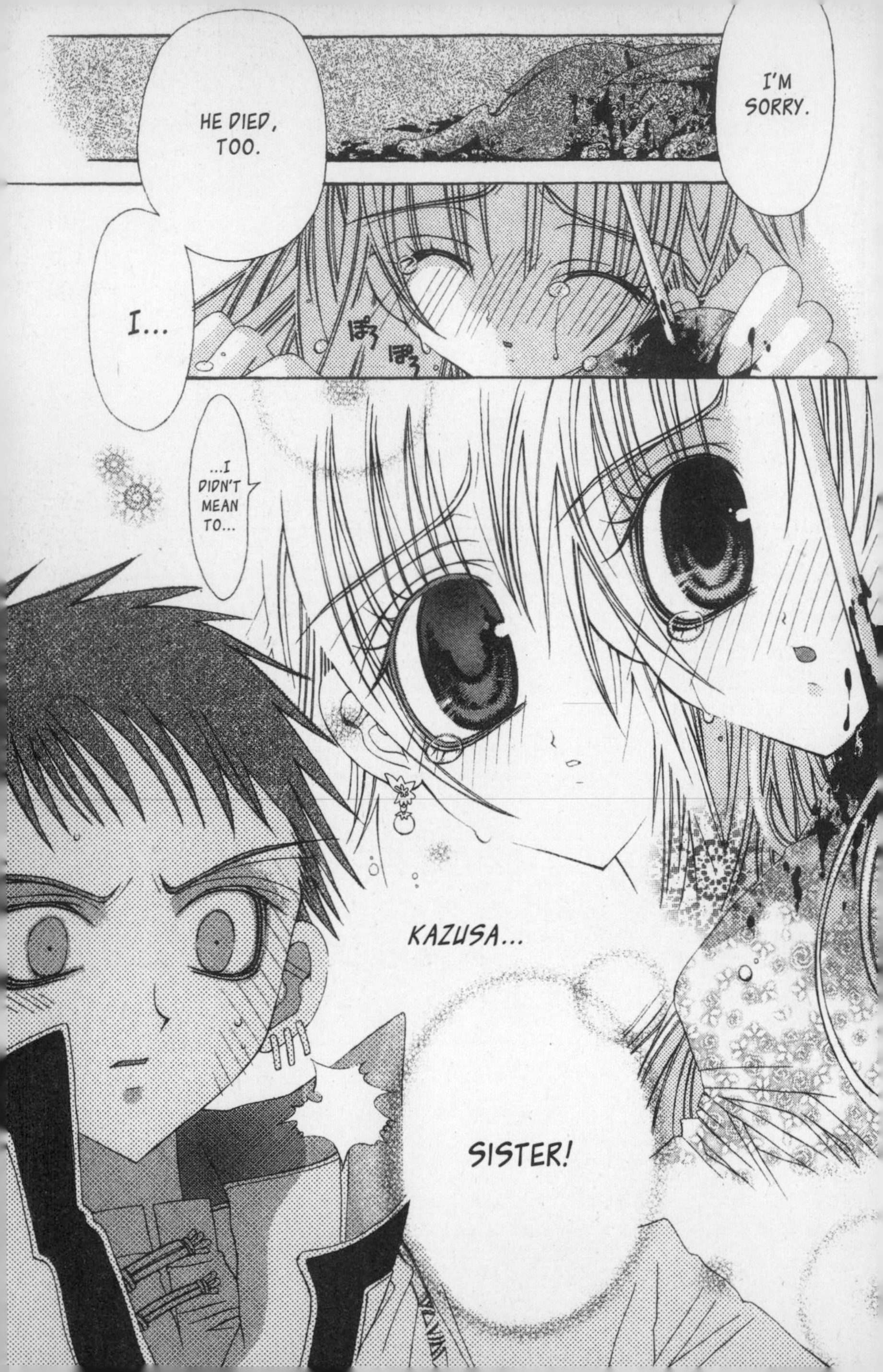
I'M SORRY.
HE DIED, TOO.
I...
ぽろ ぽろ
...I DIDN'T MEAN TO...
KAZUSA...
SISTER!

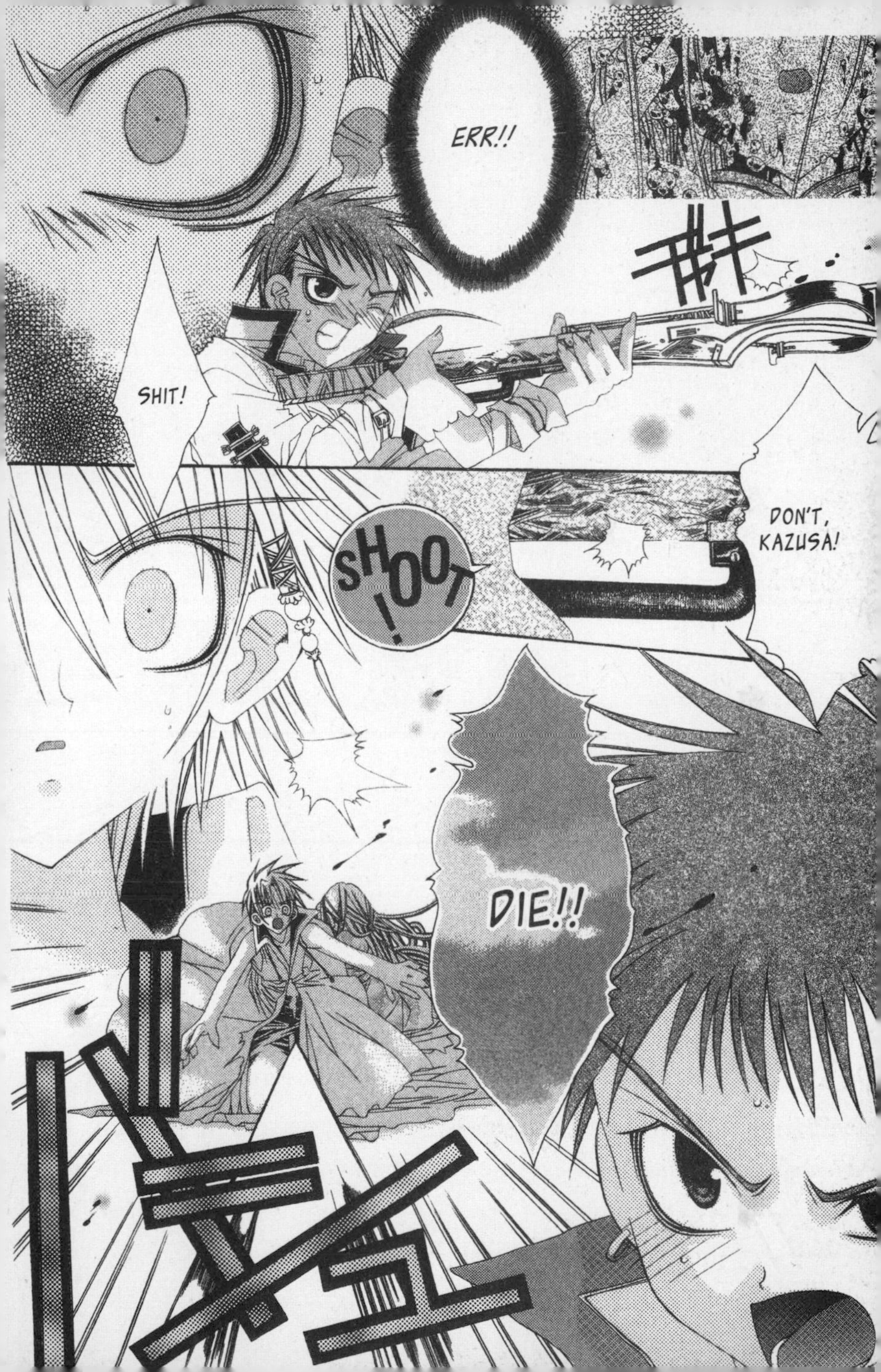
ERR!!
SHIT!
DON'T, KAZUSA!
SHOOT!
DIE!!

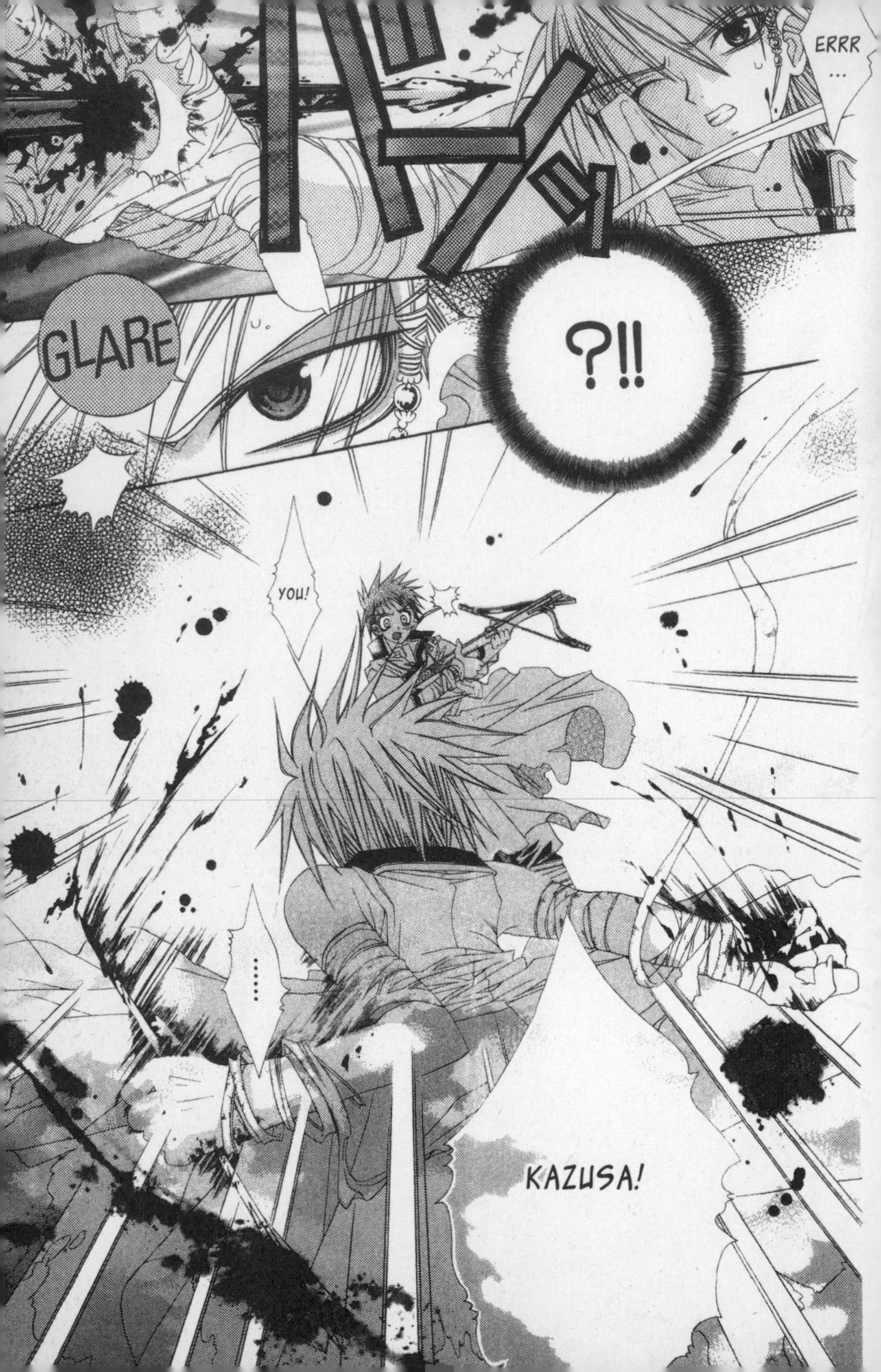
ERRR ...
?!!
GLARE
YOU!
......
KAZUSA!

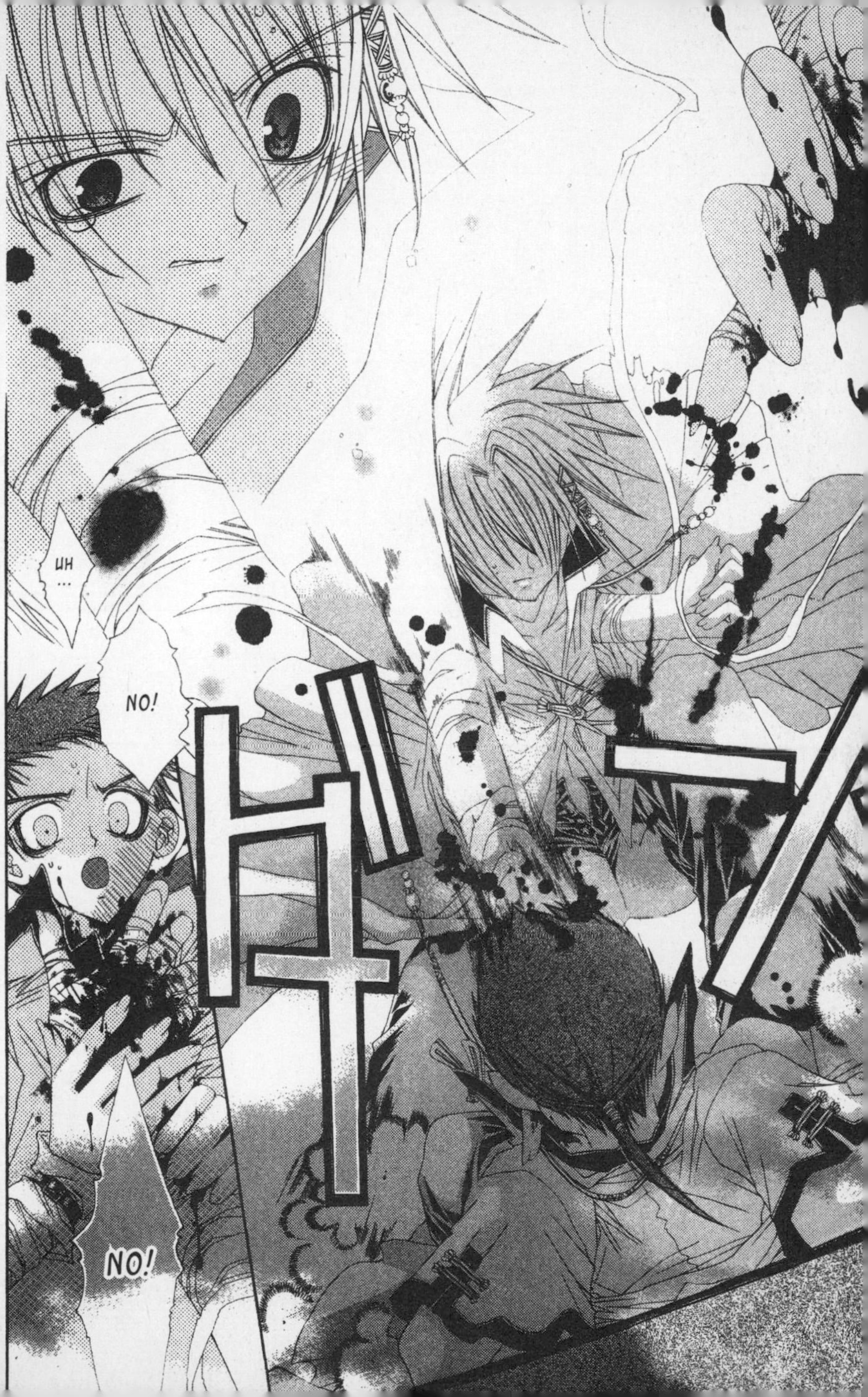
UH ...
NO!
NO!

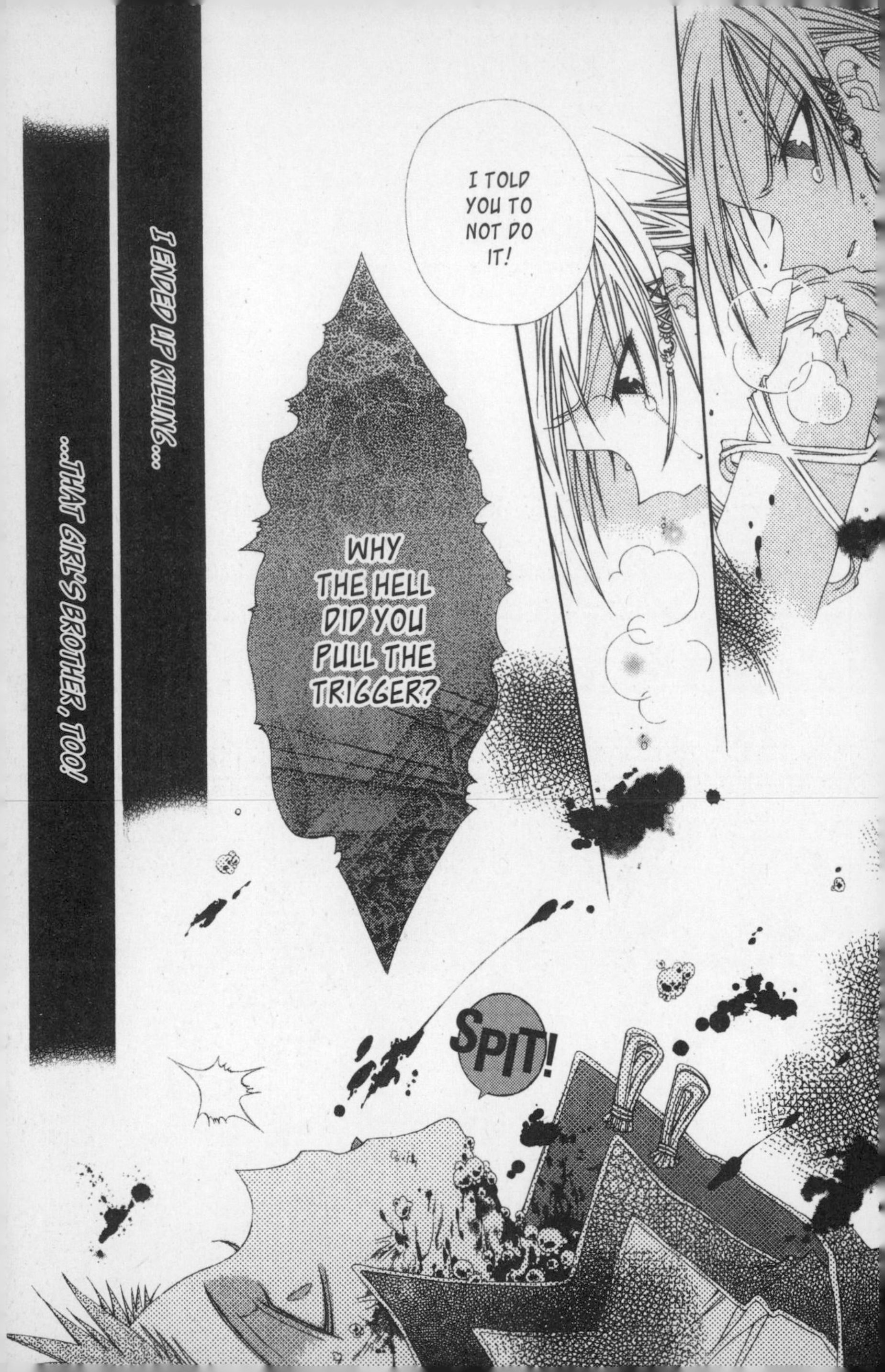
I TOLD YOU TO NOT DO IT!
WHY THE HELL DID YOU PULL THE TRIGGER?
SPIT!
I ENDED UP KILLING...
...THAT GIRL'S BROTHER, TOO!

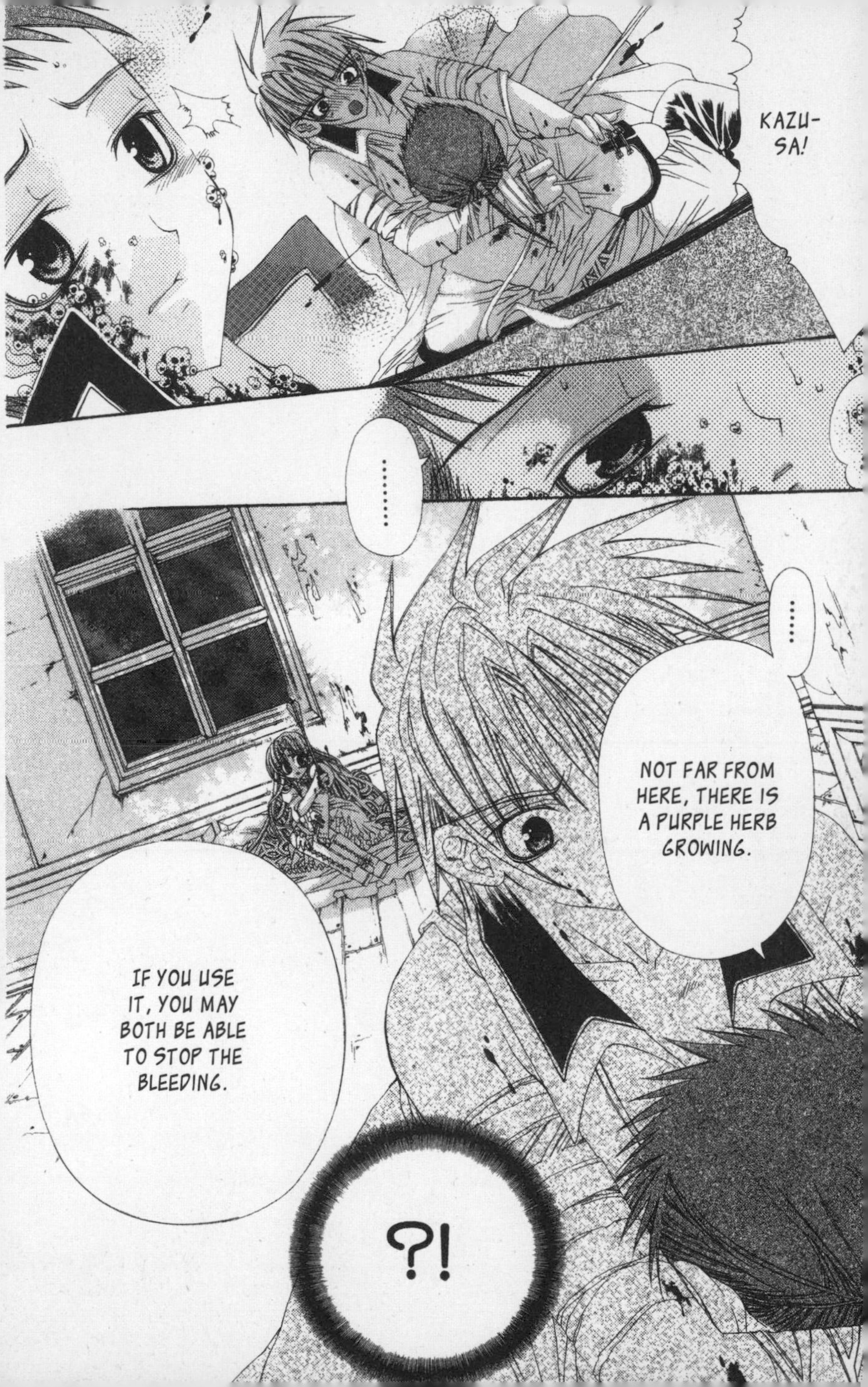
KAZU-SA!
......
......
NOT FAR FROM HERE, THERE IS A PURPLE HERB GROWING.
IF YOU USE IT, YOU MAY BOTH BE ABLE TO STOP THE BLEEDING.
?!

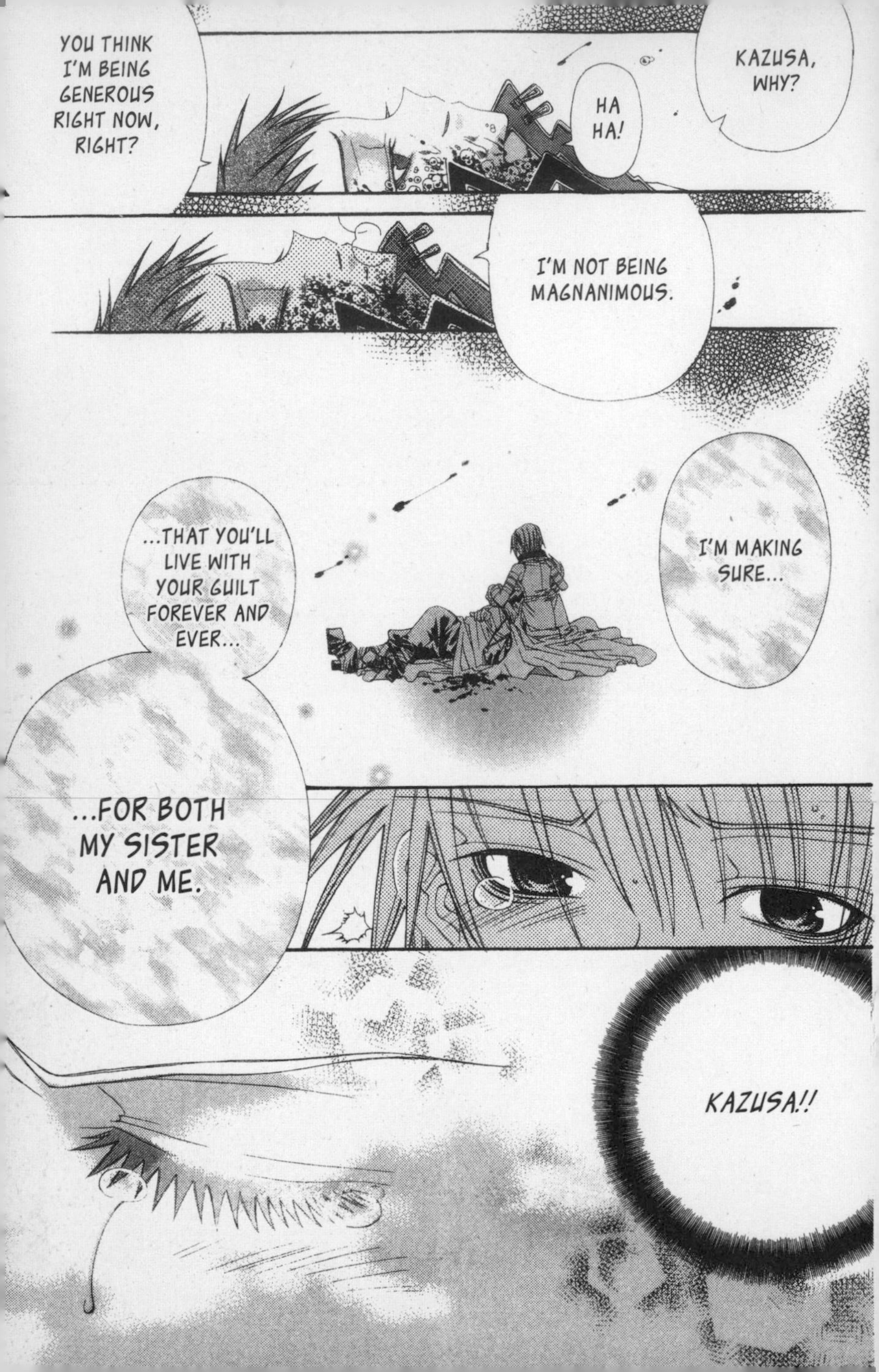
KAZUSA, WHY?
HA HA!
YOU THINK I'M BEING GENEROUS RIGHT NOW, RIGHT?
I'M NOT BEING MAGNANIMOUS.
I'M MAKING SURE...
...THAT YOU'LL LIVE WITH YOUR GUILT FOREVER AND EVER...
...FOR BOTH MY SISTER AND ME.
KAZUSA!!

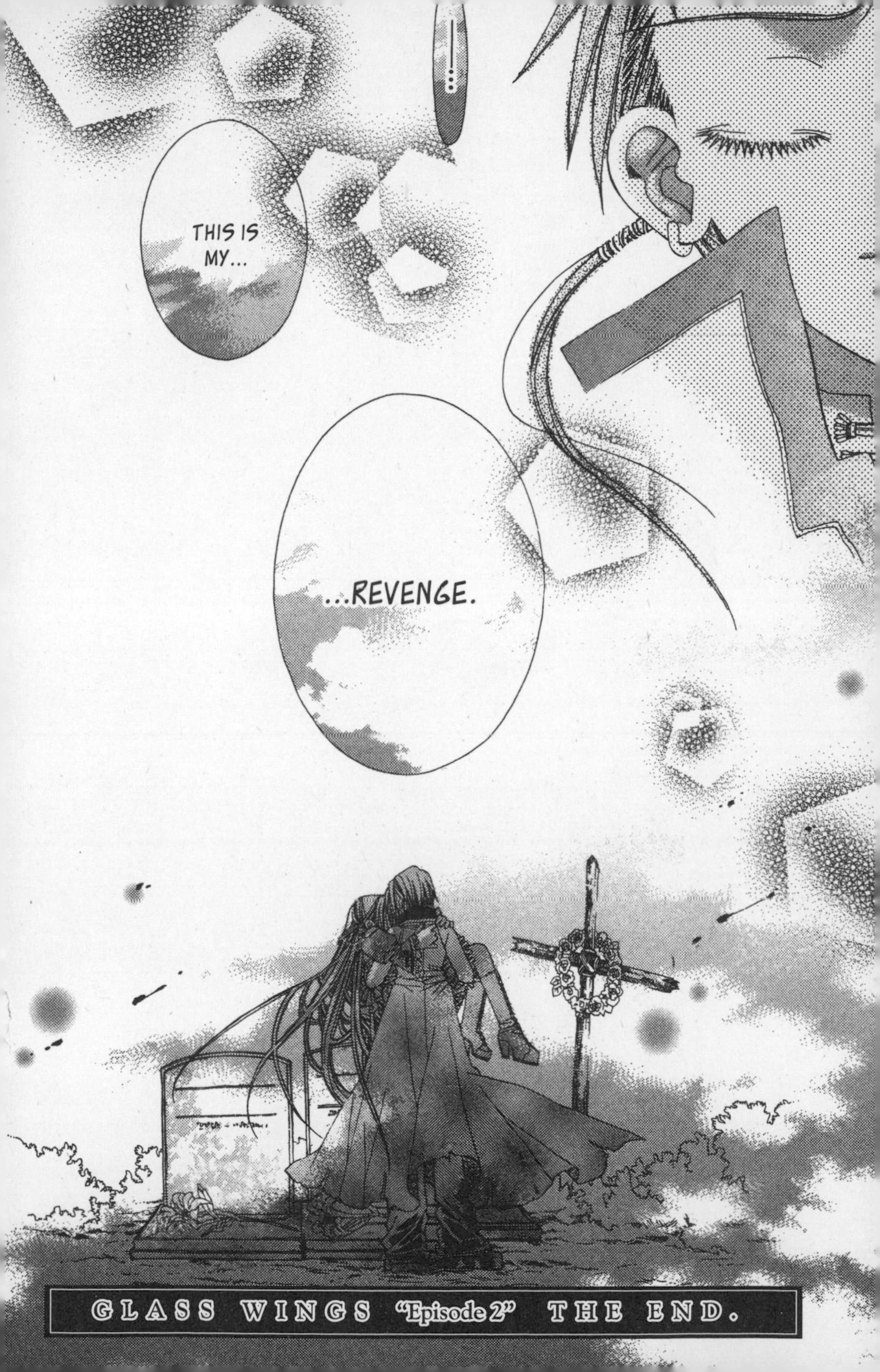
THIS IS MY...
...REVENGE.
GLASS WINGS "Episode 2" THE END.

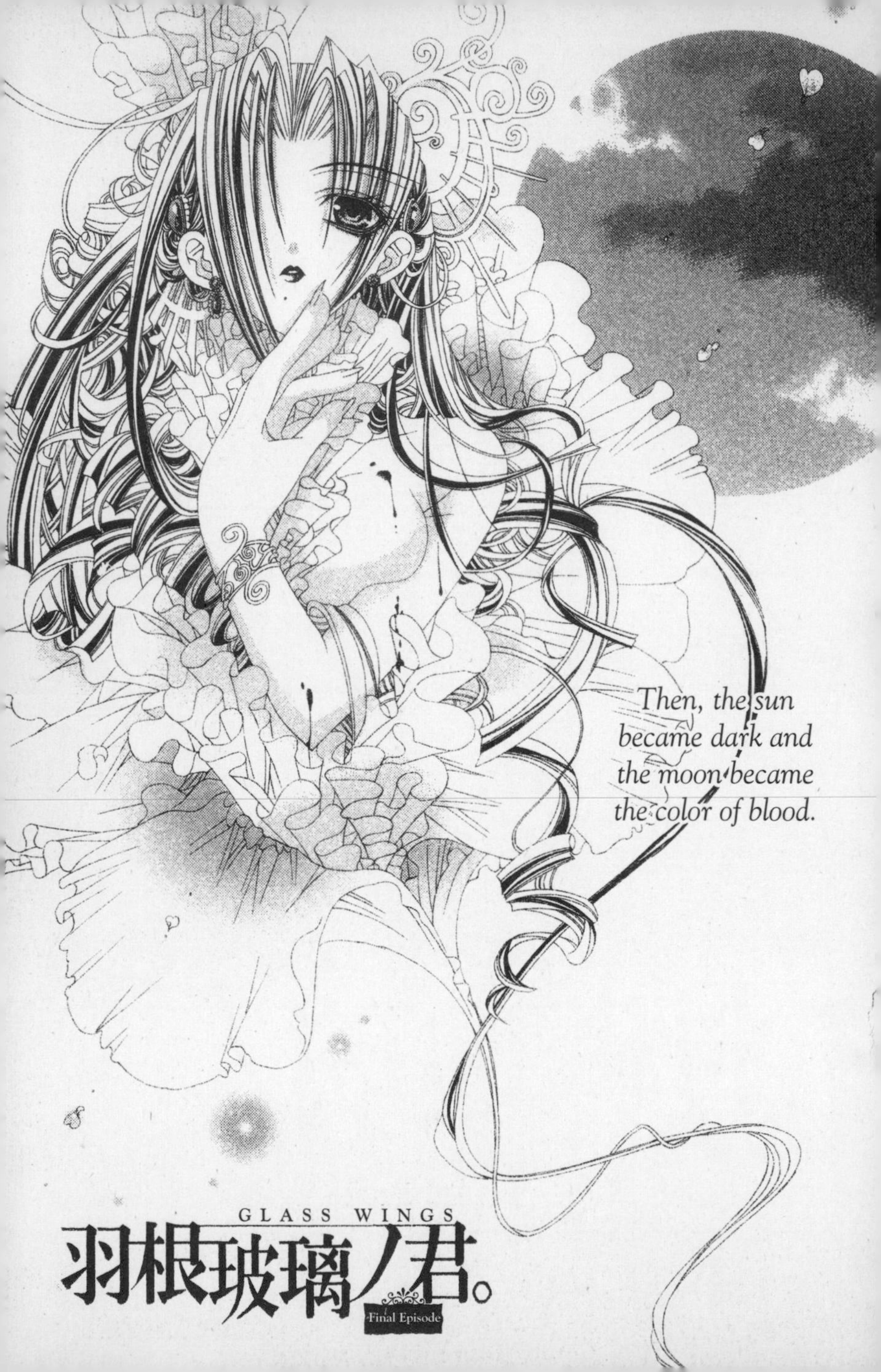
Then, the sun became dark and the moon became the color of blood.
GLASS WINGS
羽根玻璃ノ君。
Final Episode

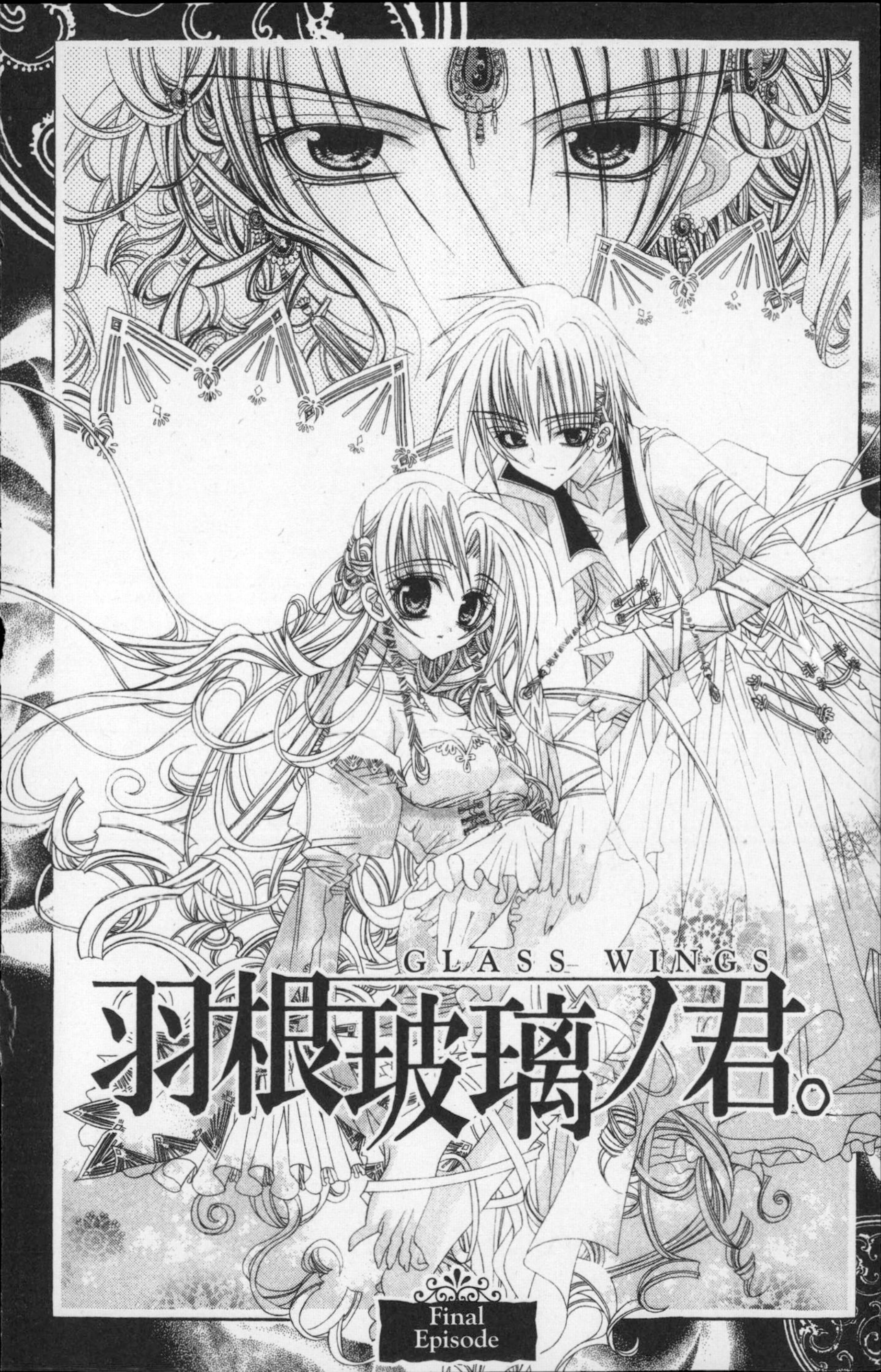
GLASS WINGS
羽根玻璃ノ君。
Final
Episode

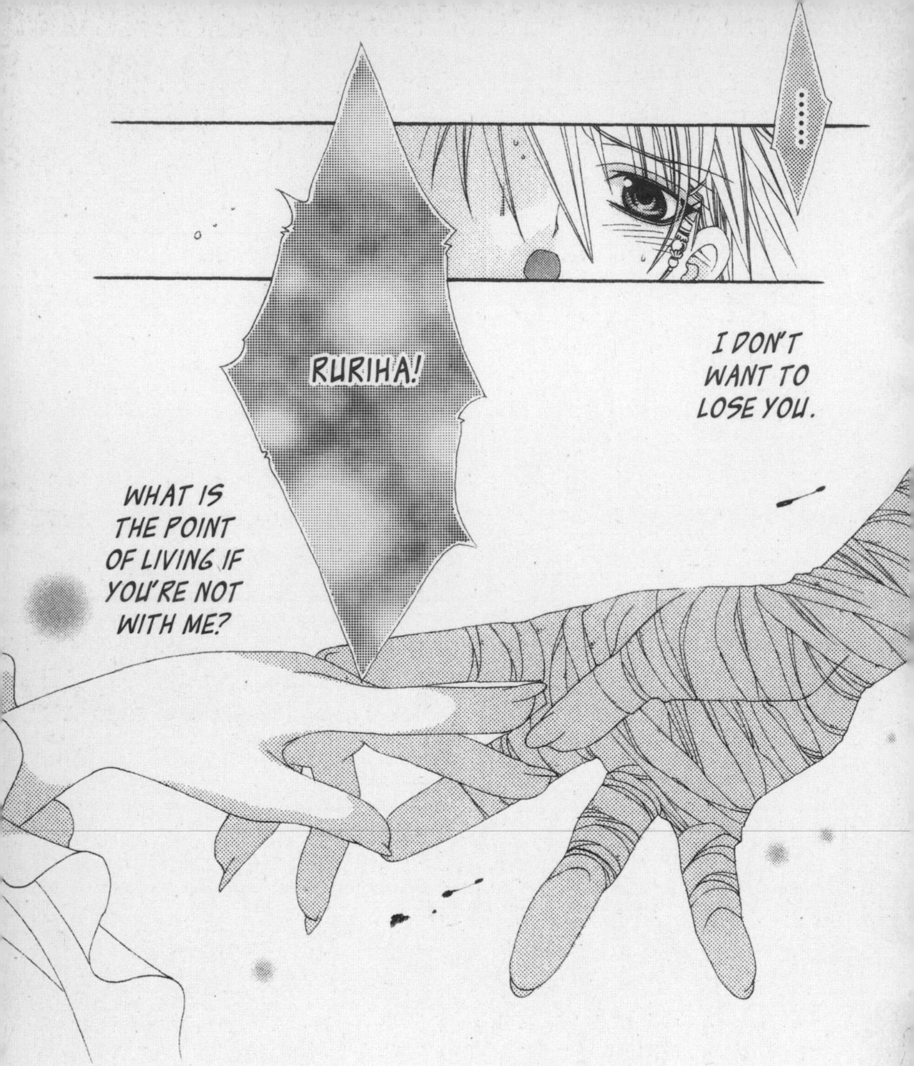
......
RURIHA!
I DON'T WANT TO LOSE YOU.
WHAT IS THE POINT OF LIVING IF YOU'RE NOT WITH ME?

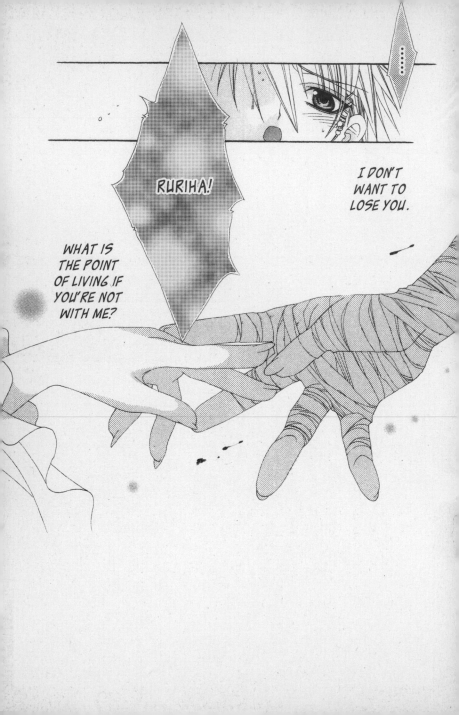

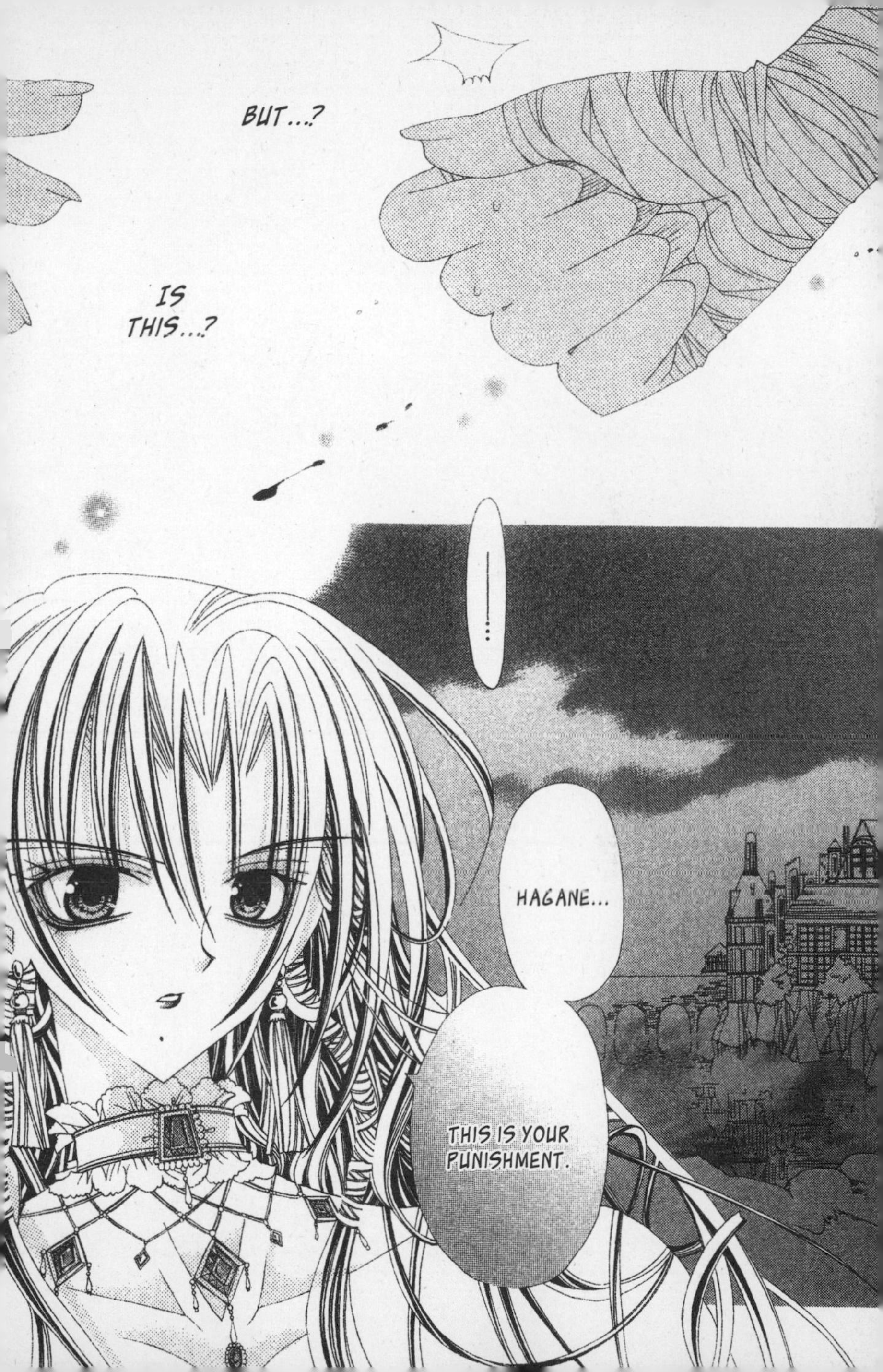
BUT...?
IS THIS...?
HAGANE...
THIS IS YOUR PUNISHMENT.

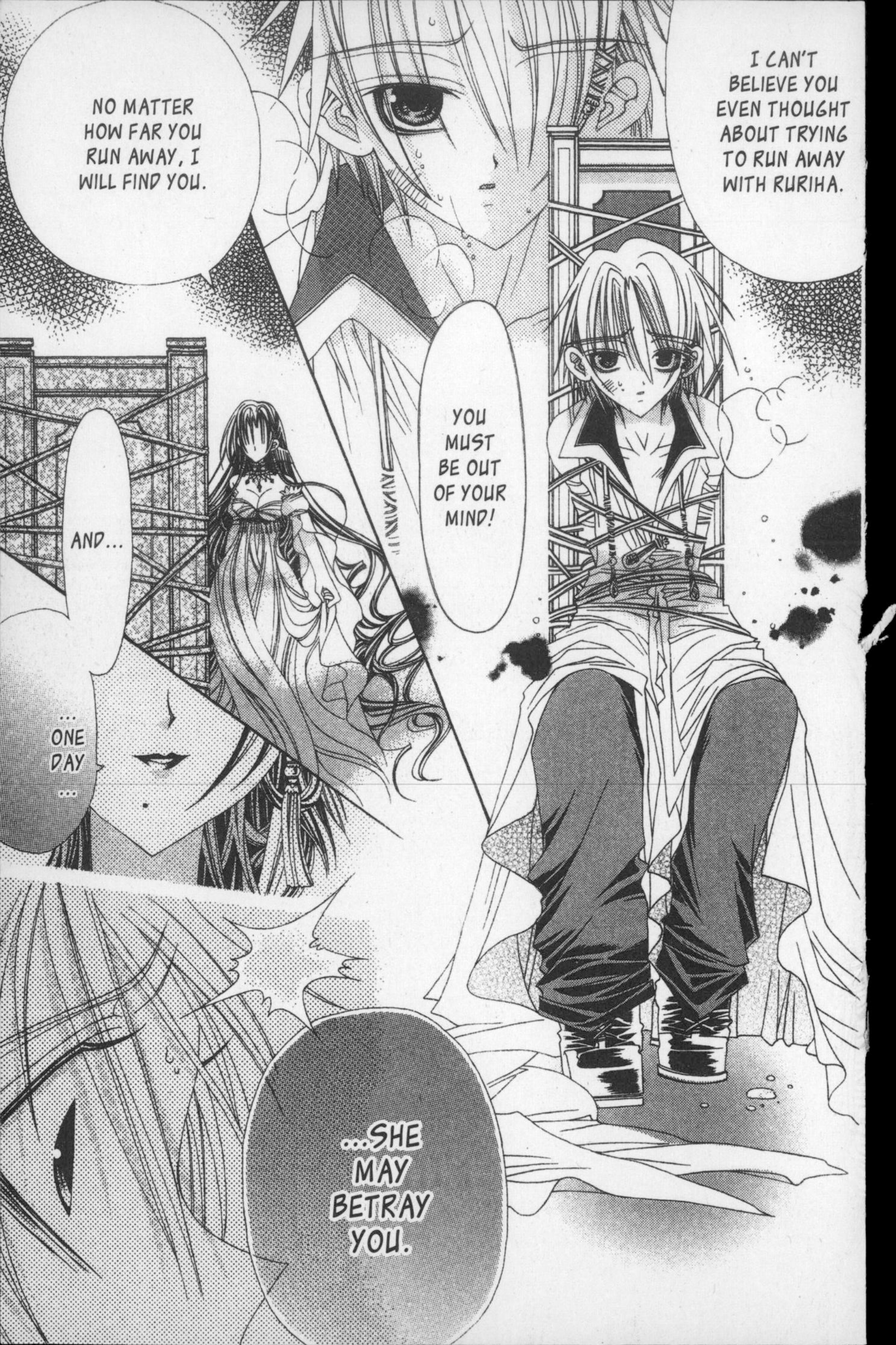
I CAN'T BELIEVE YOU EVEN THOUGHT ABOUT TRYING TO RUN AWAY WITH RURIHA.
YOU MUST BE OUT OF YOUR MIND!
NO MATTER HOW FAR YOU RUN AWAY, I WILL FIND YOU.
AND...
...ONE DAY...
...SHE MAY BETRAY YOU.

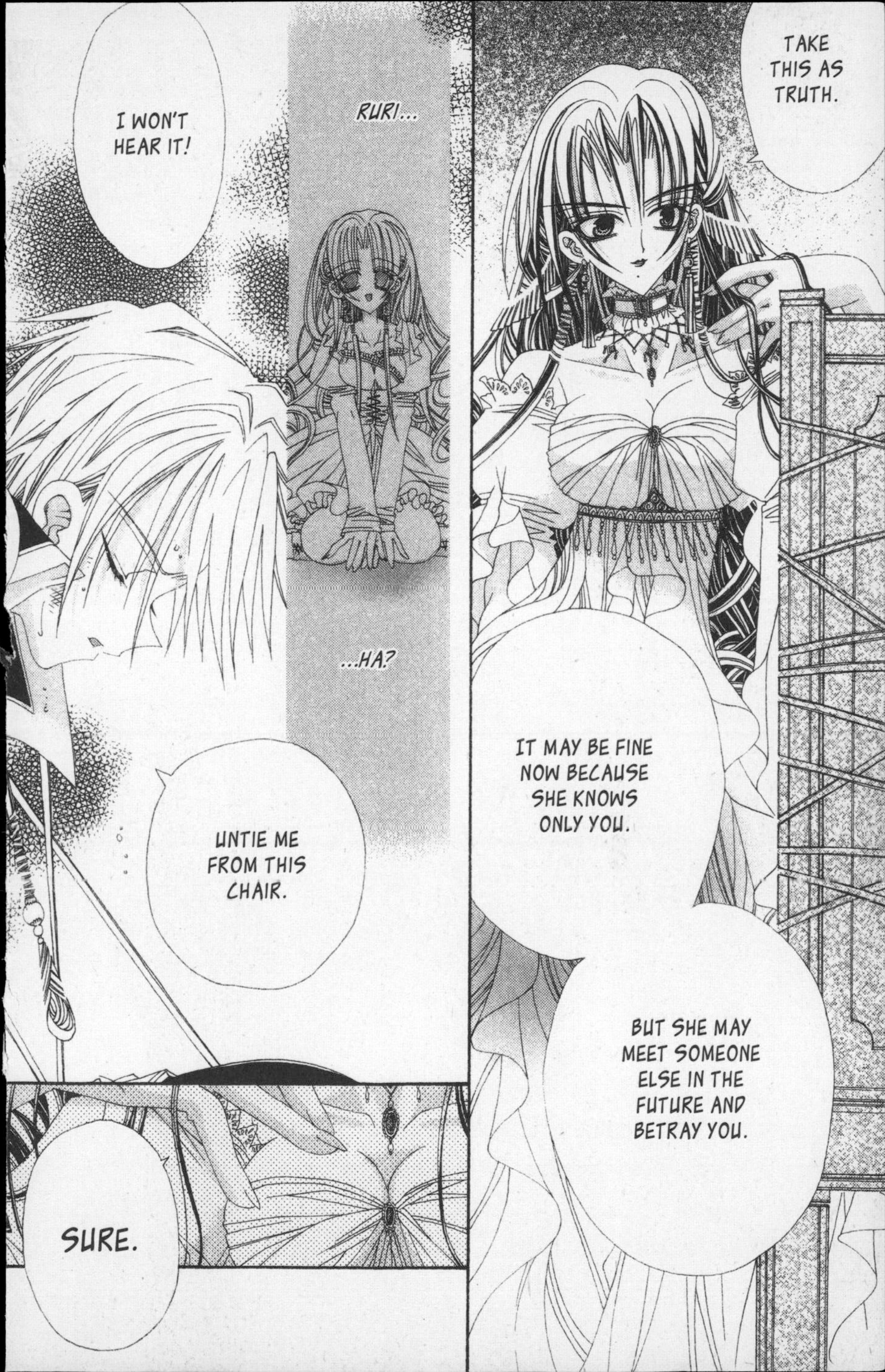

TAKE THIS AS TRUTH.
IT MAY BE FINE NOW BECAUSE SHE KNOWS ONLY YOU.
BUT SHE MAY MEET SOMEONE ELSE IN THE FUTURE AND BETRAY YOU.
RURI...
I WON'T HEAR IT!
...HA?
UNTIE ME FROM THIS CHAIR.
SURE.

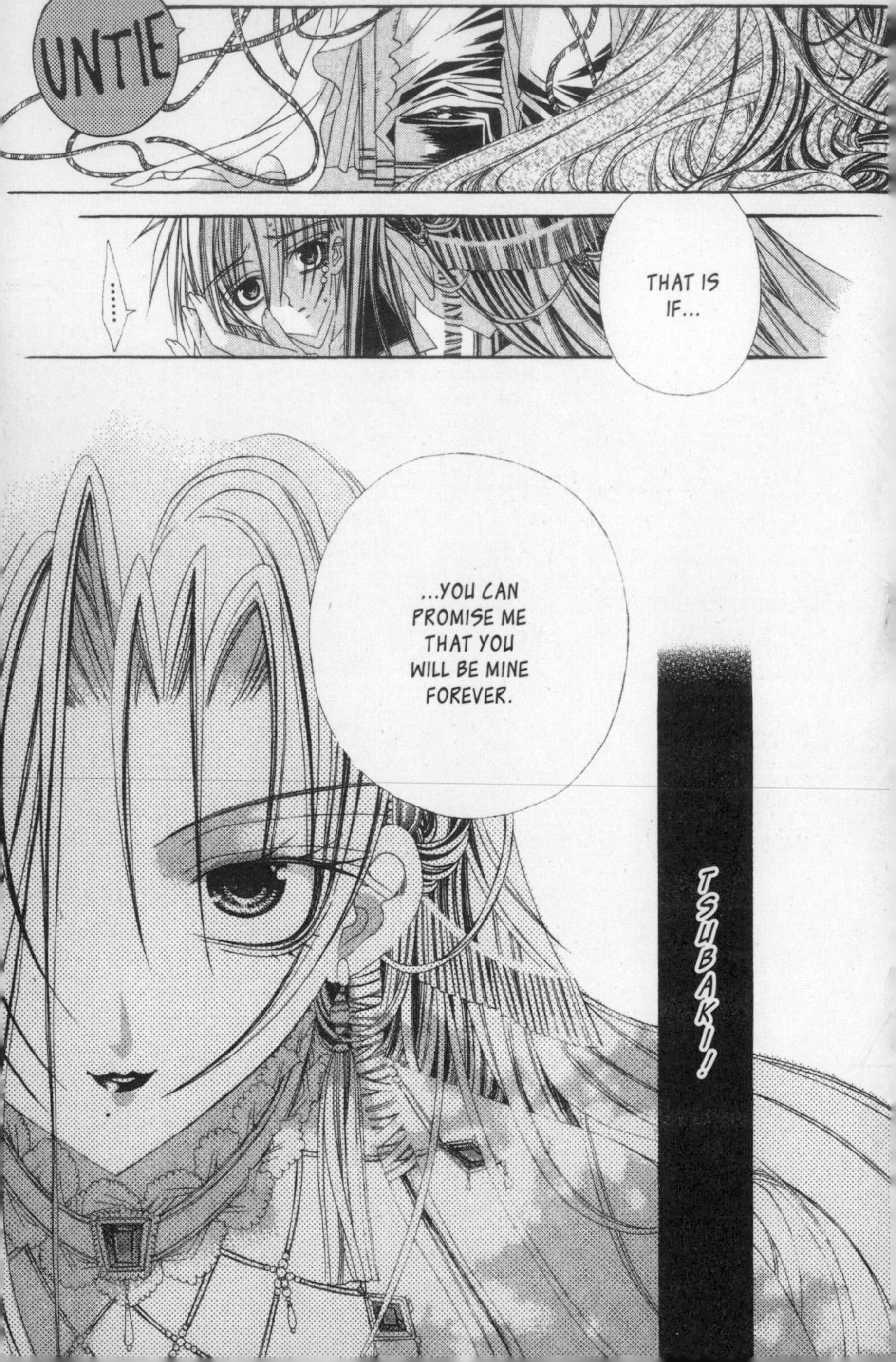
UNTIE
THAT IS IF...
......
...YOU CAN PROMISE ME THAT YOU WILL BE MINE FOREVER.
TSUBAKI!

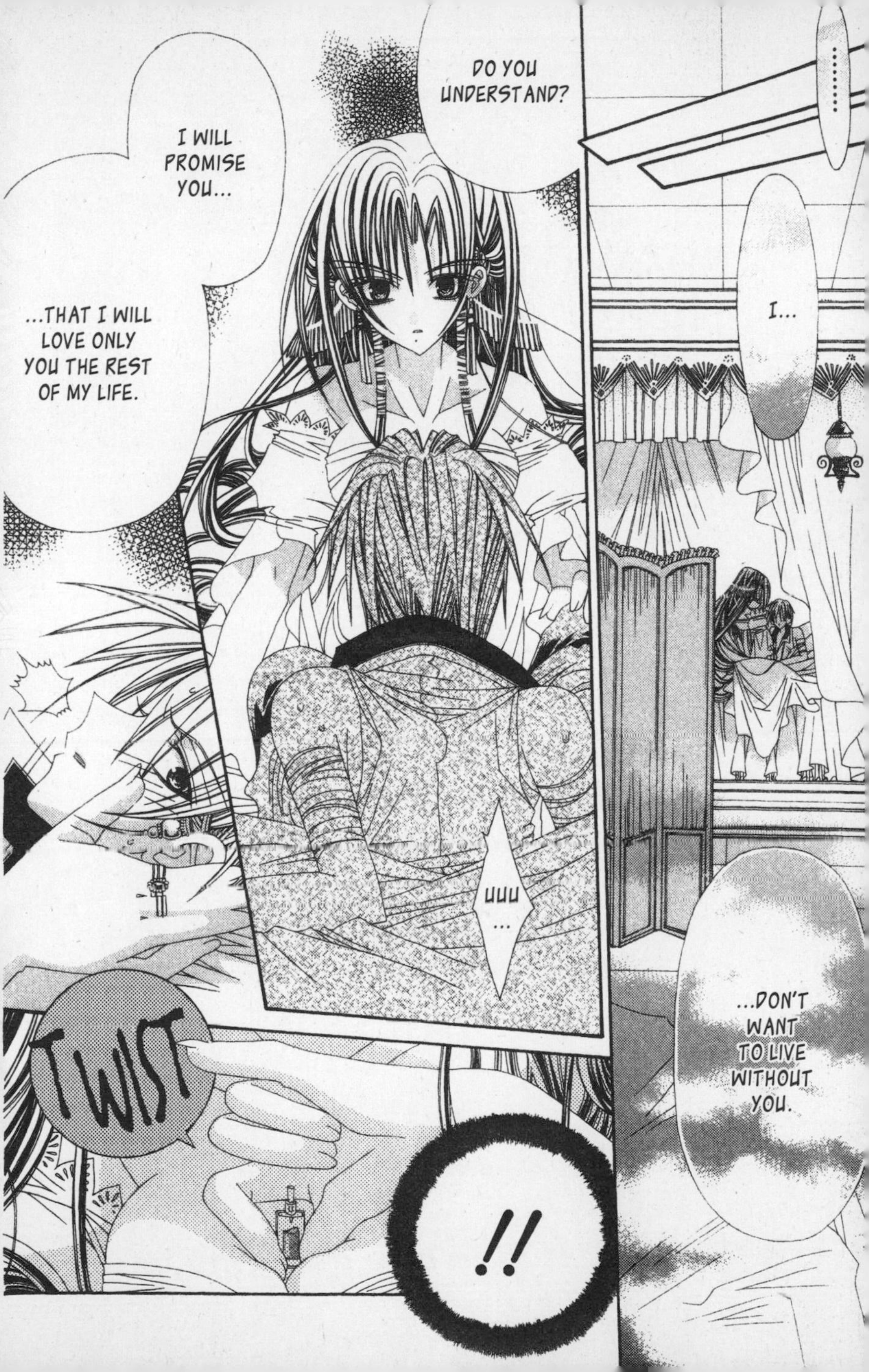
......
I...
...DON'T WANT TO LIVE WITHOUT YOU.
DO YOU UNDERSTAND?
uuu ...
I WILL PROMISE YOU...
...THAT I WILL LOVE ONLY YOU THE REST OF MY LIFE.
!!
TWIST

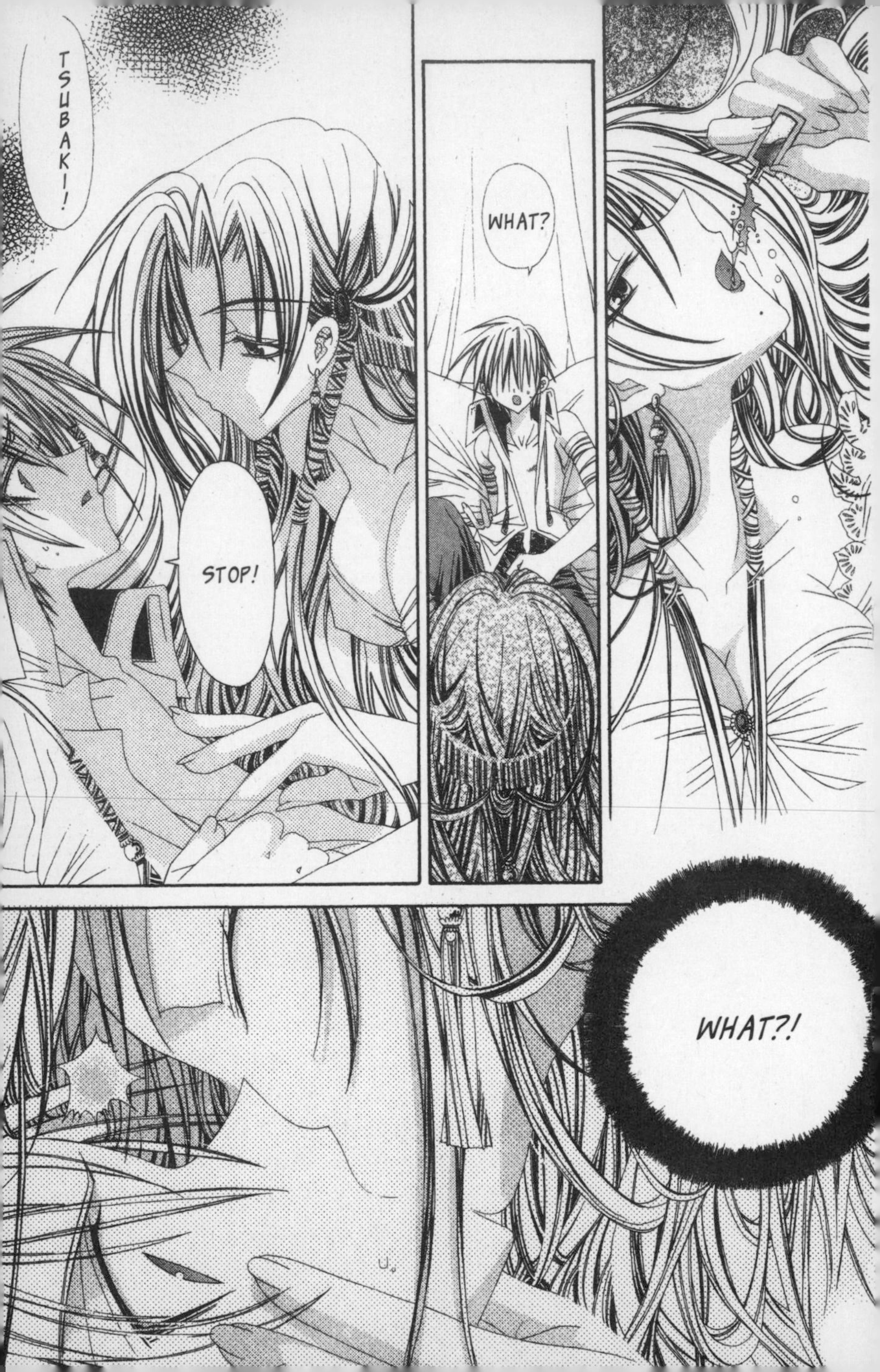
WHAT?
TSUBAKI!
STOP!
WHAT?!

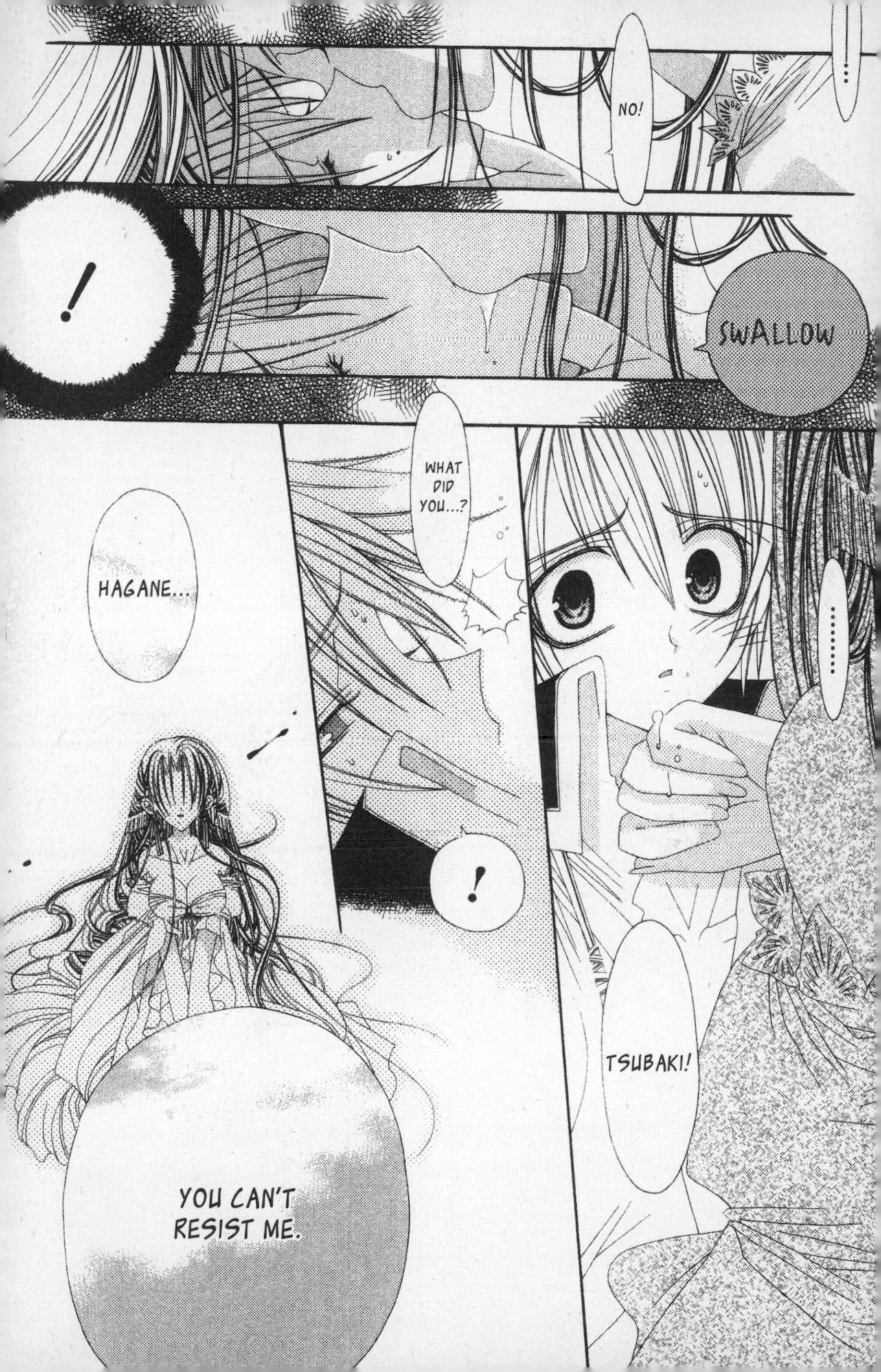
...
NO!
SWALLOW
!
......
TSUBAKI!
WHAT DID YOU...?
!
HAGANE...
YOU CAN'T RESIST ME.

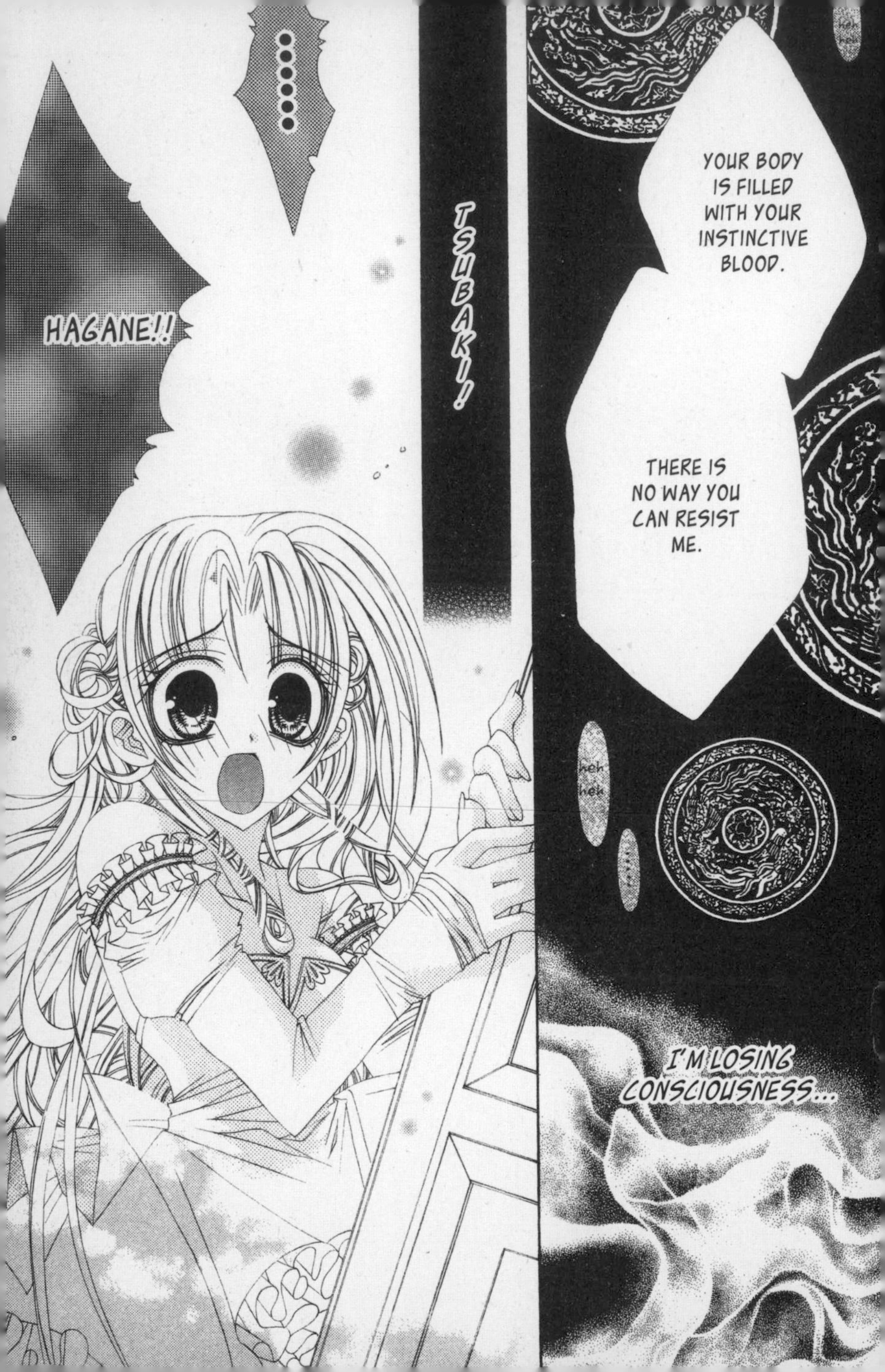
YOUR BODY IS FILLED WITH YOUR INSTINCTIVE BLOOD.
THERE IS NO WAY YOU CAN RESIST ME.
I'M LOSING CONSCIOUSNESS...
TSUBAKI!
......
HAGANE!!

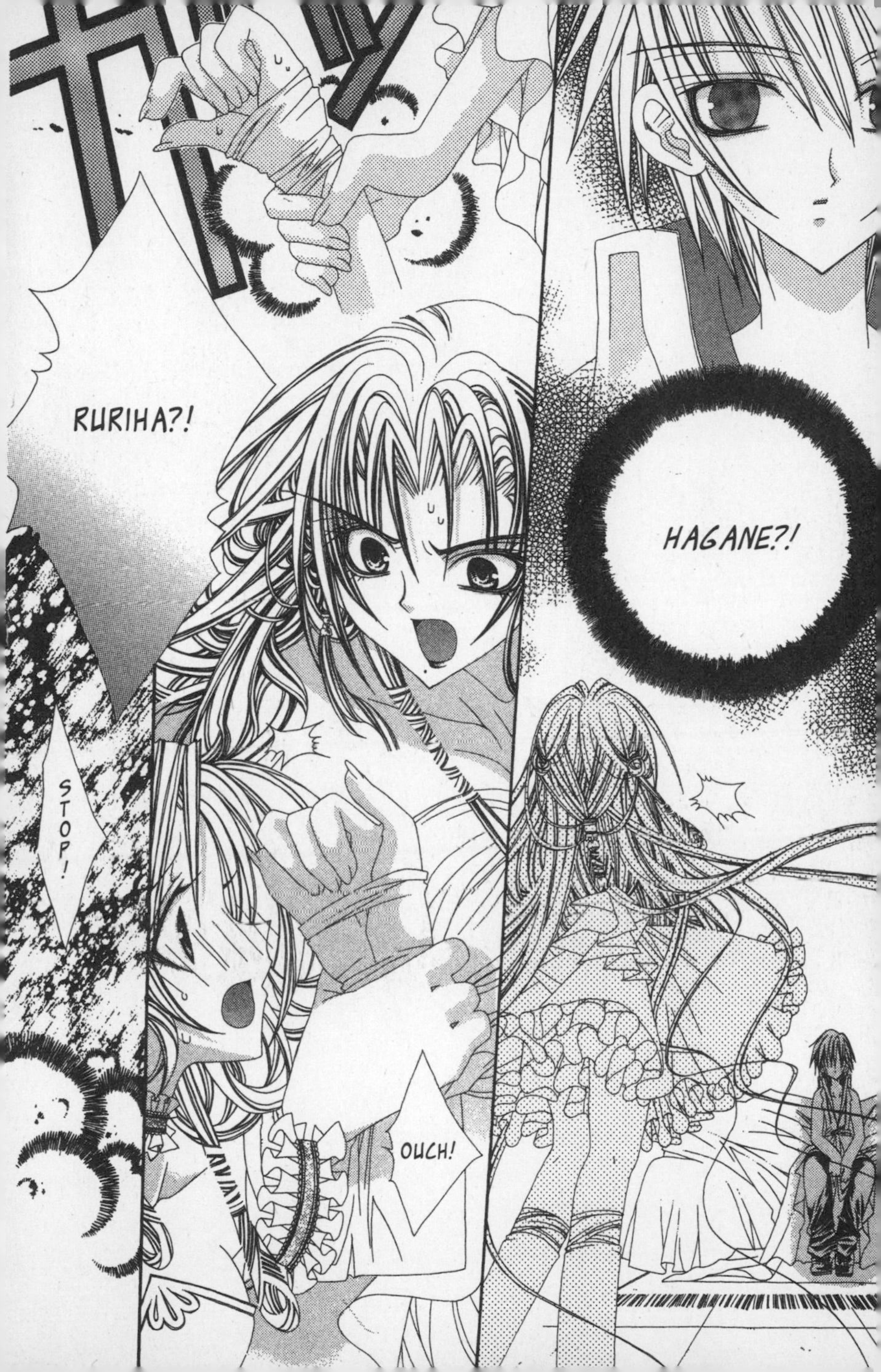
HAGANE?!
OUCH!
RURIHA?!
STOP!

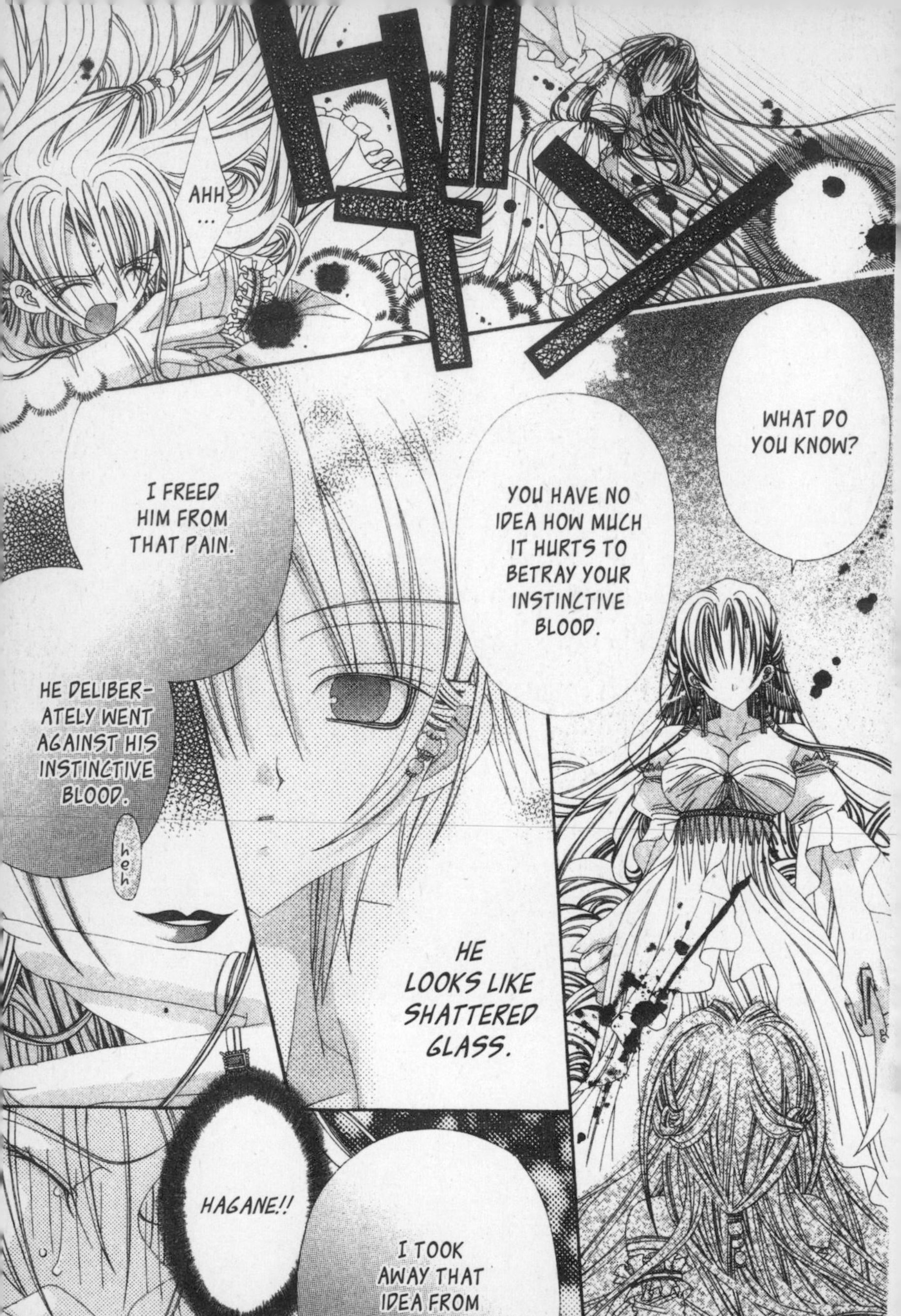
AHH ...
WHAT DO YOU KNOW?
YOU HAVE NO IDEA HOW MUCH IT HURTS TO BETRAY YOUR INSTINCTIVE BLOOD.
I FREED HIM FROM THAT PAIN.
HE DELIBER-ATELY WENT AGAINST HIS INSTINCTIVE BLOOD.
heh
HE LOOKS LIKE SHATTERED GLASS.
I TOOK AWAY THAT IDEA FROM HIM.
HAGANE!!

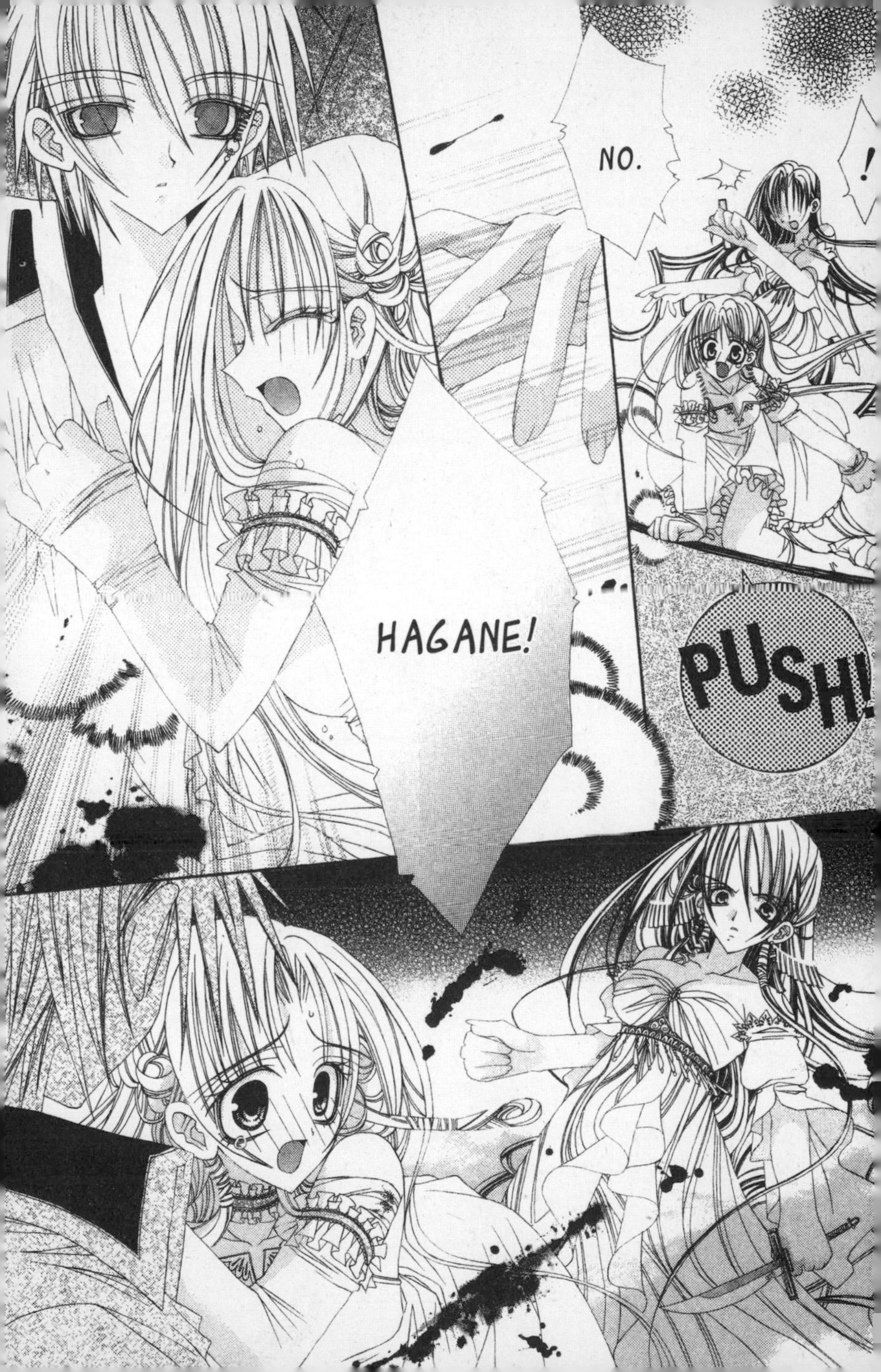
!
NO.
PUSH!
HAGANE!

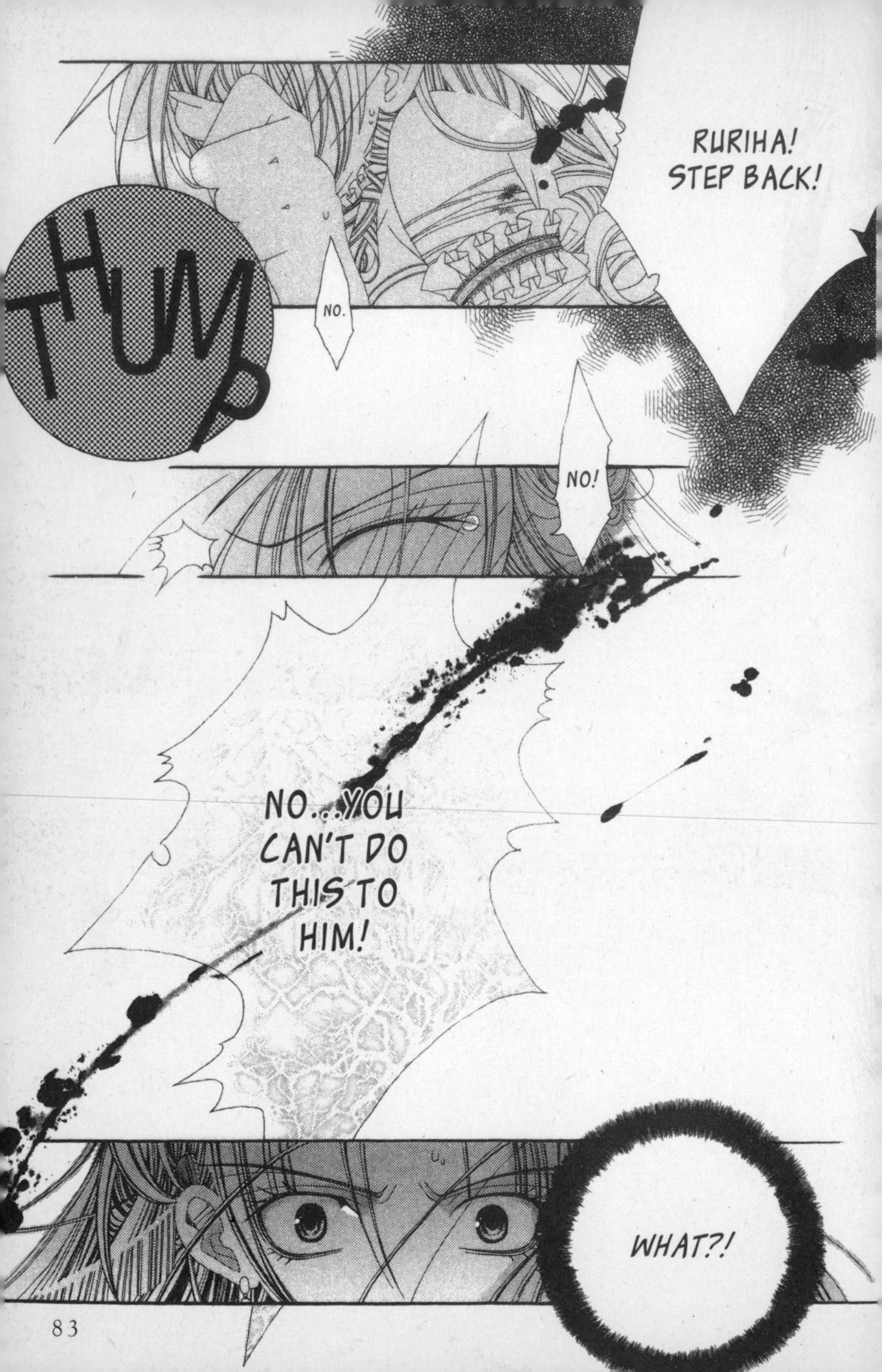
RURIHA! STEP BACK!
THUMP
NO.
NO!
NO... YOU CAN'T DO THIS TO HIM!
WHAT?!

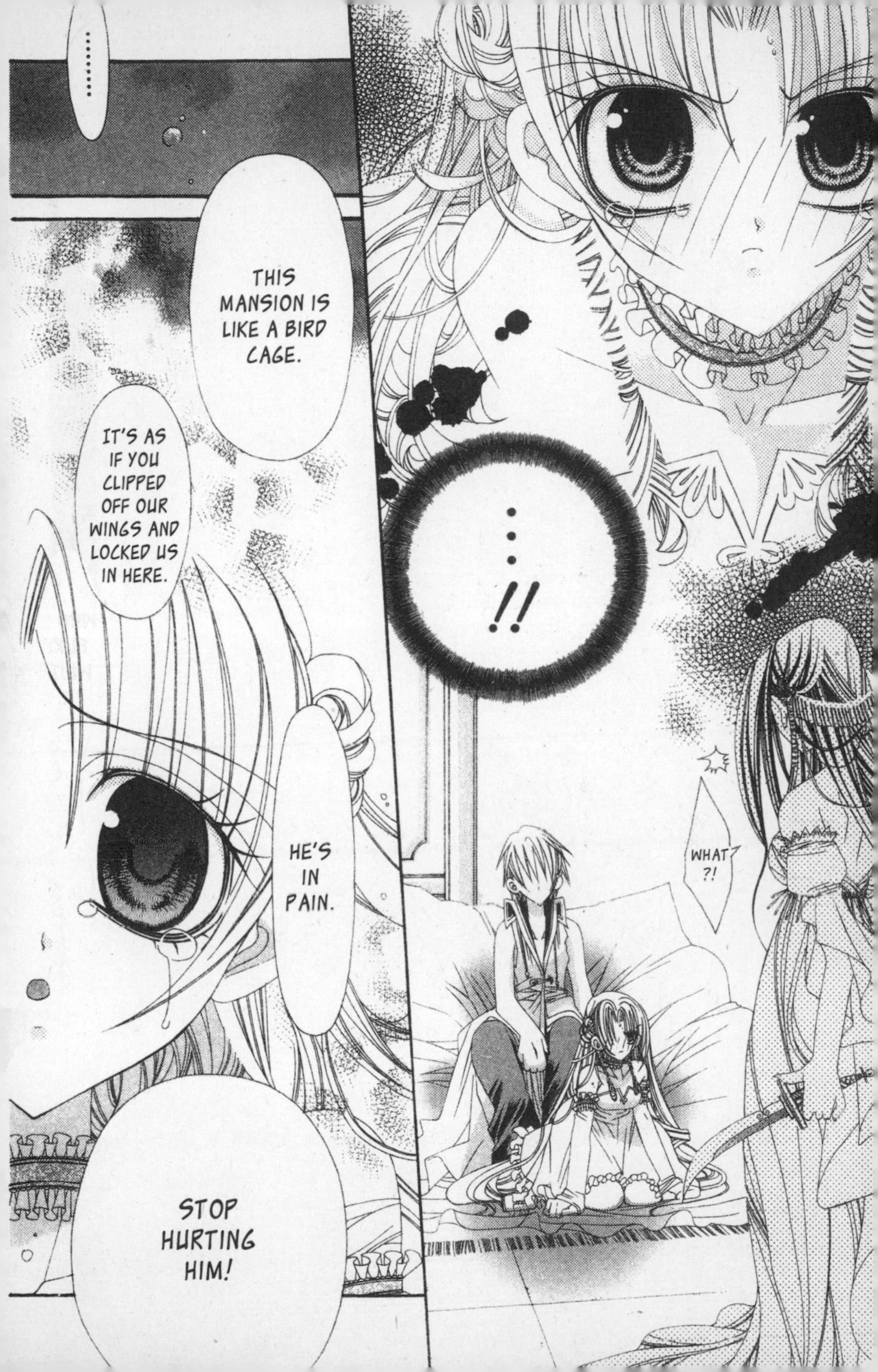
...!!
WHAT?!
......
THIS MANSION IS LIKE A BIRD CAGE.
IT'S AS IF YOU CLIPPED OFF OUR WINGS AND LOCKED US IN HERE.
HE'S IN PAIN.
STOP HURTING HIM!

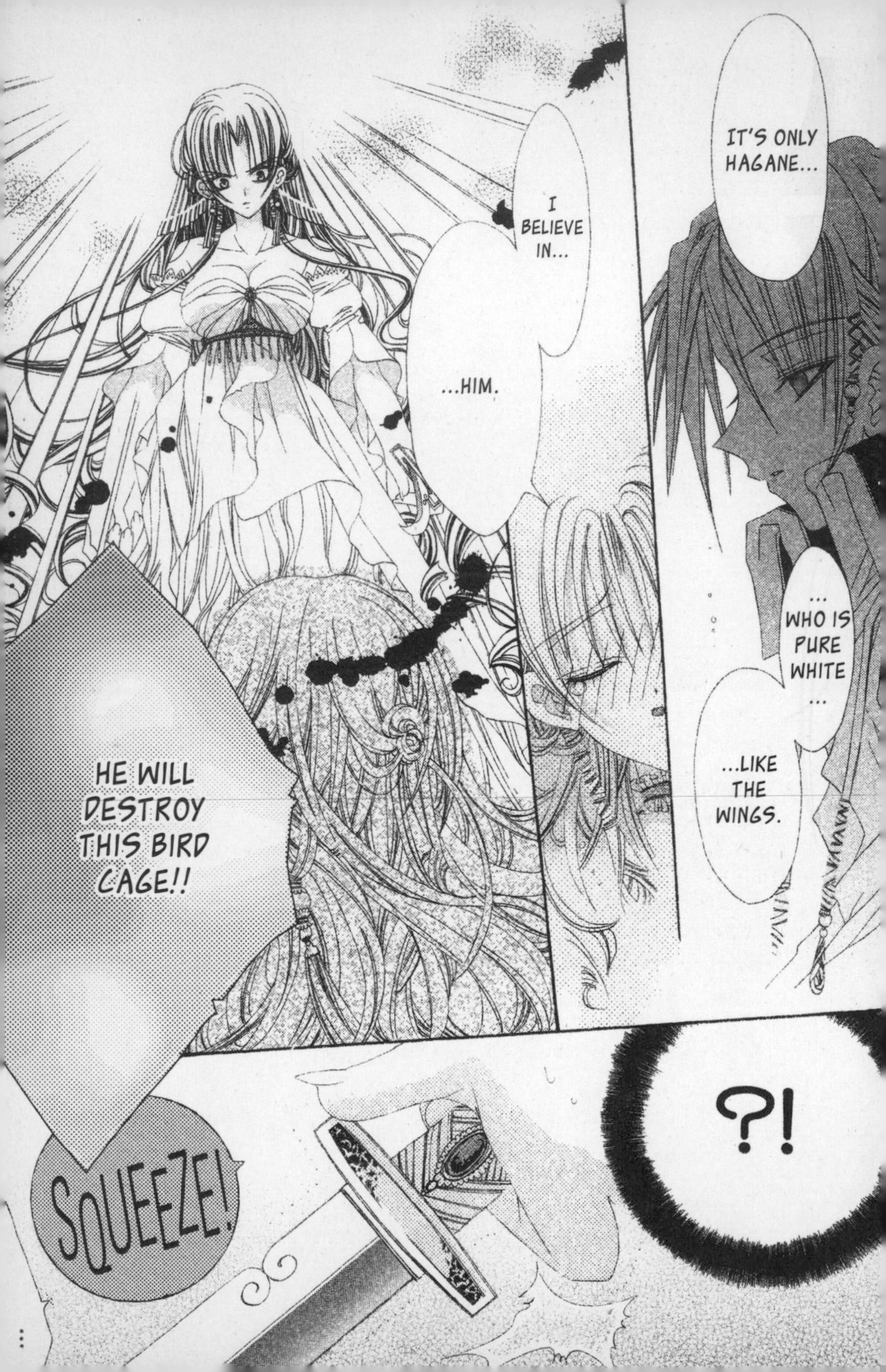
IT'S ONLY HAGANE...
... WHO IS PURE WHITE ...
...LIKE THE WINGS.
I BELIEVE IN...
...HIM.
HE WILL DESTROY THIS BIRD CAGE!!
?!
SQUEEZE!

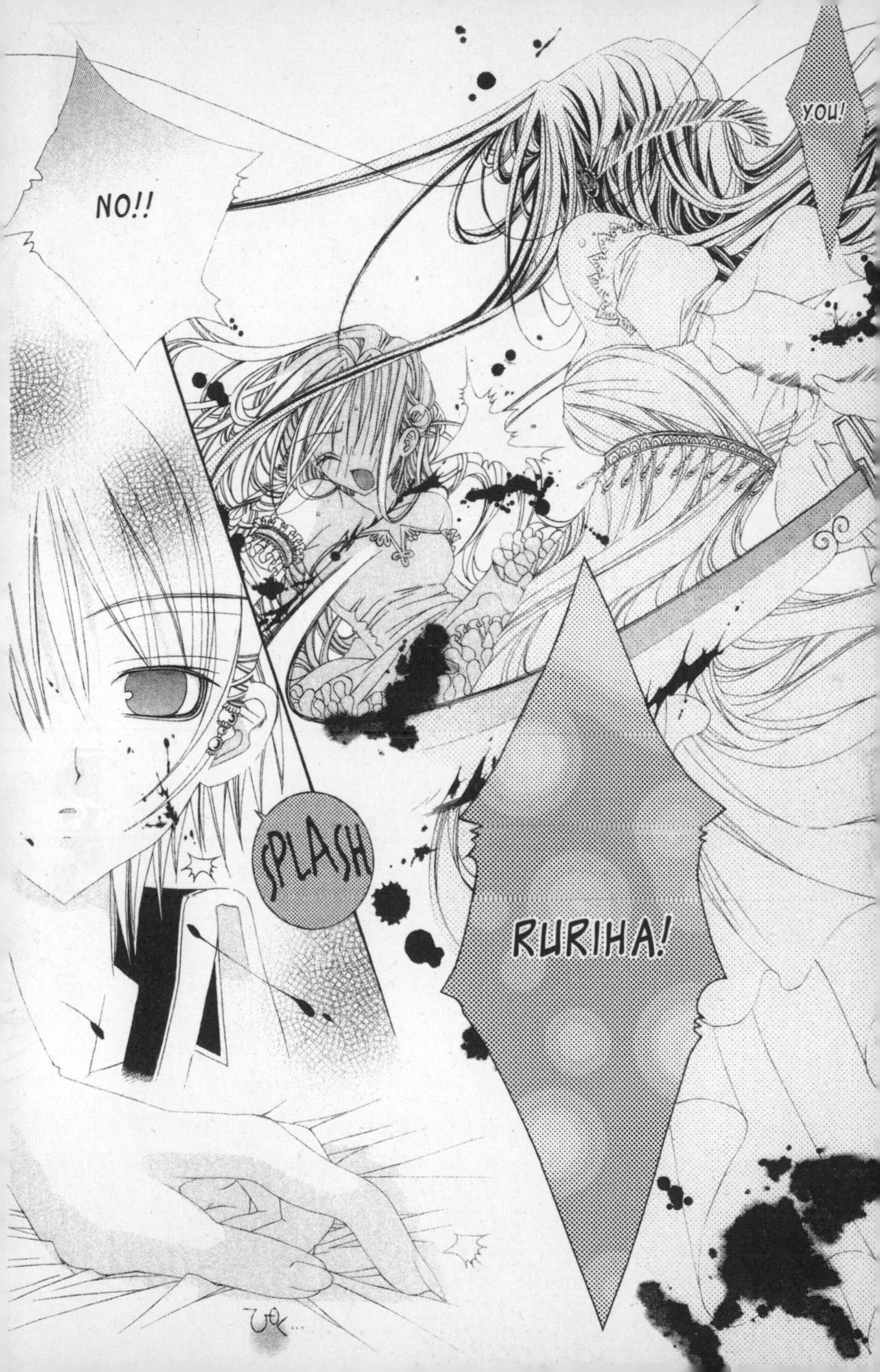
YOU!
NO!!
RURIHA!
SPLASH
ひく…

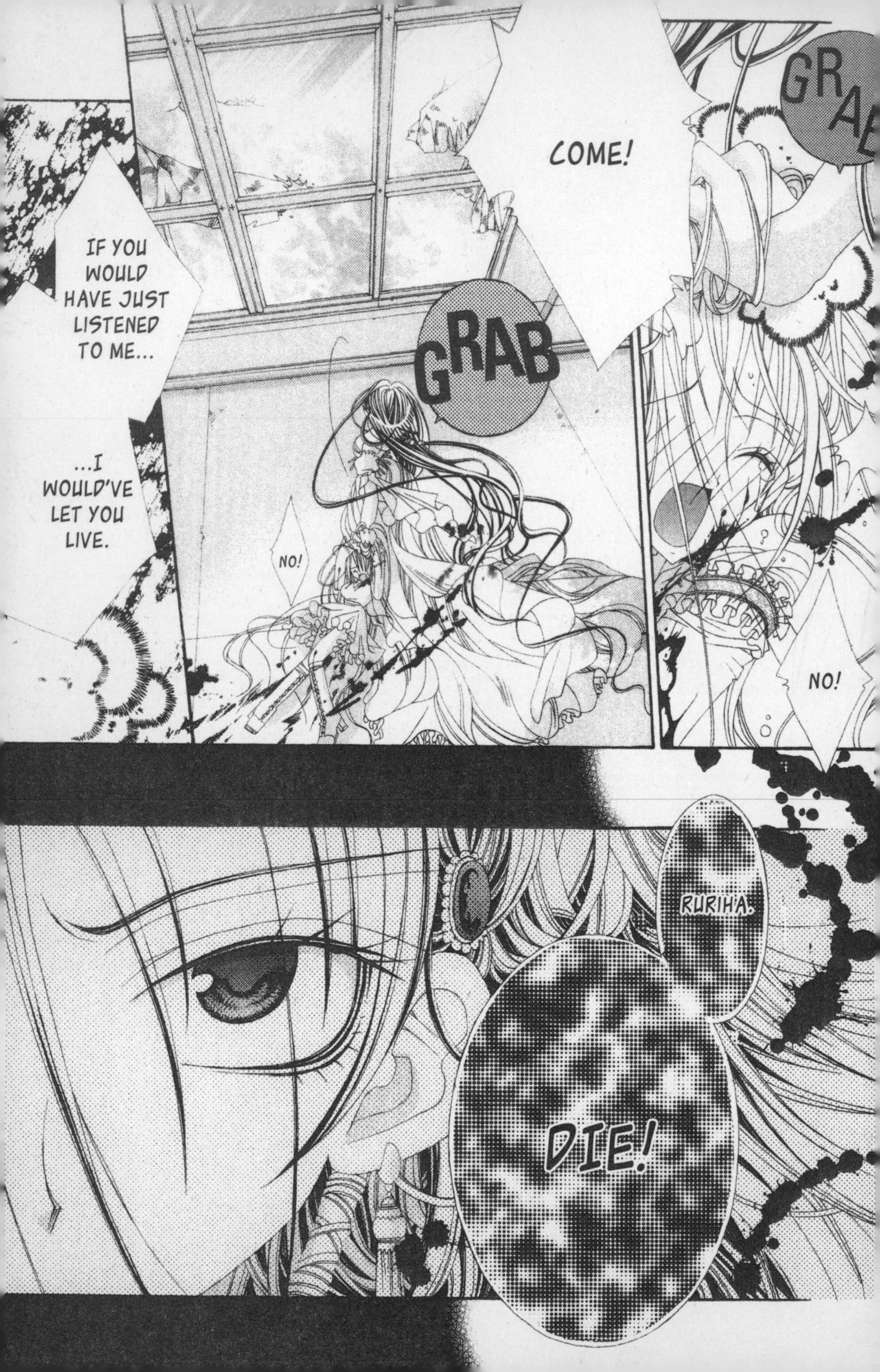
GRAB
COME!
NO!
GRAB
NO!
IF YOU WOULD HAVE JUST LISTENED TO ME...
...I WOULD'VE LET YOU LIVE.
RURIHA.
DIE!

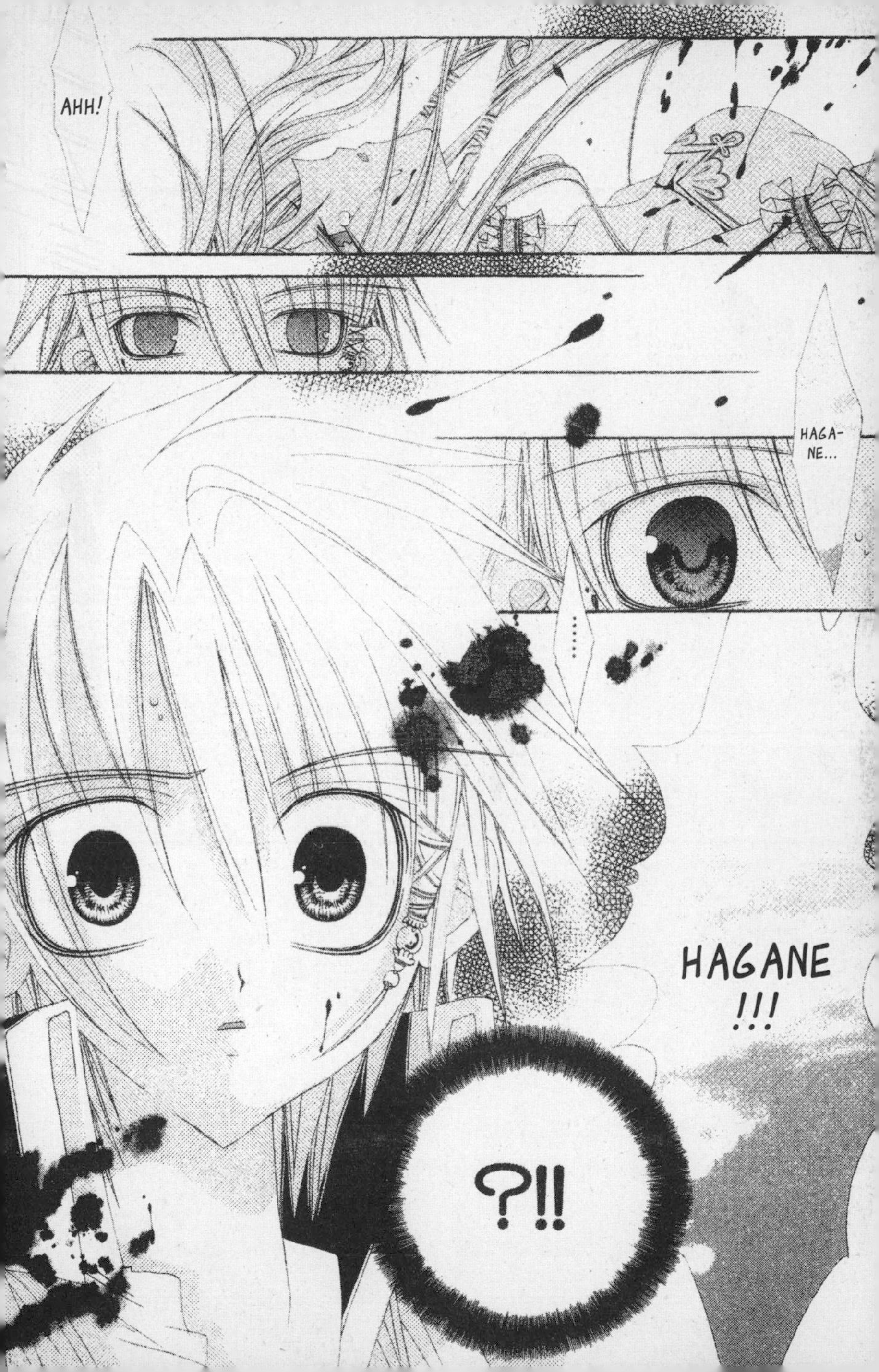
AHH!
HAGA-NE...
......
HAGANE !!!
?!!

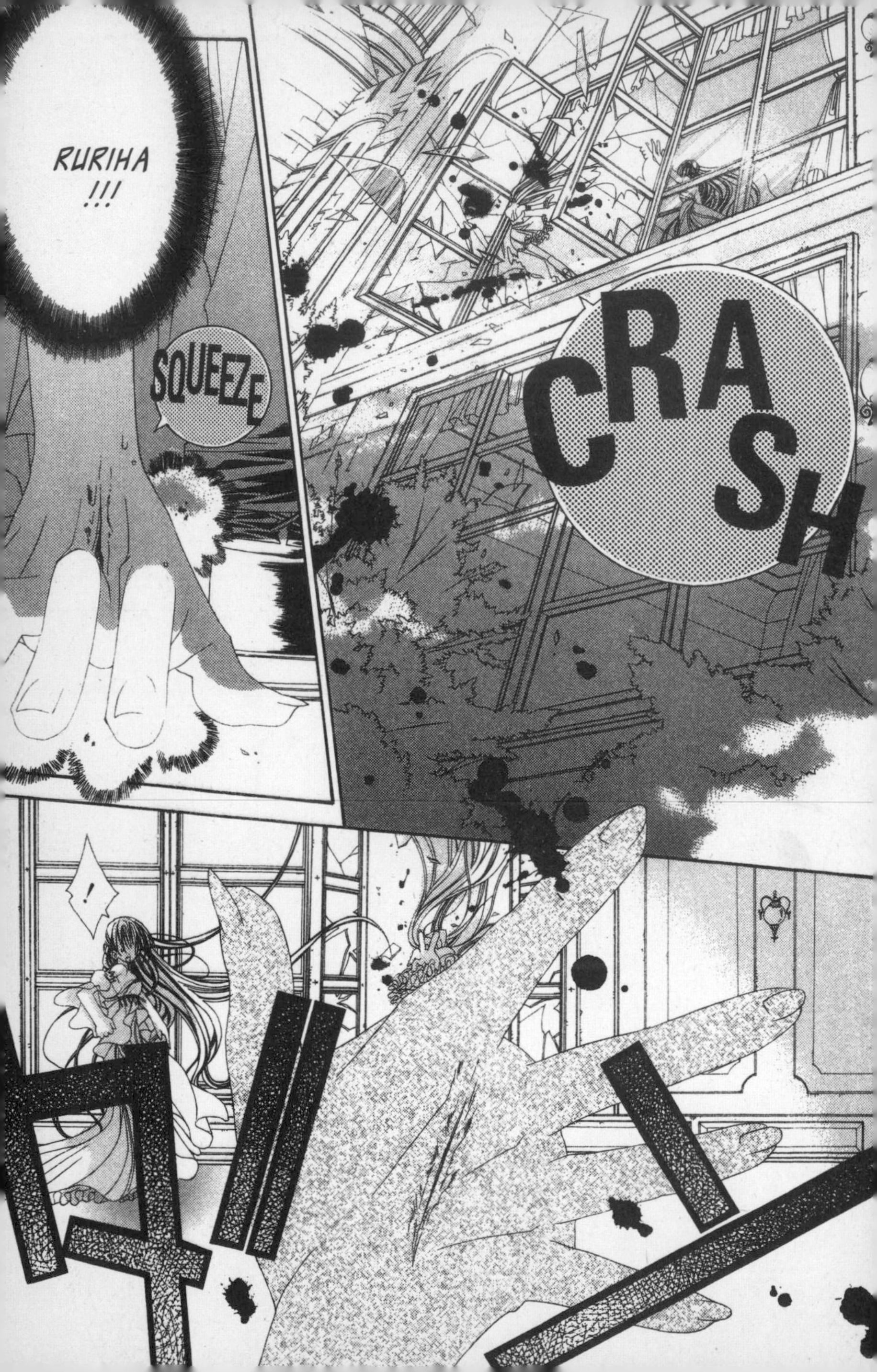
CRASH
RURIHA !!!
SQUEEZE
!

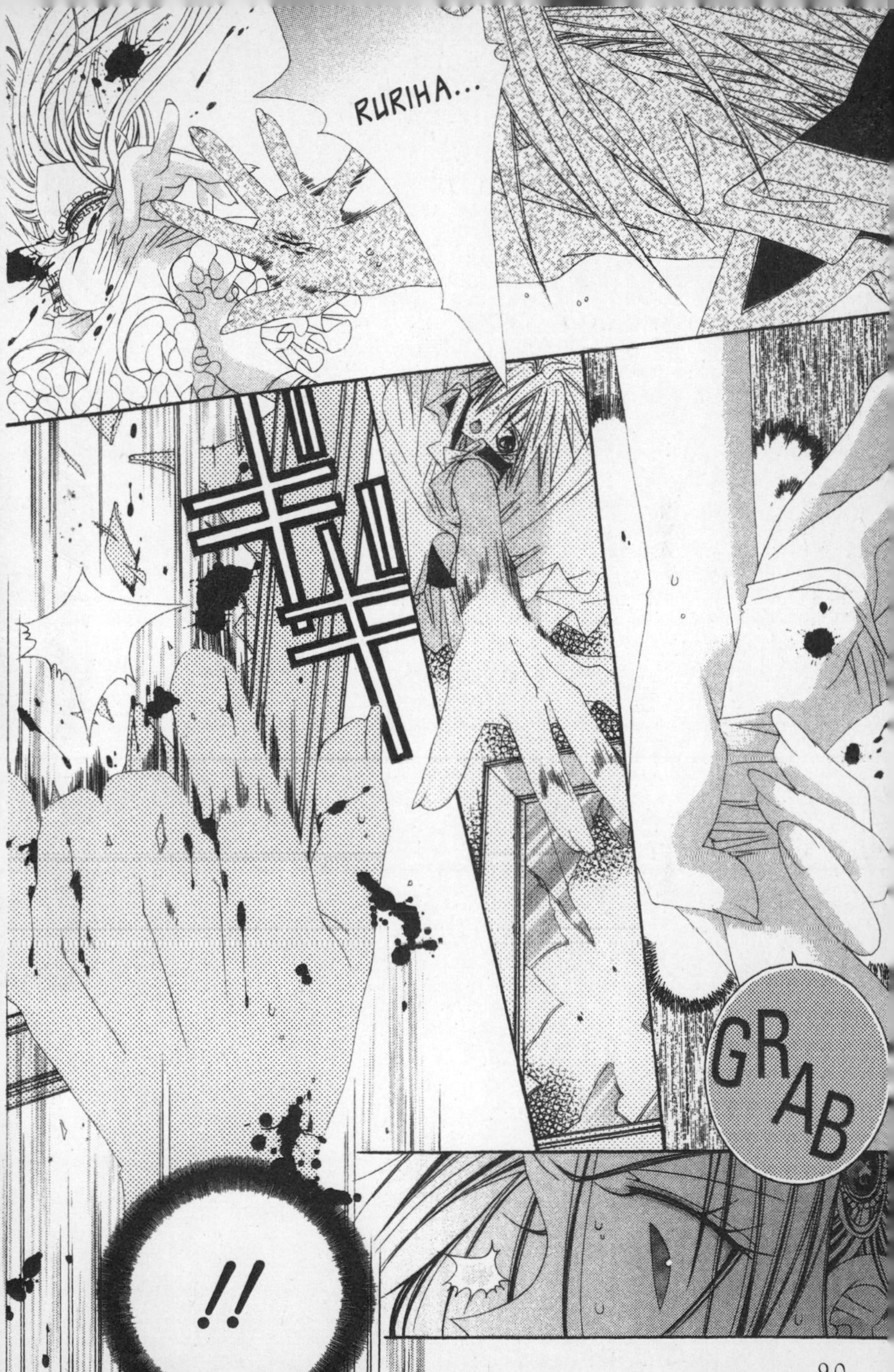
RURIHA...
GRAB
!!

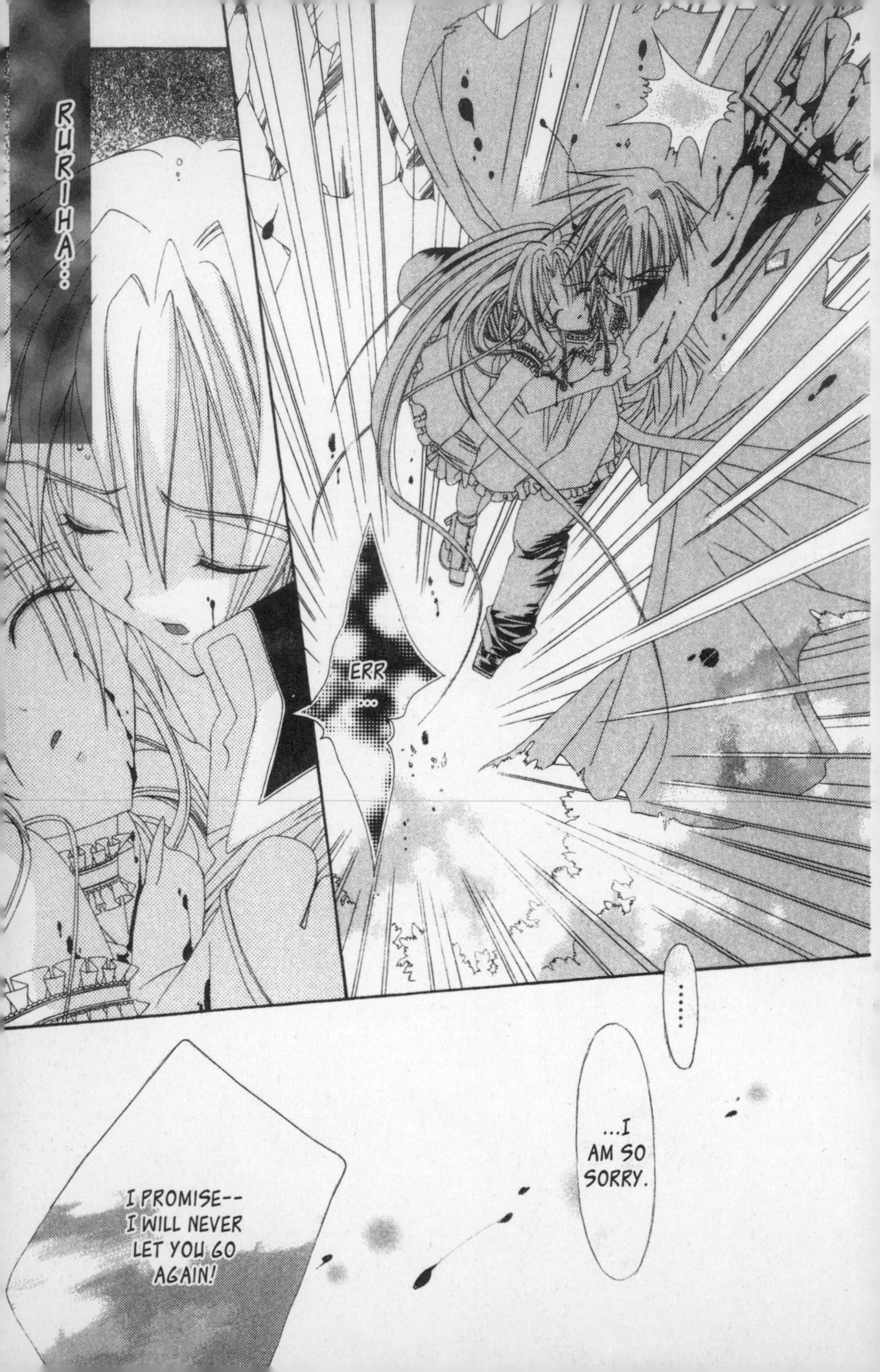
ERR...
RURIHA...
......
...I AM SO SORRY.
I PROMISE-- I WILL NEVER LET YOU GO AGAIN!

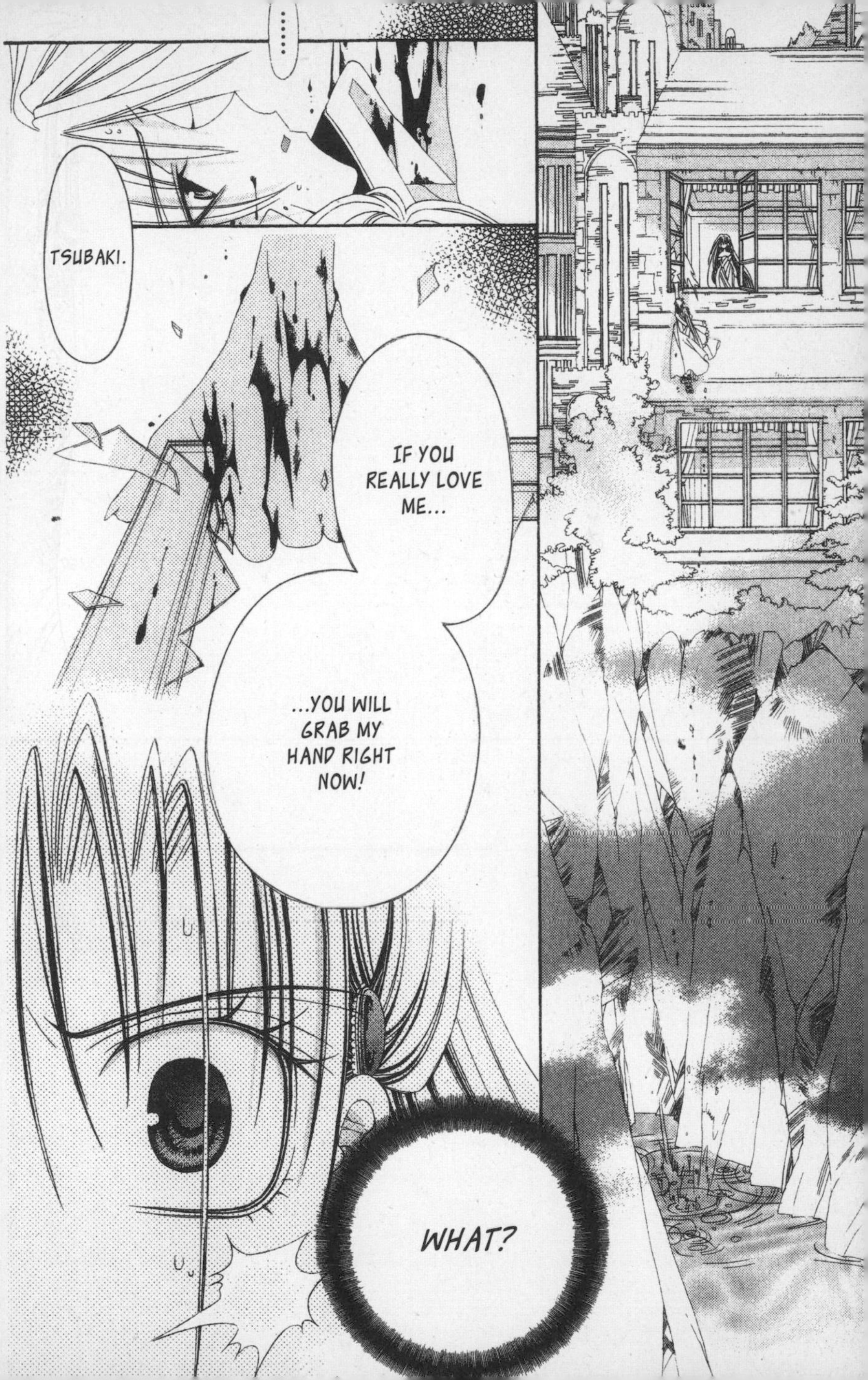
......
TSUBAKI.
IF YOU REALLY LOVE ME...
...YOU WILL GRAB MY HAND RIGHT NOW!
WHAT?

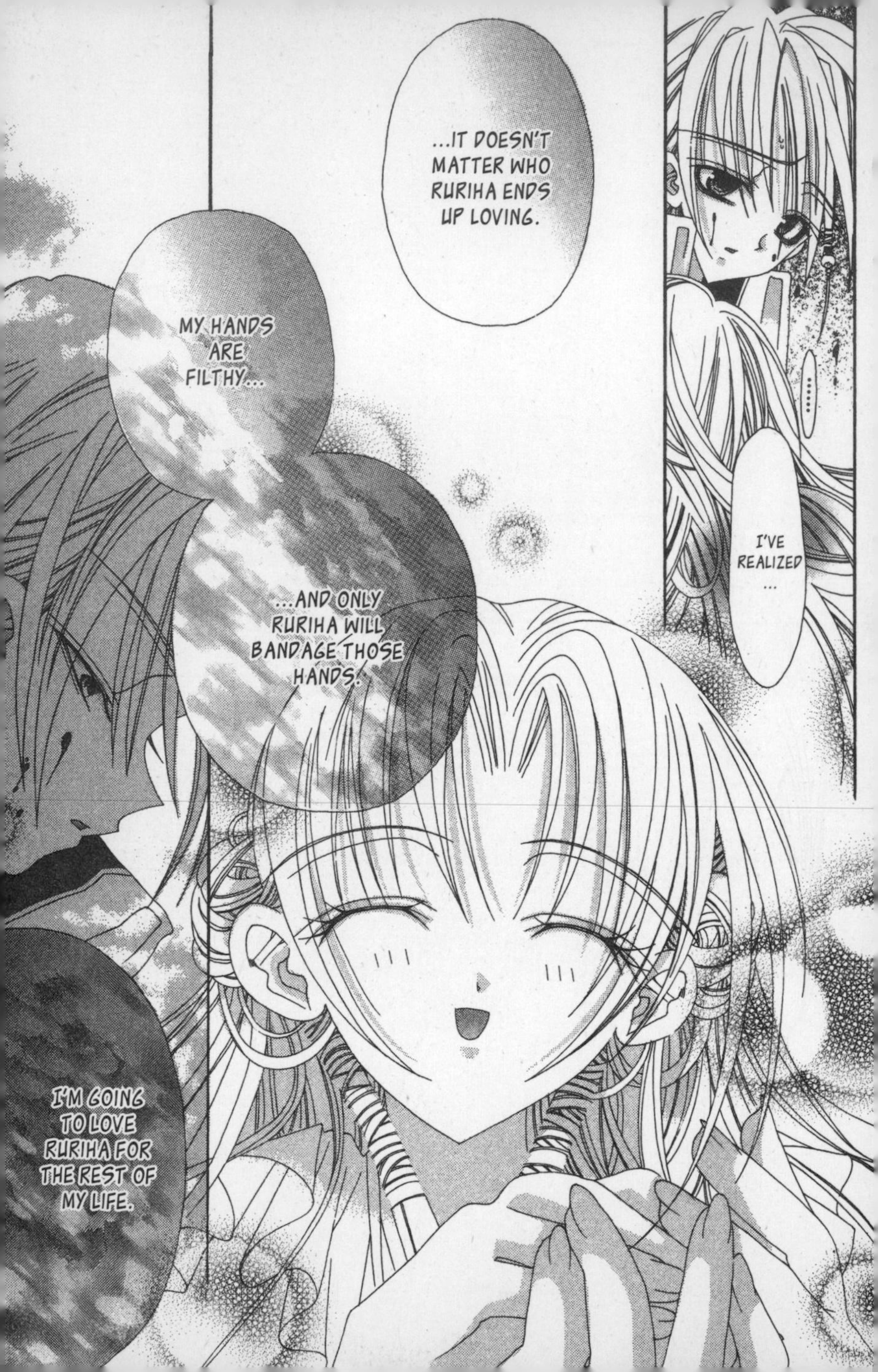
......
I'VE REALIZED ...
...IT DOESN'T MATTER WHO RURIHA ENDS UP LOVING.
MY HANDS ARE FILTHY...
...AND ONLY RURIHA WILL BANDAGE THOSE HANDS.
I'M GOING TO LOVE RURIHA FOR THE REST OF MY LIFE.

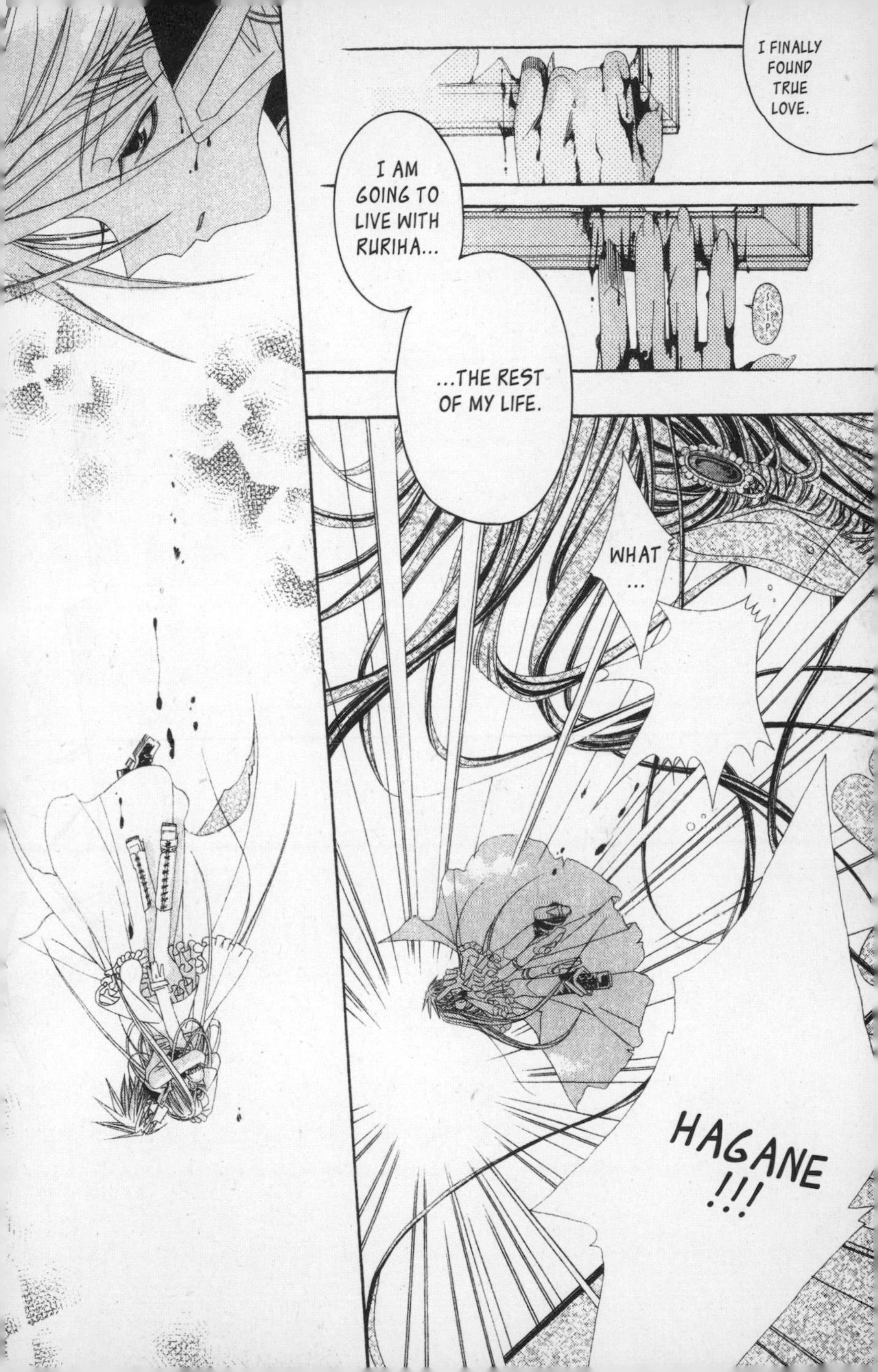
I FINALLY FOUND TRUE LOVE.
I AM GOING TO LIVE WITH RURIHA...
...THE REST OF MY LIFE.
SLIP
WHAT ...
HAGANE !!!

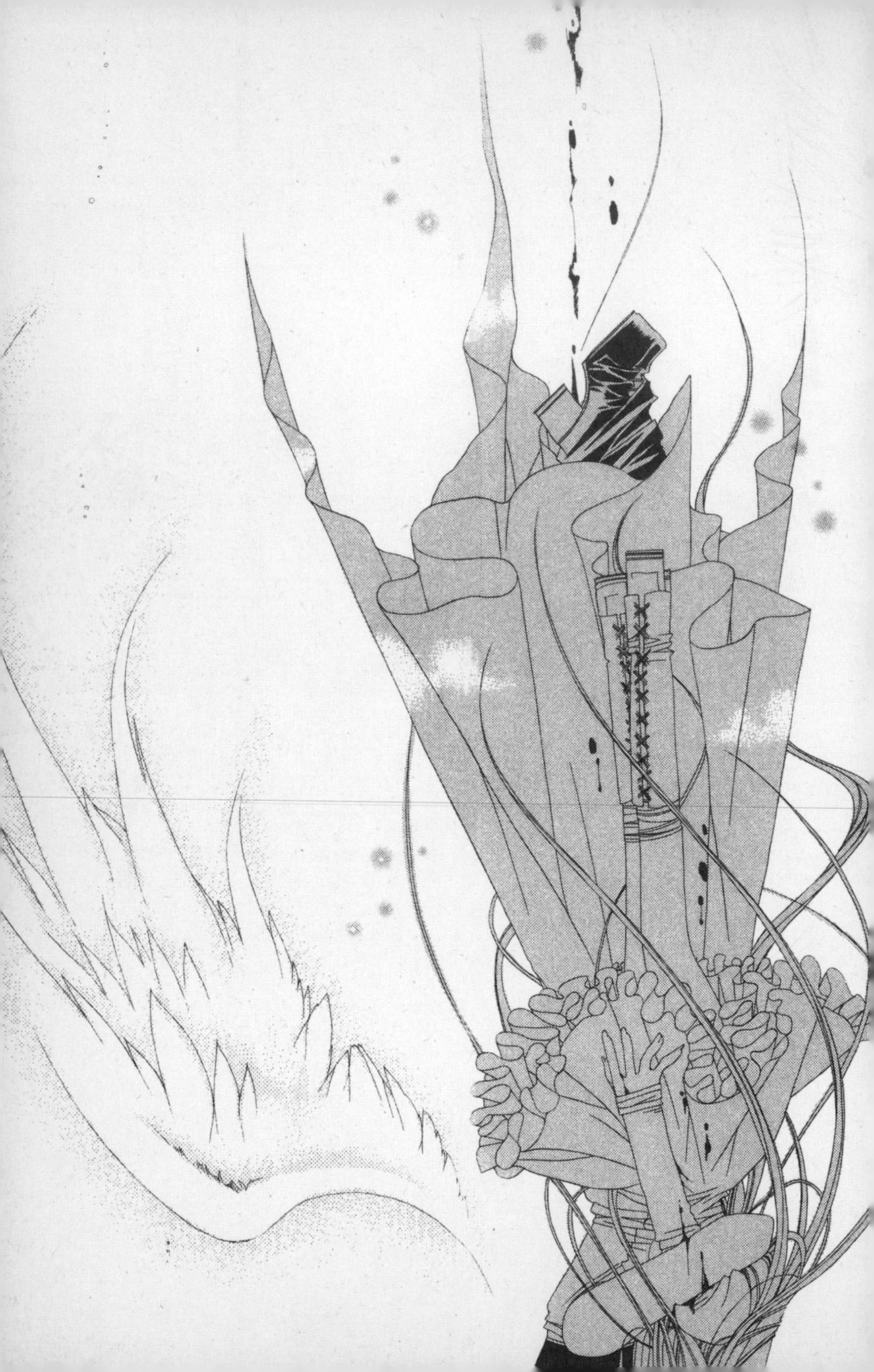

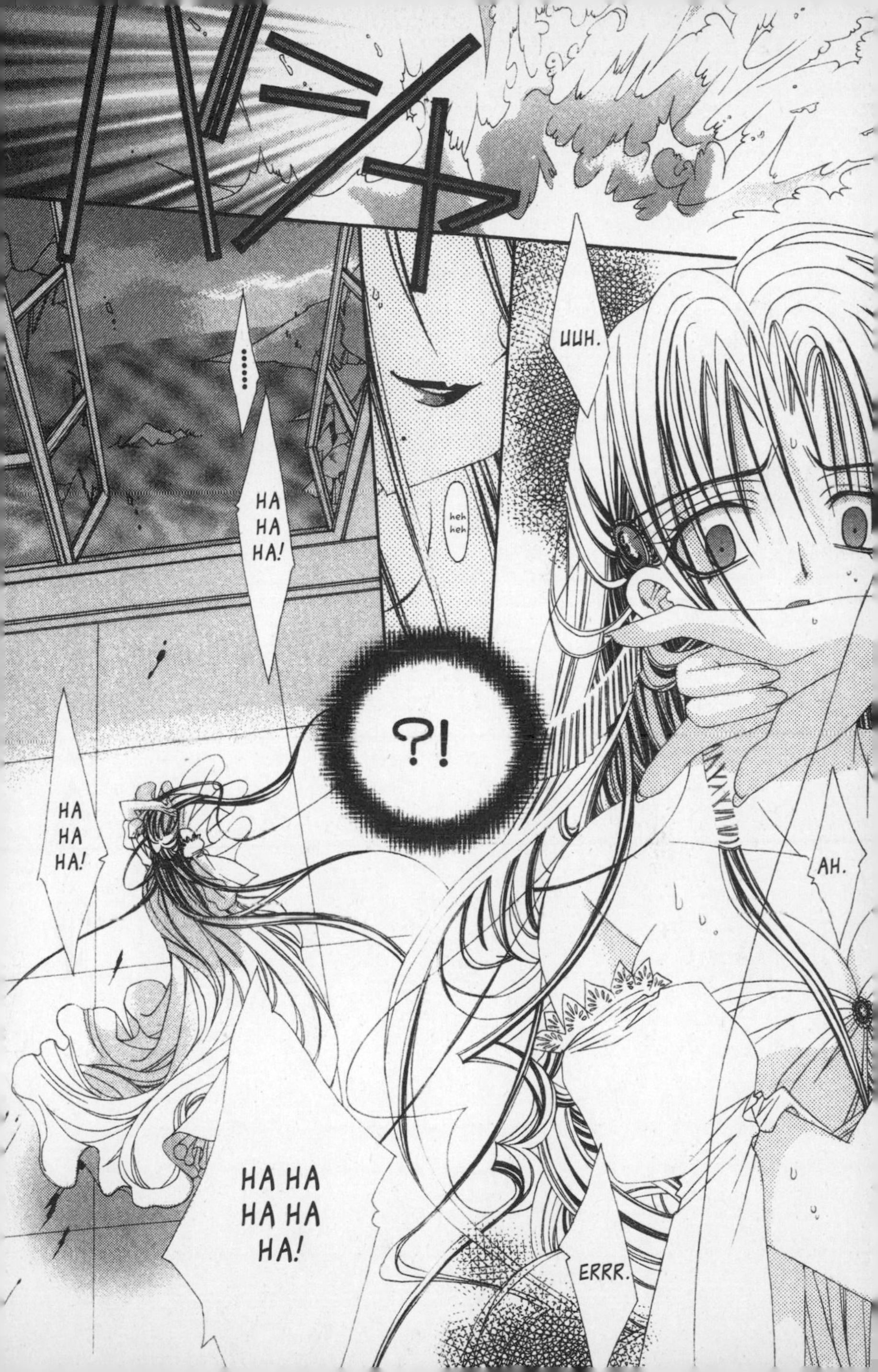
UUH.
......
heh heh
HA HA HA!
?!
AH.
HA HA HA!
HA HA HA HA HA!
ERRR.

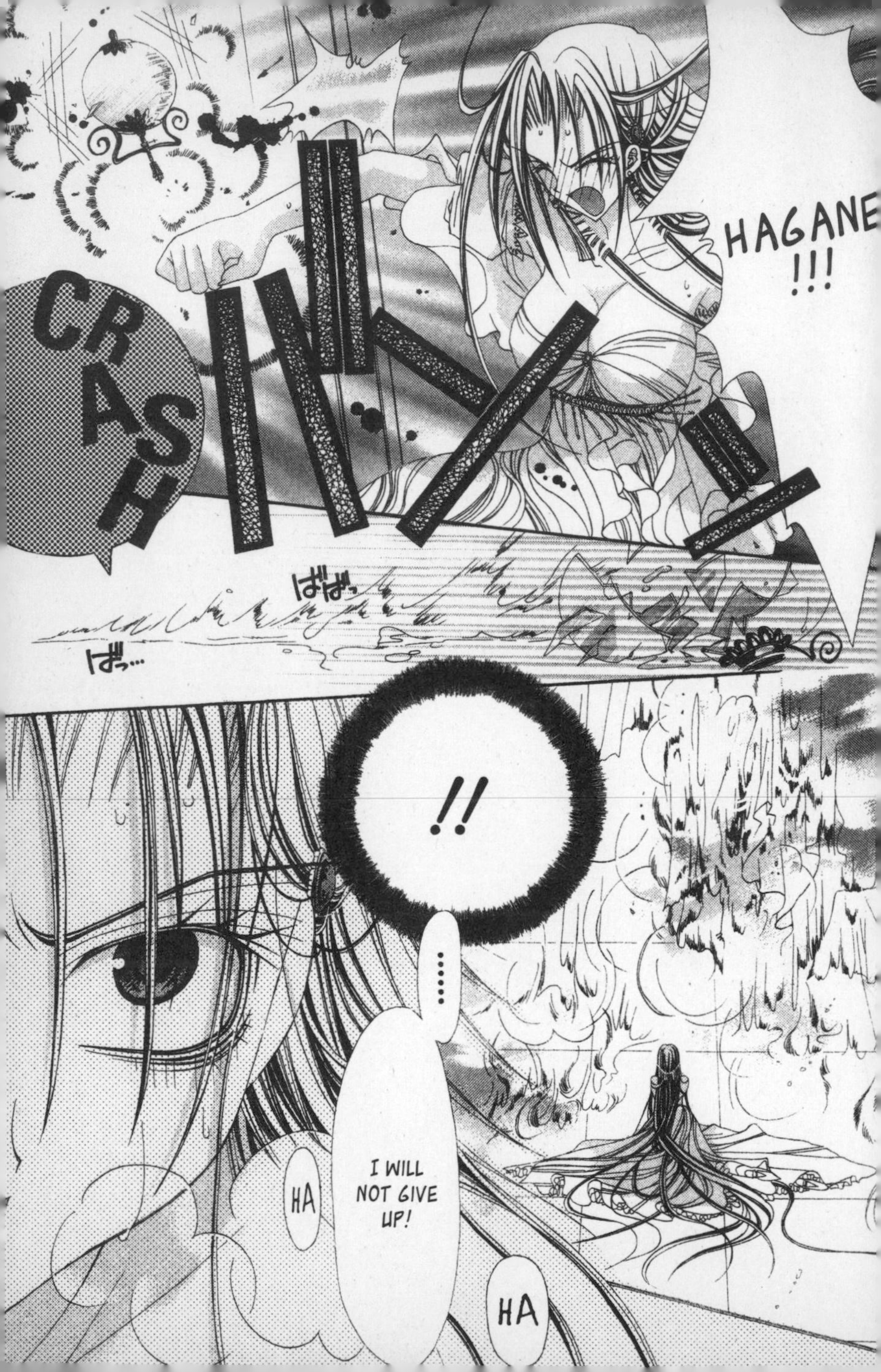
HAGANE !!!
CRASH
ばばっ
ばっ…
!!
……
I WILL NOT GIVE UP!
HA
HA

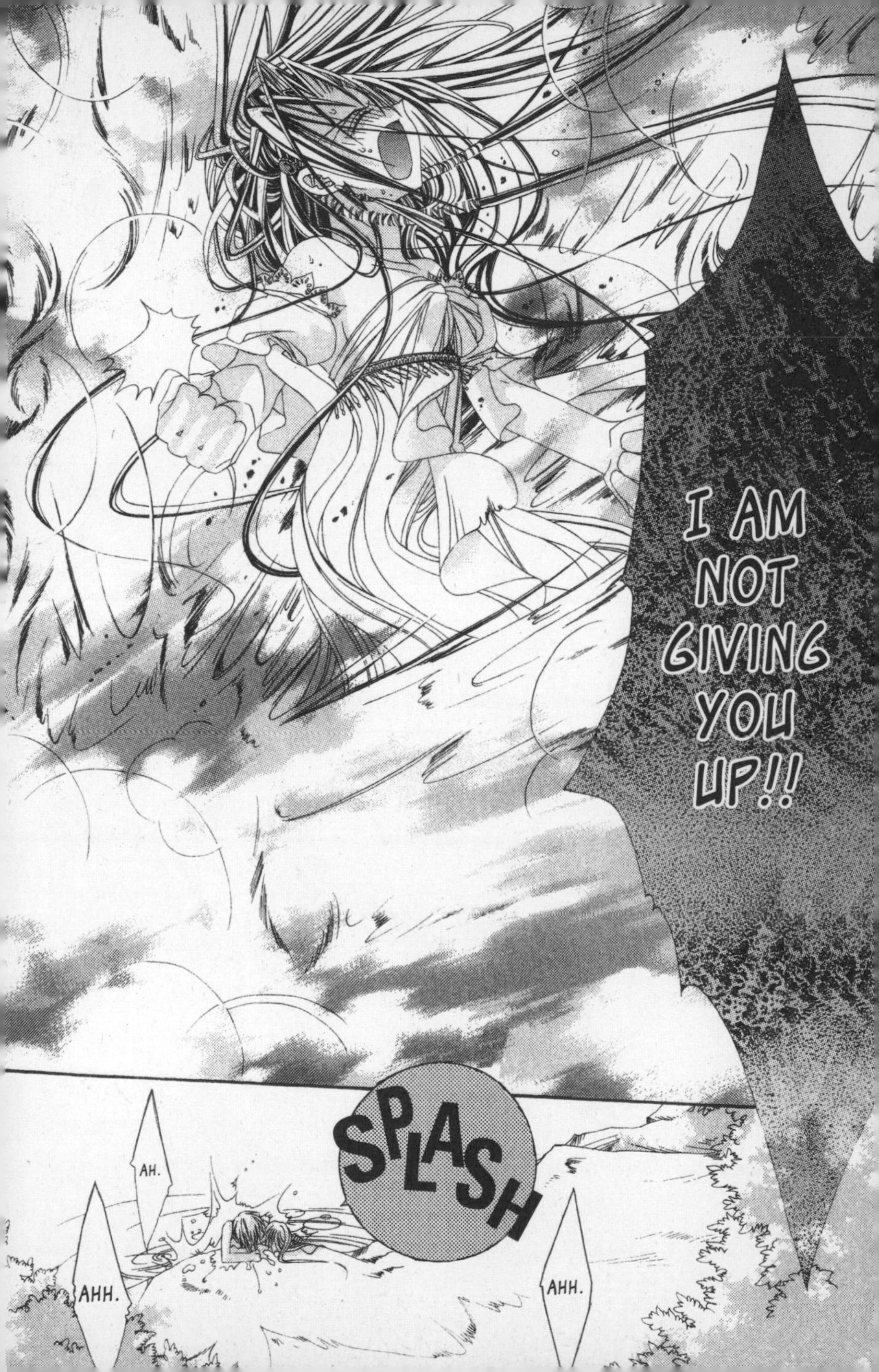
I AM NOT GIVING YOU UP!!
SPLASH
AHH.
AH.
AHH.

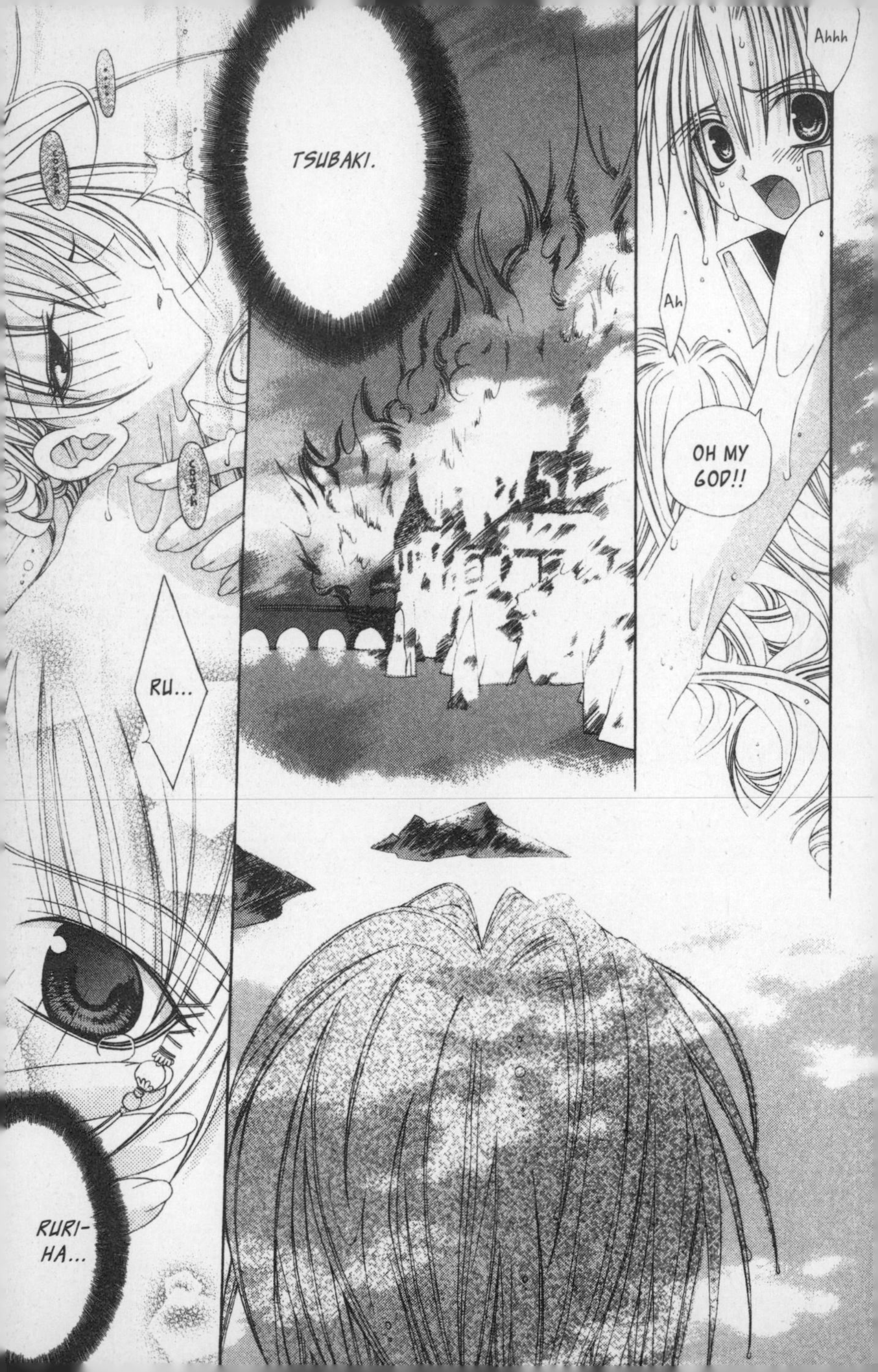
Ahhh
Ah
OH MY GOD!!
TSUBAKI.
RU...
RURI-HA...

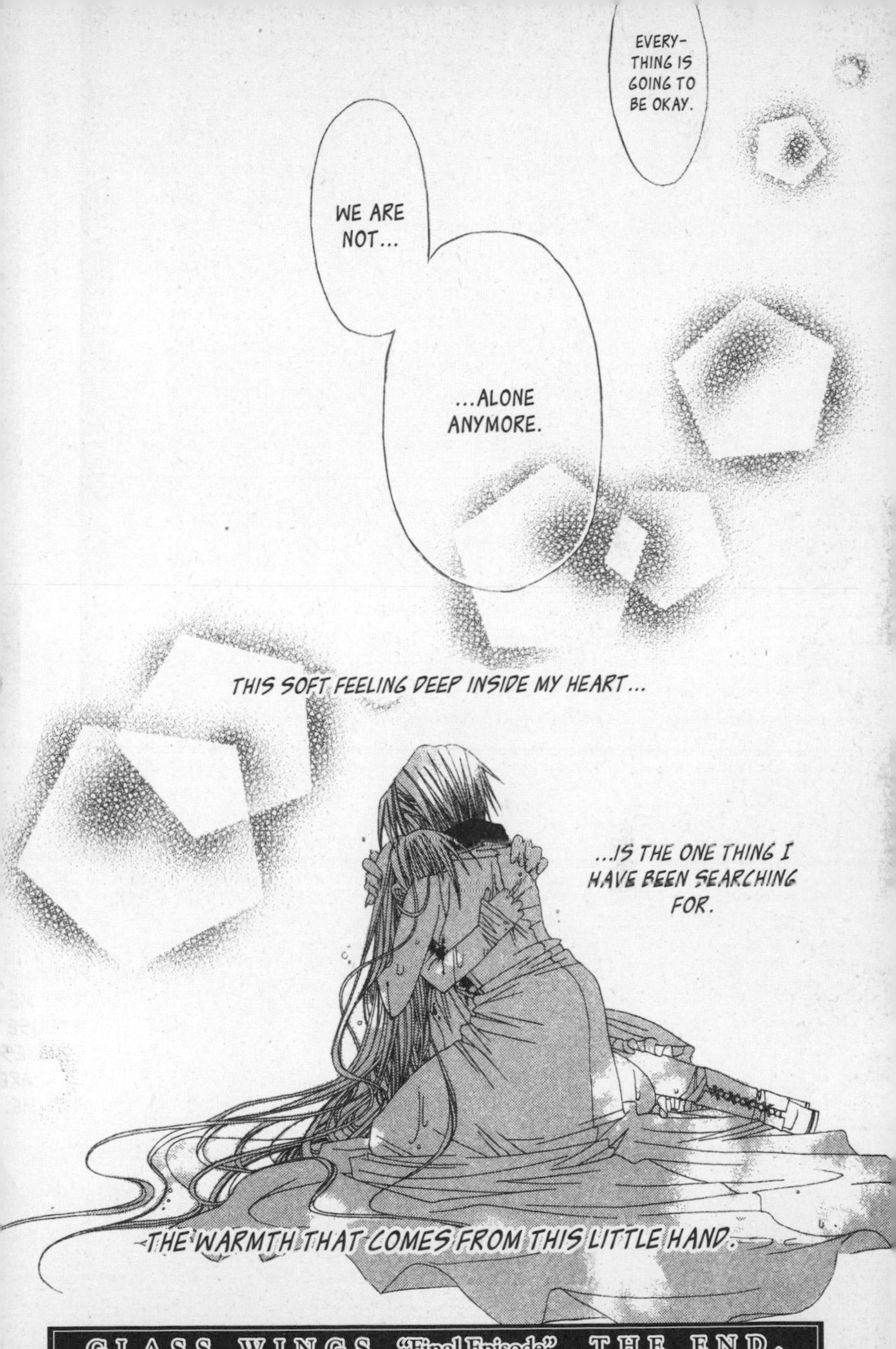
EVERY-THING IS GOING TO BE OKAY.
WE ARE NOT...
...ALONE ANYMORE.
THIS SOFT FEELING DEEP INSIDE MY HEART...
...IS THE ONE THING I HAVE BEEN SEARCHING FOR.
THE WARMTH THAT COMES FROM THIS LITTLE HAND.

GLASS WINGS "Final Episode" THE END.

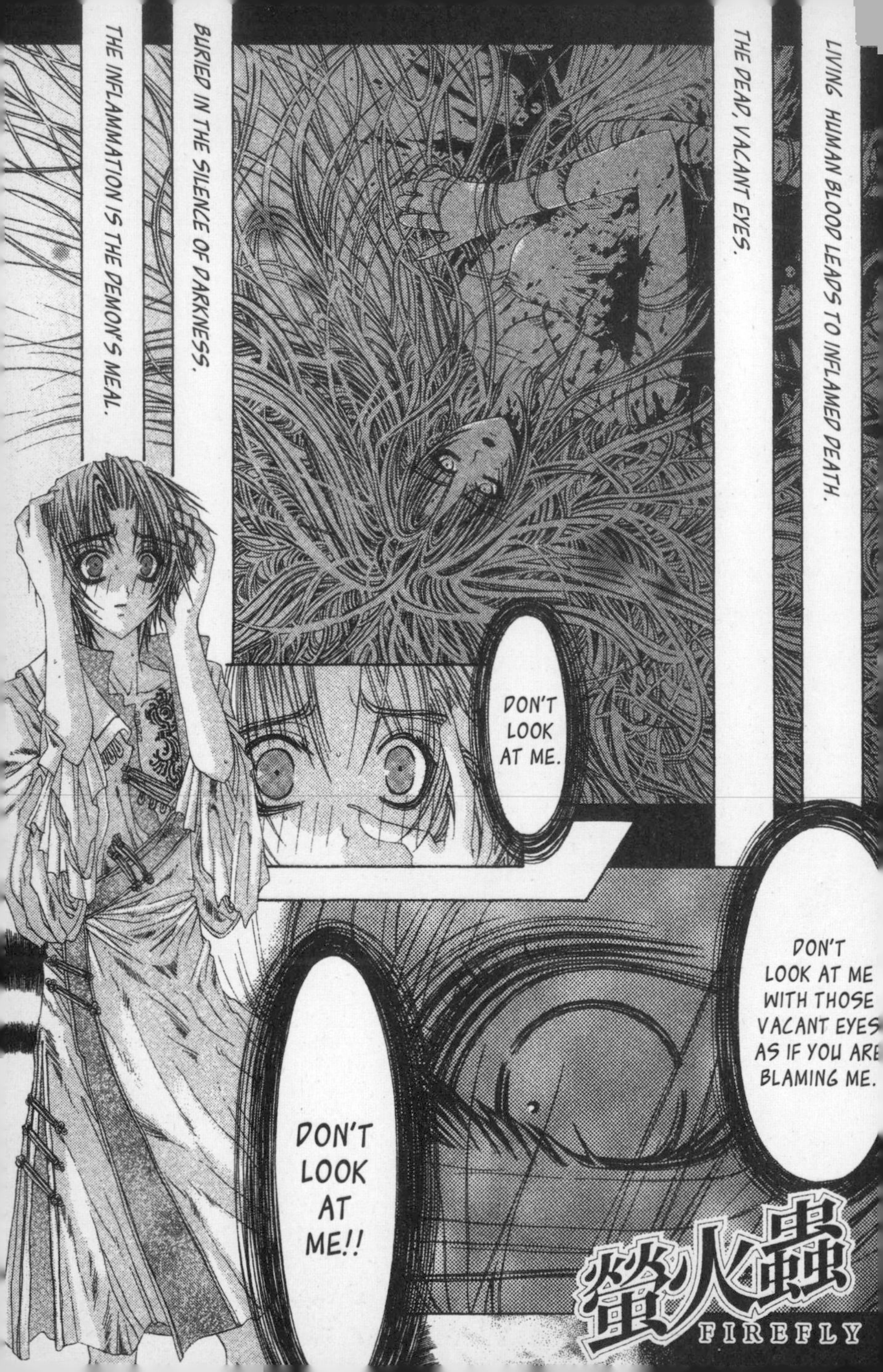
LIVING HUMAN BLOOD LEADS TO INFLAMED DEATH.
THE DEAD, VACANT EYES.
BURIED IN THE SILENCE OF DARKNESS.
THE INFLAMMATION IS THE DEMON'S MEAL.
DON'T LOOK AT ME.
DON'T LOOK AT ME WITH THOSE VACANT EYES AS IF YOU ARE BLAMING ME.
DON'T LOOK AT ME!!
螢人蟲
FIREFLY

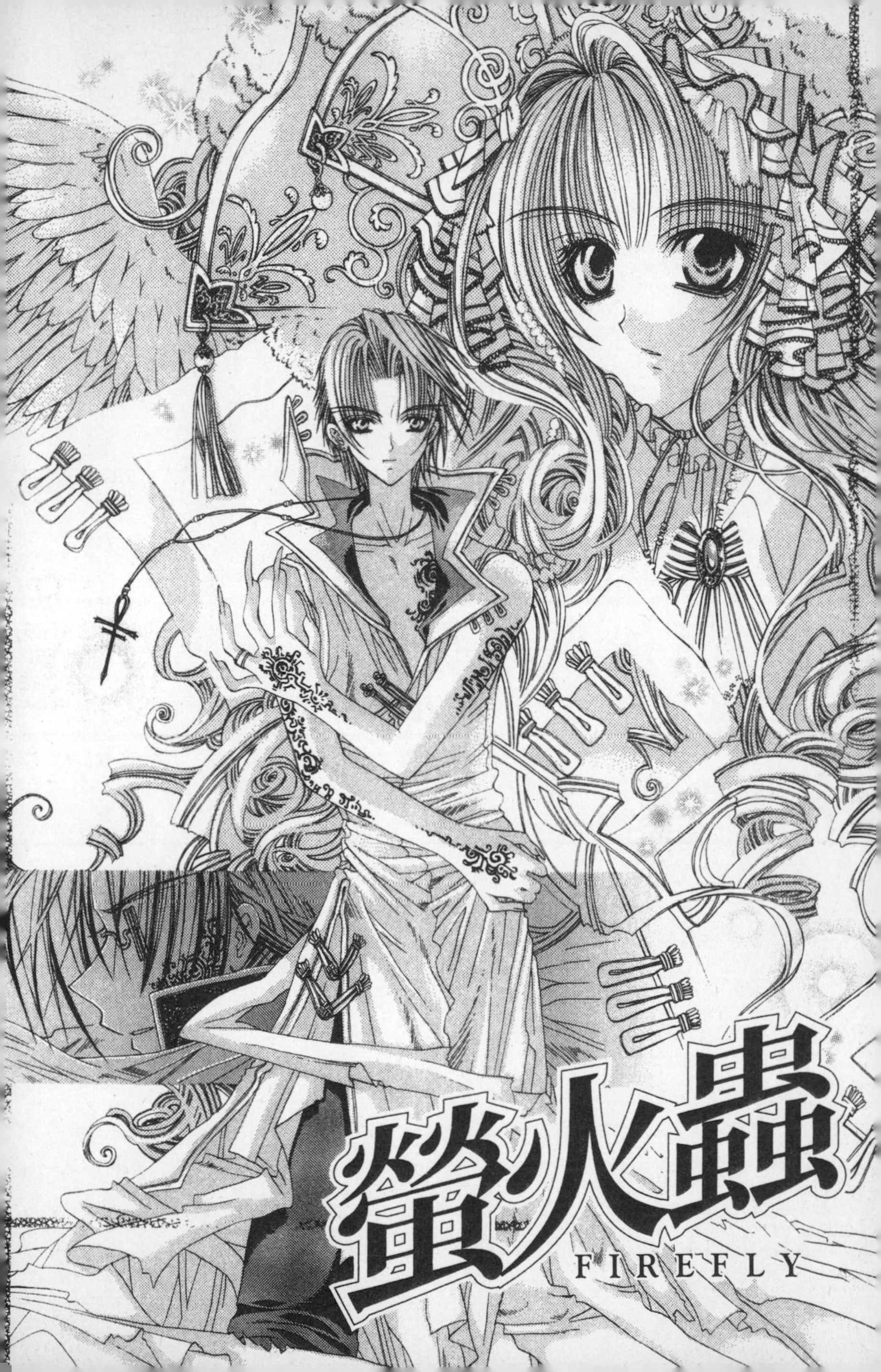
螢人蟲
FIREFLY

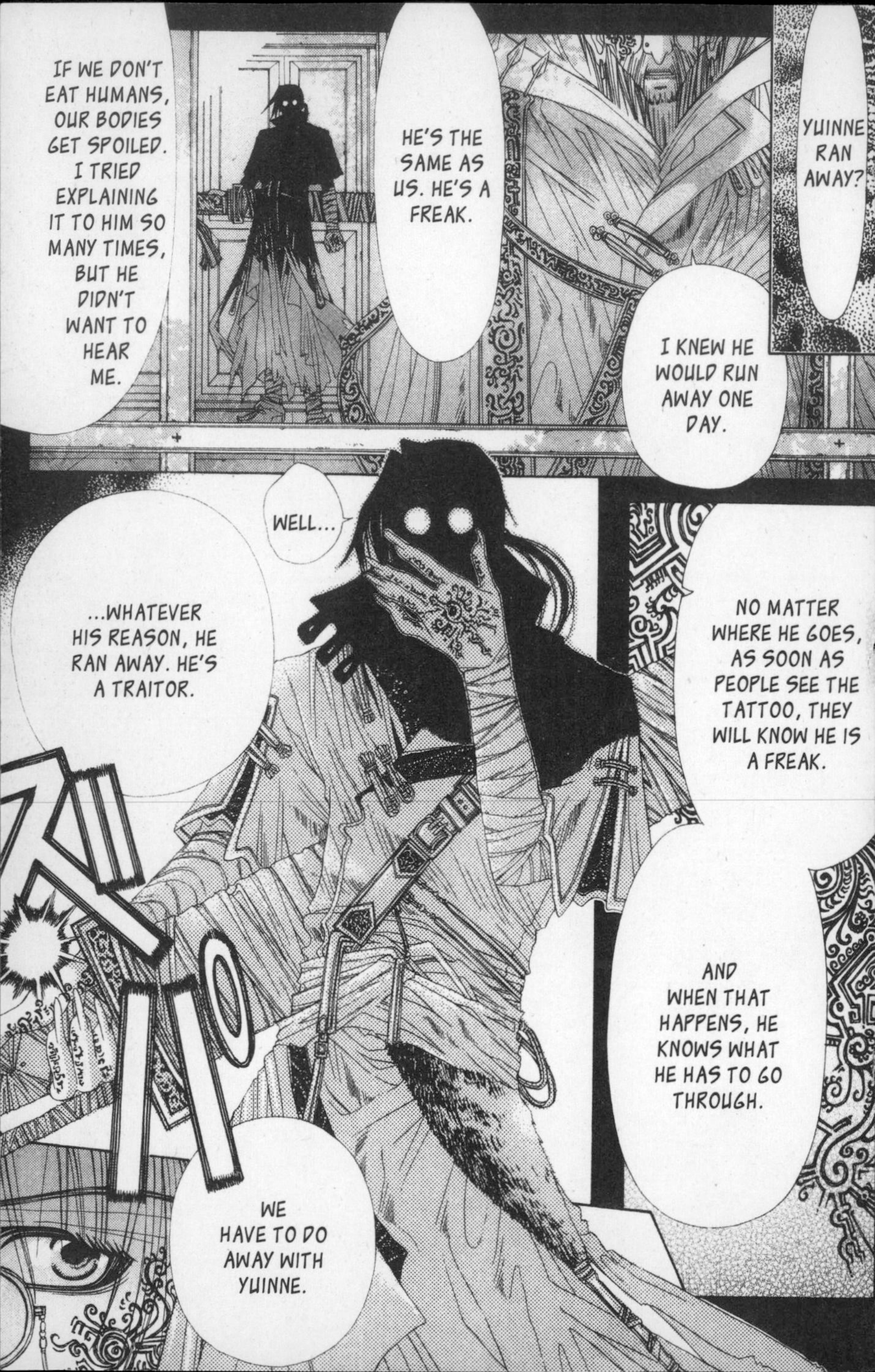
YUINNE RAN AWAY?
I KNEW HE WOULD RUN AWAY ONE DAY.
HE'S THE SAME AS US. HE'S A FREAK.
IF WE DON'T EAT HUMANS, OUR BODIES GET SPOILED. I TRIED EXPLAINING IT TO HIM SO MANY TIMES, BUT HE DIDN'T WANT TO HEAR ME.
NO MATTER WHERE HE GOES, AS SOON AS PEOPLE SEE THE TATTOO, THEY WILL KNOW HE IS A FREAK.
AND WHEN THAT HAPPENS, HE KNOWS WHAT HE HAS TO GO THROUGH.
WELL...
...WHATEVER HIS REASON, HE RAN AWAY. HE'S A TRAITOR.
WE HAVE TO DO AWAY WITH YUINNE.

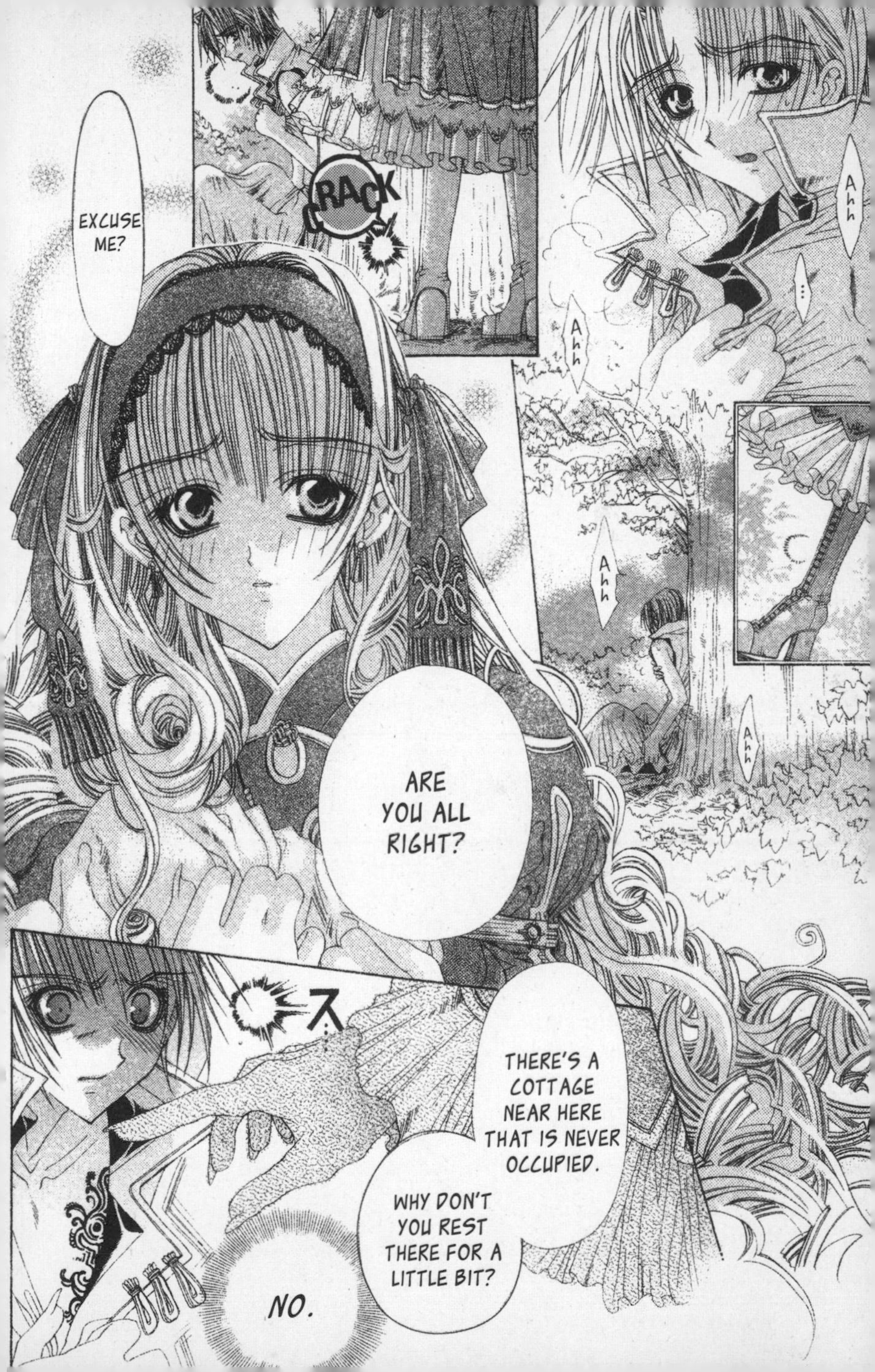
Ahh
...
Ahh
CRACK
EXCUSE ME?
Ahh
Ahh
ARE YOU ALL RIGHT?
THERE'S A COTTAGE NEAR HERE THAT IS NEVER OCCUPIED.
WHY DON'T YOU REST THERE FOR A LITTLE BIT?
NO.

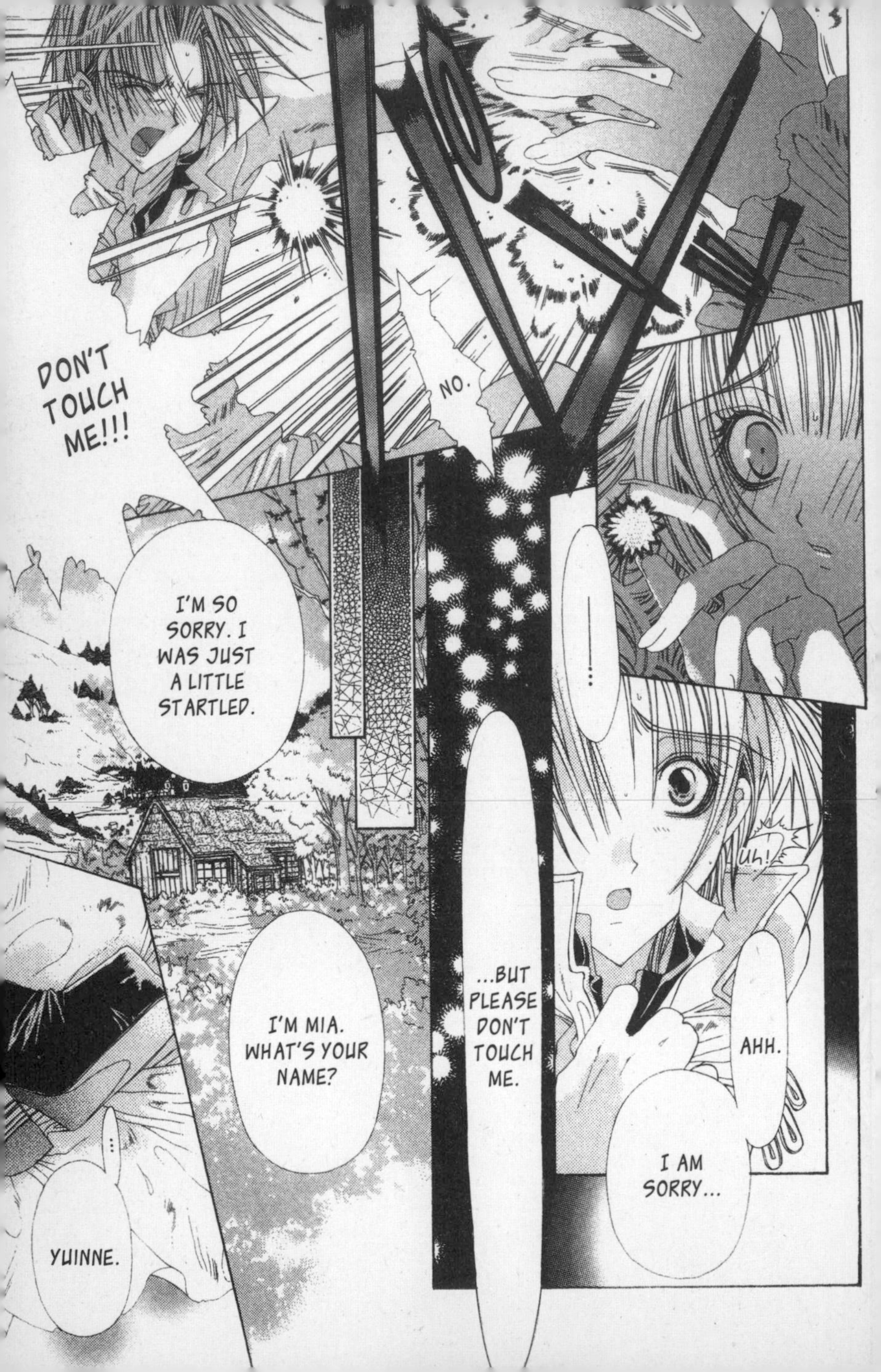

NO.
DON'T TOUCH ME!!!
...
Uh!
AHH.
I AM SORRY...
...BUT PLEASE DON'T TOUCH ME.
I'M SO SORRY. I WAS JUST A LITTLE STARTLED.
I'M MIA. WHAT'S YOUR NAME?
...
YUINNE.

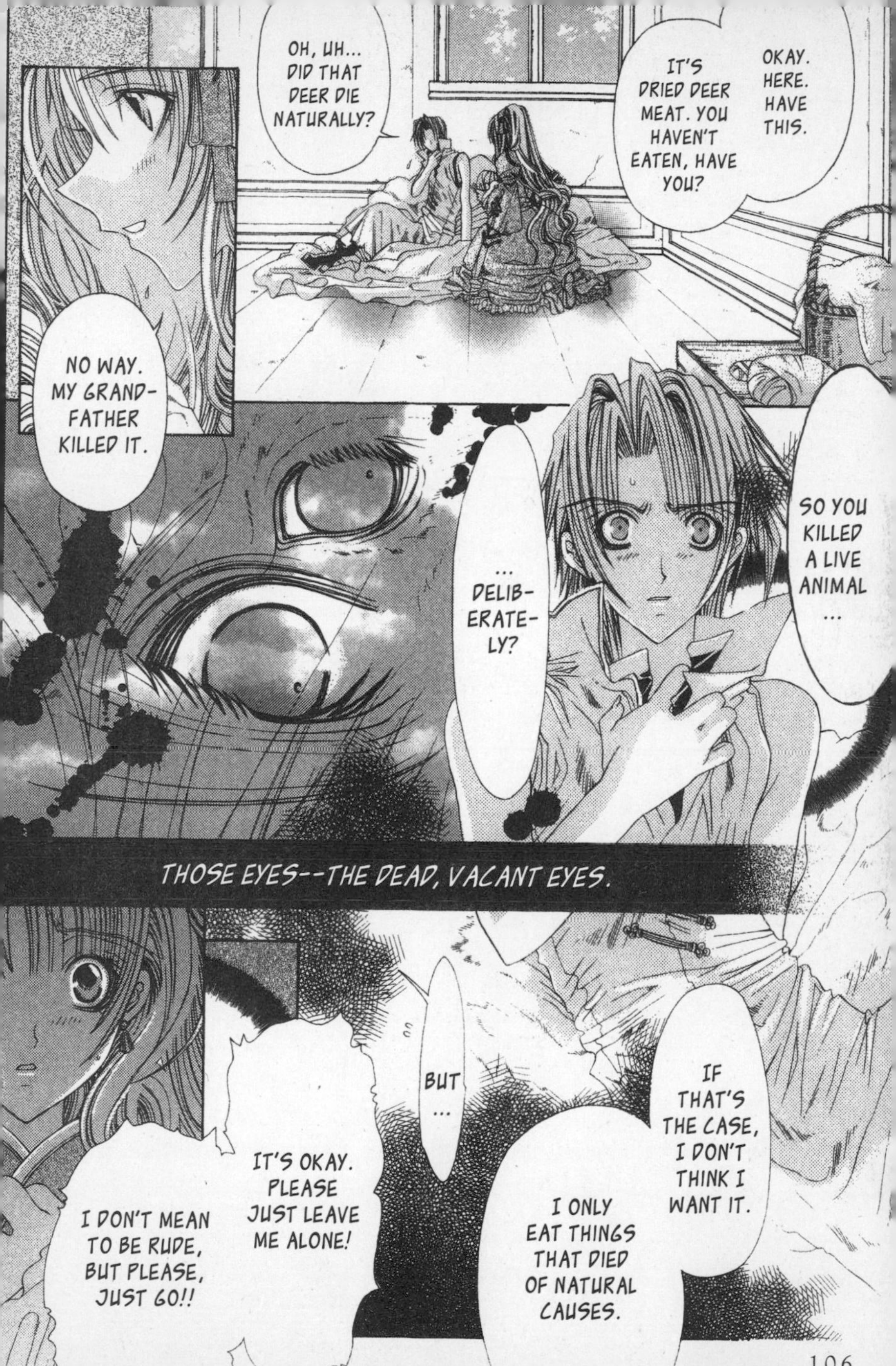
OKAY. HERE. HAVE THIS.
IT'S DRIED DEER MEAT. YOU HAVEN'T EATEN, HAVE YOU?
OH, UH... DID THAT DEER DIE NATURALLY?
NO WAY. MY GRAND-FATHER KILLED IT.
SO YOU KILLED A LIVE ANIMAL ...
... DELIB-ERATE-LY?
THOSE EYES--THE DEAD, VACANT EYES.
IF THAT'S THE CASE, I DON'T THINK I WANT IT.
I ONLY EAT THINGS THAT DIED OF NATURAL CAUSES.
BUT ...
IT'S OKAY. PLEASE JUST LEAVE ME ALONE!
I DON'T MEAN TO BE RUDE, BUT PLEASE, JUST GO!!

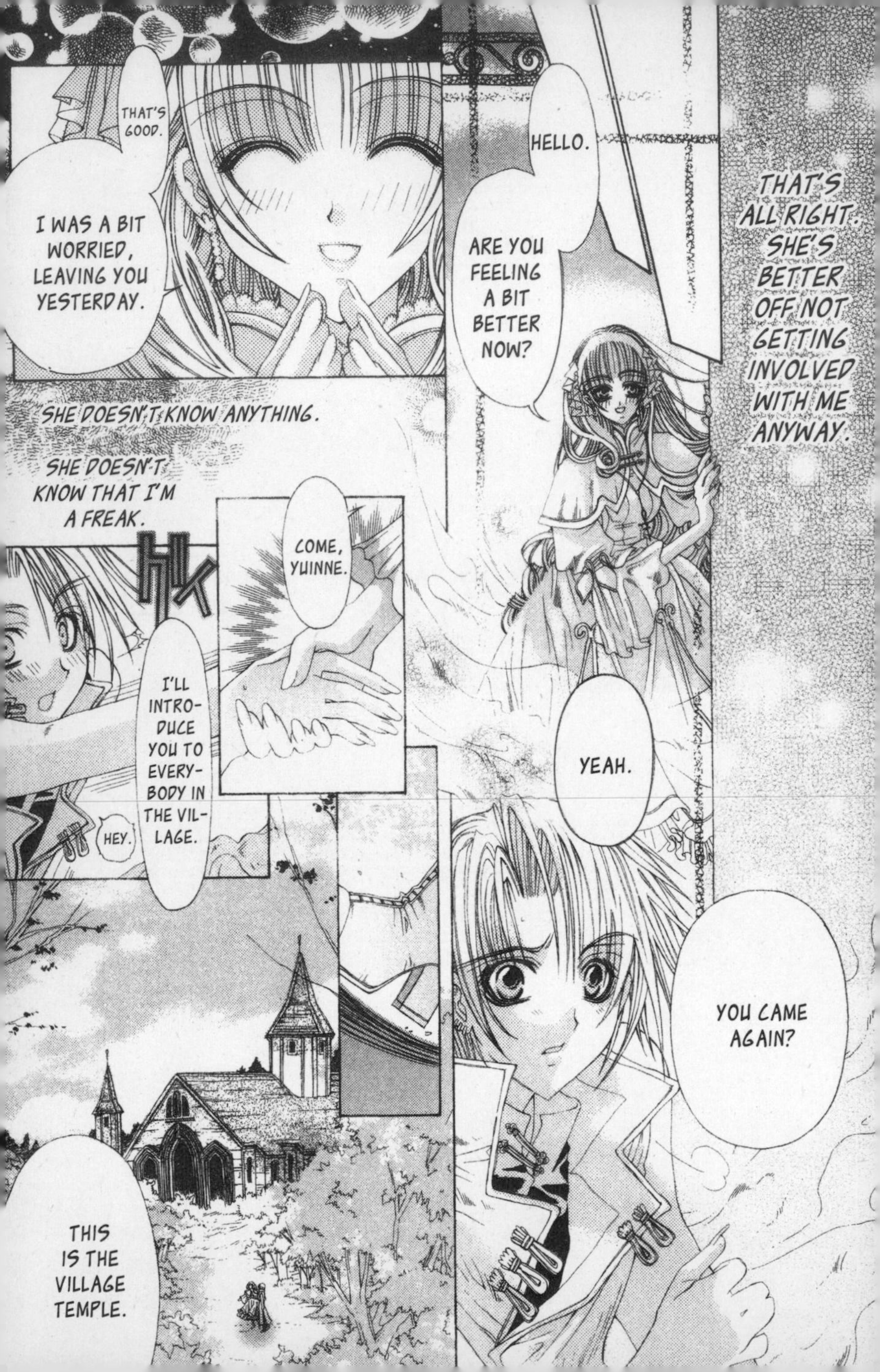
HELLO.
ARE YOU FEELING A BIT BETTER NOW?
YOU CAME AGAIN?
YEAH.
THAT'S GOOD.
I WAS A BIT WORRIED, LEAVING YOU YESTERDAY.
SHE DOESN'T KNOW ANYTHING.
SHE DOESN'T KNOW THAT I'M A FREAK.
THAT'S ALL RIGHT. SHE'S BETTER OFF NOT GETTING INVOLVED WITH ME ANYWAY.
COME, YUINNE.
HK
HEY.
I'LL INTRO-DUCE YOU TO EVERY-BODY IN THE VIL-LAGE.
THIS IS THE VILLAGE TEMPLE.

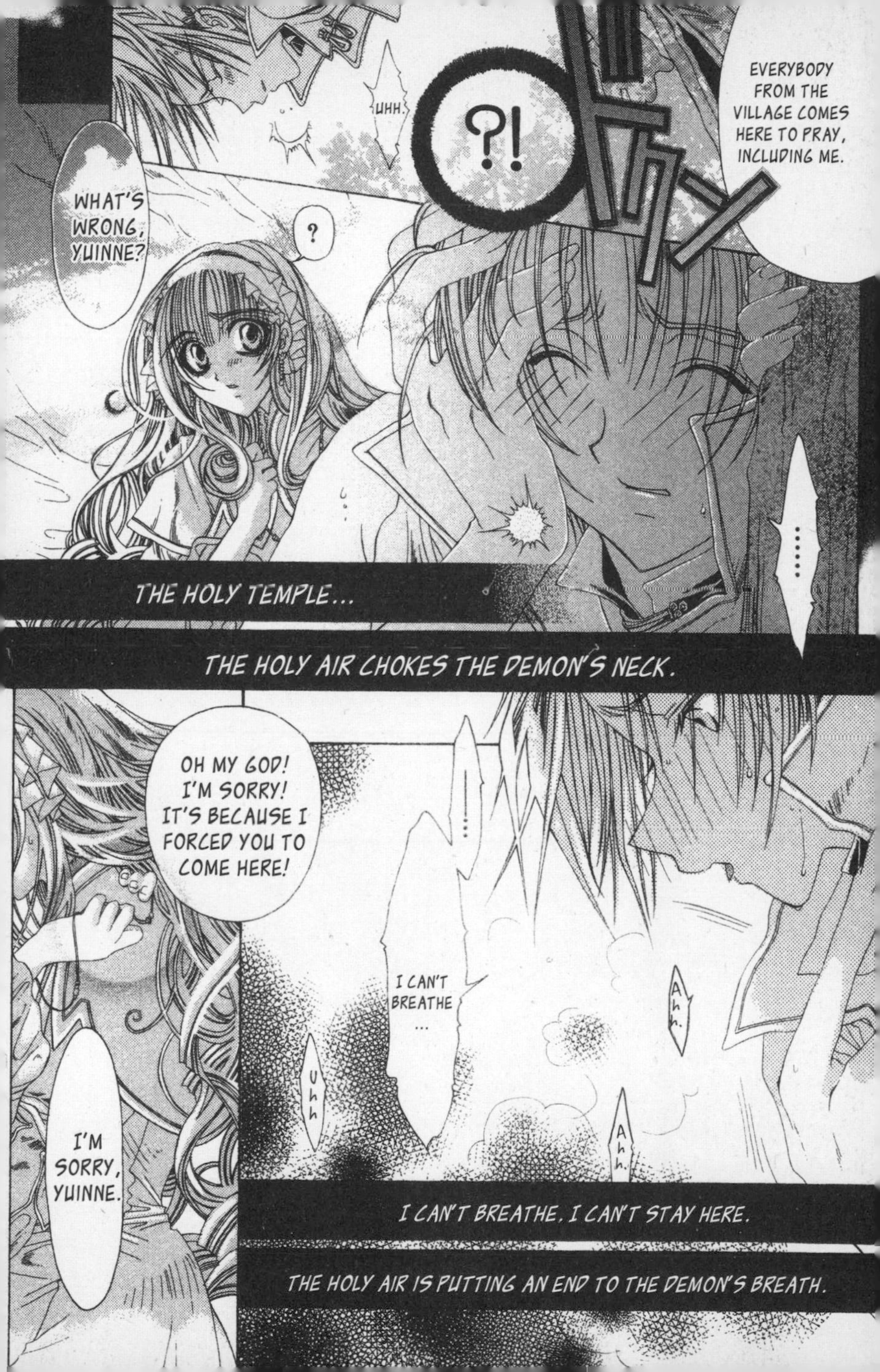
EVERYBODY FROM THE VILLAGE COMES HERE TO PRAY, INCLUDING ME.
?!
UHH.
WHAT'S WRONG, YUINNE?
?
......
THE HOLY TEMPLE...
THE HOLY AIR CHOKES THE DEMON'S NECK.
......
I CAN'T BREATHE ...
Ahh.
Uhh
Ahh.
I CAN'T BREATHE. I CAN'T STAY HERE.
THE HOLY AIR IS PUTTING AN END TO THE DEMON'S BREATH.
OH MY GOD! I'M SORRY! IT'S BECAUSE I FORCED YOU TO COME HERE!
I'M SORRY, YUINNE.

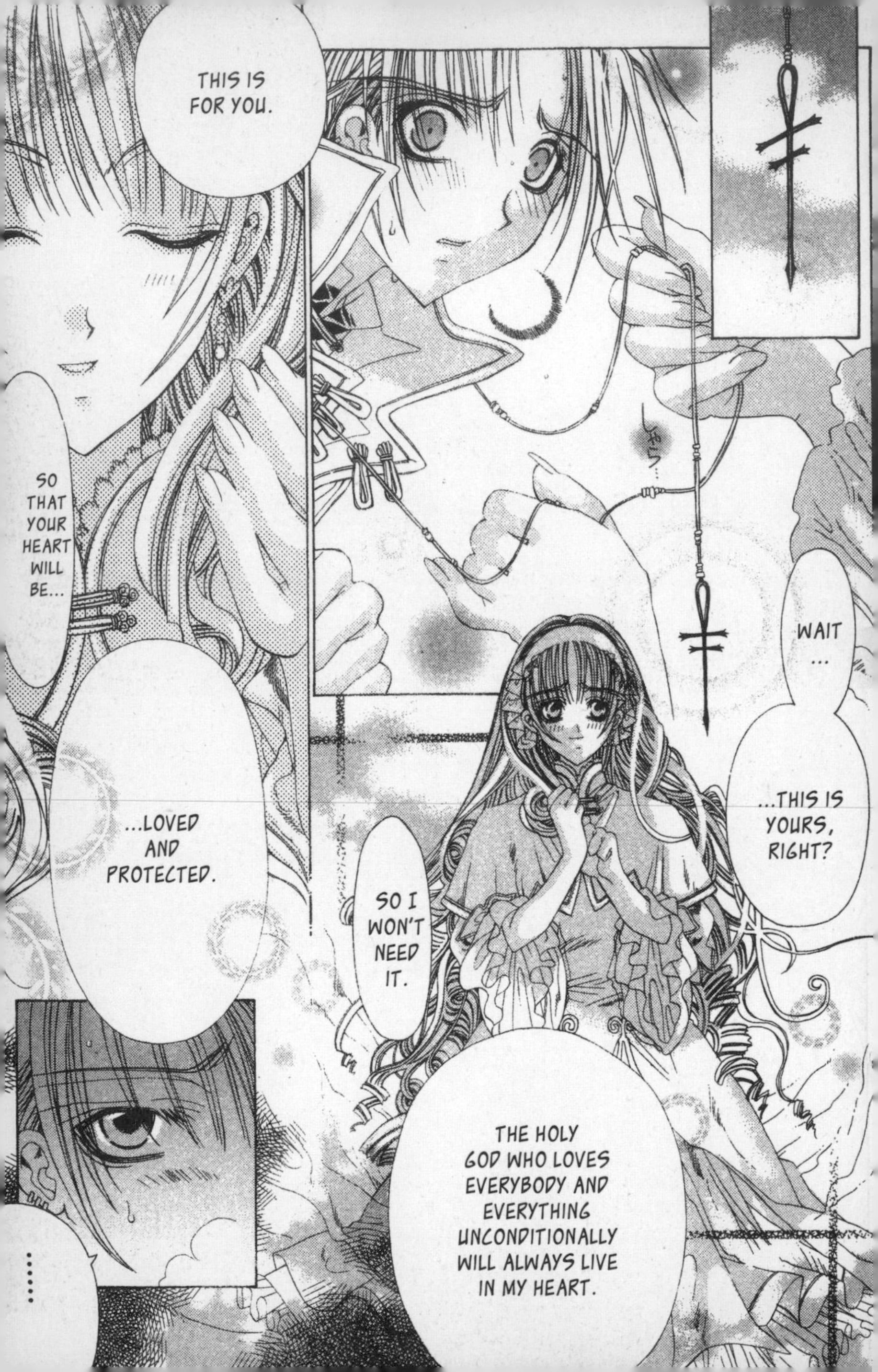
しゃら…
THIS IS FOR YOU.
SO THAT YOUR HEART WILL BE...
...LOVED AND PROTECTED.
WAIT...
...THIS IS YOURS, RIGHT?
SO I WON'T NEED IT.
THE HOLY GOD WHO LOVES EVERYBODY AND EVERYTHING UNCONDITIONALLY WILL ALWAYS LIVE IN MY HEART.
......

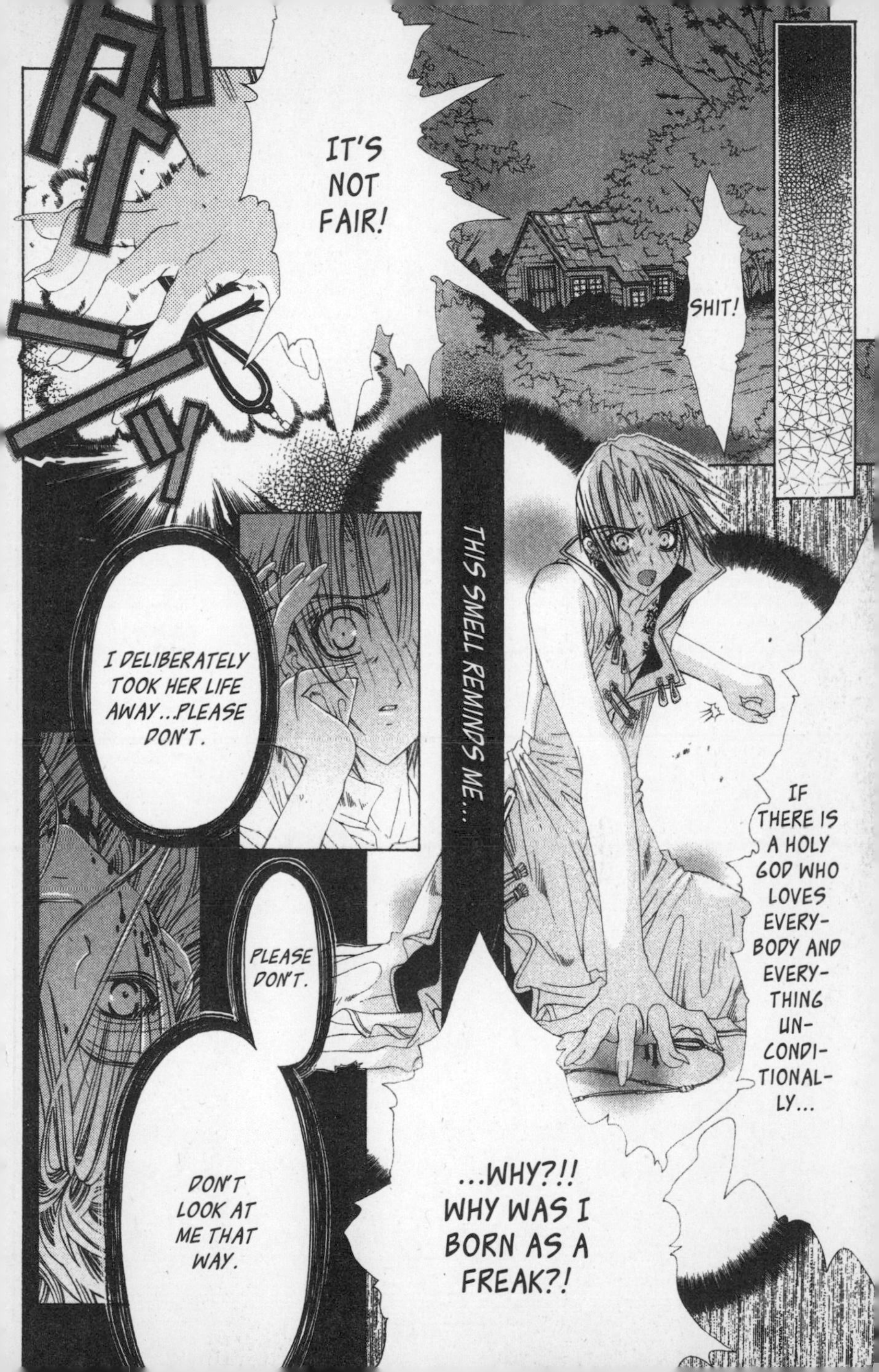
IT'S NOT FAIR!
SHIT!
IF THERE IS A HOLY GOD WHO LOVES EVERY-BODY AND EVERY-THING UN-CONDI-TIONAL-LY...
...WHY?!! WHY WAS I BORN AS A FREAK?!
THIS SMELL REMINDS ME...
I DELIBERATELY TOOK HER LIFE AWAY...PLEASE DON'T.
PLEASE DON'T.
DON'T LOOK AT ME THAT WAY.

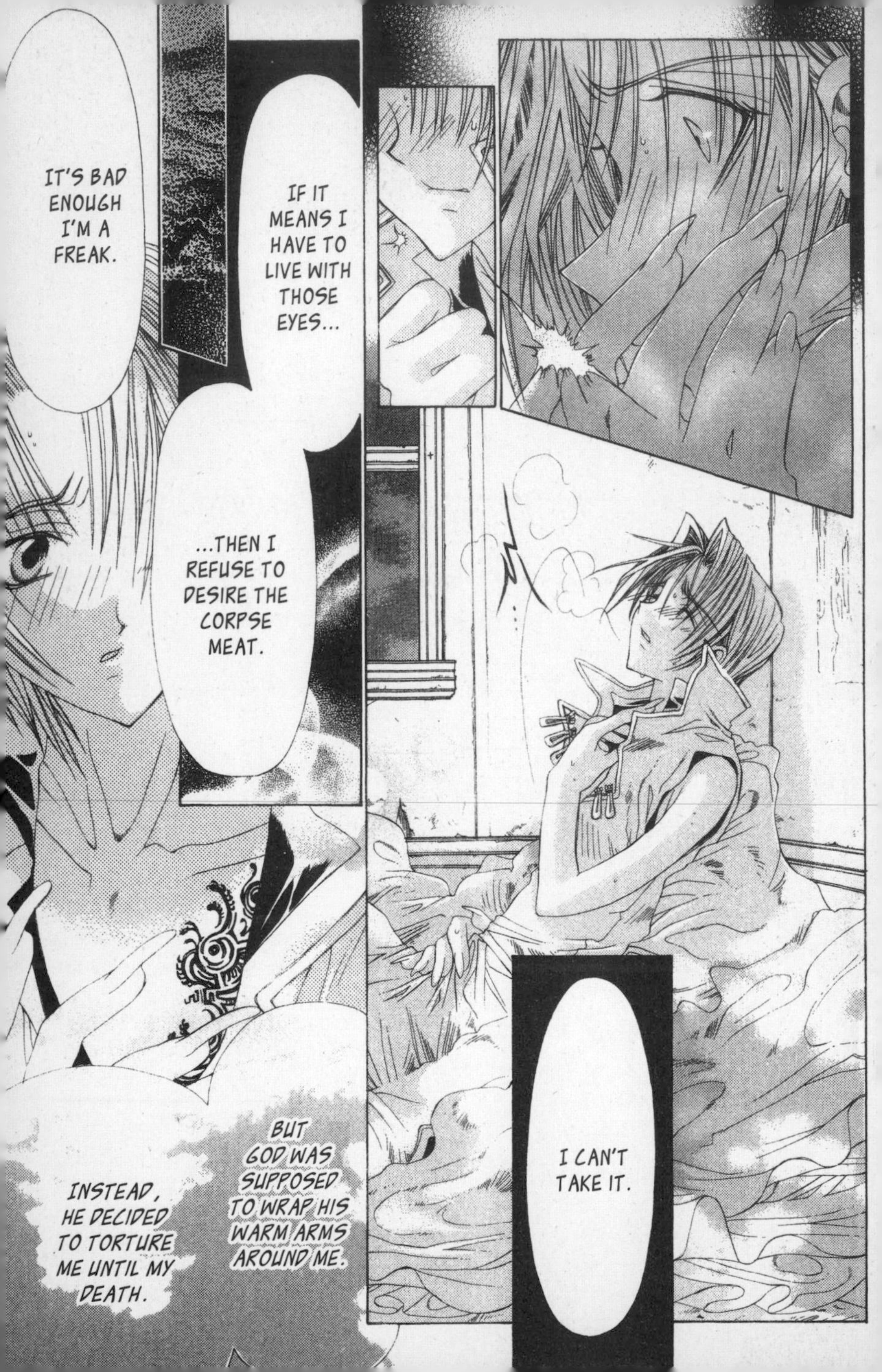
I CAN'T TAKE IT.
IF IT MEANS I HAVE TO LIVE WITH THOSE EYES...
IT'S BAD ENOUGH I'M A FREAK.
...THEN I REFUSE TO DESIRE THE CORPSE MEAT.
BUT GOD WAS SUPPOSED TO WRAP HIS WARM ARMS AROUND ME.
INSTEAD, HE DECIDED TO TORTURE ME UNTIL MY DEATH.

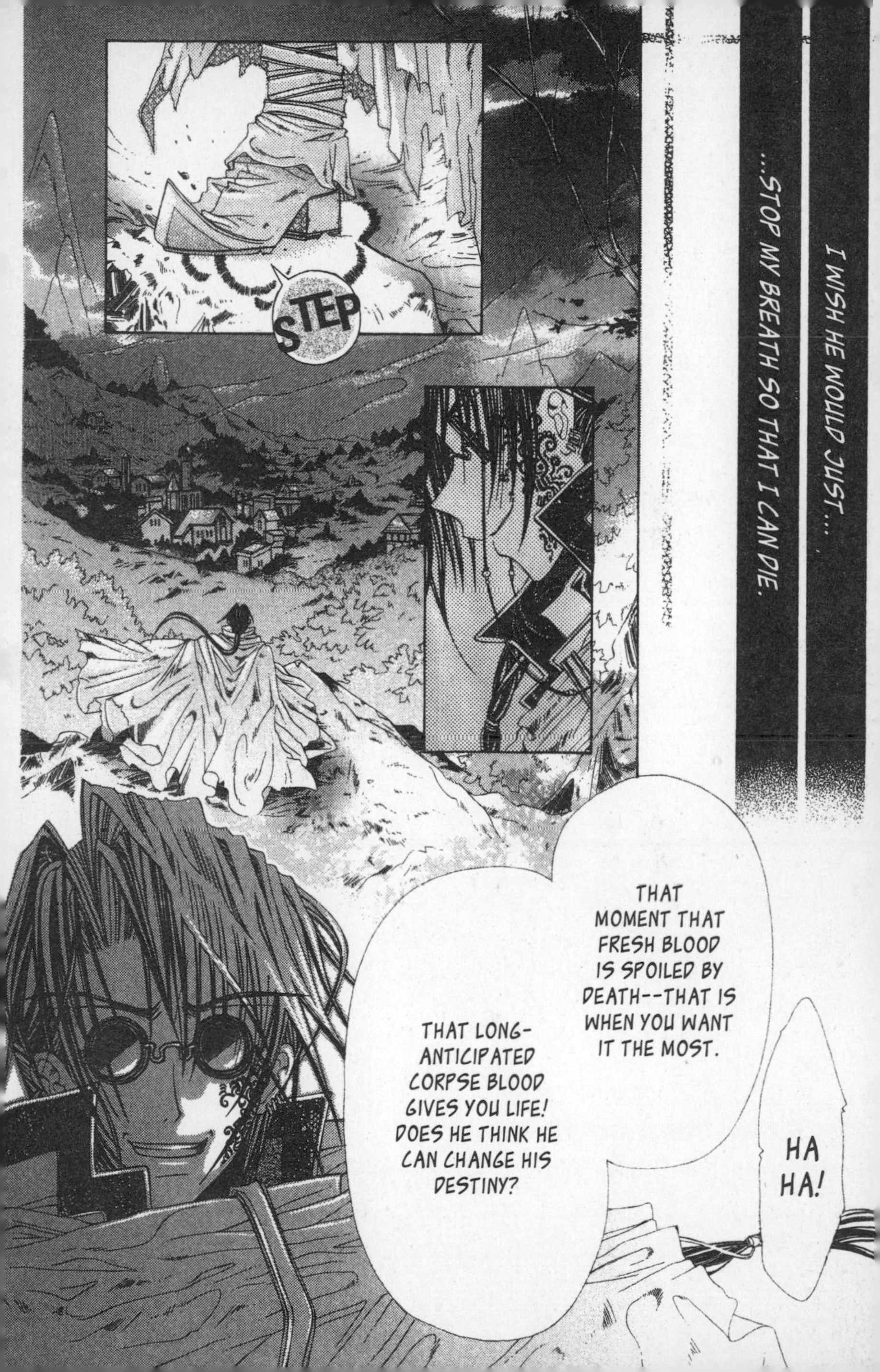
I WISH HE WOULD JUST...
...STOP MY BREATH SO THAT I CAN DIE.
STEP
THAT MOMENT THAT FRESH BLOOD IS SPOILED BY DEATH--THAT IS WHEN YOU WANT IT THE MOST.
THAT LONG-ANTICIPATED CORPSE BLOOD GIVES YOU LIFE! DOES HE THINK HE CAN CHANGE HIS DESTINY?
HA HA!

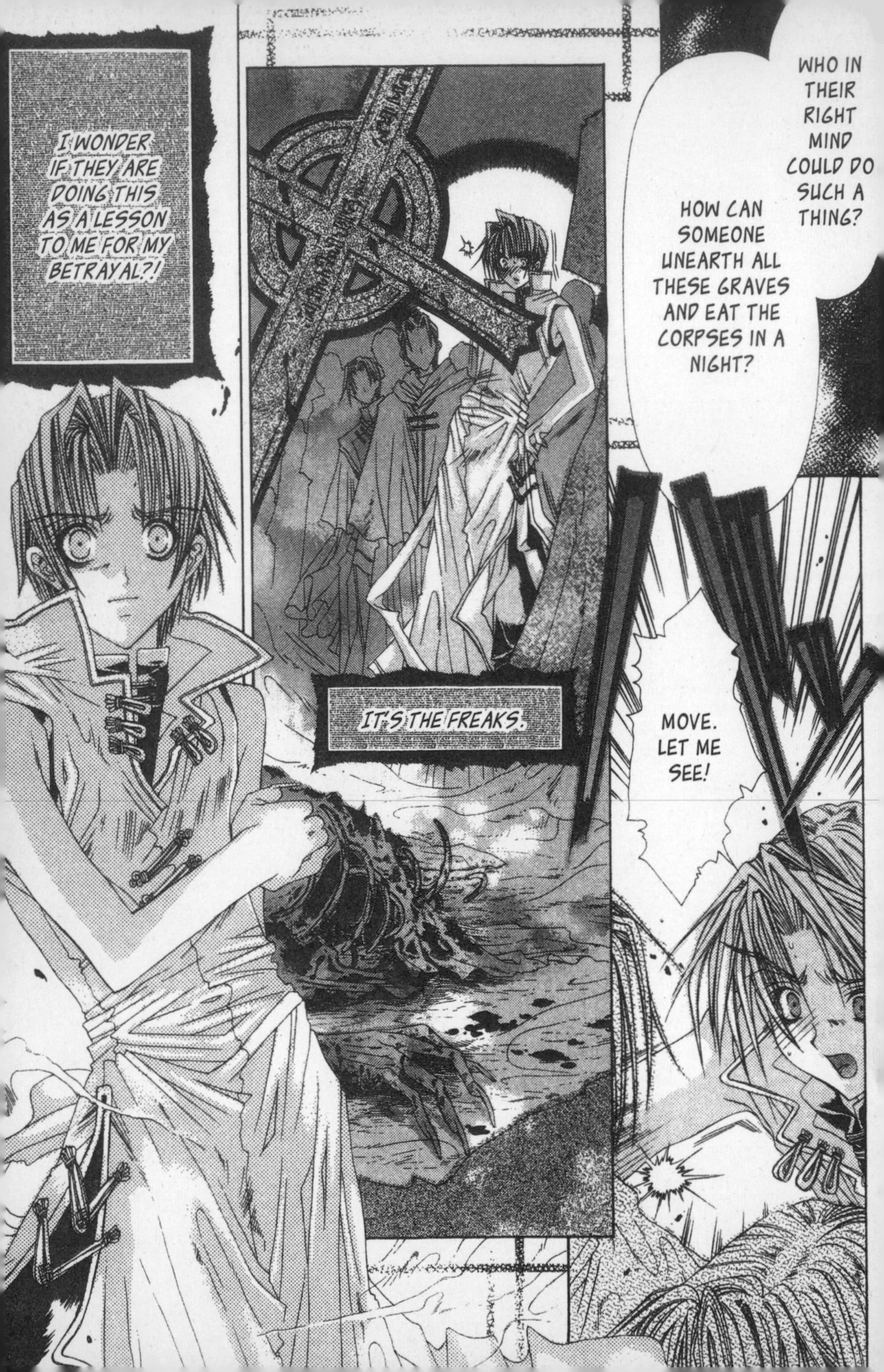
WHO IN THEIR RIGHT MIND COULD DO SUCH A THING?
HOW CAN SOMEONE UNEARTH ALL THESE GRAVES AND EAT THE CORPSES IN A NIGHT?
MOVE. LET ME SEE!
IT'S THE FREAKS.
I WONDER IF THEY ARE DOING THIS AS A LESSON TO ME FOR MY BETRAYAL?!

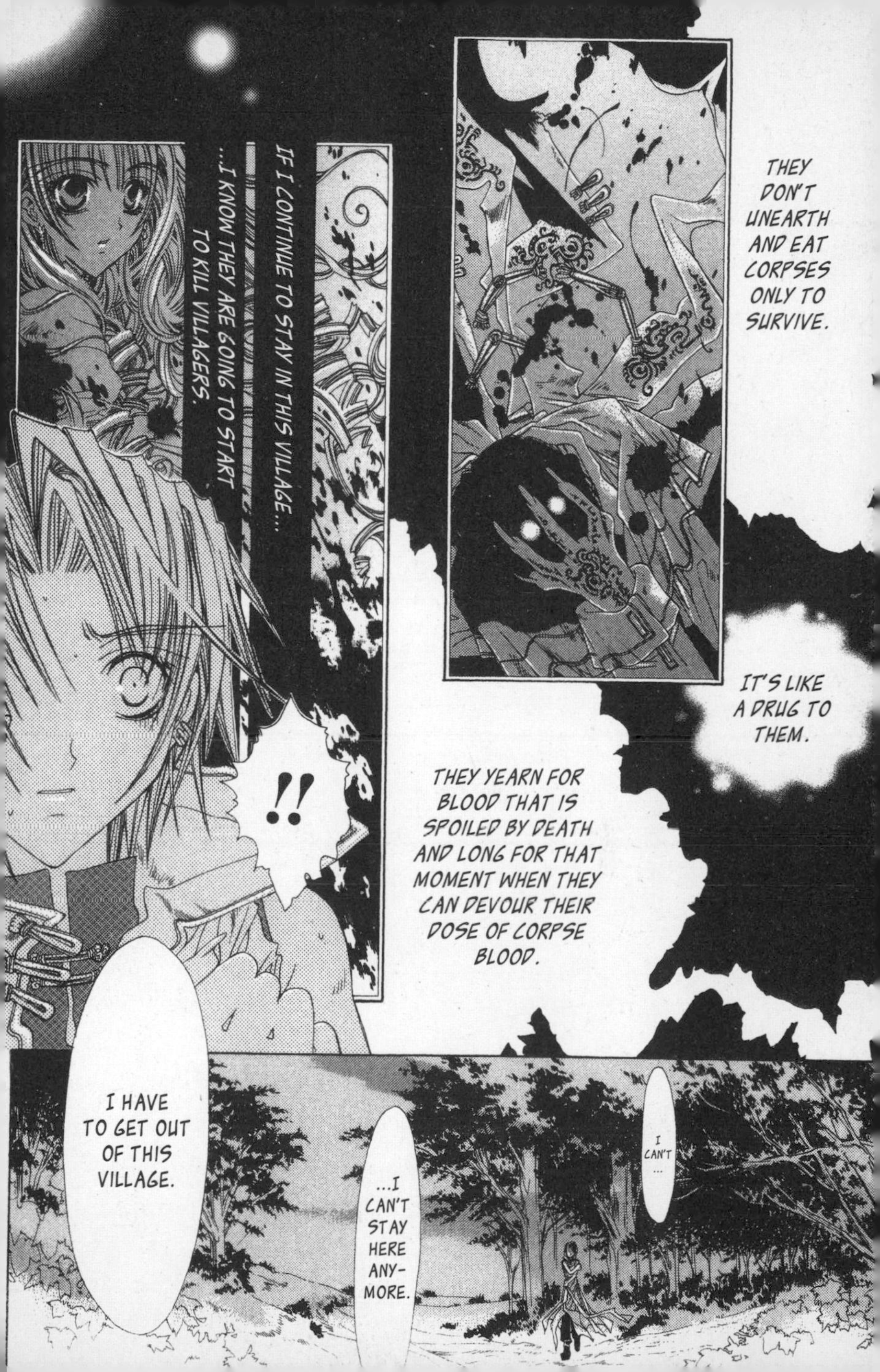
THEY DON'T UNEARTH AND EAT CORPSES ONLY TO SURVIVE.
IT'S LIKE A DRUG TO THEM.
THEY YEARN FOR BLOOD THAT IS SPOILED BY DEATH AND LONG FOR THAT MOMENT WHEN THEY CAN DEVOUR THEIR DOSE OF CORPSE BLOOD.
IF I CONTINUE TO STAY IN THIS VILLAGE...
...I KNOW THEY ARE GOING TO START TO KILL VILLAGERS.
!!
I CAN'T ...
...I CAN'T STAY HERE ANY-MORE.
I HAVE TO GET OUT OF THIS VILLAGE.

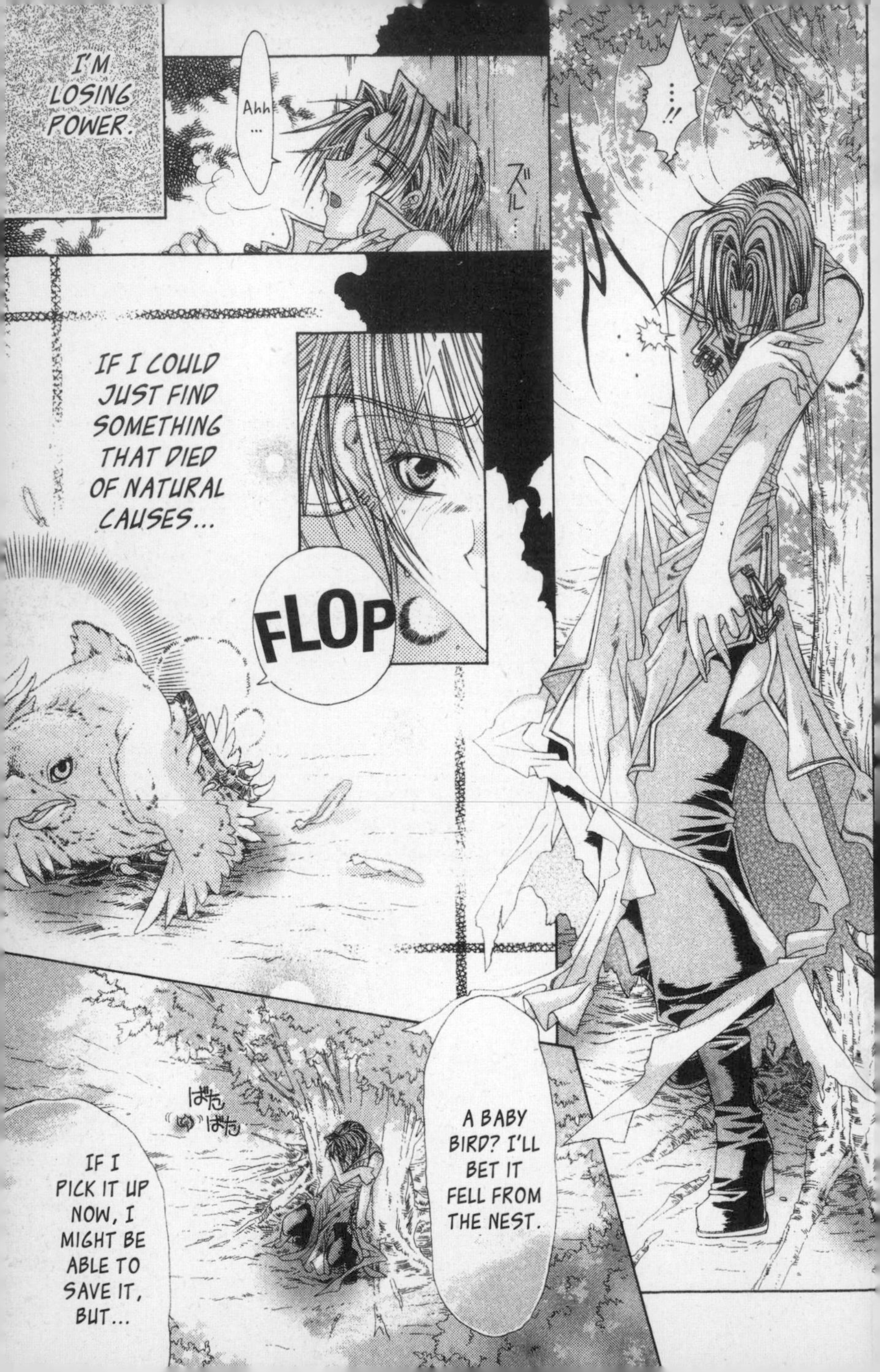

...!!
I'M LOSING POWER.
Ahh...
ズル…
IF I COULD JUST FIND SOMETHING THAT DIED OF NATURAL CAUSES...
FLOP
A BABY BIRD? I'LL BET IT FELL FROM THE NEST.
ぱた ぱた
IF I PICK IT UP NOW, I MIGHT BE ABLE TO SAVE IT, BUT...

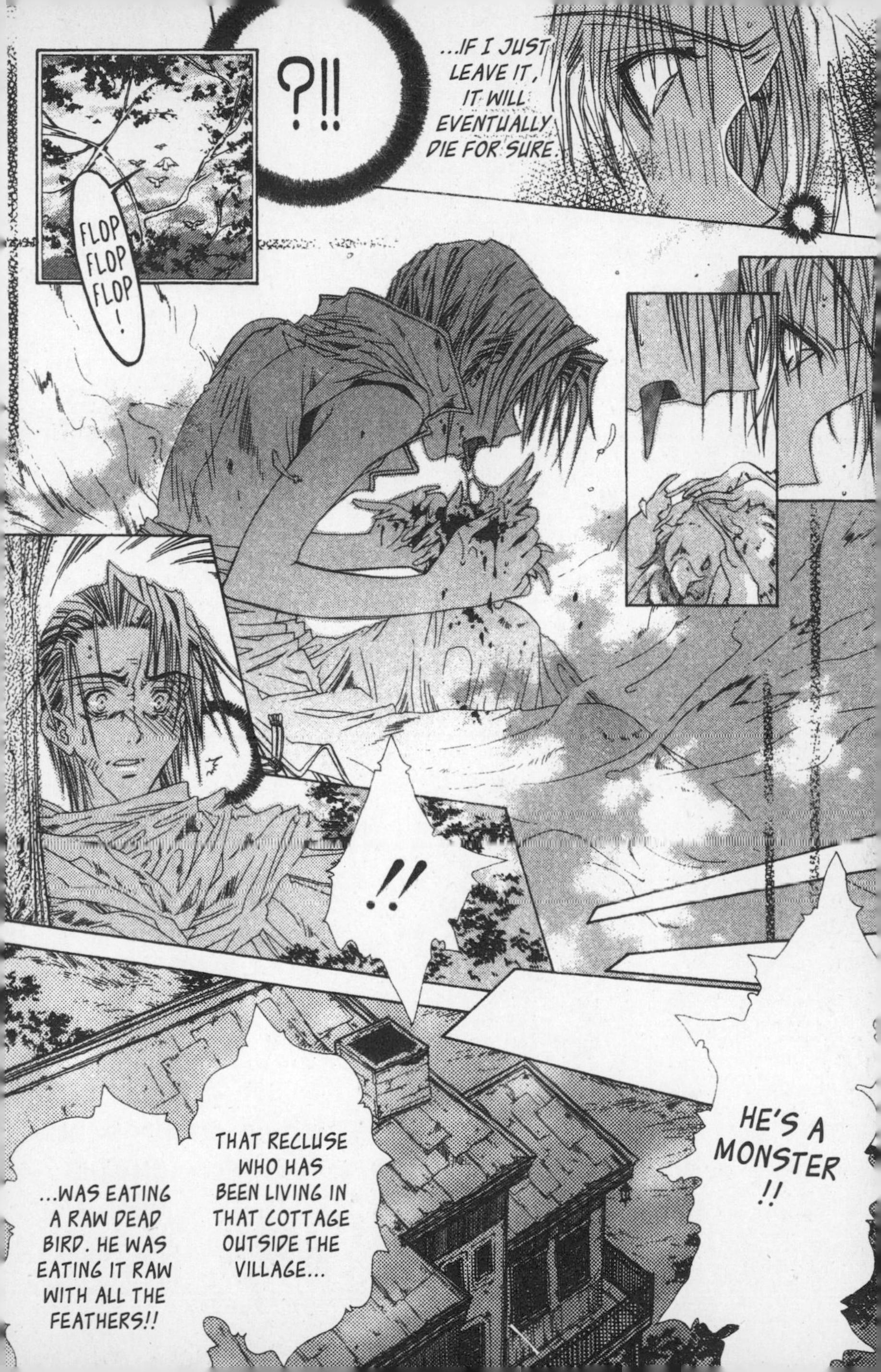
...IF I JUST LEAVE IT, IT WILL EVENTUALLY DIE FOR SURE.
?!!
FLOP FLOP FLOP!
!!
HE'S A MONSTER!!
THAT RECLUSE WHO HAS BEEN LIVING IN THAT COTTAGE OUTSIDE THE VILLAGE...
...WAS EATING A RAW DEAD BIRD. HE WAS EATING IT RAW WITH ALL THE FEATHERS!!

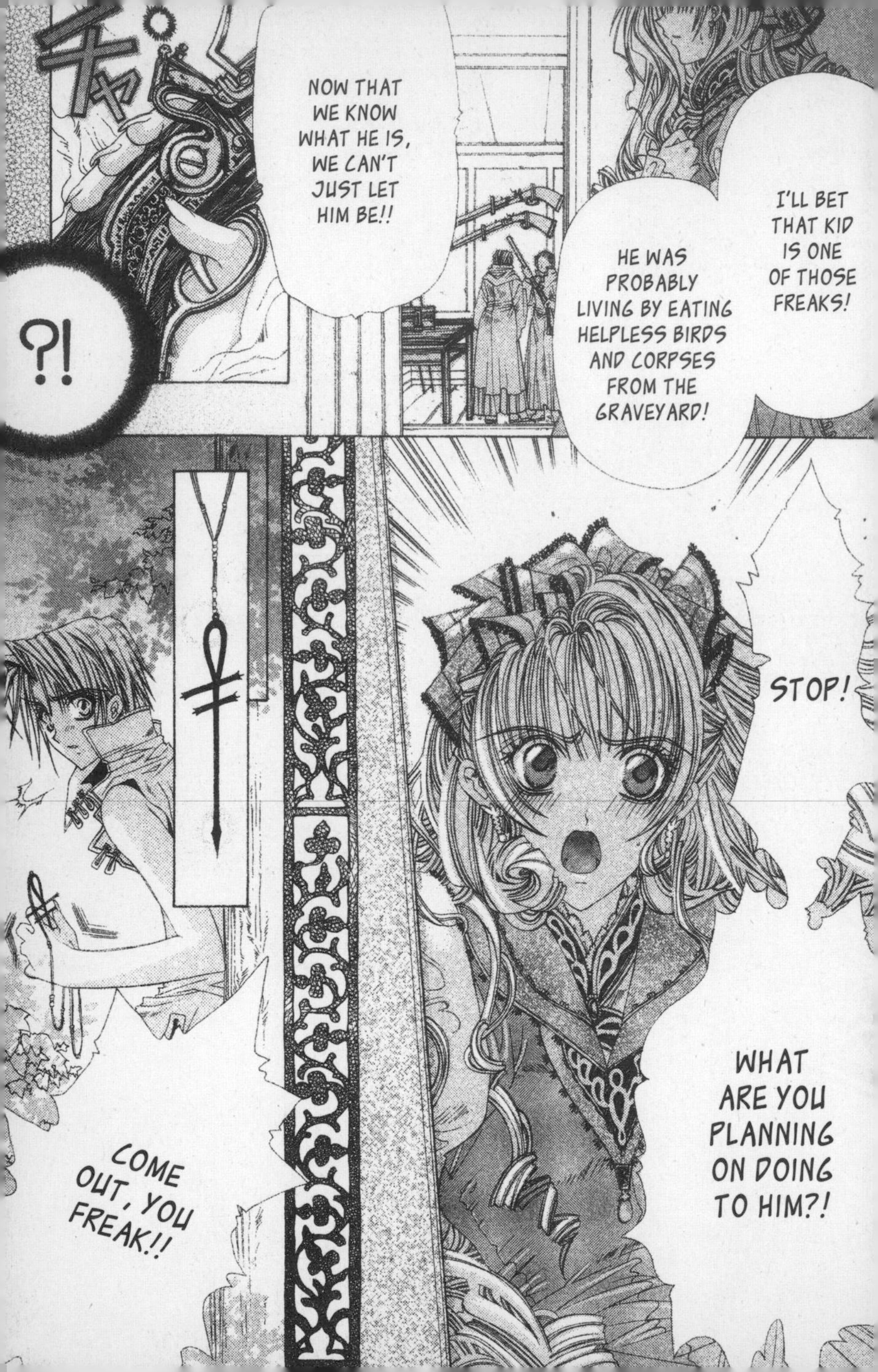

I'LL BET THAT KID IS ONE OF THOSE FREAKS!
HE WAS PROBABLY LIVING BY EATING HELPLESS BIRDS AND CORPSES FROM THE GRAVEYARD!
NOW THAT WE KNOW WHAT HE IS, WE CAN'T JUST LET HIM BE!!
チャ
?!
STOP!
WHAT ARE YOU PLANNING ON DOING TO HIM?!
COME OUT, YOU FREAK!!

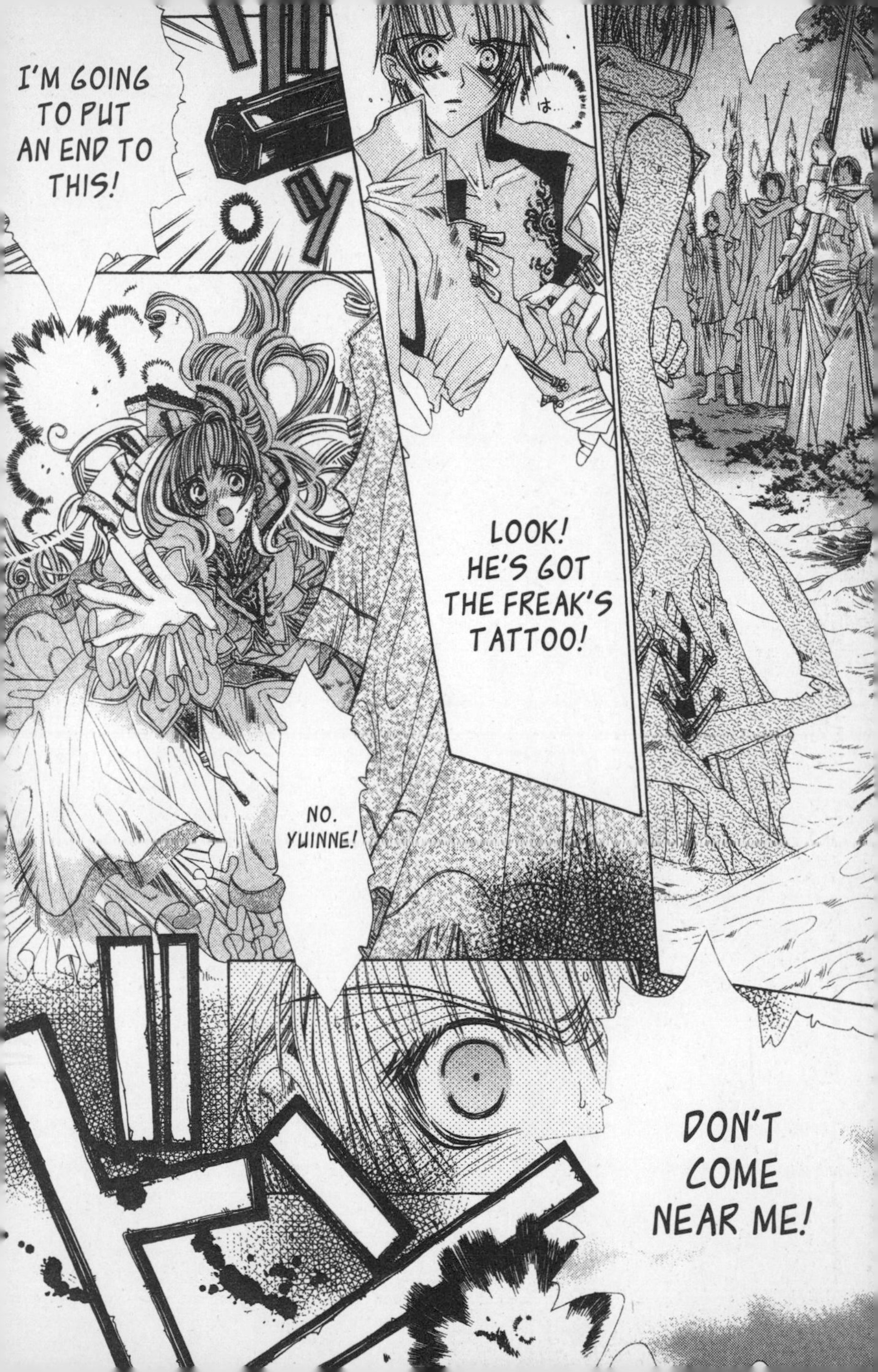
LOOK! HE'S GOT THE FREAK'S TATTOO!
は…
I'M GOING TO PUT AN END TO THIS!
NO. YUINNE!
DON'T COME NEAR ME!

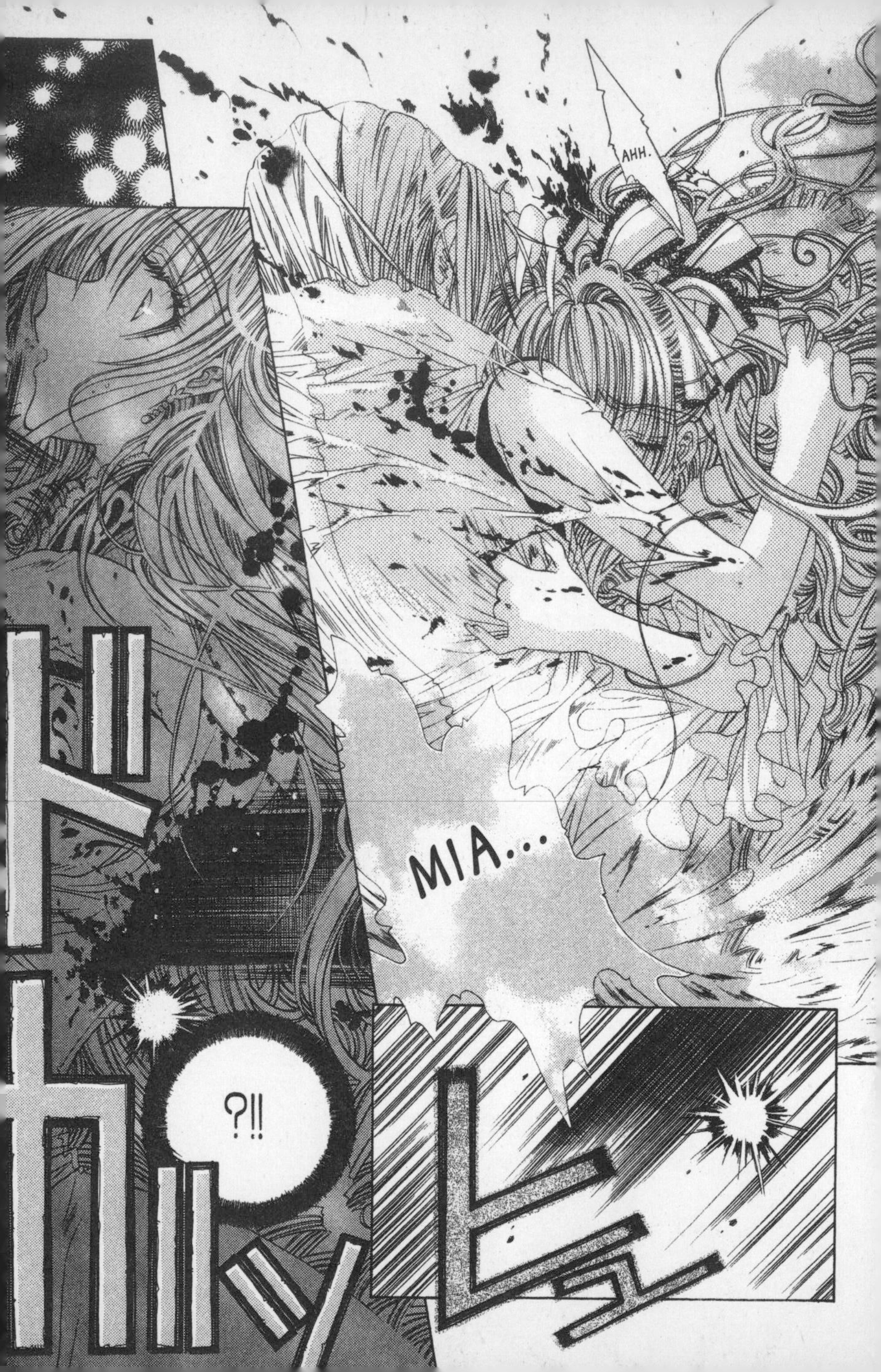
AHH.
MIA...
?!!

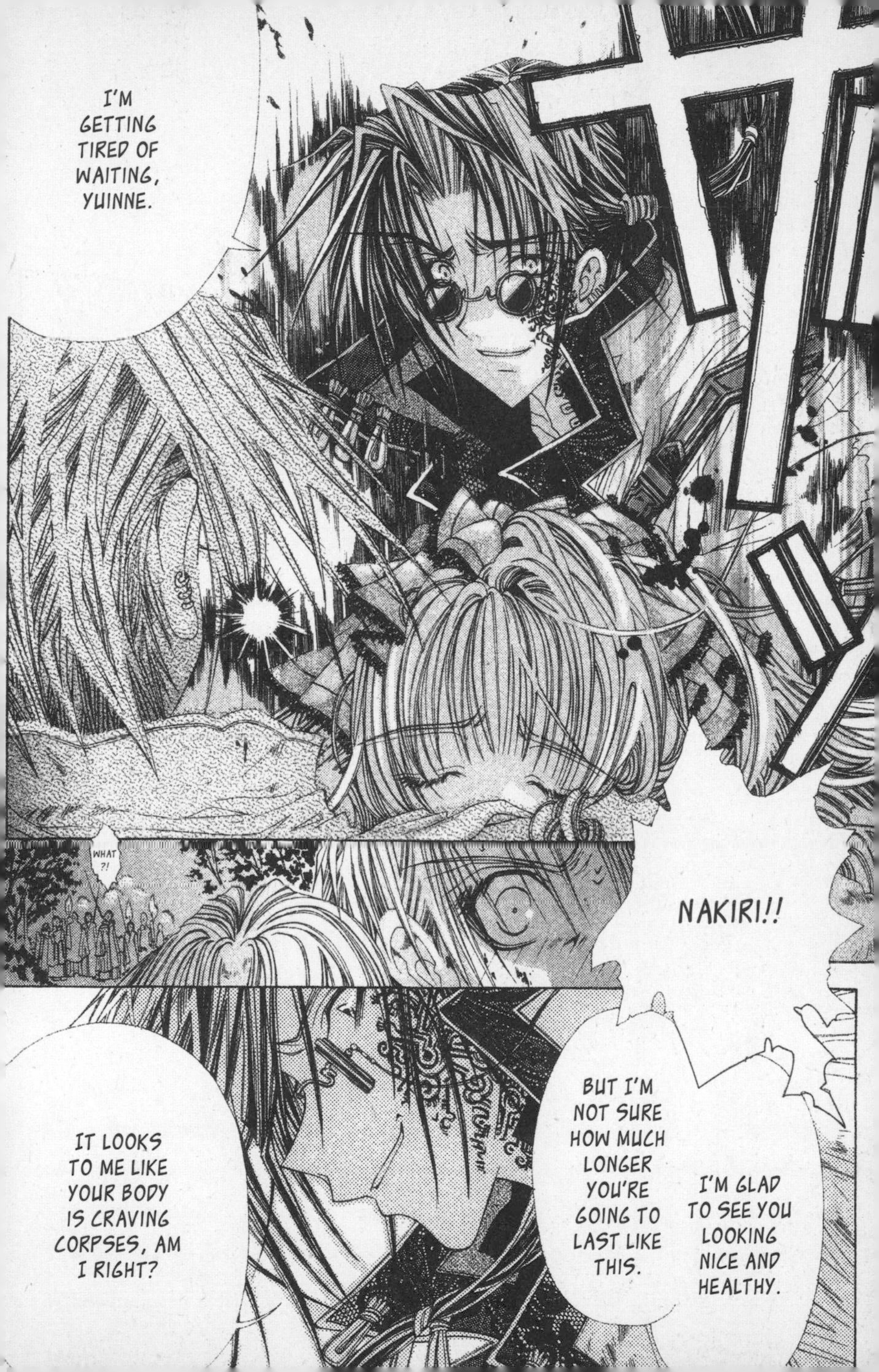
I'M GETTING TIRED OF WAITING, YUINNE.
NAKIRI!!
WHAT?!
I'M GLAD TO SEE YOU LOOKING NICE AND HEALTHY.
BUT I'M NOT SURE HOW MUCH LONGER YOU'RE GOING TO LAST LIKE THIS.
IT LOOKS TO ME LIKE YOUR BODY IS CRAVING CORPSES, AM I RIGHT?

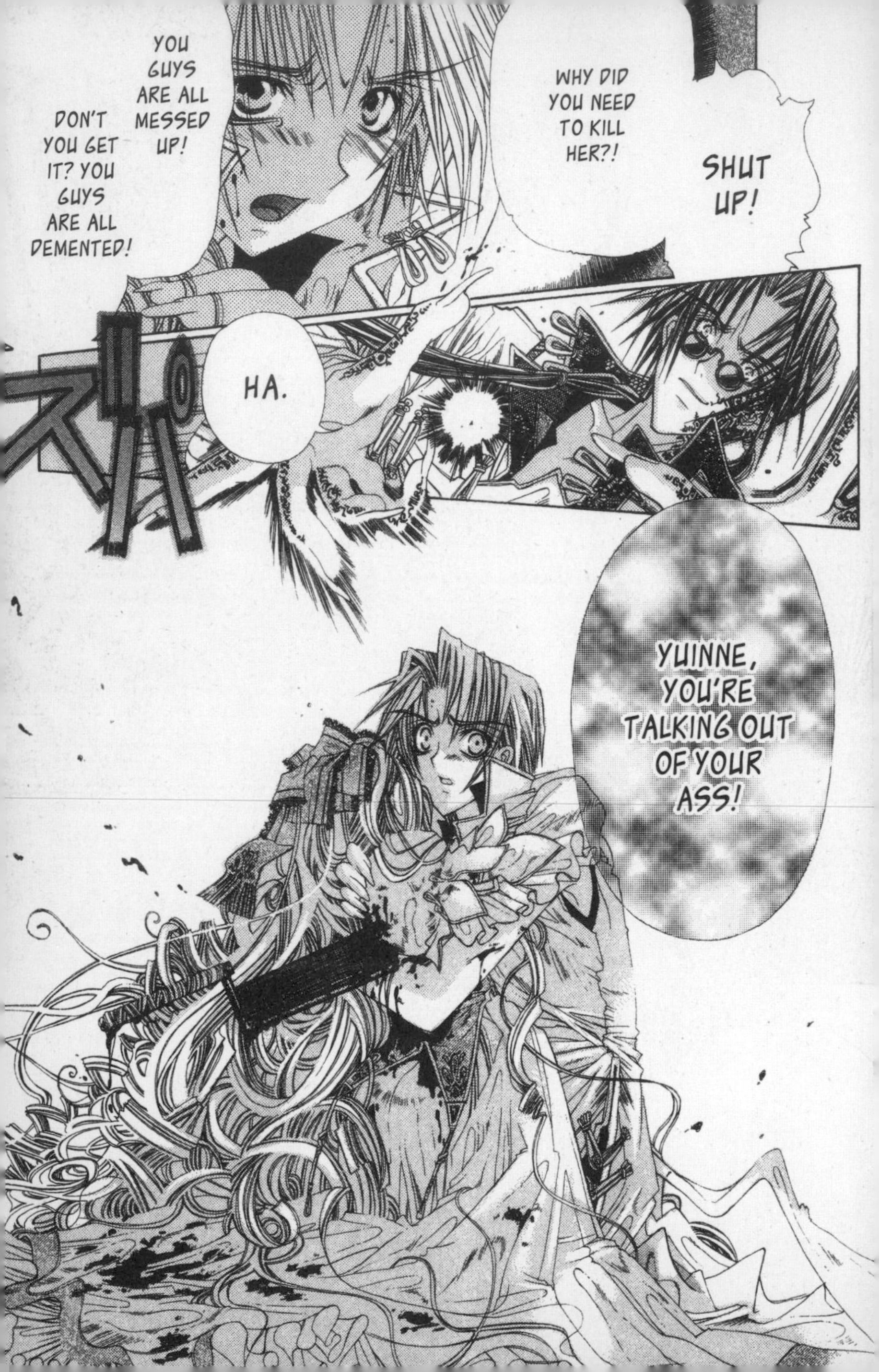
SHUT UP!
WHY DID YOU NEED TO KILL HER?!
YOU GUYS ARE ALL MESSED UP!
DON'T YOU GET IT? YOU GUYS ARE ALL DEMENTED!
HA.
YUINNE, YOU'RE TALKING OUT OF YOUR ASS!

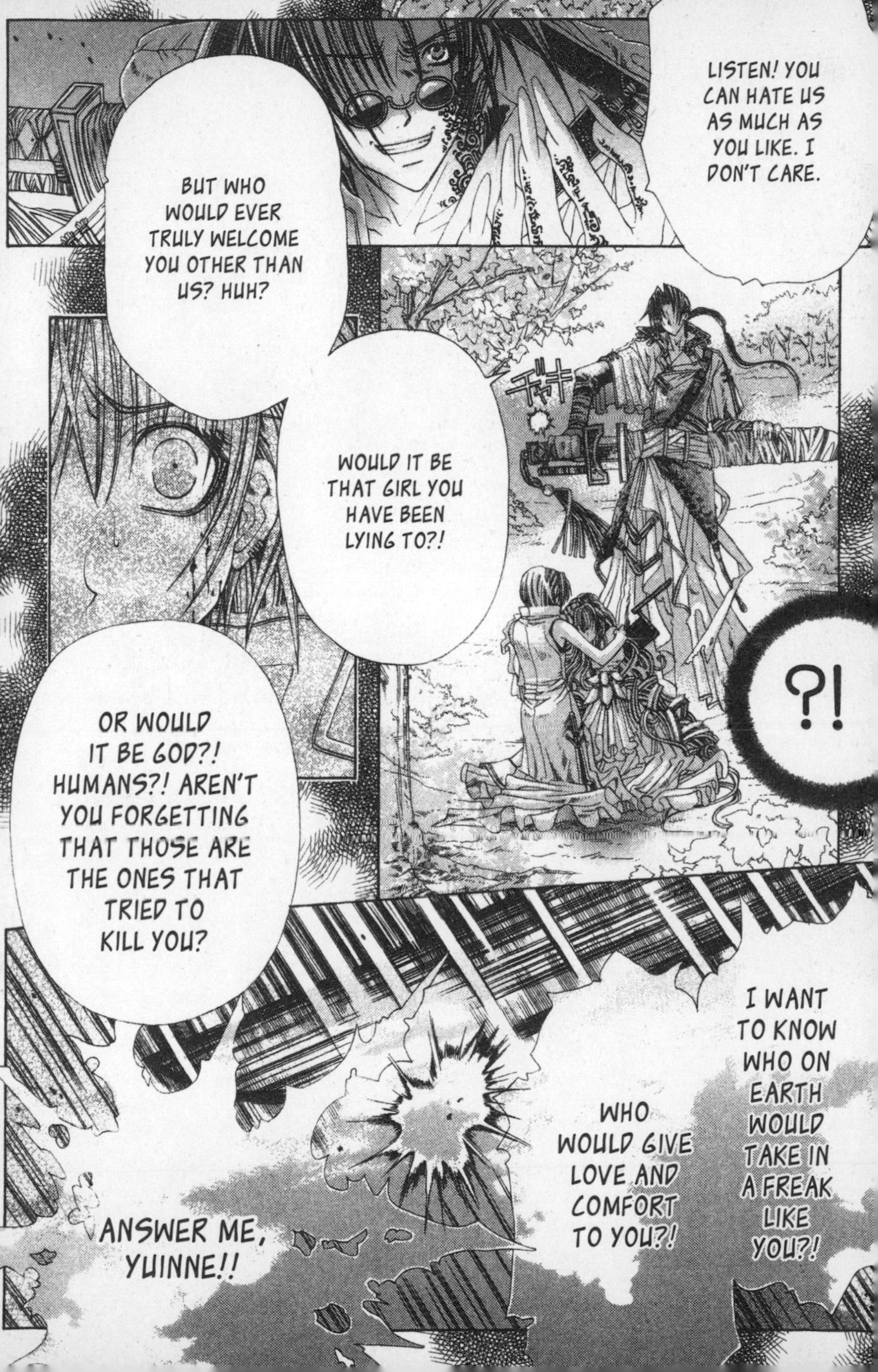
LISTEN! YOU CAN HATE US AS MUCH AS YOU LIKE. I DON'T CARE.
BUT WHO WOULD EVER TRULY WELCOME YOU OTHER THAN US? HUH?
WOULD IT BE THAT GIRL YOU HAVE BEEN LYING TO?!
?!
OR WOULD IT BE GOD?! HUMANS?! AREN'T YOU FORGETTING THAT THOSE ARE THE ONES THAT TRIED TO KILL YOU?
I WANT TO KNOW WHO ON EARTH WOULD TAKE IN A FREAK LIKE YOU?!
WHO WOULD GIVE LOVE AND COMFORT TO YOU?!
ANSWER ME, YUINNE!!

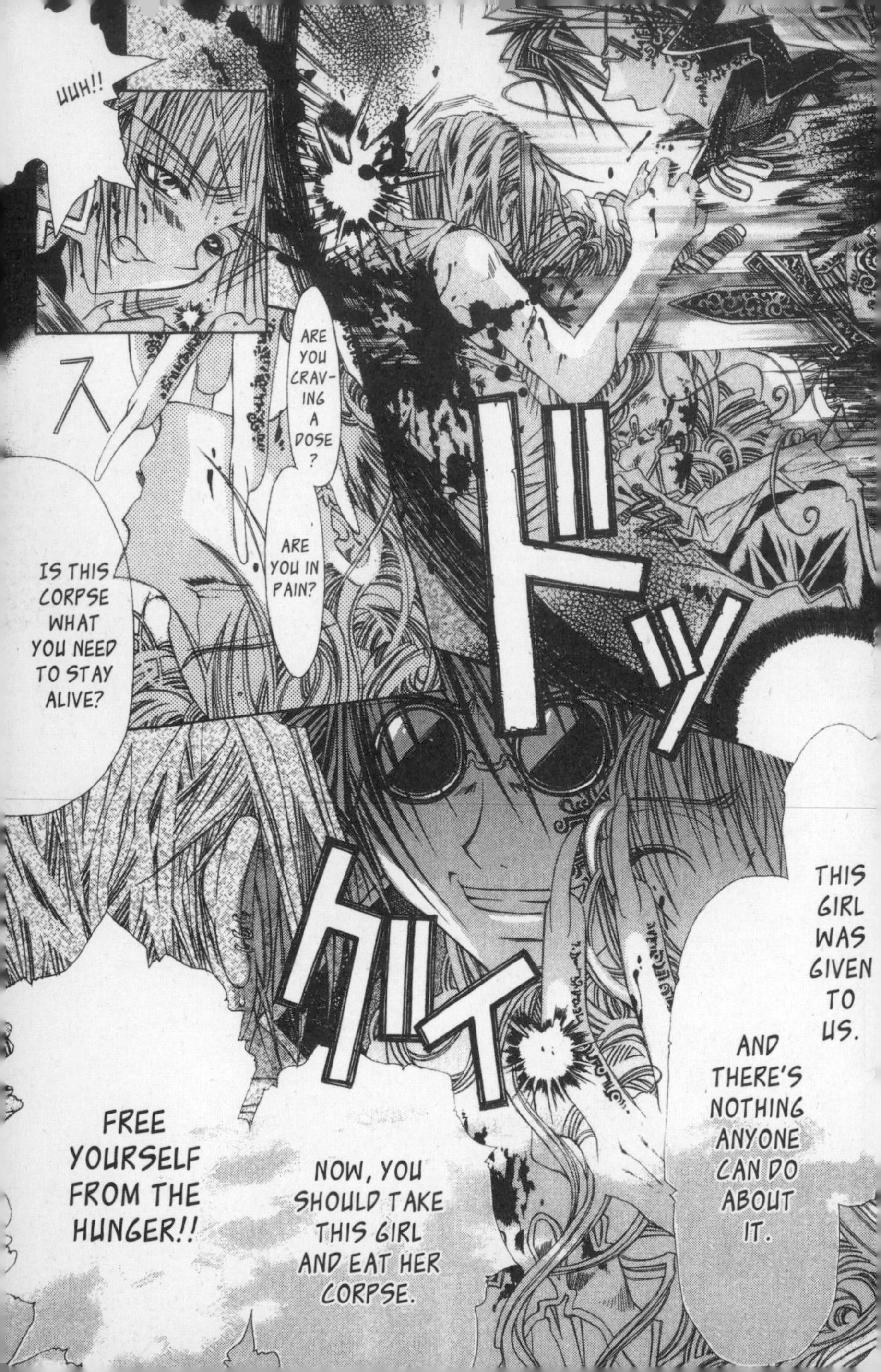
ARE YOU CRAVING A DOSE?
ARE YOU IN PAIN?
UUH!!
ドッ
ス
IS THIS CORPSE WHAT YOU NEED TO STAY ALIVE?
THIS GIRL WAS GIVEN TO US.
AND THERE'S NOTHING ANYONE CAN DO ABOUT IT.
NOW, YOU SHOULD TAKE THIS GIRL AND EAT HER CORPSE.
FREE YOURSELF FROM THE HUNGER!!

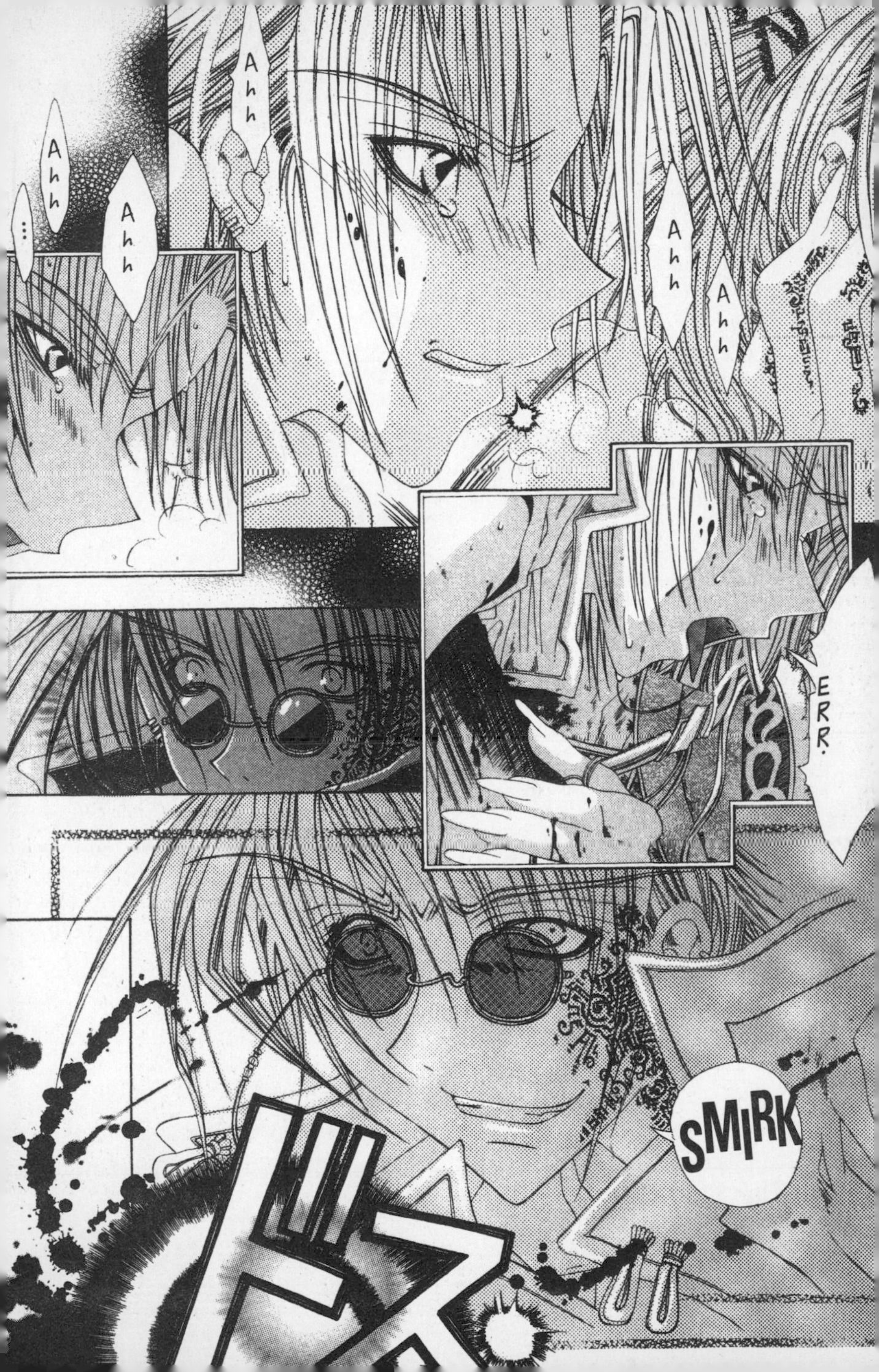

Ahh
Ahh
Ahh
Ahh
Ahh
...
ERR.
SMIRK
ドス

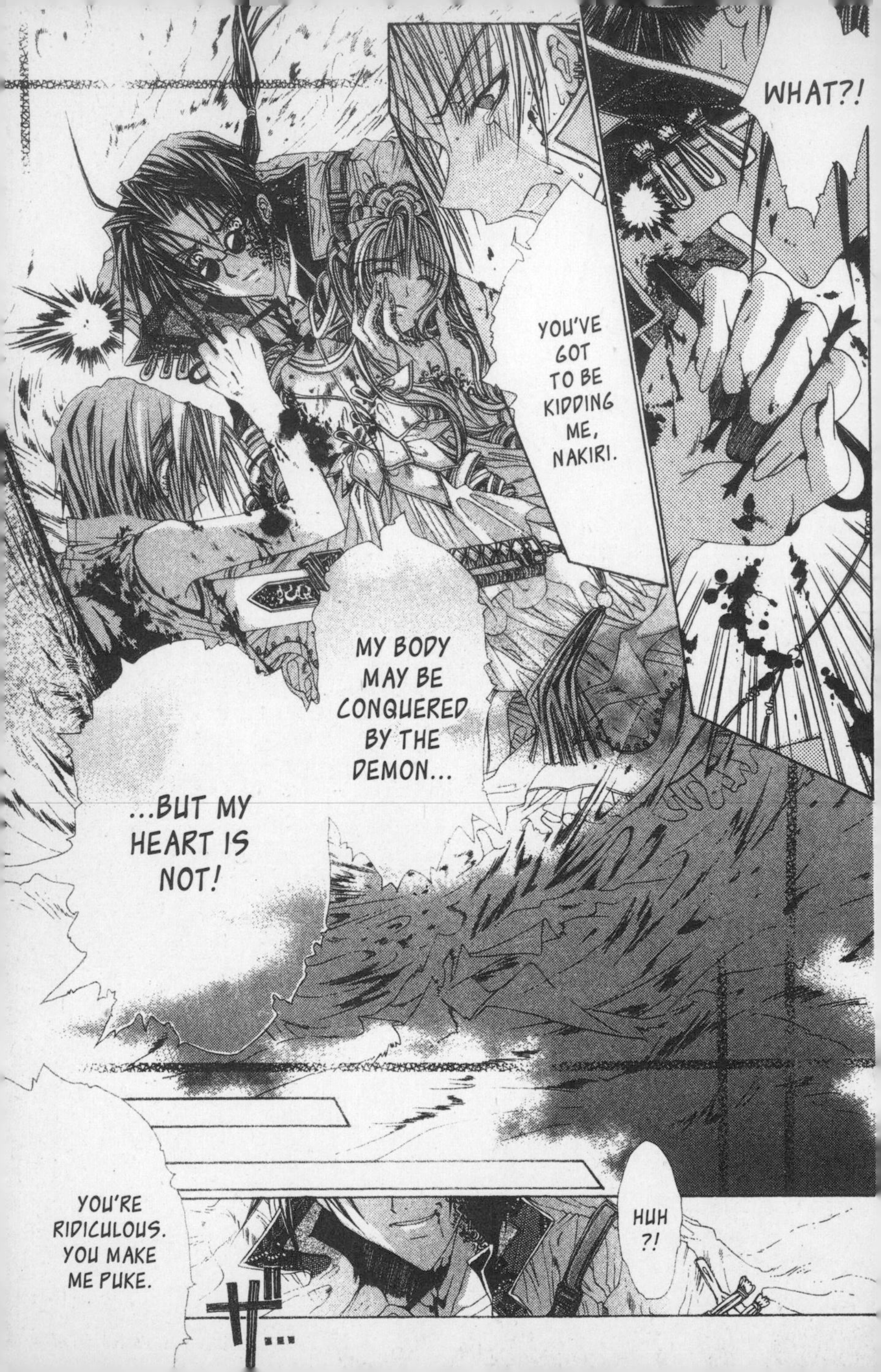
WHAT?!
YOU'VE GOT TO BE KIDDING ME, NAKIRI.
MY BODY MAY BE CONQUERED BY THE DEMON...
...BUT MY HEART IS NOT!
HUH?!
YOU'RE RIDICULOUS. YOU MAKE ME PUKE.

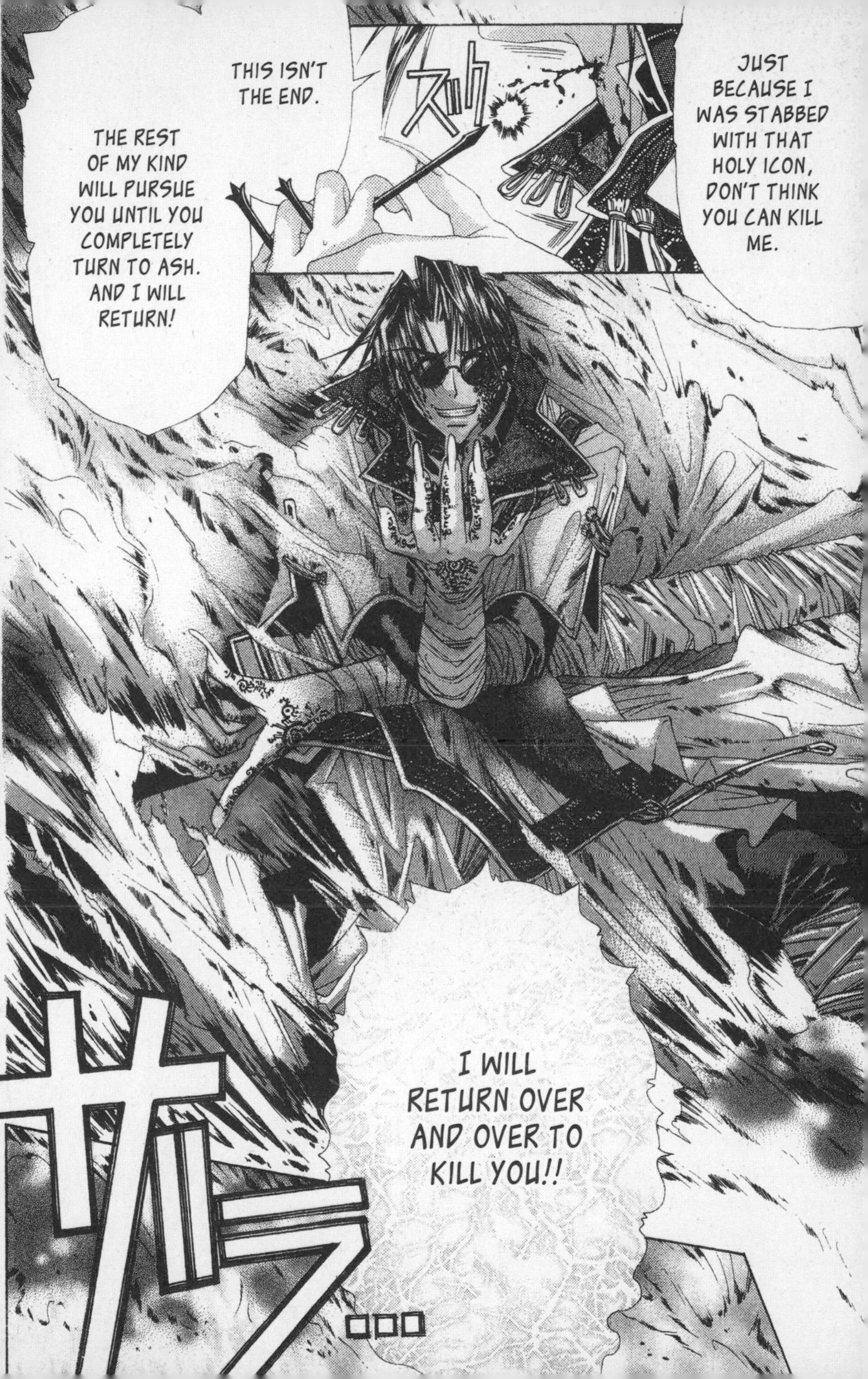
JUST BECAUSE I WAS STABBED WITH THAT HOLY ICON, DON'T THINK YOU CAN KILL ME.
THIS ISN'T THE END.
THE REST OF MY KIND WILL PURSUE YOU UNTIL YOU COMPLETELY TURN TO ASH. AND I WILL RETURN!
I WILL RETURN OVER AND OVER TO KILL YOU!!

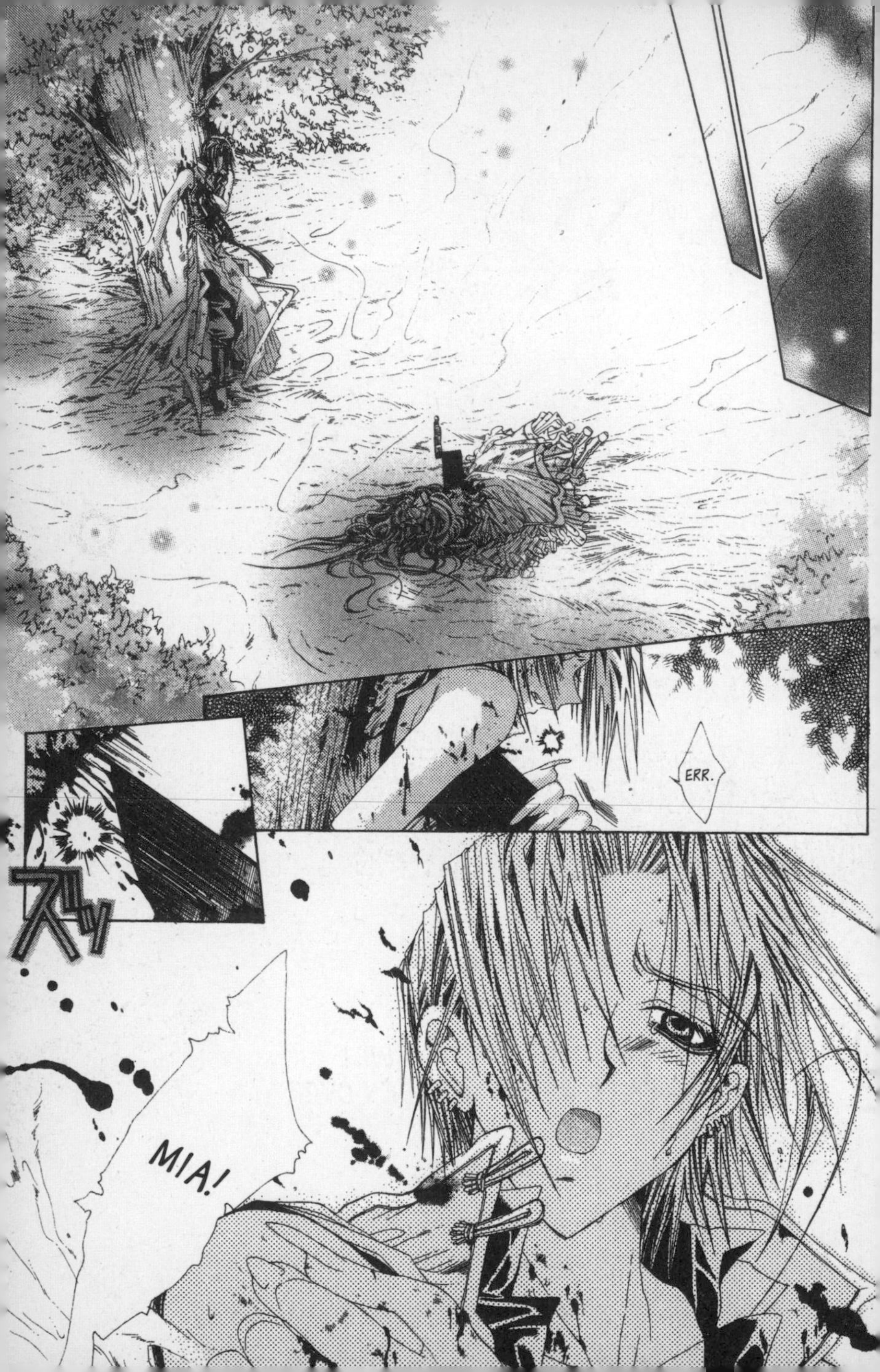
ERR.
スッ
MIA!

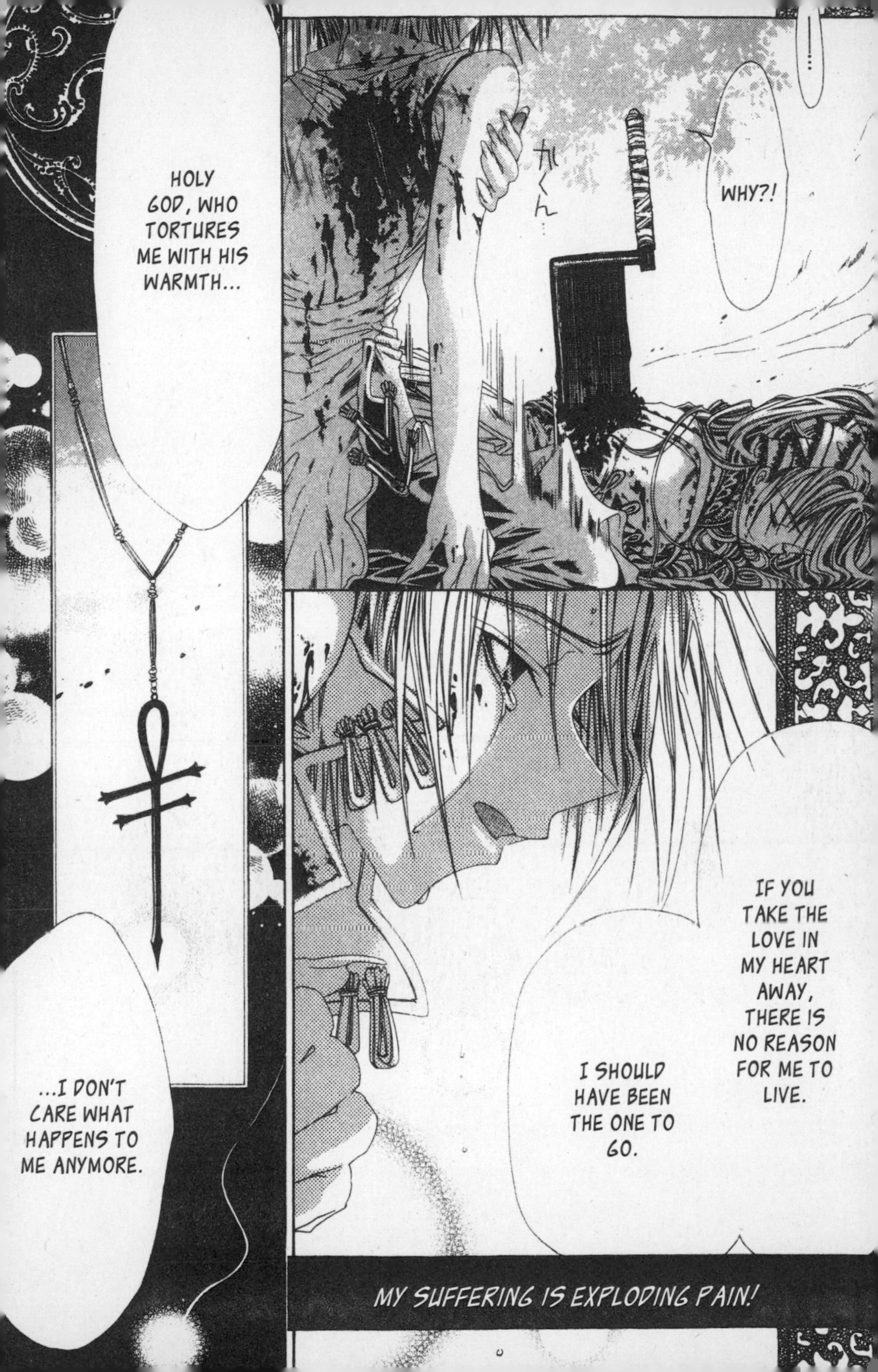
…!
WHY?!
IF YOU TAKE THE LOVE IN MY HEART AWAY, THERE IS NO REASON FOR ME TO LIVE.
I SHOULD HAVE BEEN THE ONE TO GO.
MY SUFFERING IS EXPLODING PAIN!
HOLY GOD, WHO TORTURES ME WITH HIS WARMTH...
...I DON'T CARE WHAT HAPPENS TO ME ANYMORE.

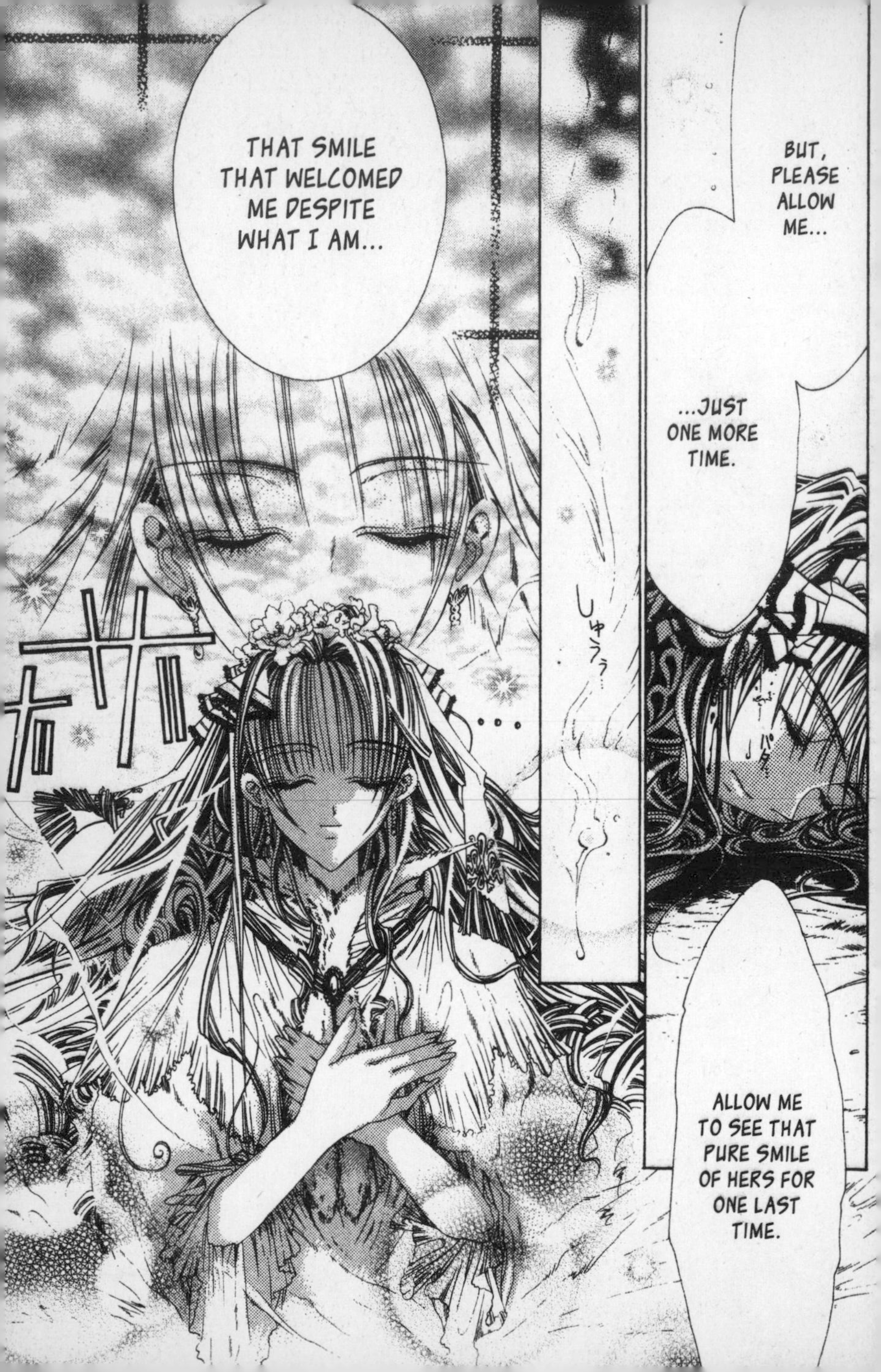
BUT, PLEASE ALLOW ME...
...JUST ONE MORE TIME.
ALLOW ME TO SEE THAT PURE SMILE OF HERS FOR ONE LAST TIME.
THAT SMILE THAT WELCOMED ME DESPITE WHAT I AM...

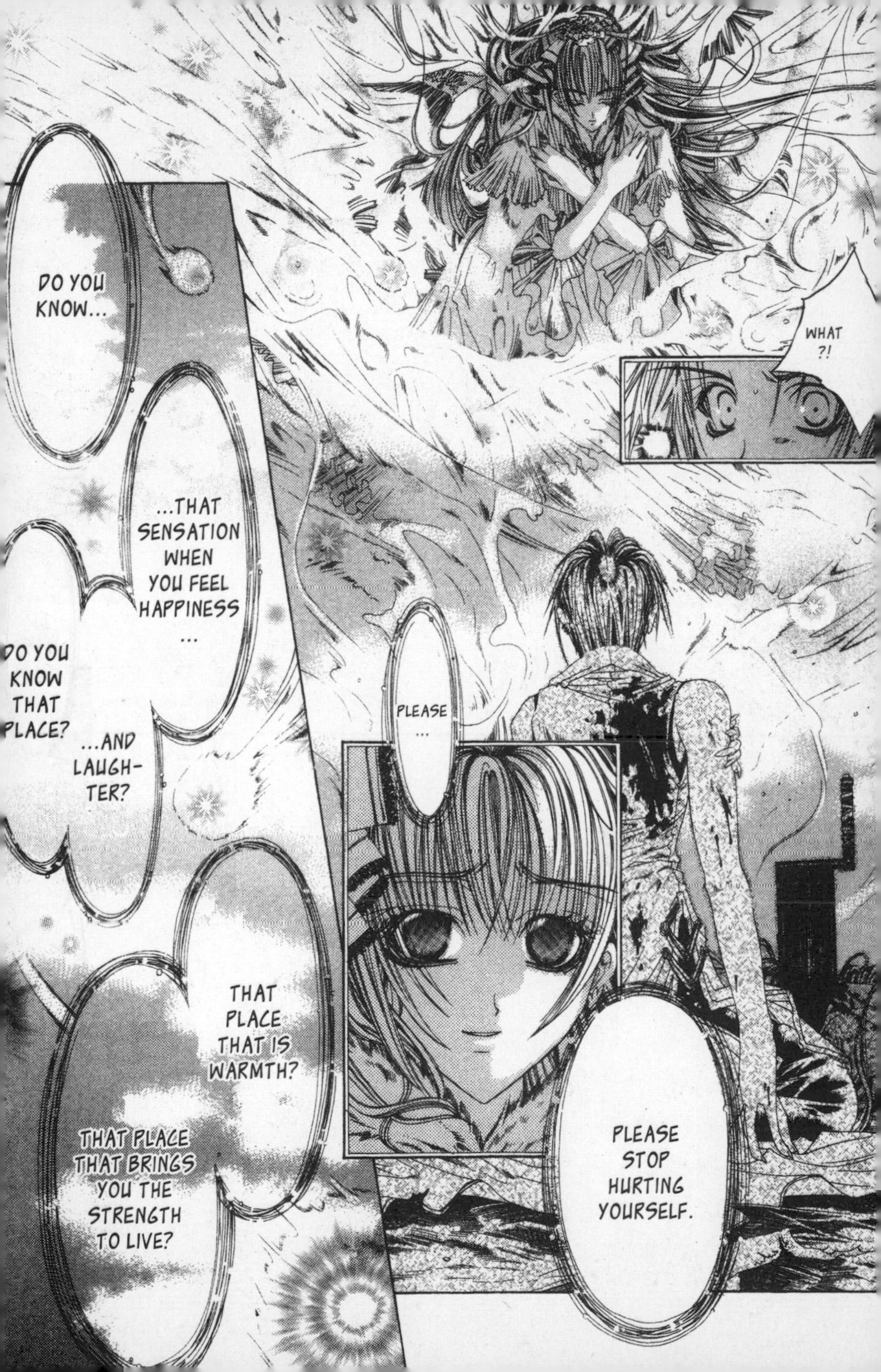
WHAT ?!
PLEASE ...
PLEASE STOP HURTING YOURSELF.
DO YOU KNOW...
...THAT SENSATION WHEN YOU FEEL HAPPINESS ...
DO YOU KNOW THAT PLACE?
...AND LAUGHTER?
THAT PLACE THAT IS WARMTH?
THAT PLACE THAT BRINGS YOU THE STRENGTH TO LIVE?

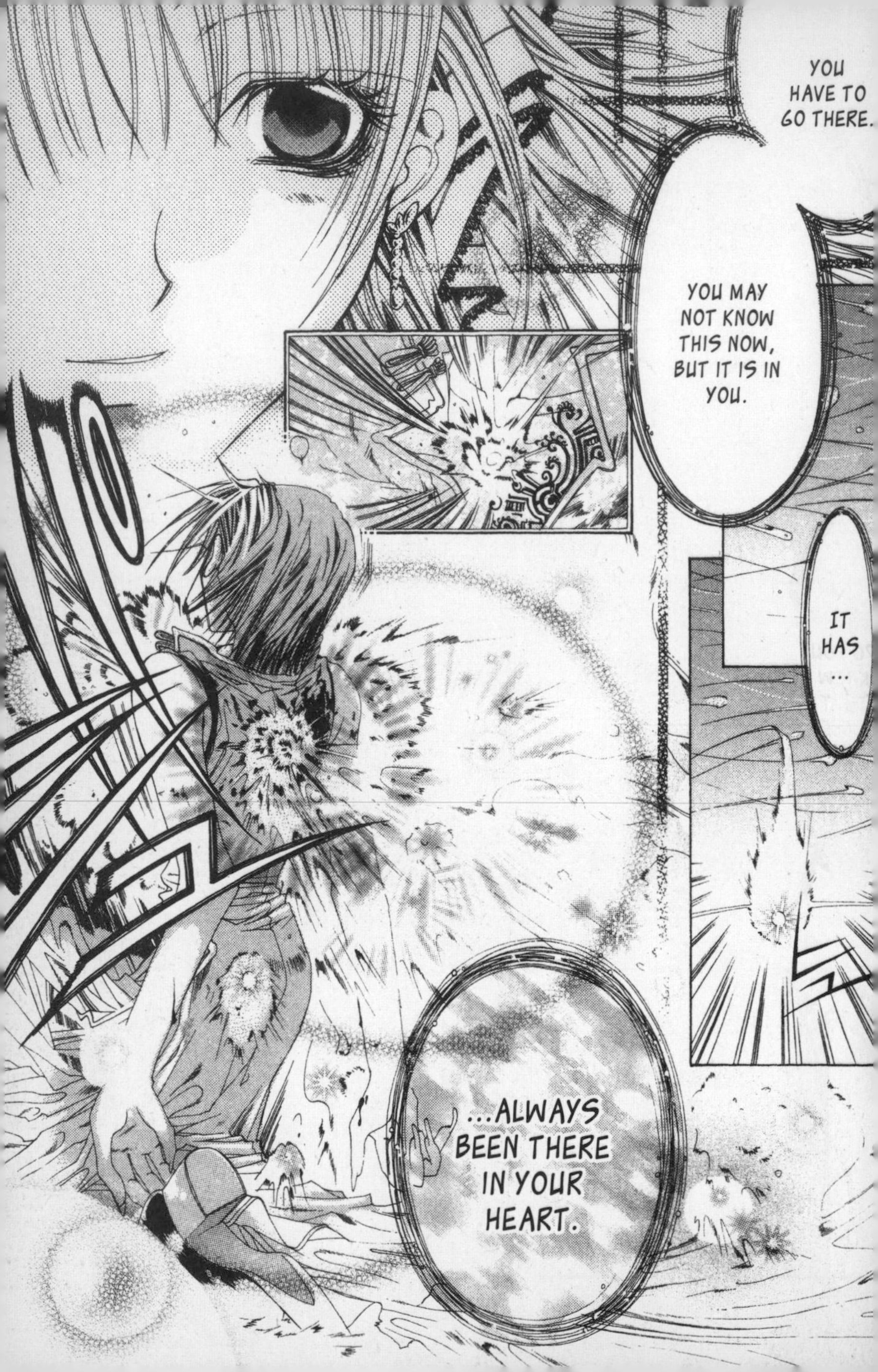
YOU HAVE TO GO THERE.
YOU MAY NOT KNOW THIS NOW, BUT IT IS IN YOU.
IT HAS ...
...ALWAYS BEEN THERE IN YOUR HEART.

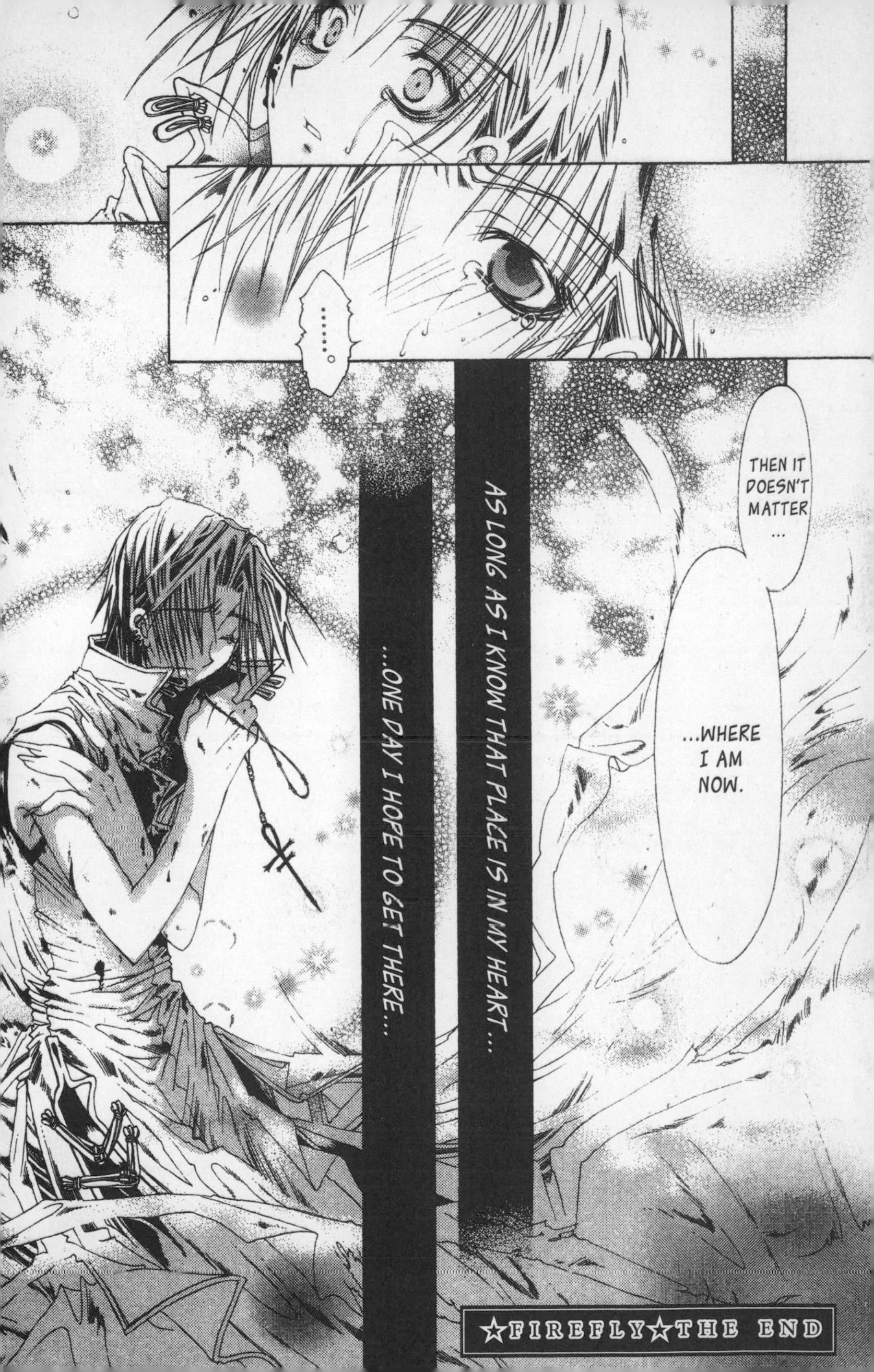
......
THEN IT DOESN'T MATTER ...
...WHERE I AM NOW.
AS LONG AS I KNOW THAT PLACE IS IN MY HEART...
...ONE DAY I HOPE TO GET THERE...
☆FIREFLY☆THE END

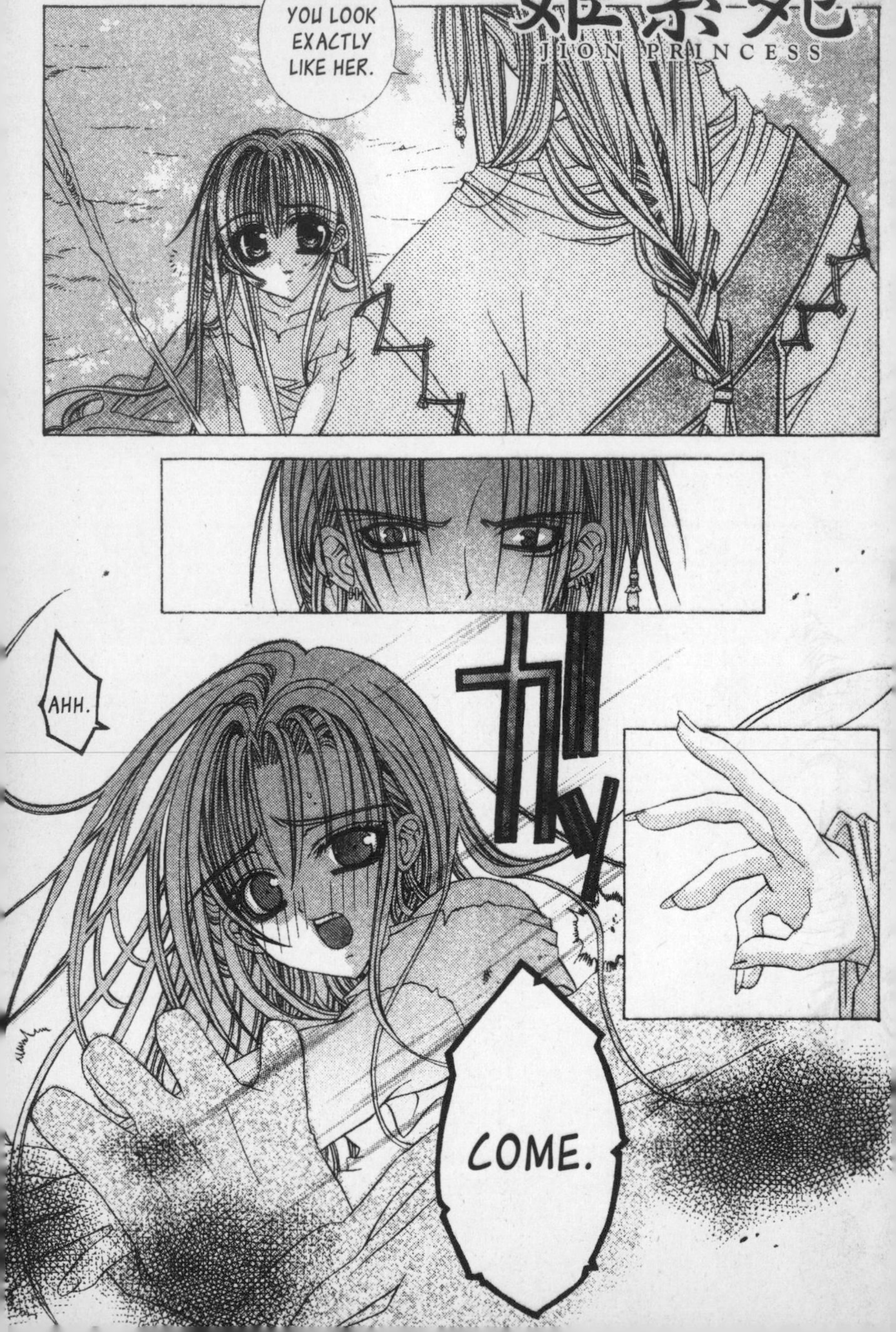
YOU LOOK EXACTLY LIKE HER.
AHH.
COME.

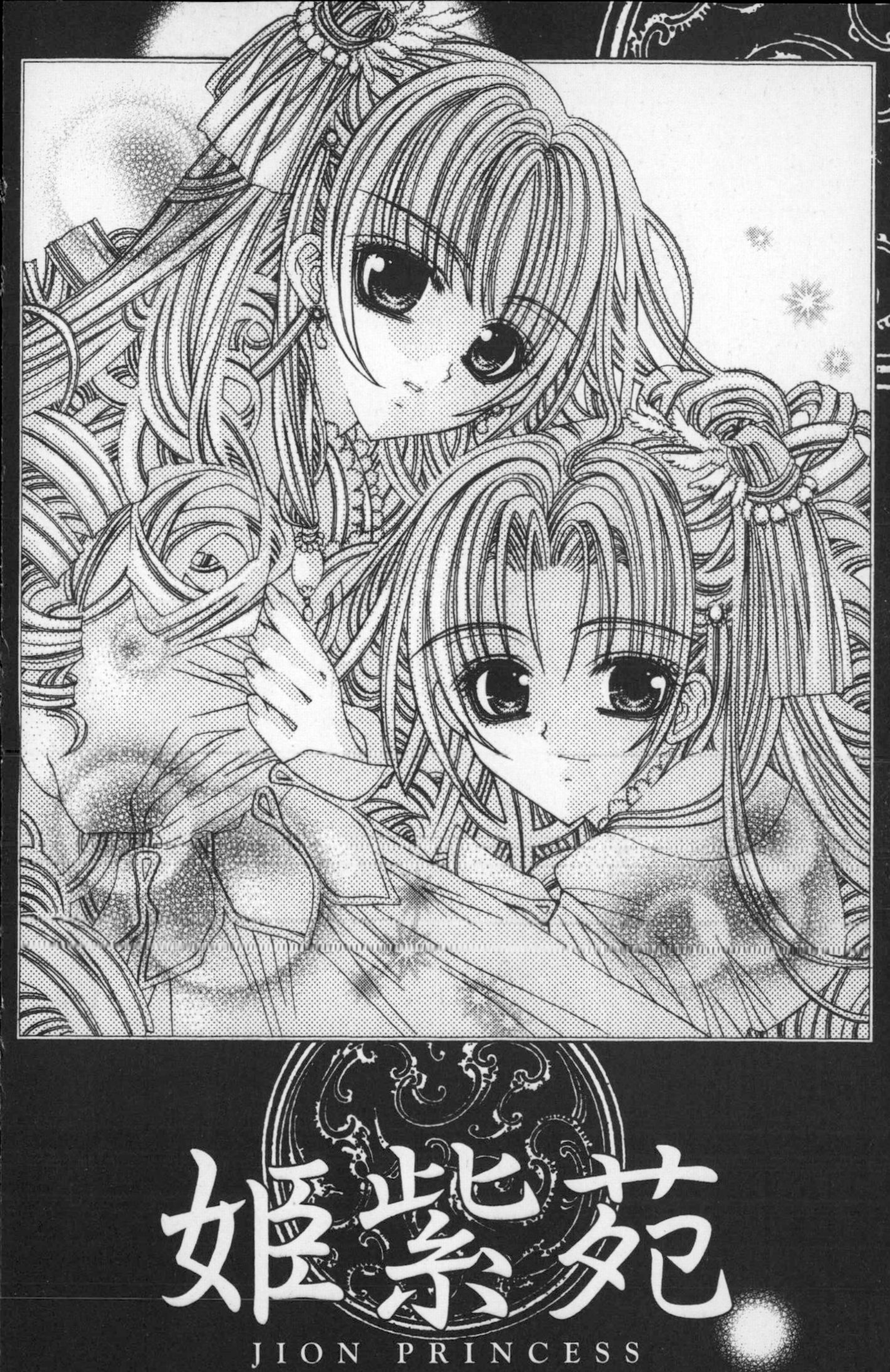
姫紫苑
JION PRINCESS

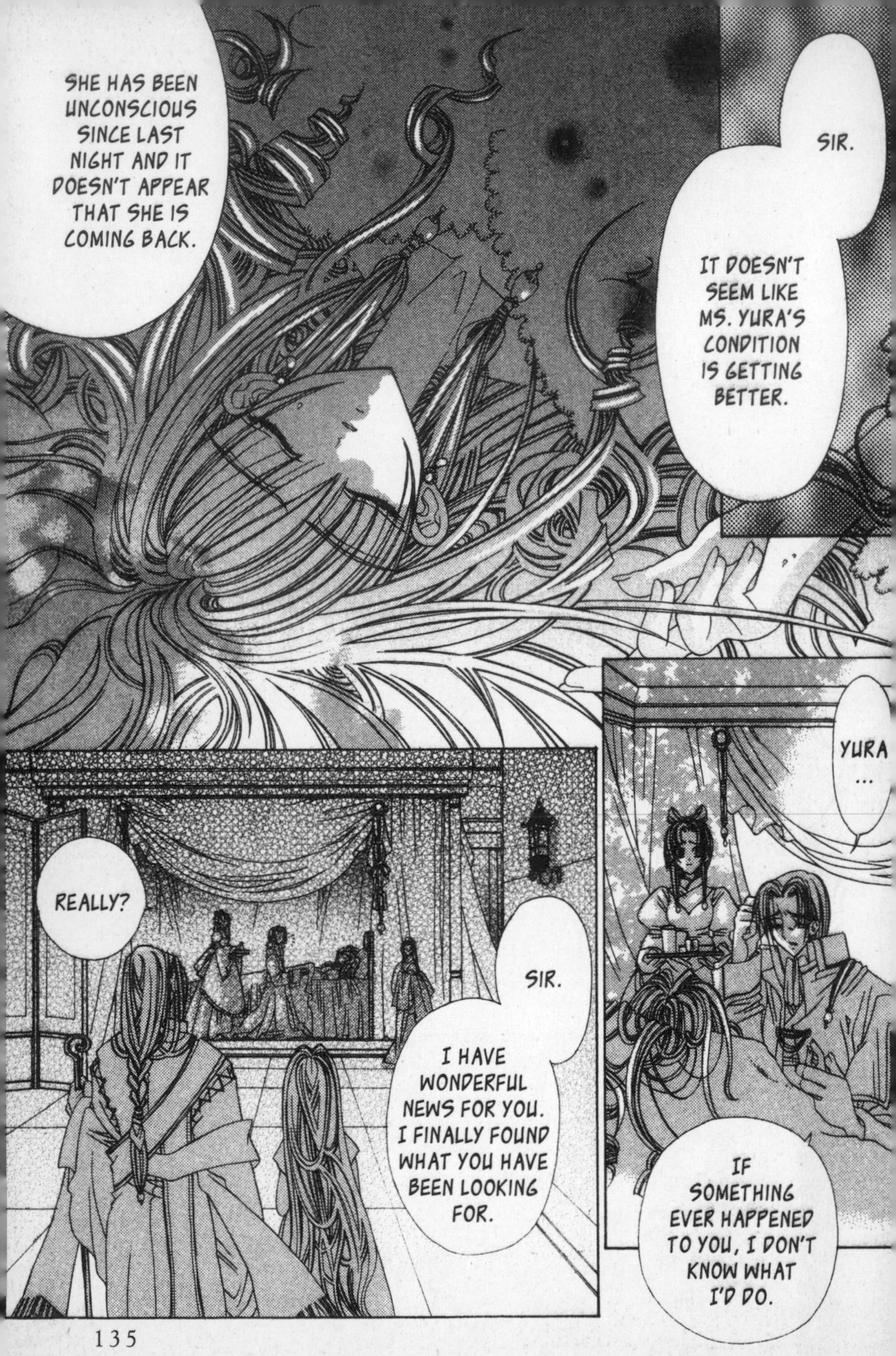
SIR.
IT DOESN'T SEEM LIKE MS. YURA'S CONDITION IS GETTING BETTER.
SHE HAS BEEN UNCONSCIOUS SINCE LAST NIGHT AND IT DOESN'T APPEAR THAT SHE IS COMING BACK.
YURA ...
IF SOMETHING EVER HAPPENED TO YOU, I DON'T KNOW WHAT I'D DO.
SIR.
I HAVE WONDERFUL NEWS FOR YOU. I FINALLY FOUND WHAT YOU HAVE BEEN LOOKING FOR.
REALLY?

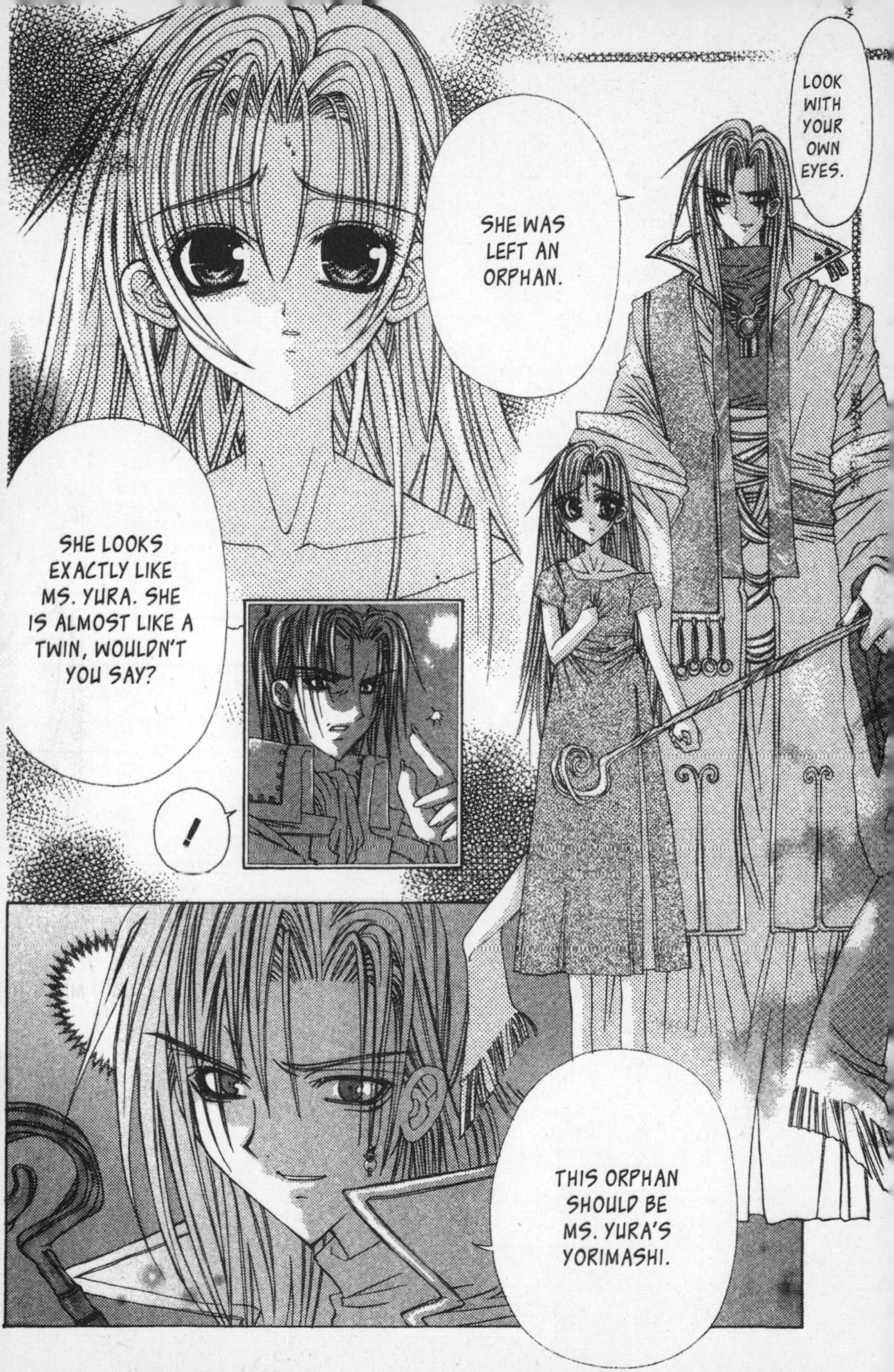
LOOK WITH YOUR OWN EYES.
SHE WAS LEFT AN ORPHAN.
SHE LOOKS EXACTLY LIKE MS. YURA. SHE IS ALMOST LIKE A TWIN, WOULDN'T YOU SAY?
!
THIS ORPHAN SHOULD BE MS. YURA'S YORIMASHI.

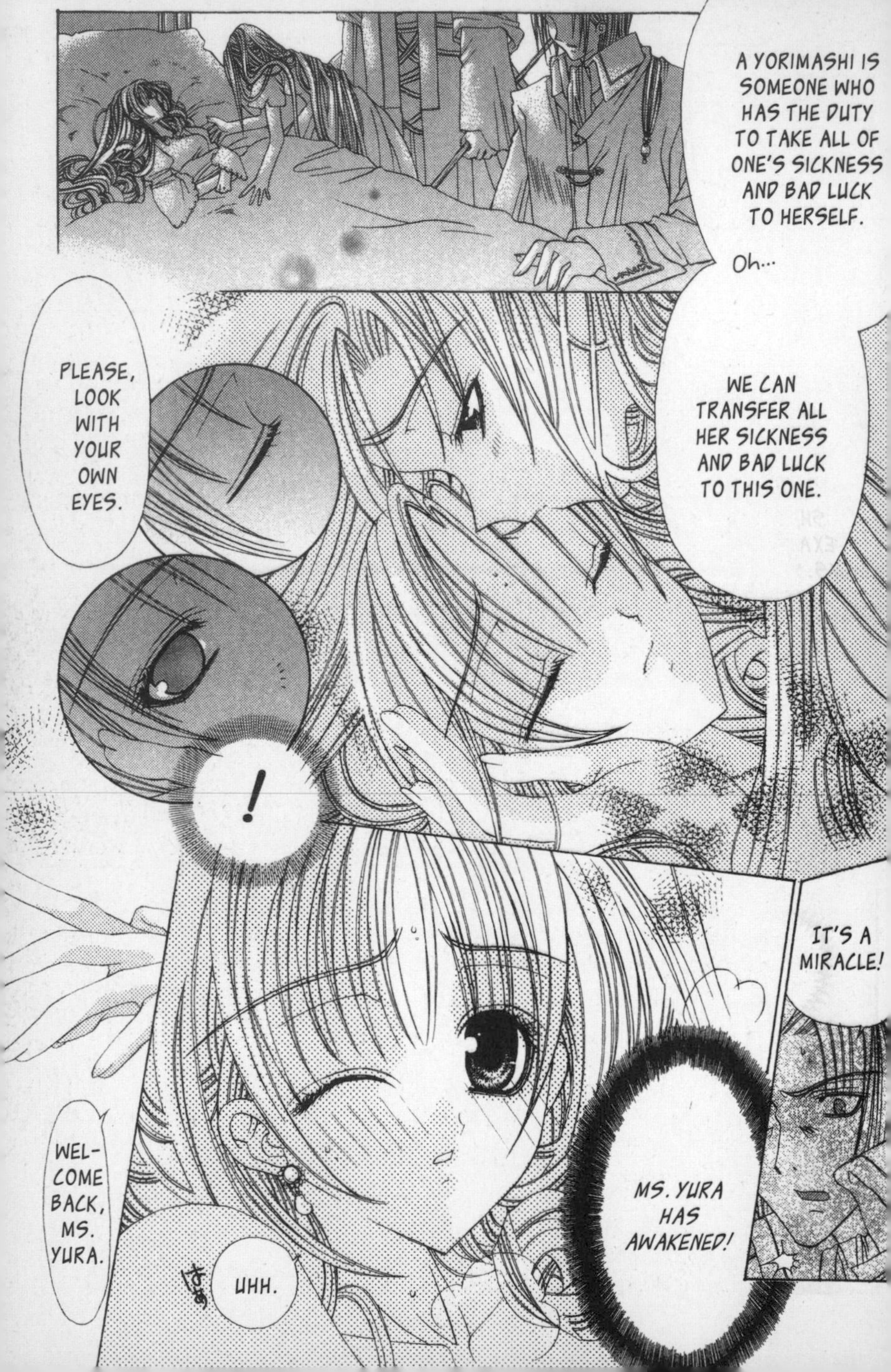
A YORIMASHI IS SOMEONE WHO HAS THE DUTY TO TAKE ALL OF ONE'S SICKNESS AND BAD LUCK TO HERSELF.
Oh...
WE CAN TRANSFER ALL HER SICKNESS AND BAD LUCK TO THIS ONE.
PLEASE, LOOK WITH YOUR OWN EYES.
!
IT'S A MIRACLE!
MS. YURA HAS AWAKENED!
UHH.
WEL-COME BACK, MS. YURA.

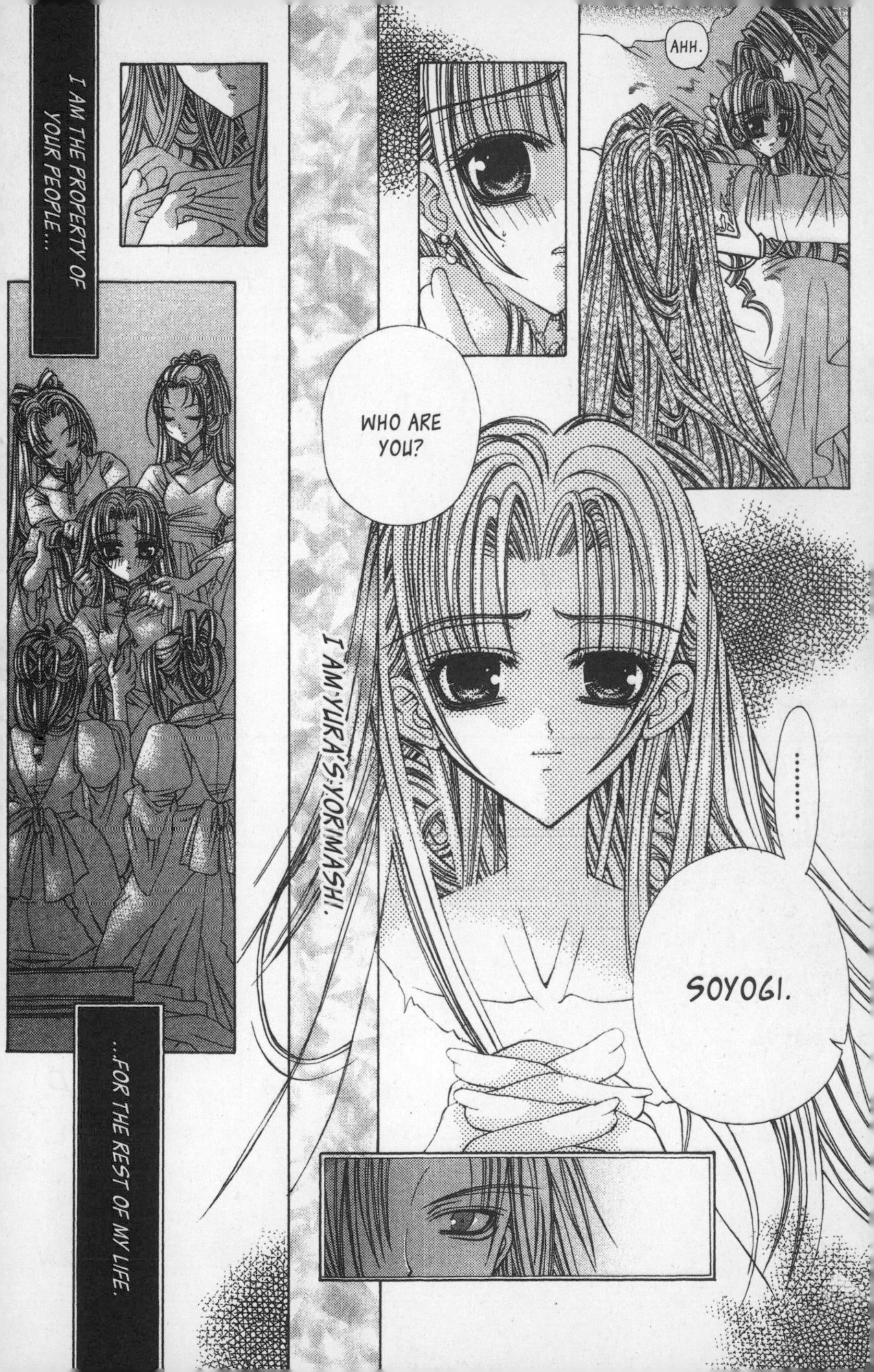
AHH.
WHO ARE YOU?
......
SOYOGI.
I AM YURA'S YORIMASHI.
I AM THE PROPERTY OF YOUR PEOPLE...
...FOR THE REST OF MY LIFE.

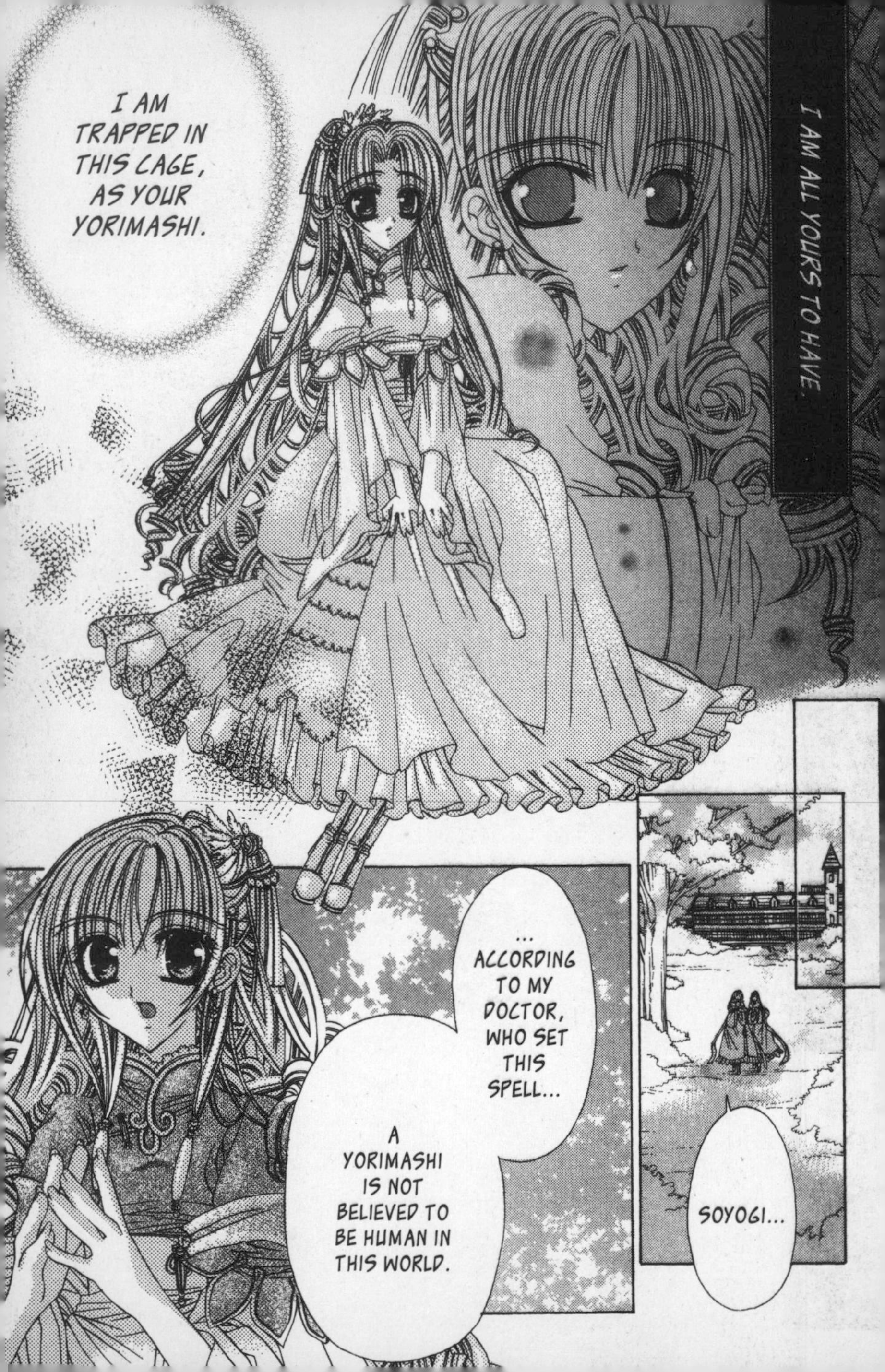
I AM ALL YOURS TO HAVE.
I AM TRAPPED IN THIS CAGE, AS YOUR YORIMASHI.
SOYOGI...
...ACCORDING TO MY DOCTOR, WHO SET THIS SPELL...
A YORIMASHI IS NOT BELIEVED TO BE HUMAN IN THIS WORLD.

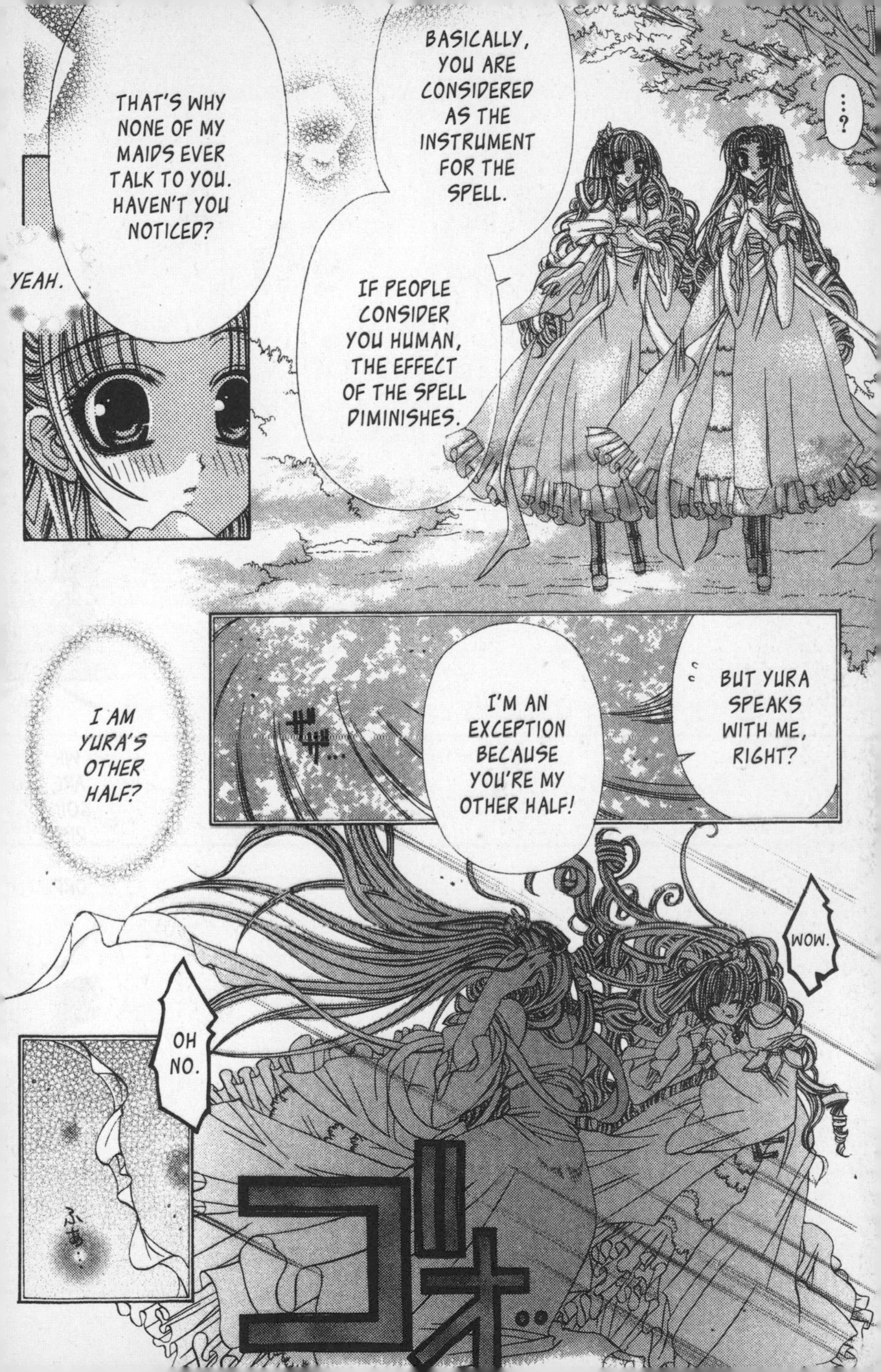
…?
BASICALLY, YOU ARE CONSIDERED AS THE INSTRUMENT FOR THE SPELL.
IF PEOPLE CONSIDER YOU HUMAN, THE EFFECT OF THE SPELL DIMINISHES.
THAT'S WHY NONE OF MY MAIDS EVER TALK TO YOU. HAVEN'T YOU NOTICED?
YEAH.
BUT YURA SPEAKS WITH ME, RIGHT?
I'M AN EXCEPTION BECAUSE YOU'RE MY OTHER HALF!
I AM YURA'S OTHER HALF?
WOW.
OH NO.

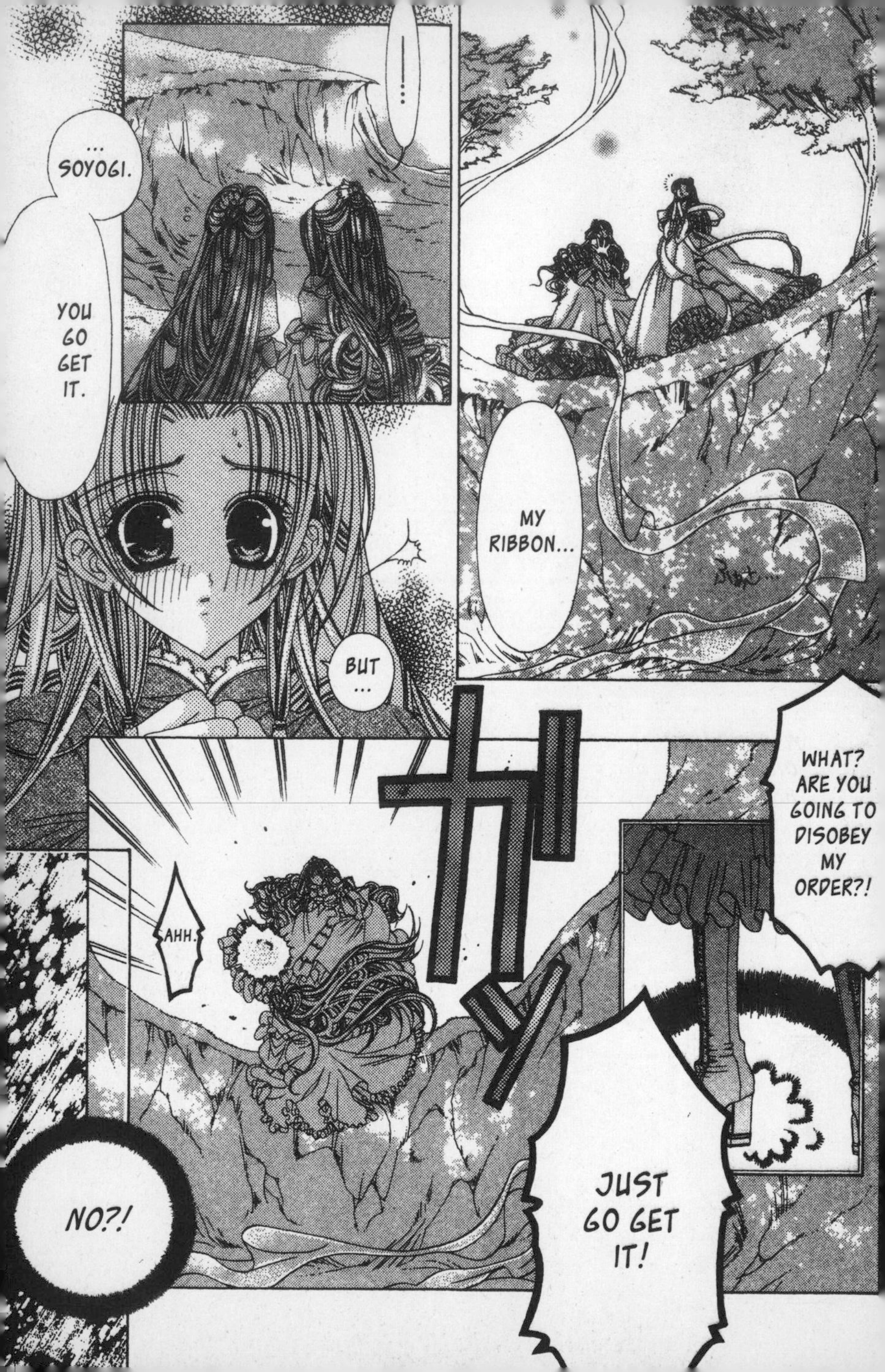
MY RIBBON...
!...
... SOYOGI.
YOU GO GET IT.
BUT ...
WHAT? ARE YOU GOING TO DISOBEY MY ORDER?!
ガッ
AHH.
JUST GO GET IT!
NO?!

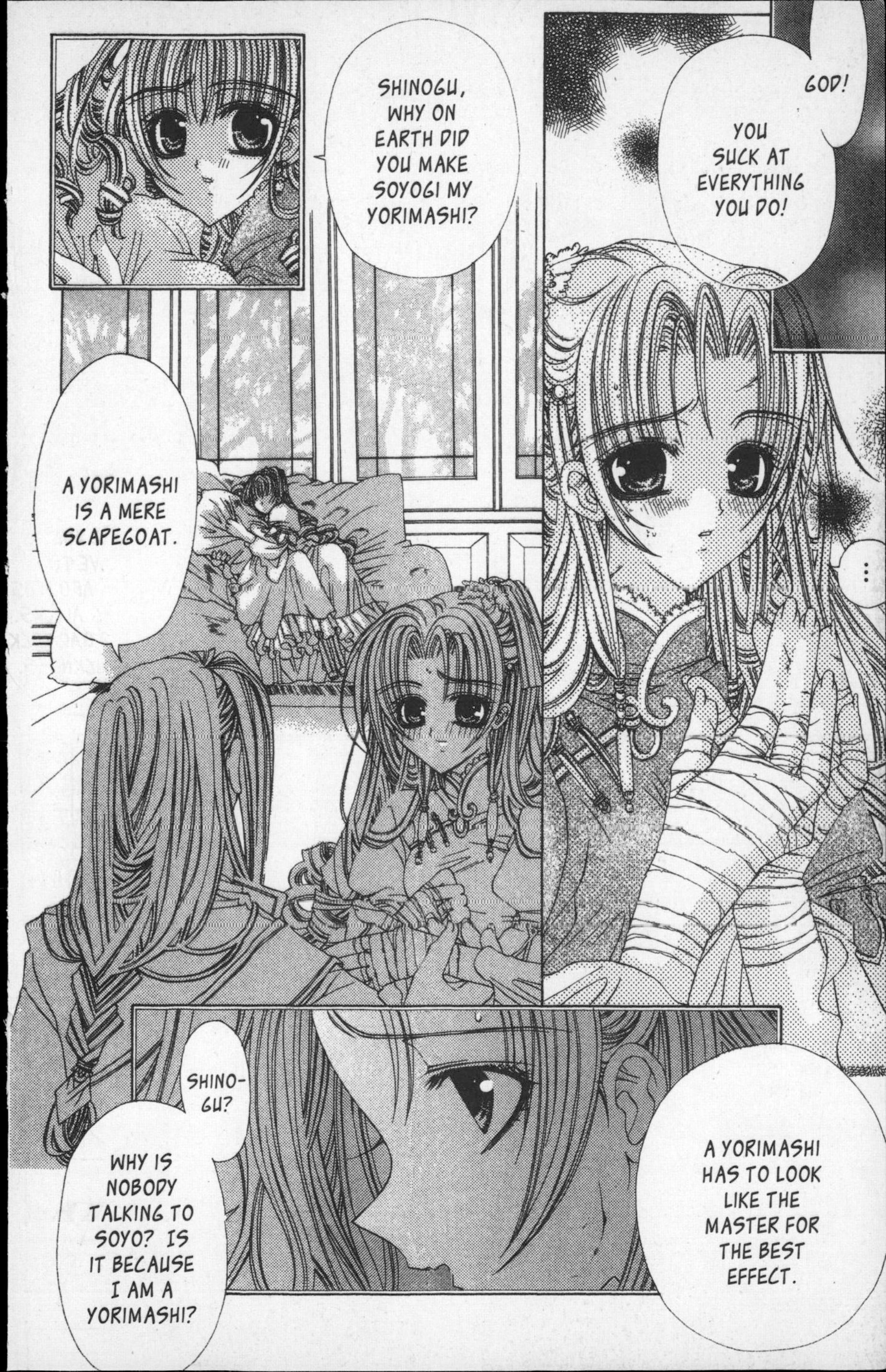
GOD!
YOU SUCK AT EVERYTHING YOU DO!
...
SHINOGU, WHY ON EARTH DID YOU MAKE SOYOGI MY YORIMASHI?
A YORIMASHI IS A MERE SCAPEGOAT.
A YORIMASHI HAS TO LOOK LIKE THE MASTER FOR THE BEST EFFECT.
SHINO-GU?
WHY IS NOBODY TALKING TO SOYO? IS IT BECAUSE I AM A YORIMASHI?

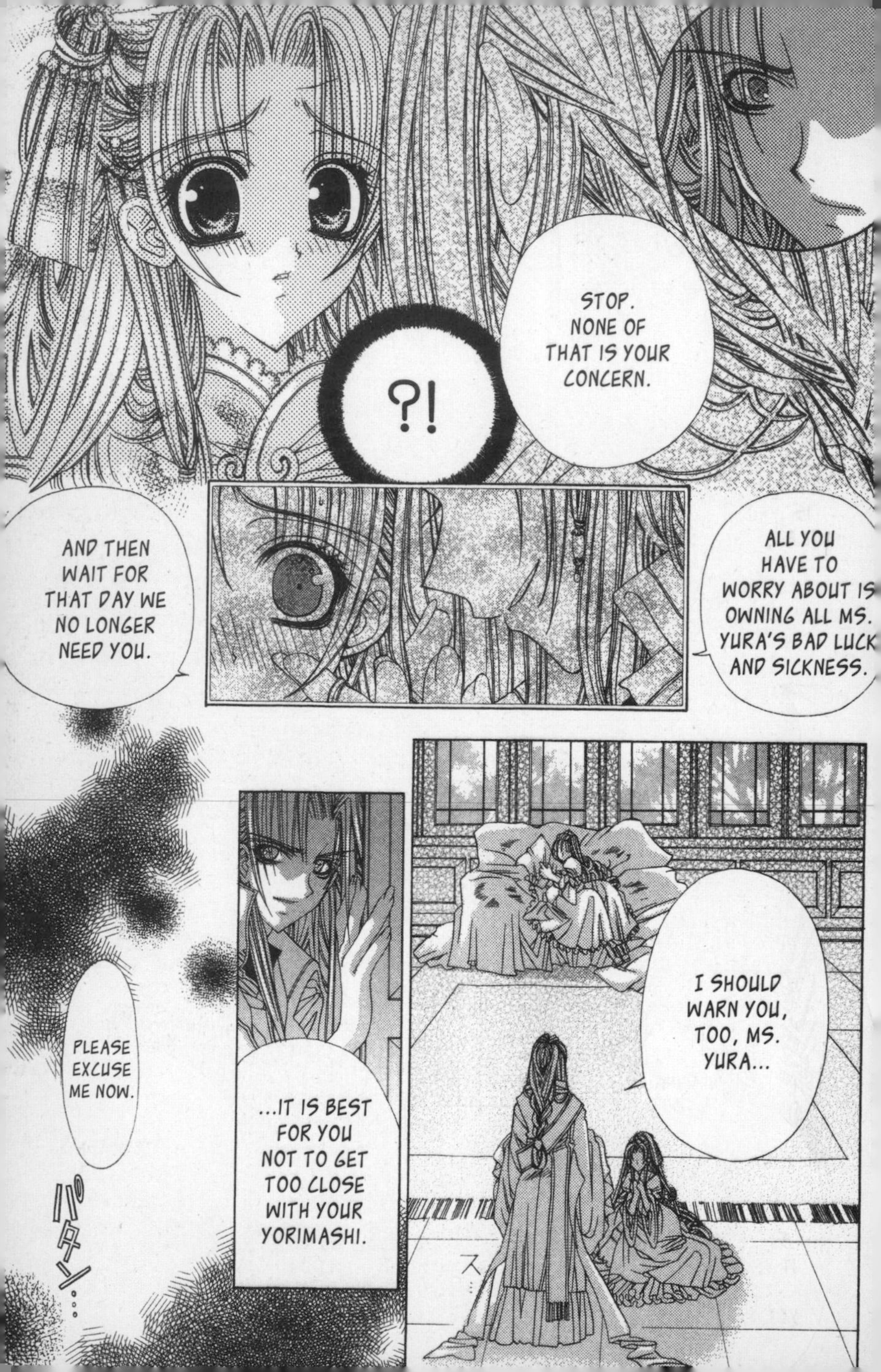
STOP. NONE OF THAT IS YOUR CONCERN.
?!
ALL YOU HAVE TO WORRY ABOUT IS OWNING ALL MS. YURA'S BAD LUCK AND SICKNESS.
AND THEN WAIT FOR THAT DAY WE NO LONGER NEED YOU.
I SHOULD WARN YOU, TOO, MS. YURA...
ス…
...IT IS BEST FOR YOU NOT TO GET TOO CLOSE WITH YOUR YORIMASHI.
PLEASE EXCUSE ME NOW.
パタン…

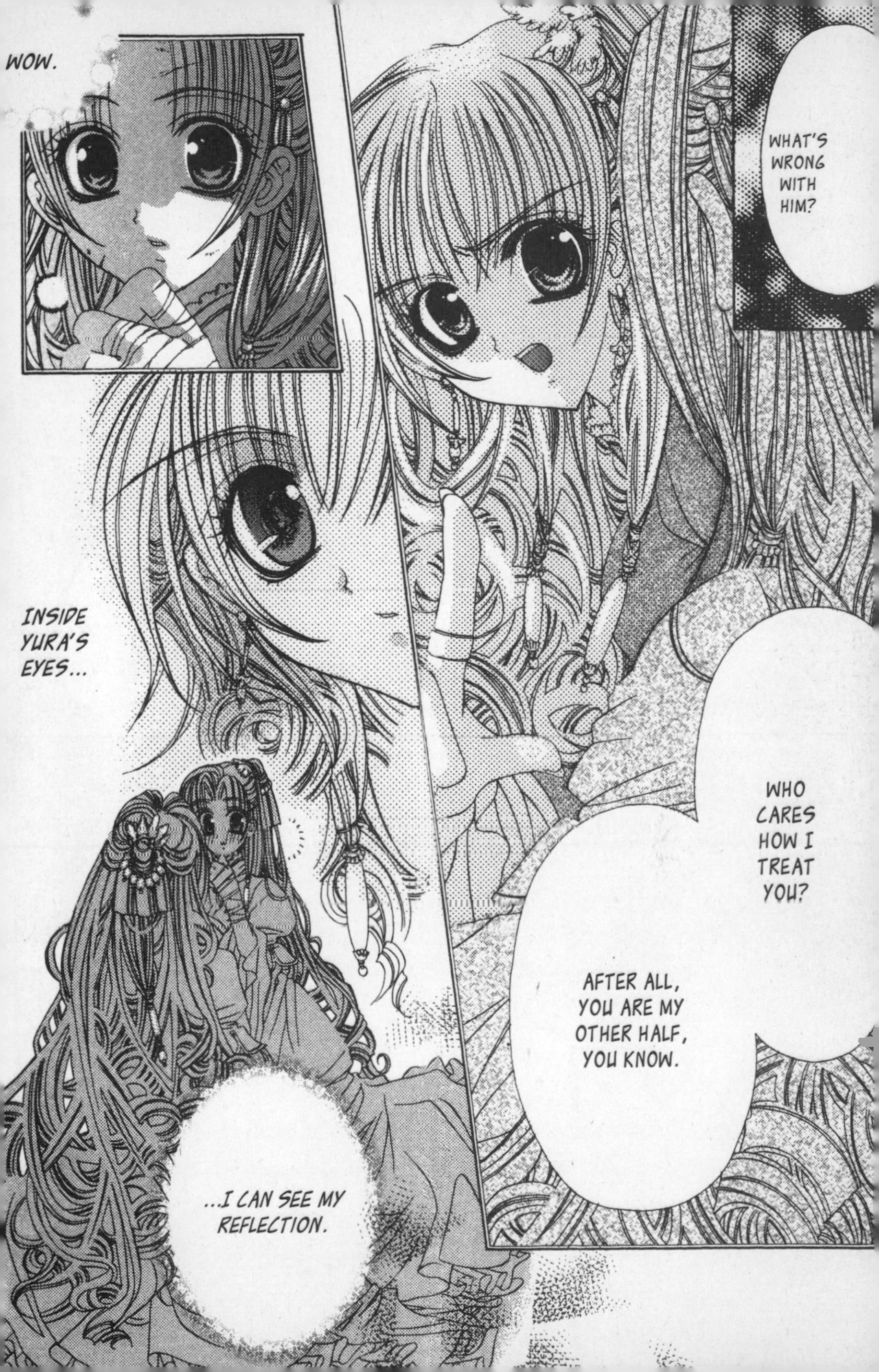
WHAT'S WRONG WITH HIM?
WOW.
WHO CARES HOW I TREAT YOU?
AFTER ALL, YOU ARE MY OTHER HALF, YOU KNOW.
INSIDE YURA'S EYES...
...I CAN SEE MY REFLECTION.

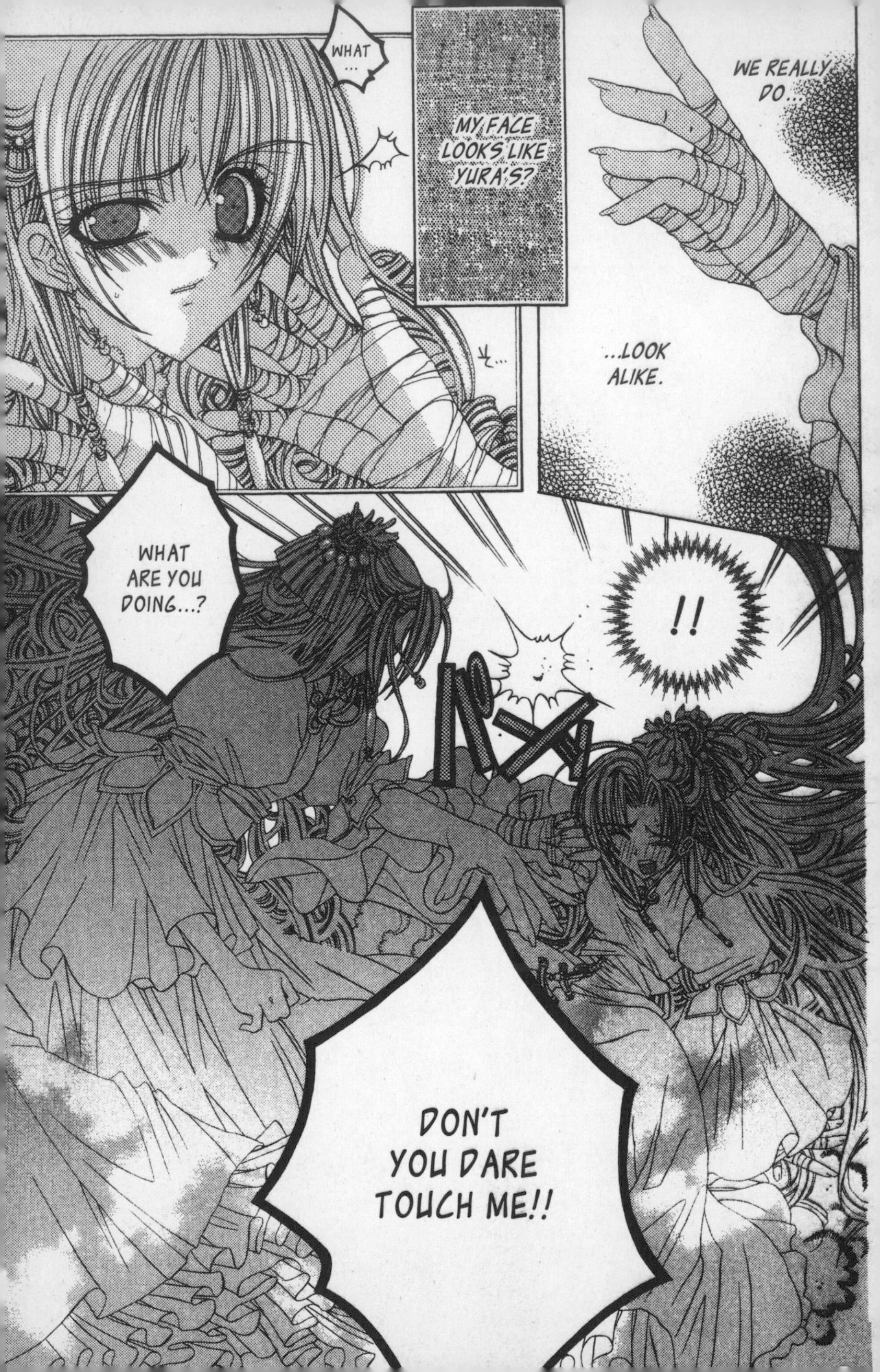
WE REALLY DO...
...LOOK ALIKE.
WHAT ...
MY FACE LOOKS LIKE YURA'S?
!!
WHAT ARE YOU DOING...?
DON'T YOU DARE TOUCH ME!!

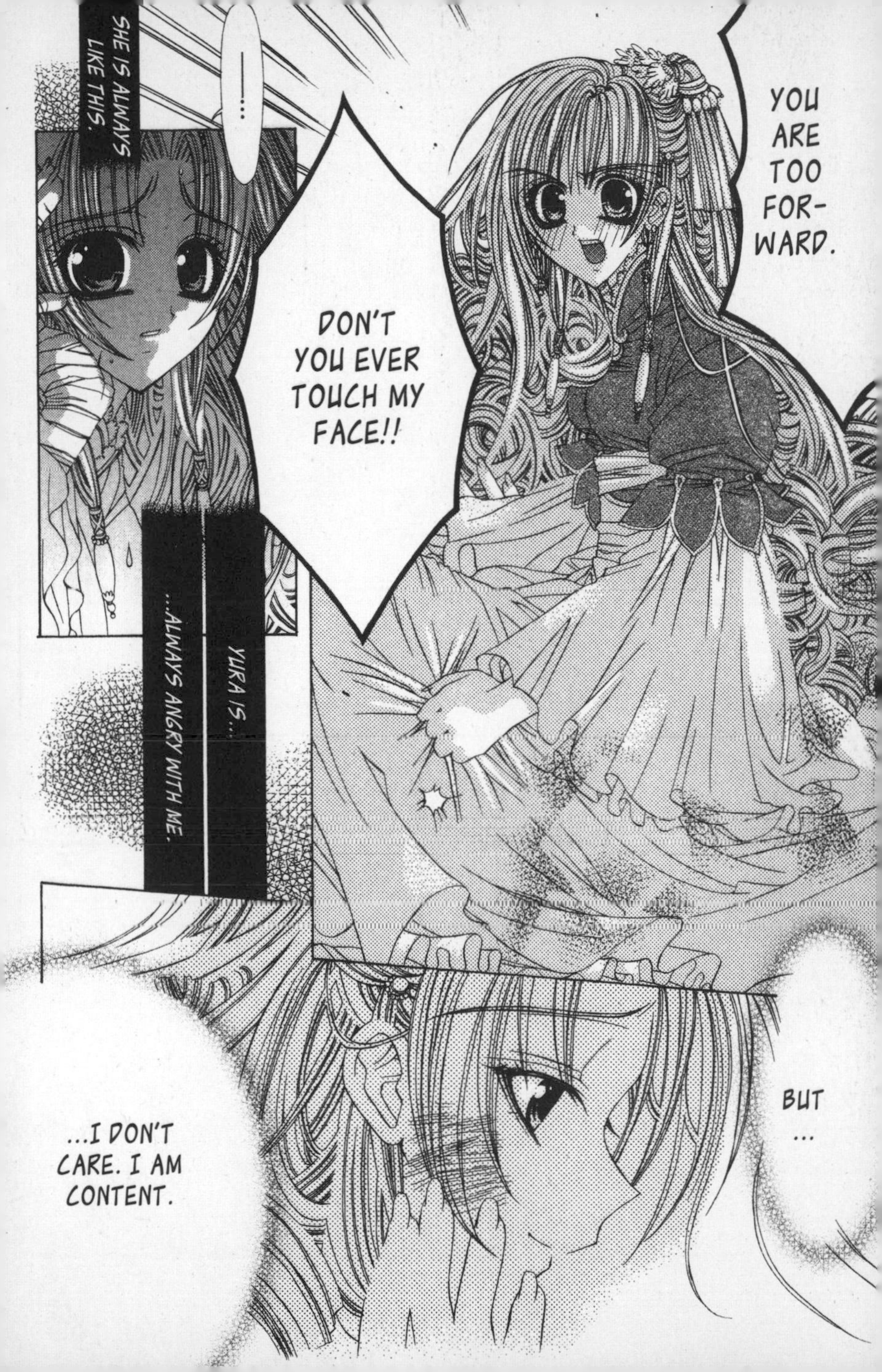
YOU ARE TOO FOR-WARD.
DON'T YOU EVER TOUCH MY FACE!!
—...
SHE IS ALWAYS LIKE THIS.
YURA IS...
...ALWAYS ANGRY WITH ME.
BUT...
...I DON'T CARE. I AM CONTENT.

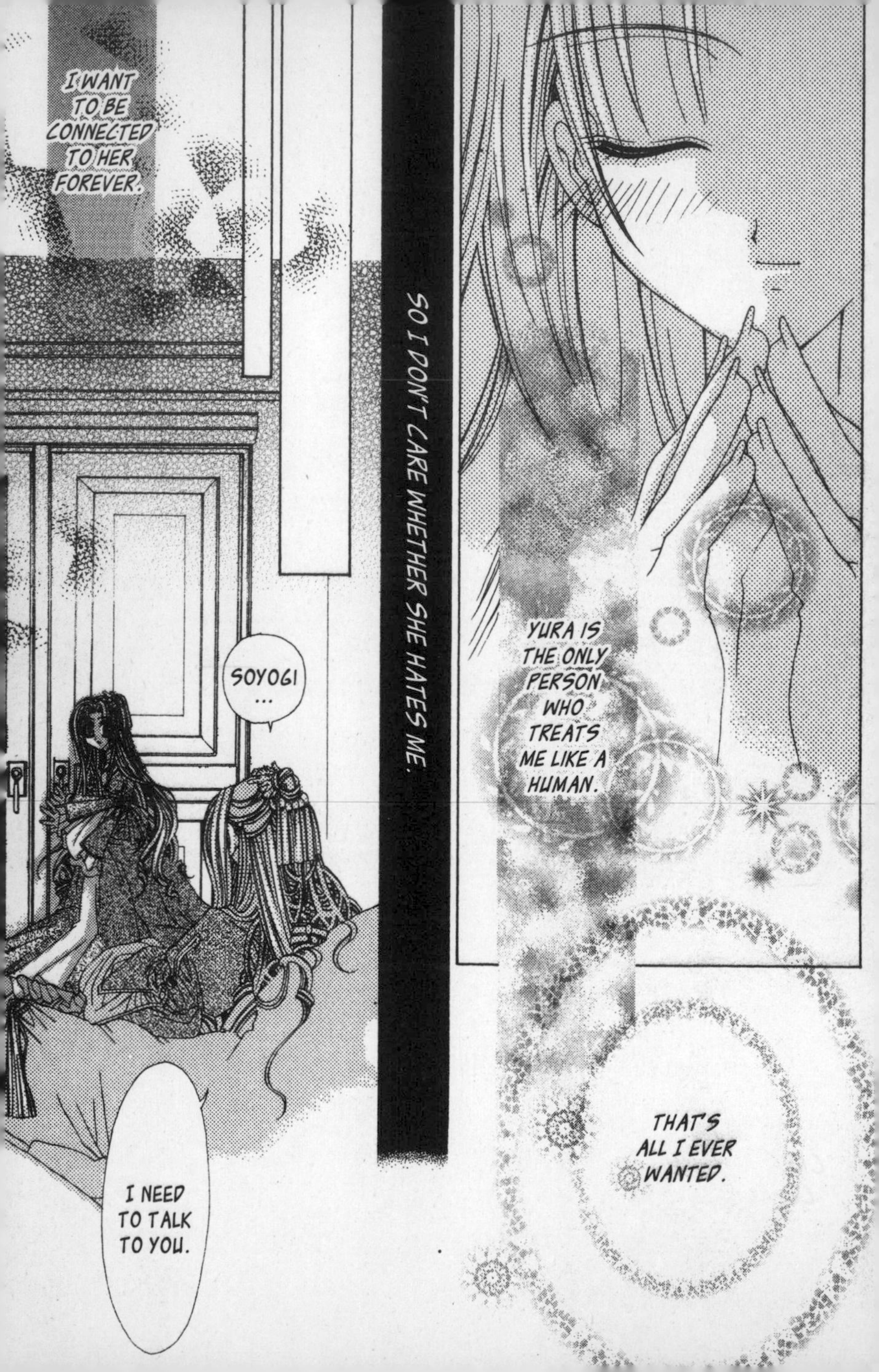
YURA IS THE ONLY PERSON WHO TREATS ME LIKE A HUMAN.
THAT'S ALL I EVER WANTED.
SO I DON'T CARE WHETHER SHE HATES ME.
I WANT TO BE CONNECTED TO HER FOREVER.
SOYOGI ...
I NEED TO TALK TO YOU.

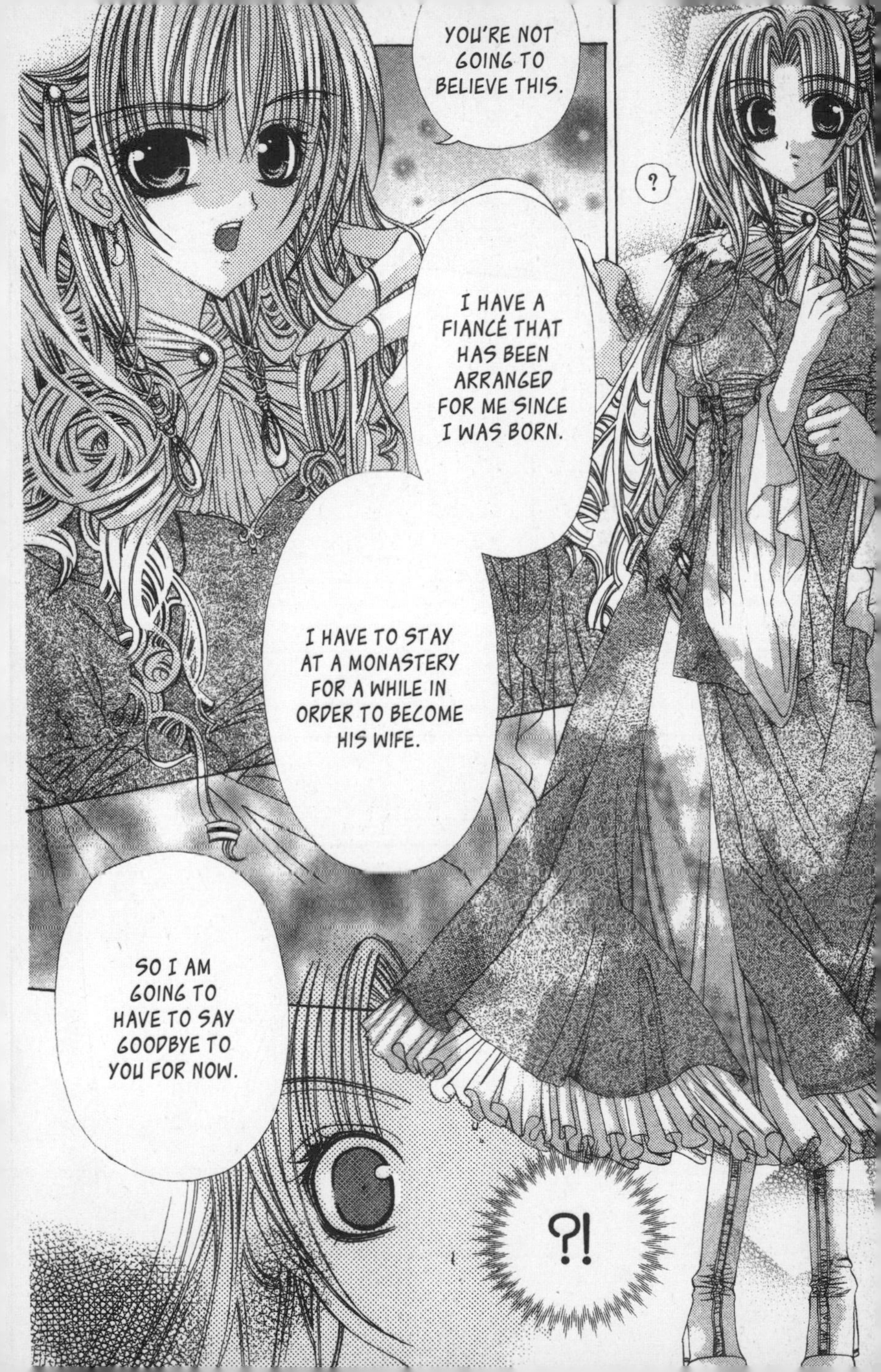
?
YOU'RE NOT GOING TO BELIEVE THIS.
I HAVE A FIANCÉ THAT HAS BEEN ARRANGED FOR ME SINCE I WAS BORN.
I HAVE TO STAY AT A MONASTERY FOR A WHILE IN ORDER TO BECOME HIS WIFE.
SO I AM GOING TO HAVE TO SAY GOODBYE TO YOU FOR NOW.
?!

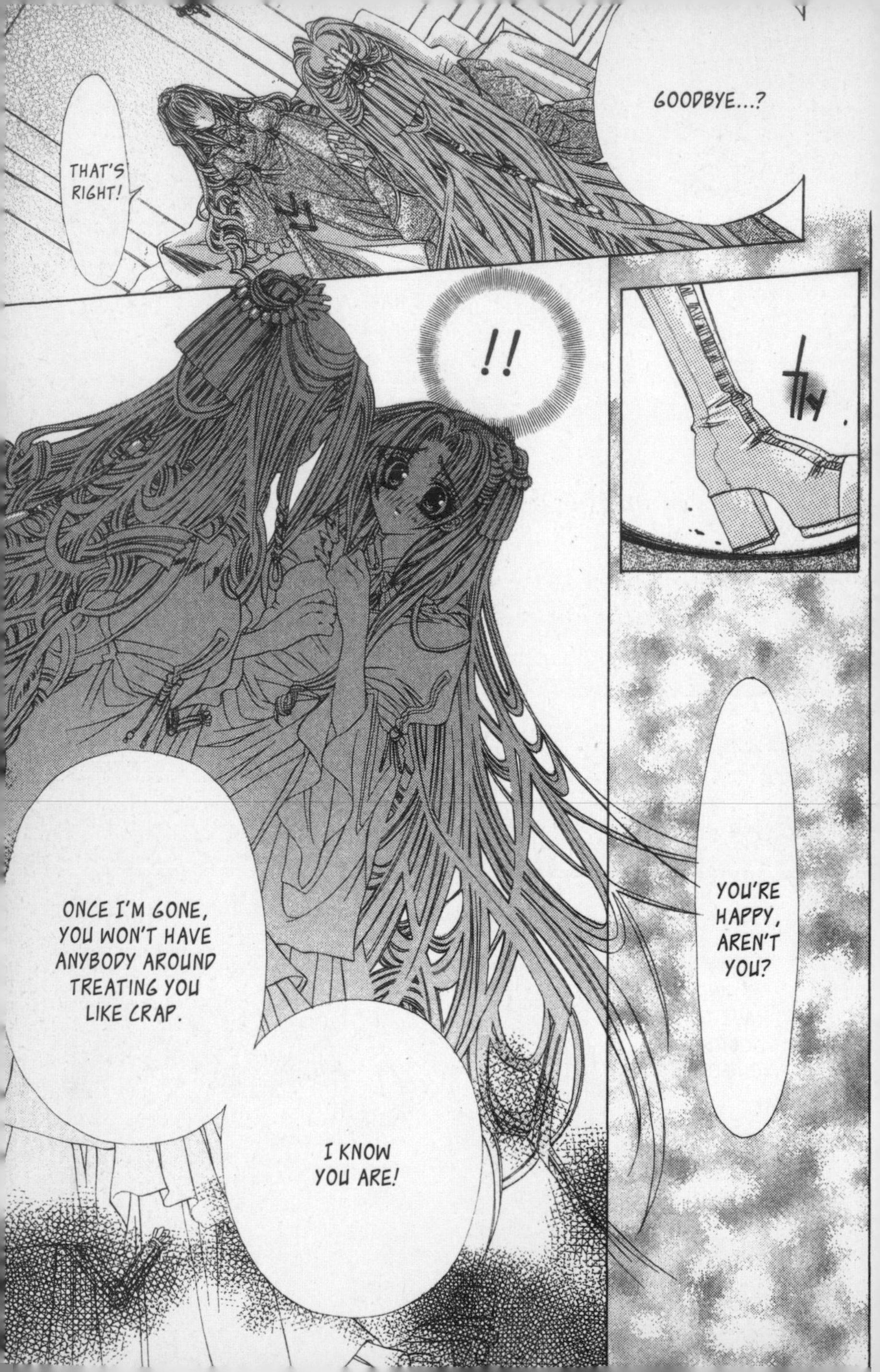
GOODBYE...?
THAT'S RIGHT!
!!
YOU'RE HAPPY, AREN'T YOU?
ONCE I'M GONE, YOU WON'T HAVE ANYBODY AROUND TREATING YOU LIKE CRAP.
I KNOW YOU ARE!

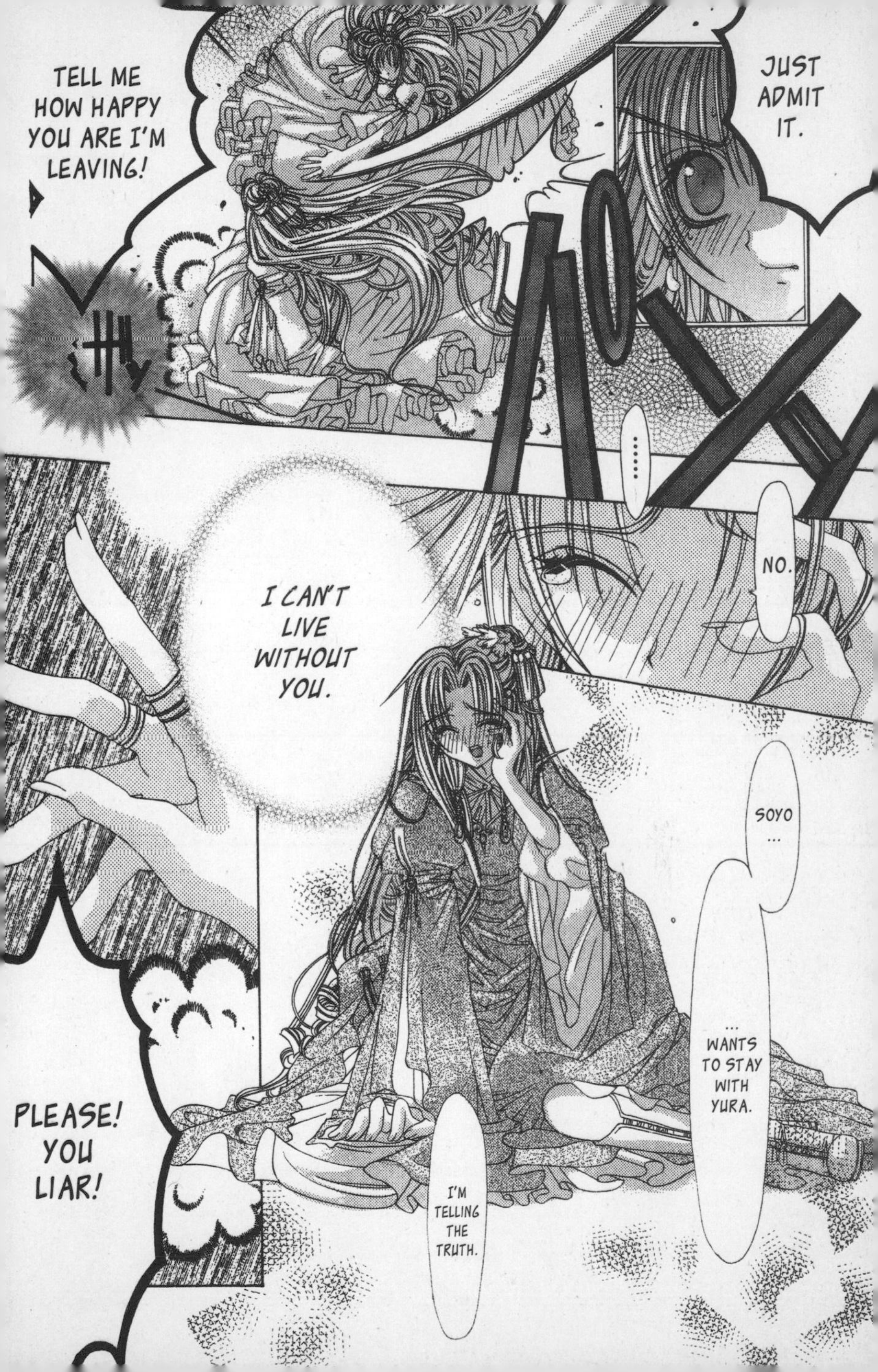
JUST ADMIT IT.
TELL ME HOW HAPPY YOU ARE I'M LEAVING!
......
NO.
SOYO ...
... WANTS TO STAY WITH YURA.
I'M TELLING THE TRUTH.
I CAN'T LIVE WITHOUT YOU.
PLEASE! YOU LIAR!

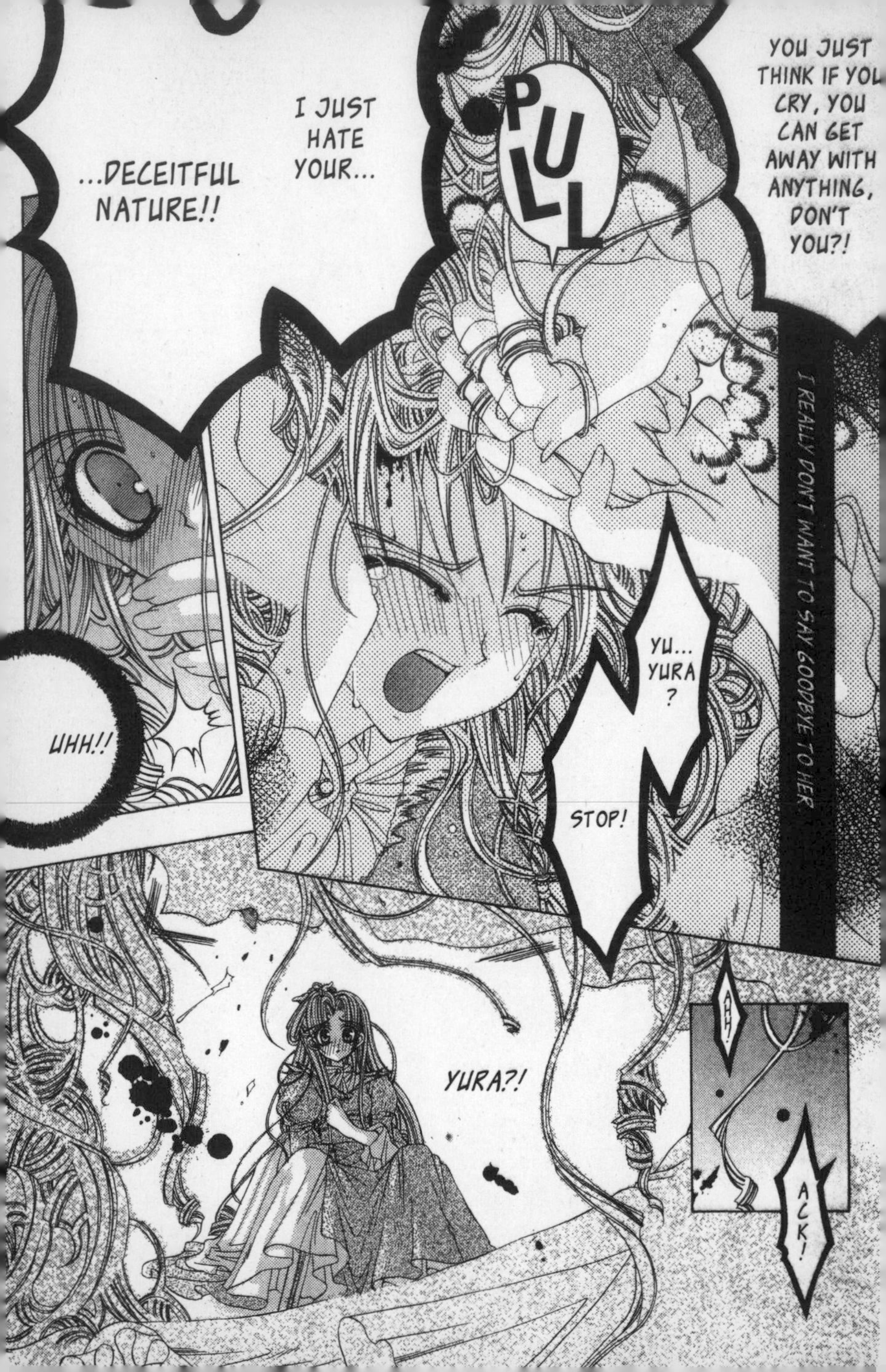
YOU JUST THINK IF YOU CRY, YOU CAN GET AWAY WITH ANYTHING, DON'T YOU?!
PULL
I JUST HATE YOUR...
...DECEITFUL NATURE!!
I REALLY DON'T WANT TO SAY GOODBYE TO HER
YU... YURA?
STOP!
UHH!!
AHH!
ACK!
YURA?!

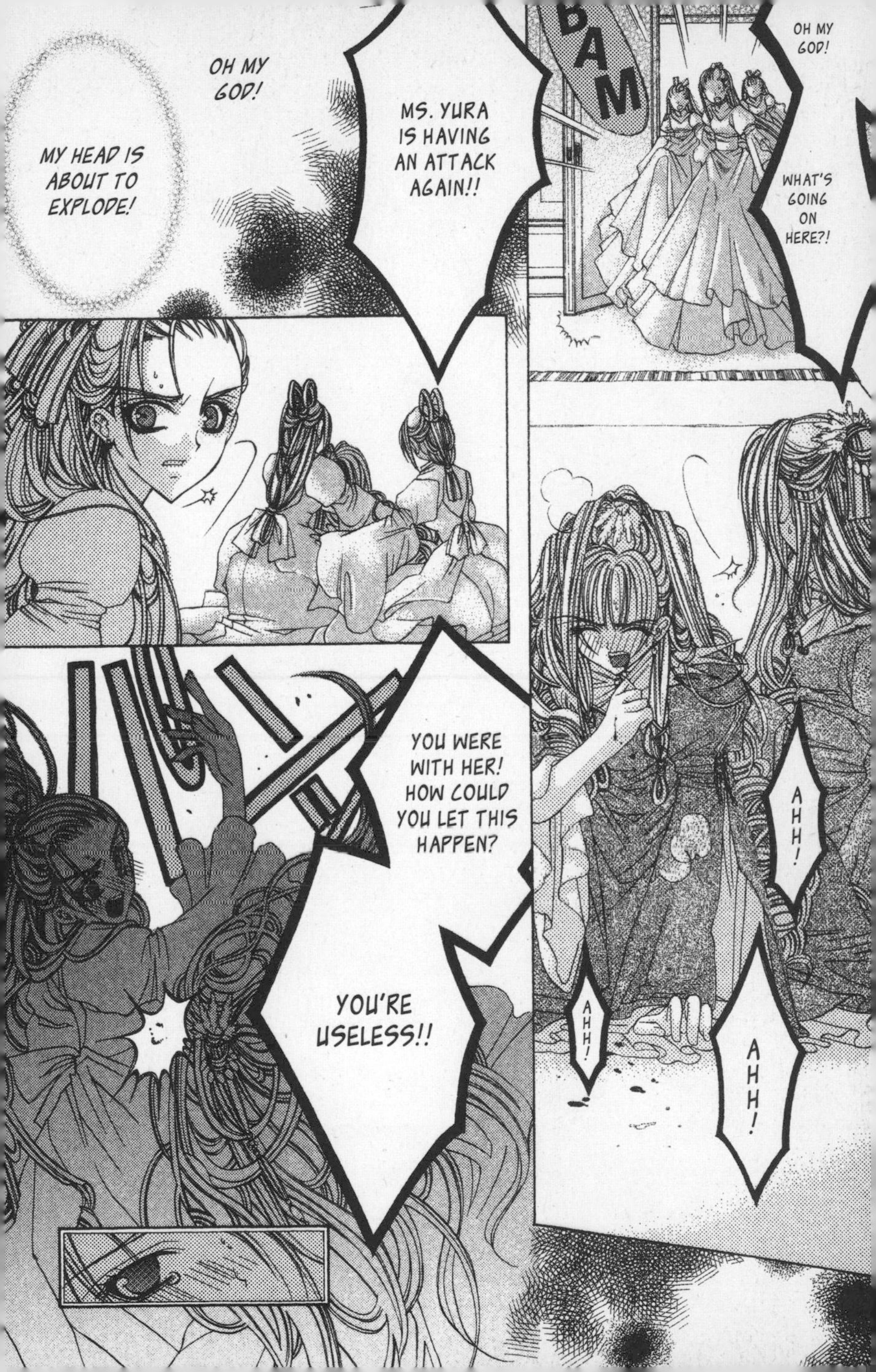
BAM
OH MY GOD!
WHAT'S GOING ON HERE?!
MS. YURA IS HAVING AN ATTACK AGAIN!!
OH MY GOD!
MY HEAD IS ABOUT TO EXPLODE!
AHH!
AHH!
AHH!
YOU WERE WITH HER! HOW COULD YOU LET THIS HAPPEN?
YOU'RE USELESS!!

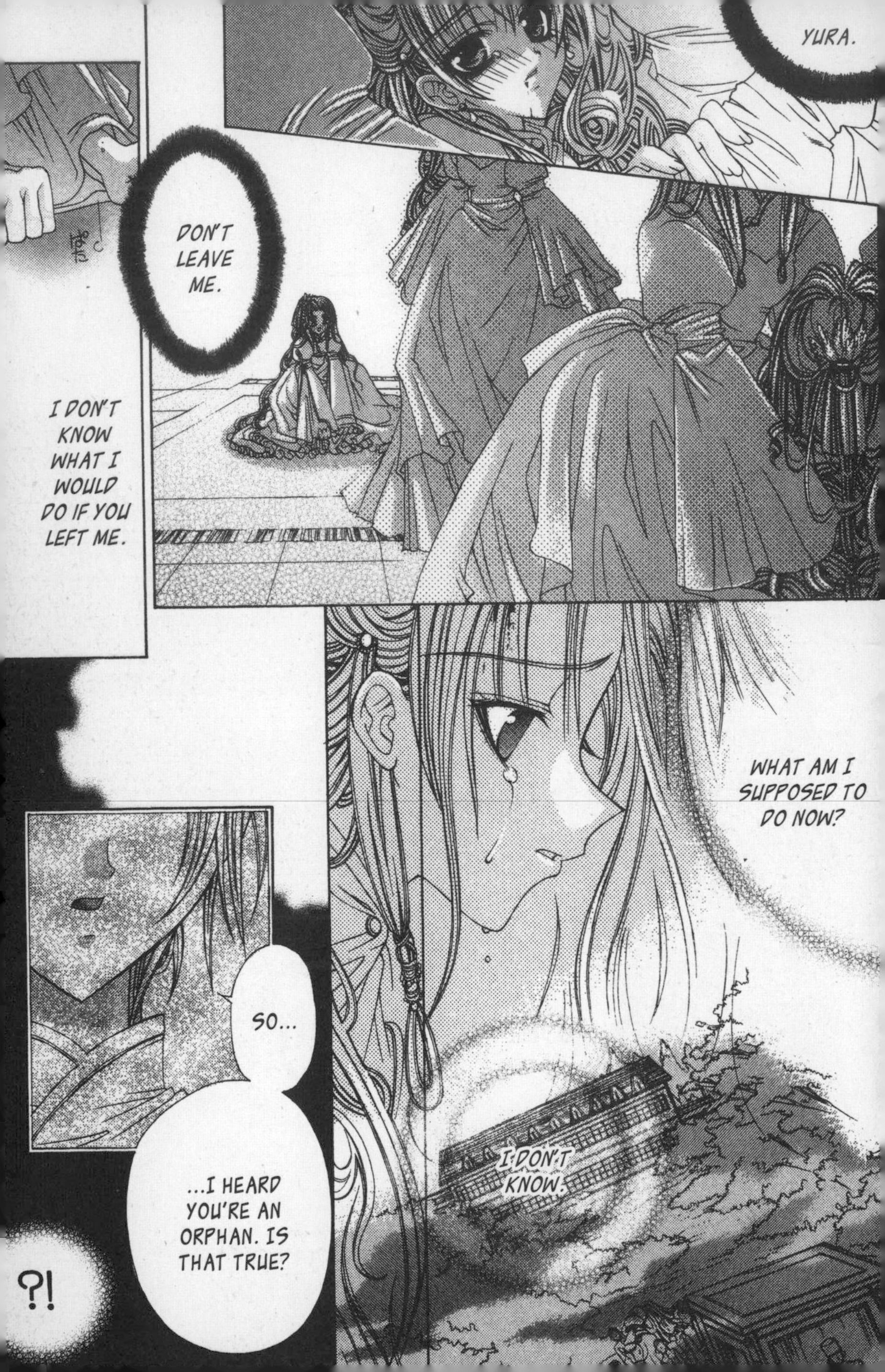
YURA.
DON'T LEAVE ME.
I DON'T KNOW WHAT I WOULD DO IF YOU LEFT ME.
WHAT AM I SUPPOSED TO DO NOW?
I DON'T KNOW.
SO...
...I HEARD YOU'RE AN ORPHAN. IS THAT TRUE?
?!

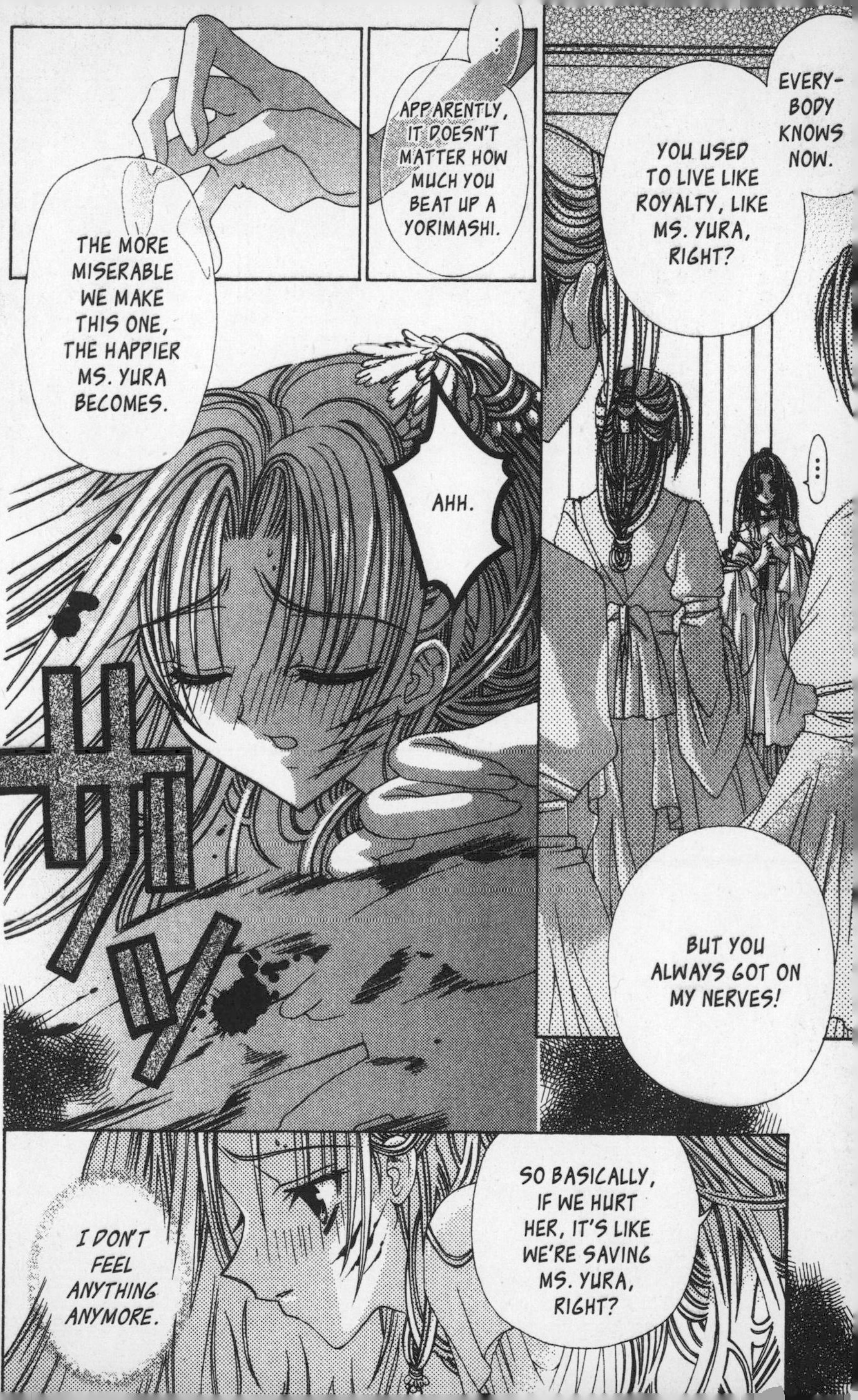
EVERYBODY KNOWS NOW.
YOU USED TO LIVE LIKE ROYALTY, LIKE MS. YURA, RIGHT?
...
BUT YOU ALWAYS GOT ON MY NERVES!
...
APPARENTLY, IT DOESN'T MATTER HOW MUCH YOU BEAT UP A YORIMASHI.
THE MORE MISERABLE WE MAKE THIS ONE, THE HAPPIER MS. YURA BECOMES.
AHH.
ザッ
SO BASICALLY, IF WE HURT HER, IT'S LIKE WE'RE SAVING MS. YURA, RIGHT?
I DON'T FEEL ANYTHING ANYMORE.

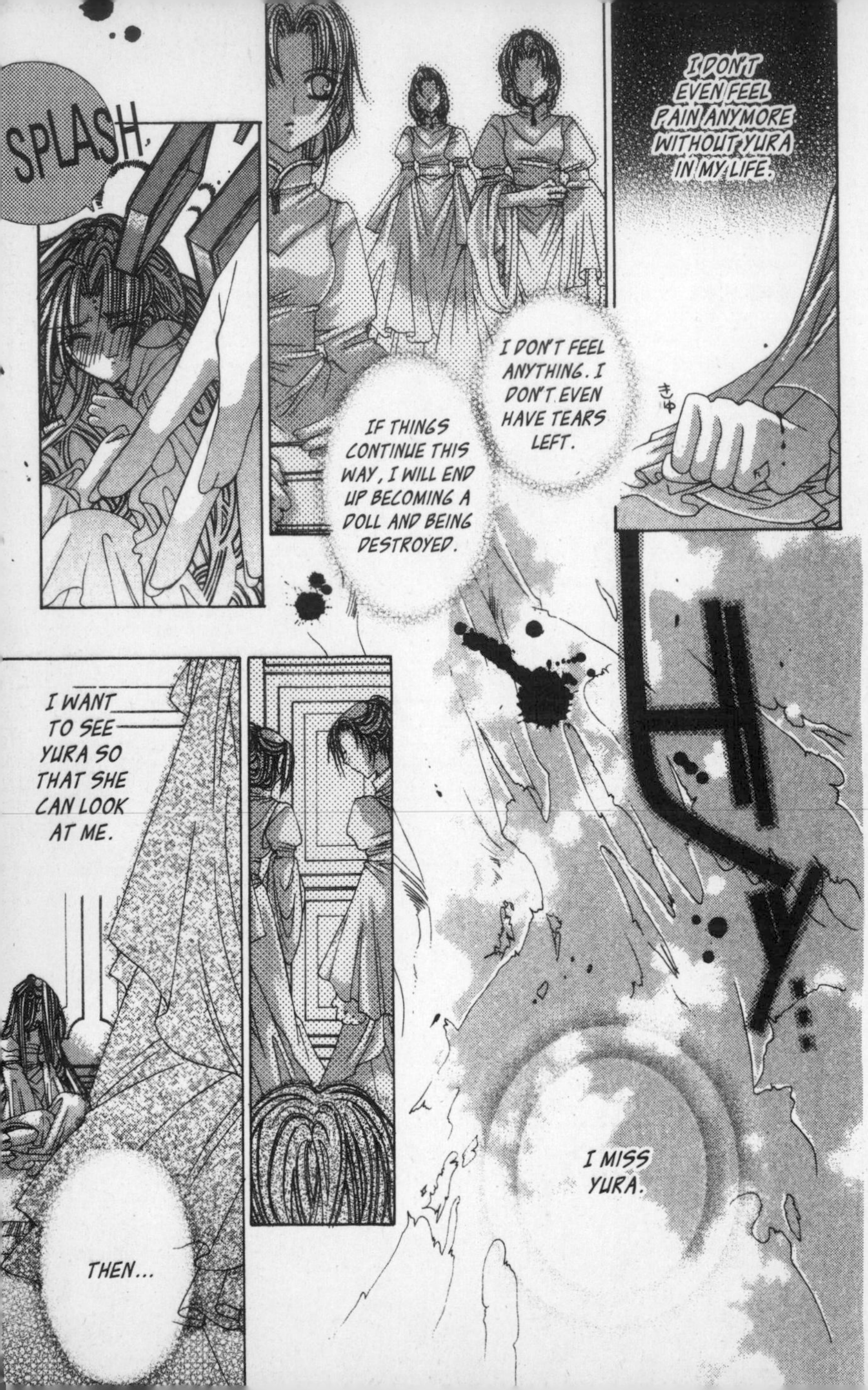
I DON'T EVEN FEEL PAIN ANYMORE WITHOUT YURA IN MY LIFE.
きゅ
I DON'T FEEL ANYTHING. I DON'T EVEN HAVE TEARS LEFT.
IF THINGS CONTINUE THIS WAY, I WILL END UP BECOMING A DOLL AND BEING DESTROYED.
SPLASH
I MISS YURA.
I WANT TO SEE YURA SO THAT SHE CAN LOOK AT ME.
THEN...

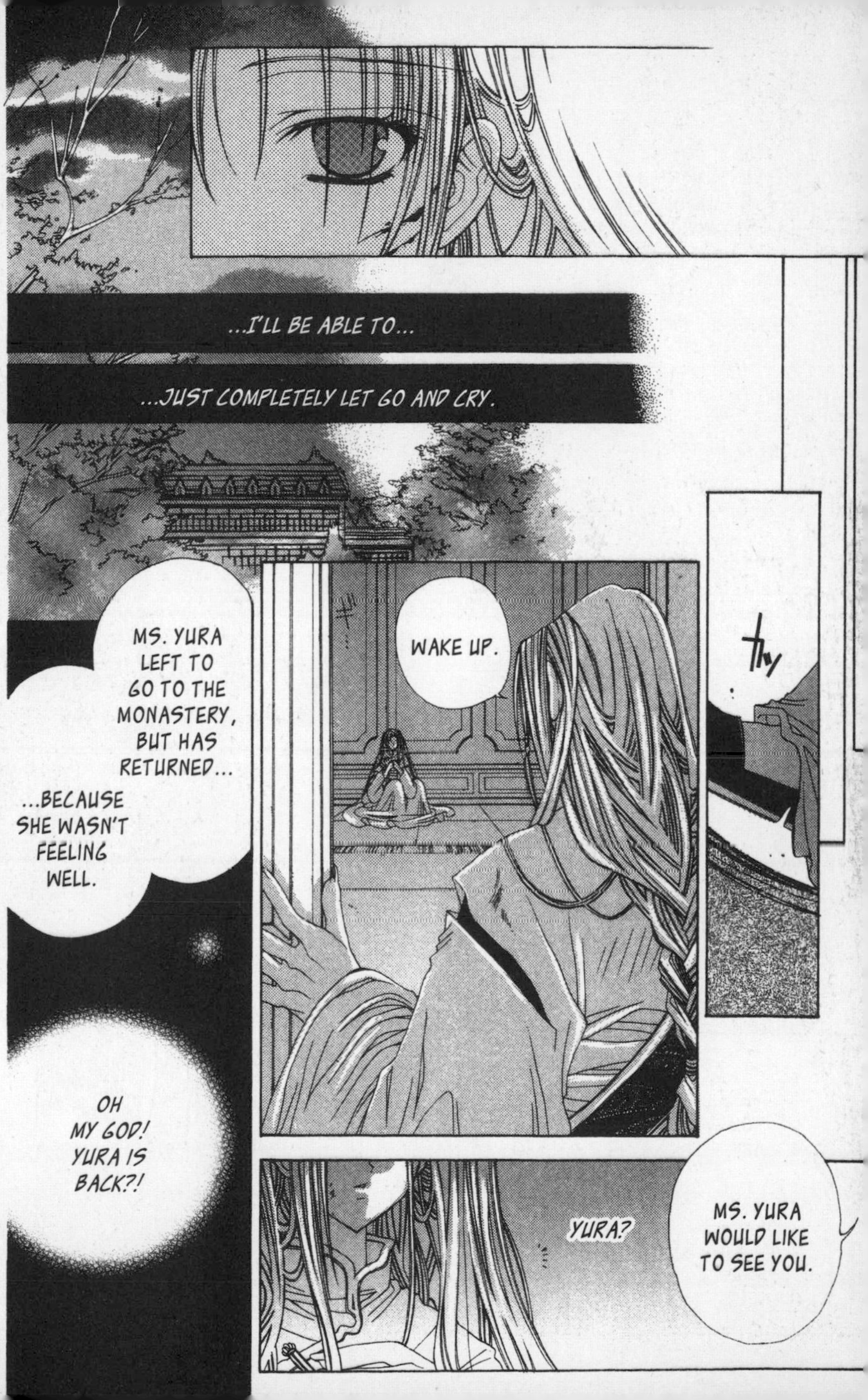
...I'LL BE ABLE TO...
...JUST COMPLETELY LET GO AND CRY.
WAKE UP.
MS. YURA WOULD LIKE TO SEE YOU.
YURA?
MS. YURA LEFT TO GO TO THE MONASTERY, BUT HAS RETURNED...
...BECAUSE SHE WASN'T FEELING WELL.
OH MY GOD! YURA IS BACK?!

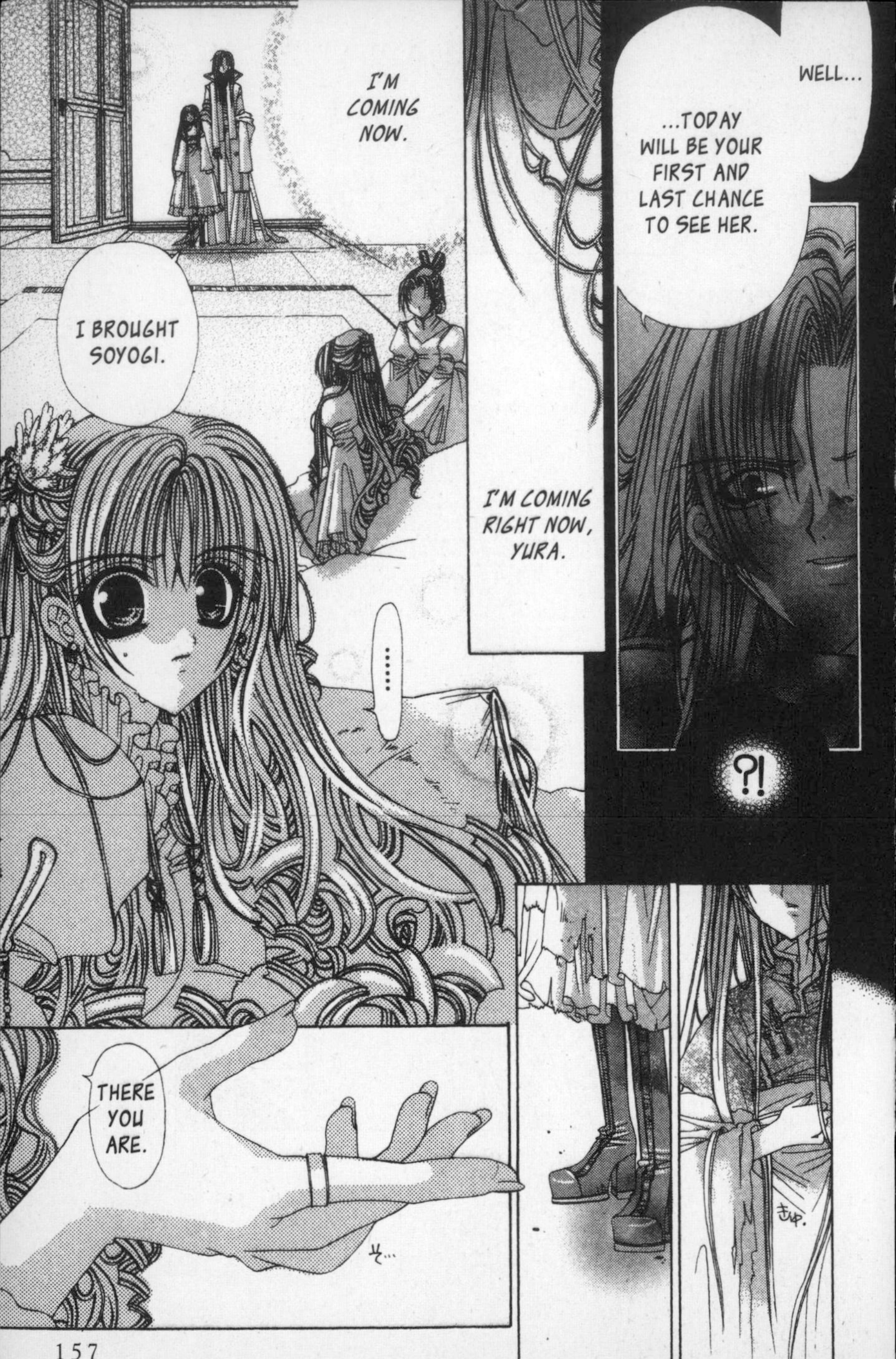
WELL...
...TODAY WILL BE YOUR FIRST AND LAST CHANCE TO SEE HER.
?!
I'M COMING RIGHT NOW, YURA.
I'M COMING NOW.
I BROUGHT SOYOGI.
......
THERE YOU ARE.

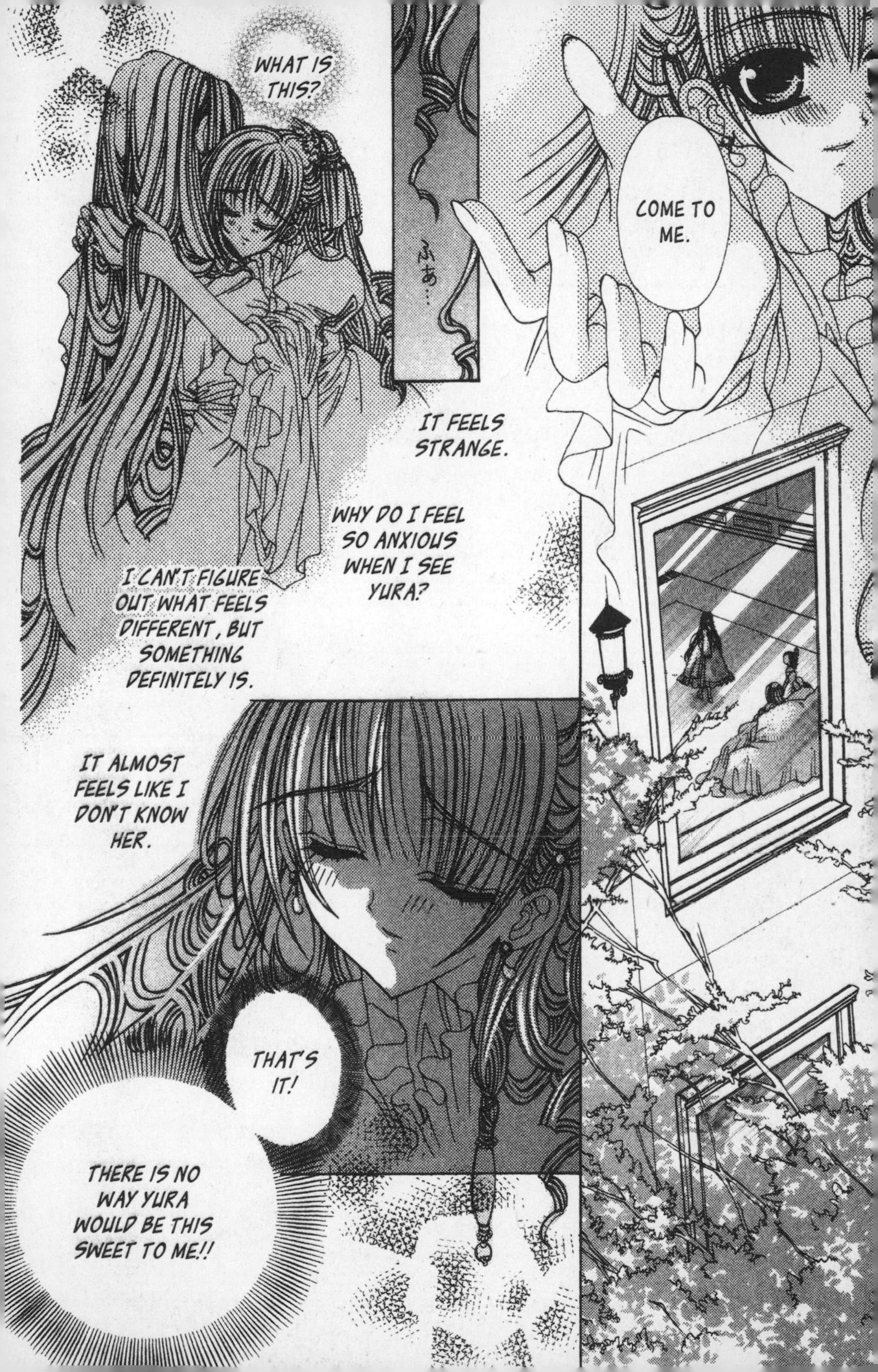
COME TO ME.
ふぁ…
WHAT IS THIS?
IT FEELS STRANGE.
WHY DO I FEEL SO ANXIOUS WHEN I SEE YURA?
I CAN'T FIGURE OUT WHAT FEELS DIFFERENT, BUT SOMETHING DEFINITELY IS.
IT ALMOST FEELS LIKE I DON'T KNOW HER.
THAT'S IT!
THERE IS NO WAY YURA WOULD BE THIS SWEET TO ME!!

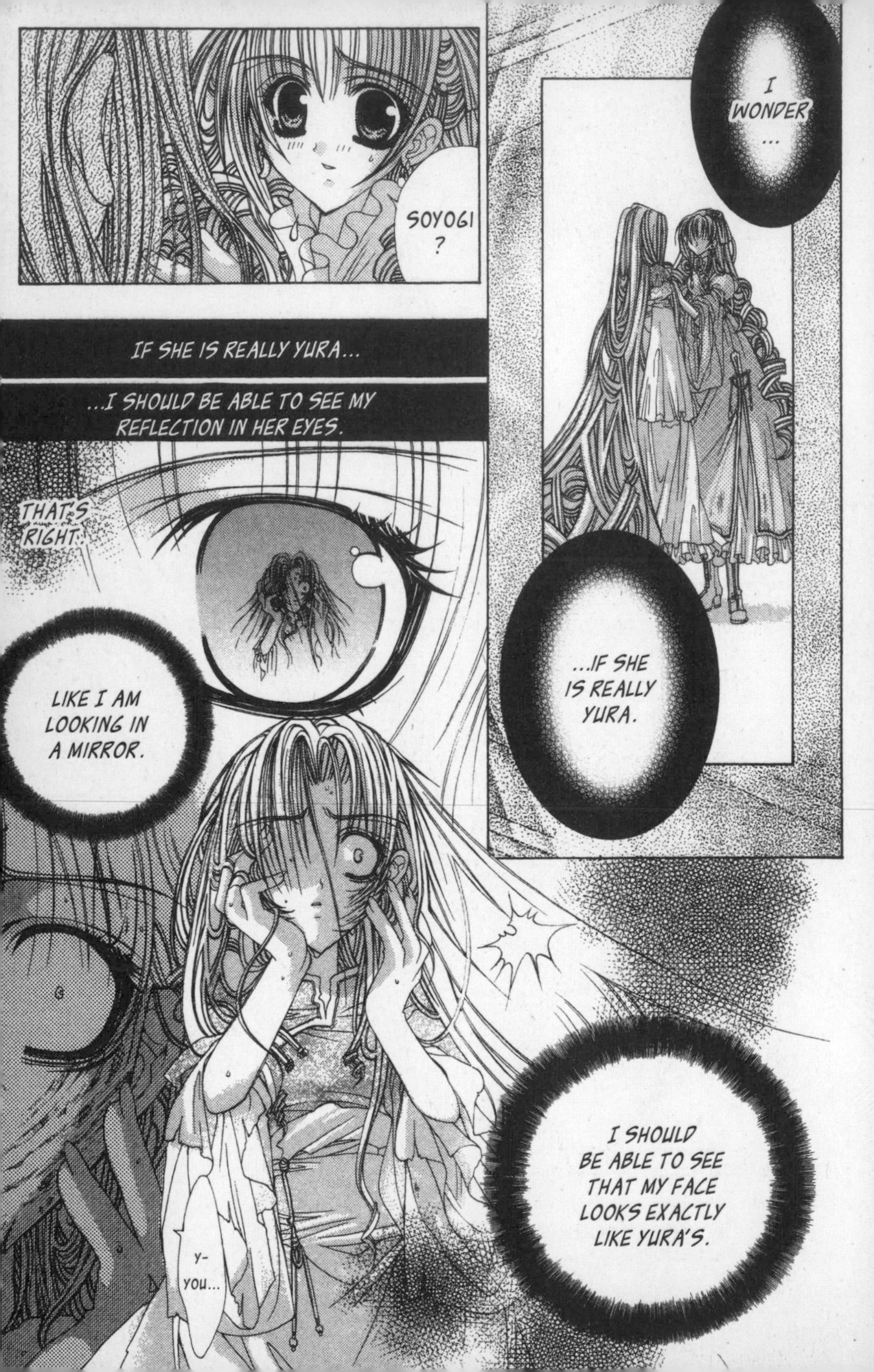

I WONDER ...
...IF SHE IS REALLY YURA.
SOYOGI ?
IF SHE IS REALLY YURA...
...I SHOULD BE ABLE TO SEE MY REFLECTION IN HER EYES.
THAT'S RIGHT.
LIKE I AM LOOKING IN A MIRROR.
I SHOULD BE ABLE TO SEE THAT MY FACE LOOKS EXACTLY LIKE YURA'S.
Y- YOU...

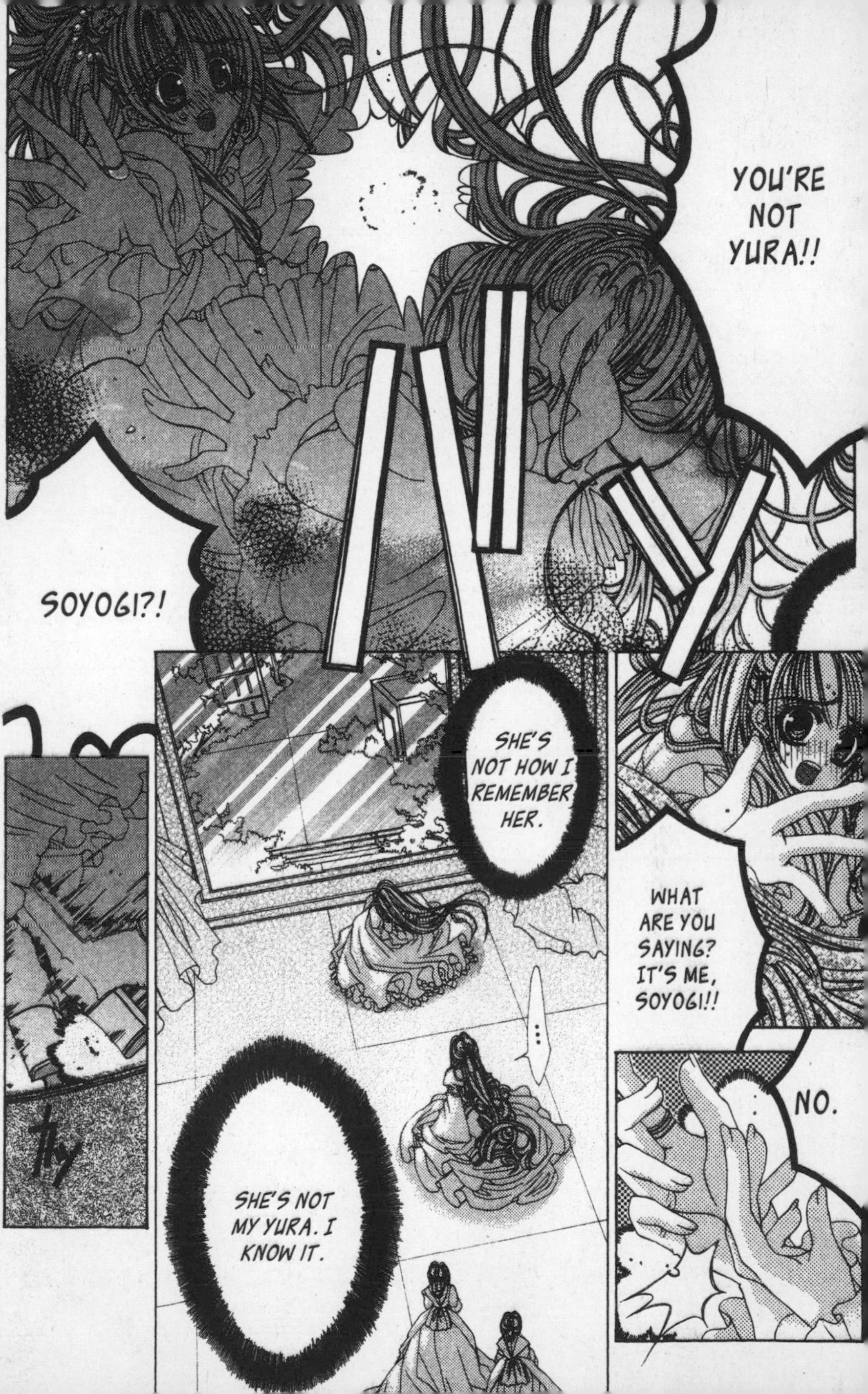
YOU'RE NOT YURA!!
SOYOGI?!
WHAT ARE YOU SAYING? IT'S ME, SOYOGI!!
NO.
SHE'S NOT HOW I REMEMBER HER.
...
SHE'S NOT MY YURA. I KNOW IT.

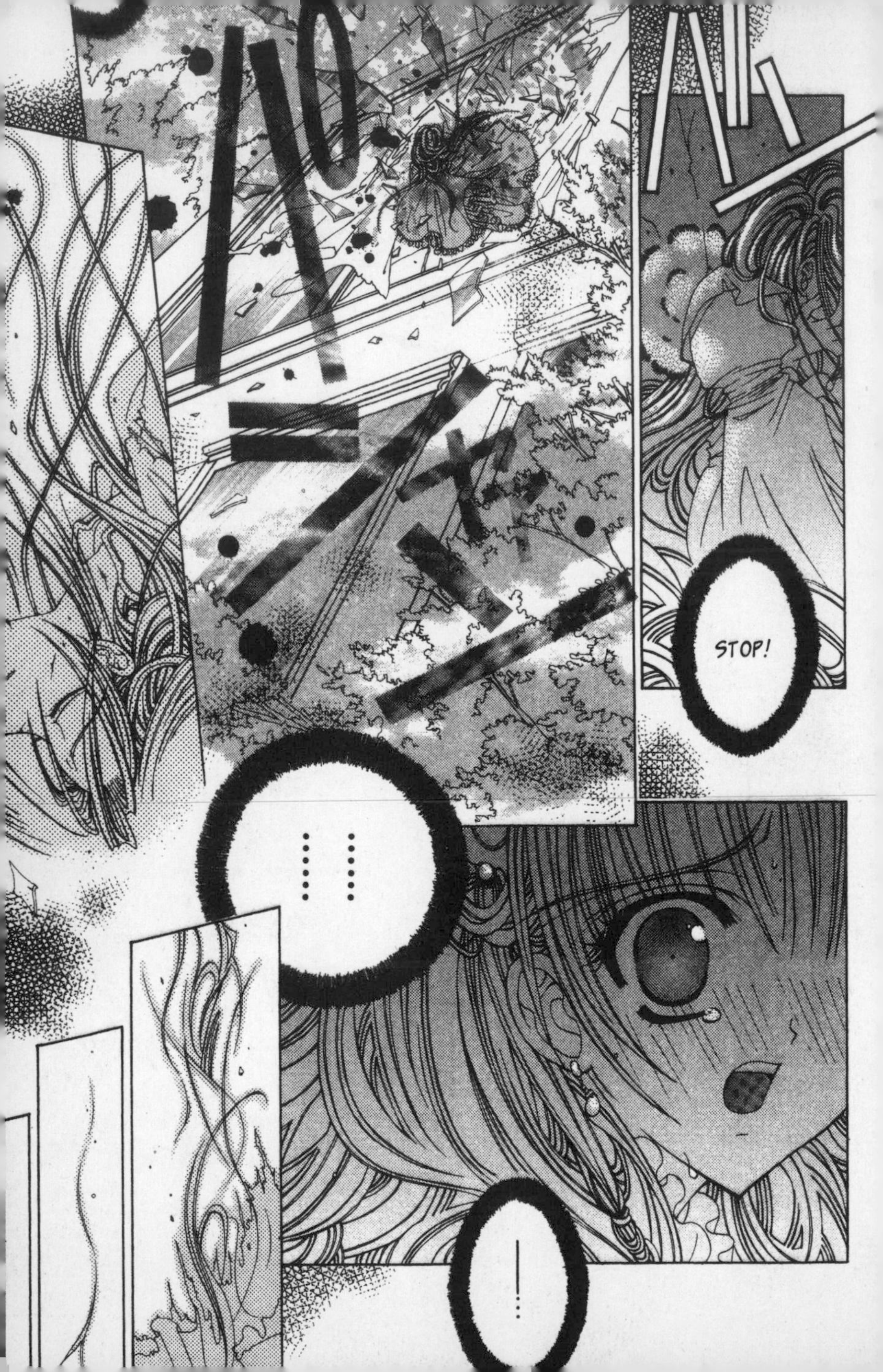
STOP!

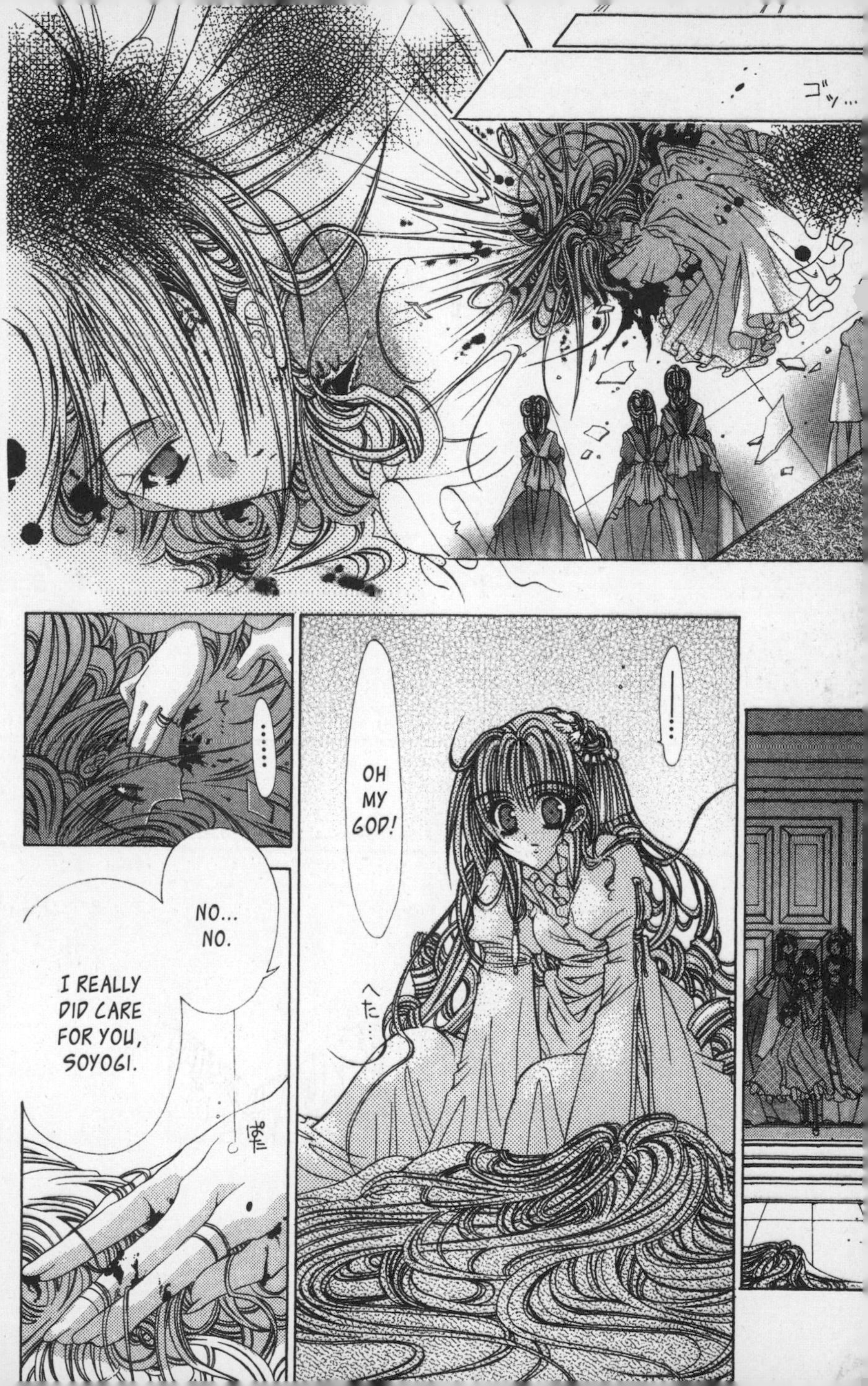
ゴッ…
!
OH MY GOD!
へた…
……
NO... NO.
I REALLY DID CARE FOR YOU, SOYOGI.

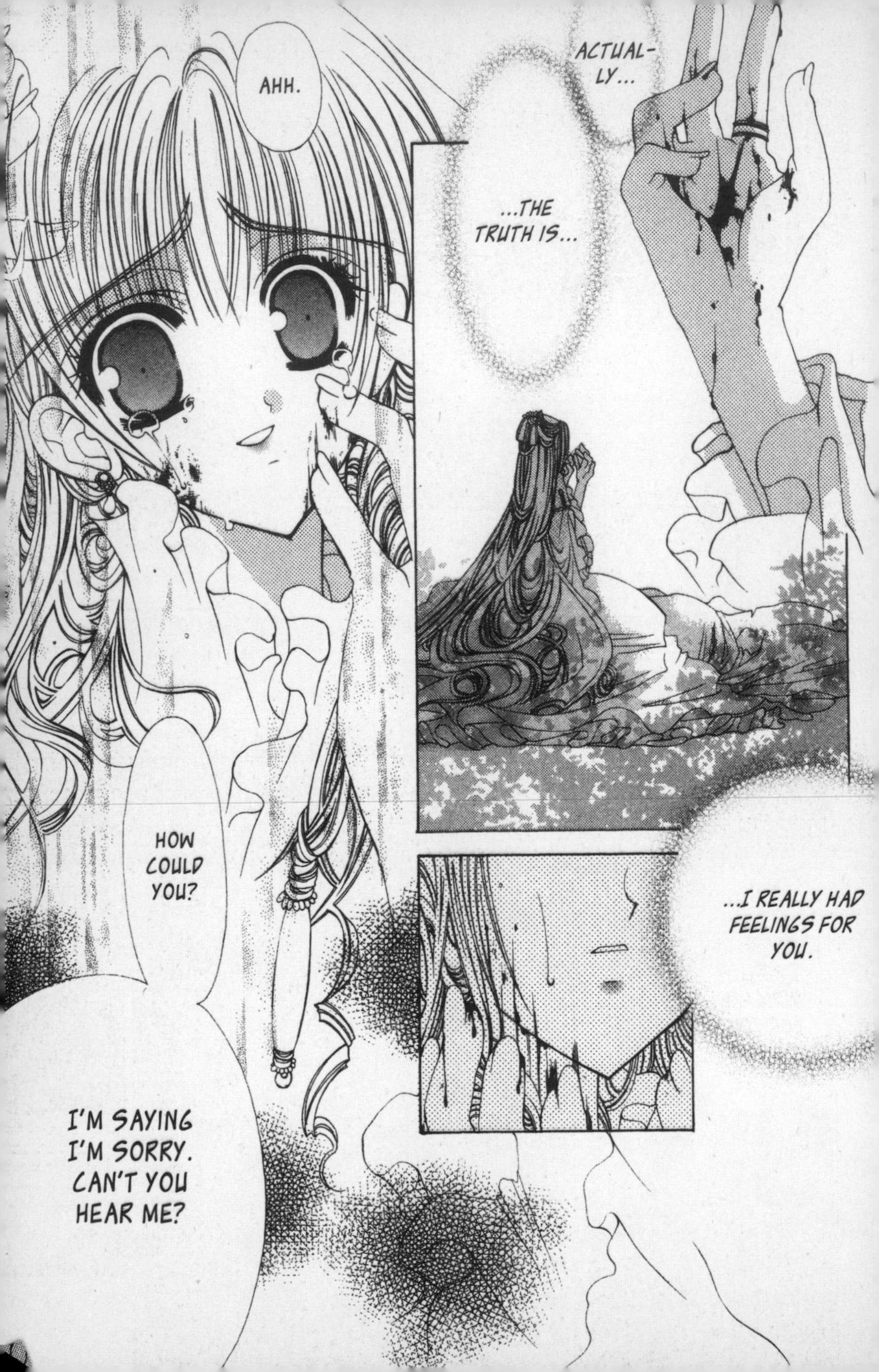
ACTUAL-LY...
...THE TRUTH IS...
...I REALLY HAD FEELINGS FOR YOU.
AHH.
HOW COULD YOU?
I'M SAYING I'M SORRY. CAN'T YOU HEAR ME?

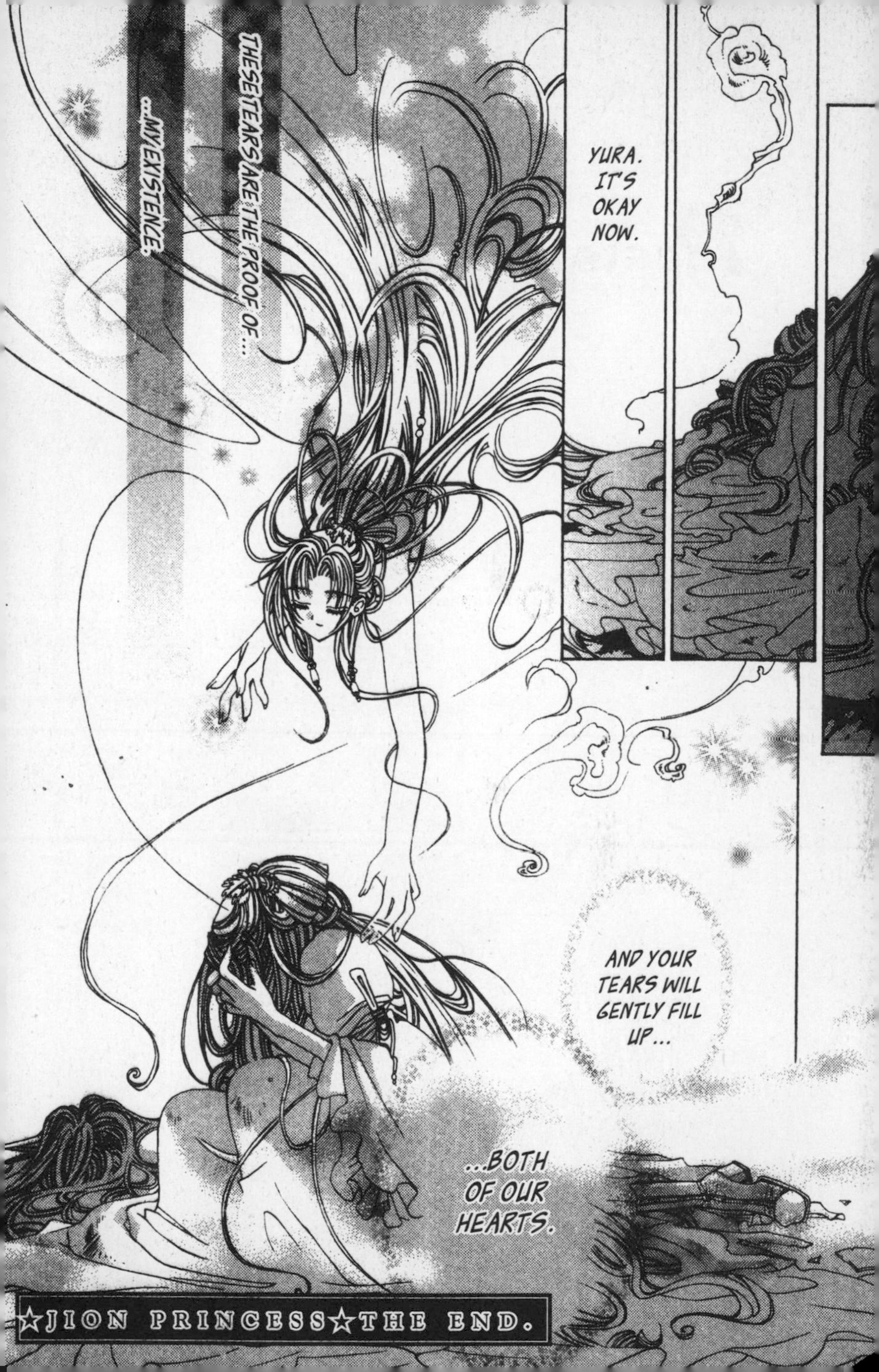
YURA. IT'S OKAY NOW.
THESE TEARS ARE THE PROOF OF...
...MY EXISTENCE.
AND YOUR TEARS WILL GENTLY FILL UP...
...BOTH OF OUR HEARTS.
☆JION PRINCESS☆THE END.

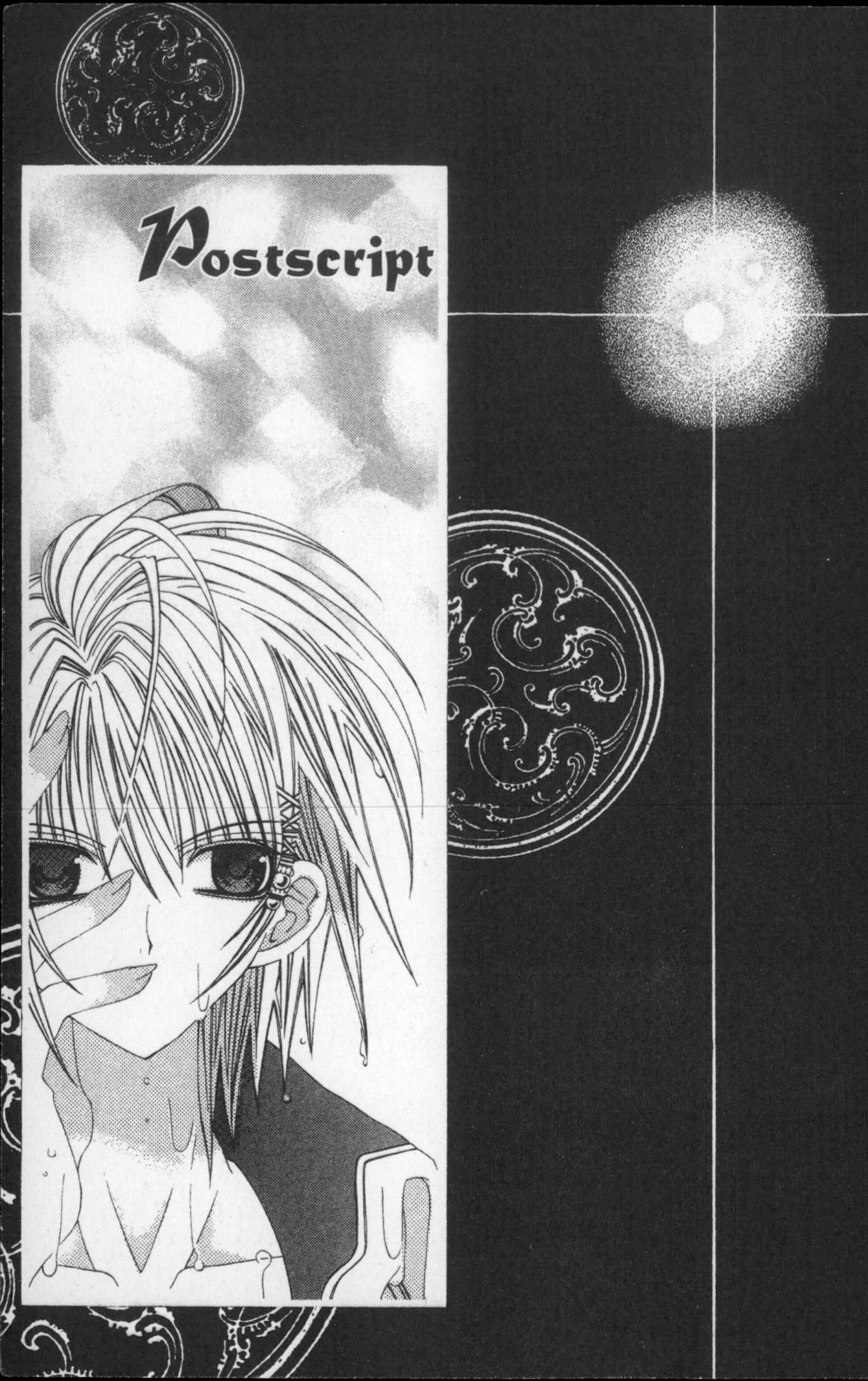
Postscript

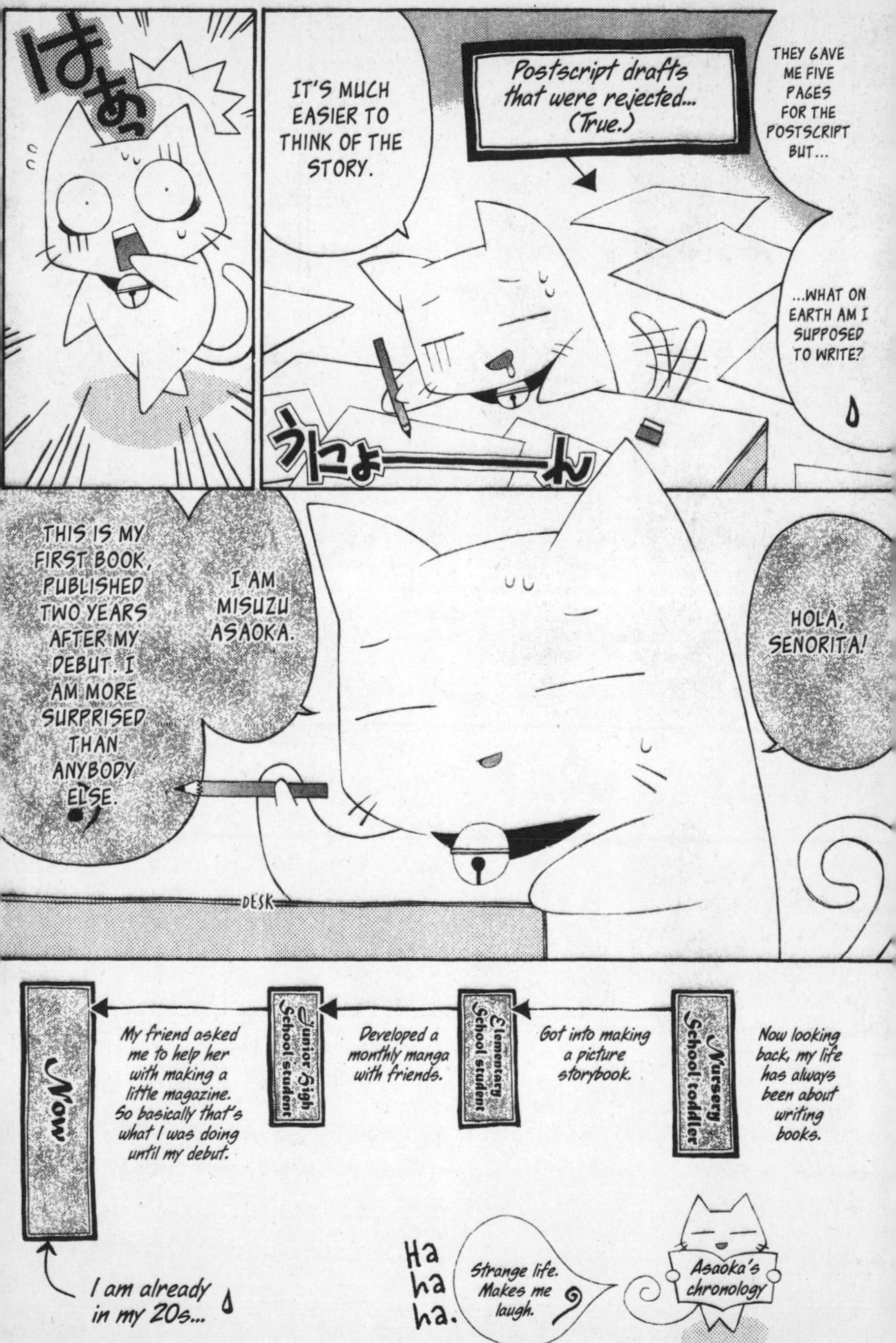
THEY GAVE ME FIVE PAGES FOR THE POSTSCRIPT BUT...
Postscript drafts that were rejected... (True.)
IT'S MUCH EASIER TO THINK OF THE STORY.
...WHAT ON EARTH AM I SUPPOSED TO WRITE?
うにょーーーん
はあっ
HOLA, SENORITA!
I AM MISUZU ASAOKA.
THIS IS MY FIRST BOOK, PUBLISHED TWO YEARS AFTER MY DEBUT. I AM MORE SURPRISED THAN ANYBODY ELSE.
DESK
Now looking back, my life has always been about writing books.
Nursery School toddler
Got into making a picture storybook.
Elementary School student
Developed a monthly manga with friends.
Junior High School student
My friend asked me to help her with making a little magazine. So basically that's what I was doing until my debut.
Now
I am already in my 20s...
Asaoka's chronology
Strange life. Makes me laugh.
Ha ha ha.

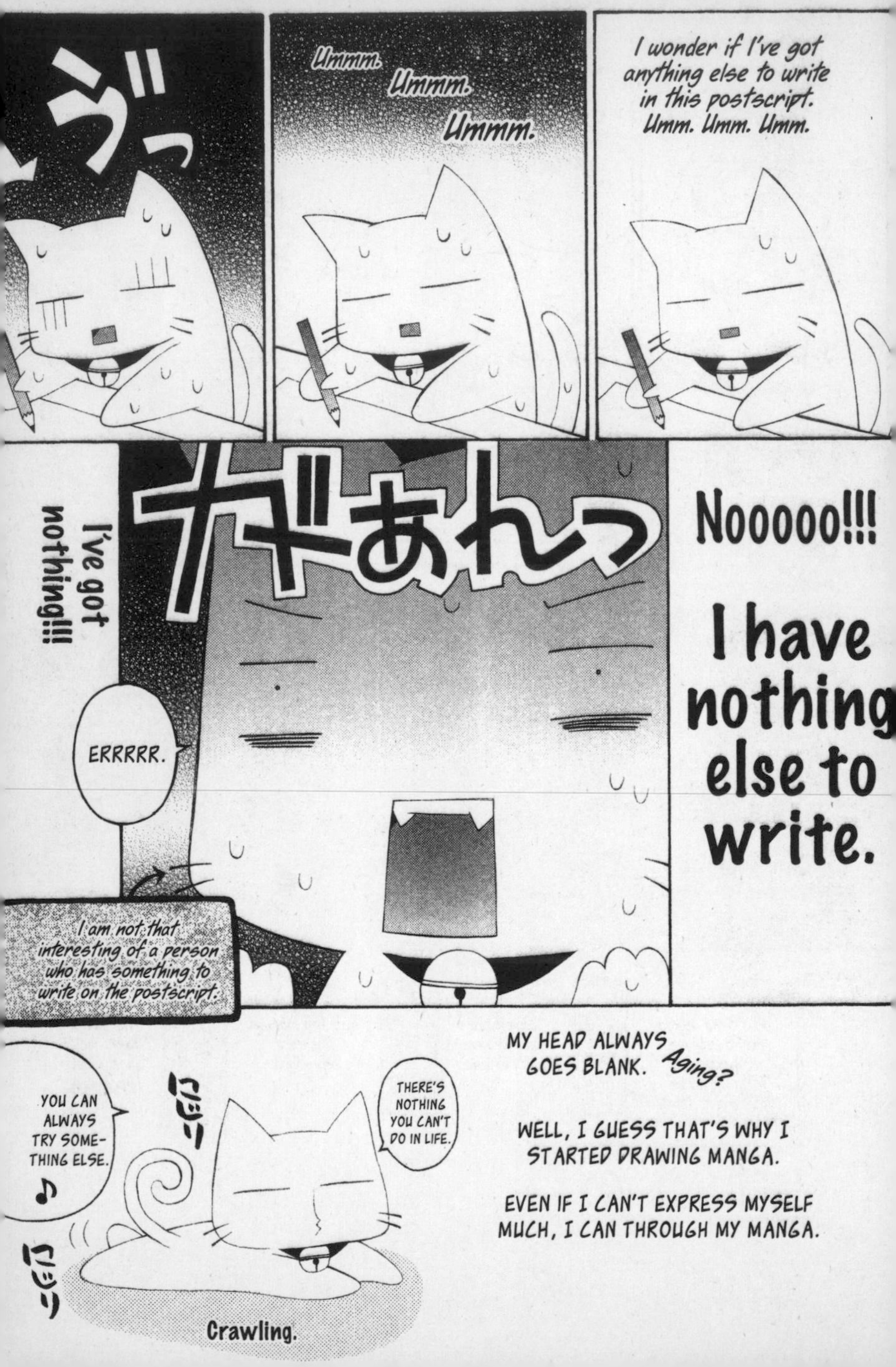

I wonder if I've got anything else to write in this postscript. Umm. Umm. Umm.
Ummm. Ummm. Ummm.
Nooooo!!!
I have nothing else to write.
ERRRRR.
I've got nothing!!!
I am not that interesting of a person who has something to write on the postscript.
MY HEAD ALWAYS GOES BLANK.
Aging?
WELL, I GUESS THAT'S WHY I STARTED DRAWING MANGA.
EVEN IF I CAN'T EXPRESS MYSELF MUCH, I CAN THROUGH MY MANGA.
THERE'S NOTHING YOU CAN'T DO IN LIFE.
YOU CAN ALWAYS TRY SOME-THING ELSE. ♪
Crawling.

I was putting effort into drawing Hagane and Ruriha's bodies rather than their faces.

I always have this ideal body image in my head. I can't draw it out precisely yet, but have been working on it every day.

Regardless of the age and sex, it has to look sexy, you know.

Yeah. When I compare that ideal body image in my head to what I am capable of drawing at this point, I realize I still have a lot to work on.

I don't like it to be wild and sexy. (Well, it depends on the story.)

I always want to draw something that is sexy yet intelligent looking.

When I am drawing Hagane's waistline and thinking about Ruriha's costumes, I am the happiest person on earth.

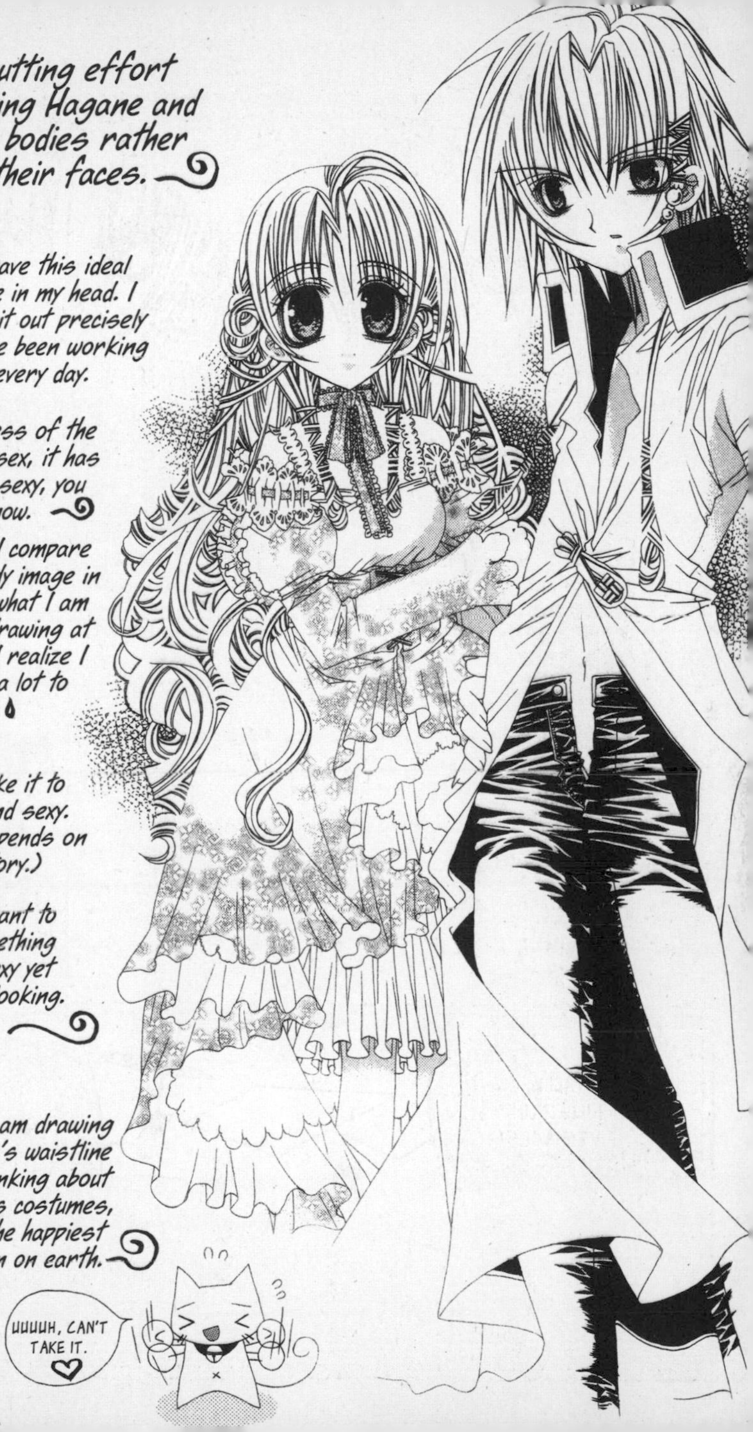
UUUUH, CAN'T TAKE IT.